D1594453

THE
FUGGERS
of
AUGSBURG

STUDIES IN

EARLY MODERN GERMAN HISTORY

H. C. Erik Midelfort, Editor

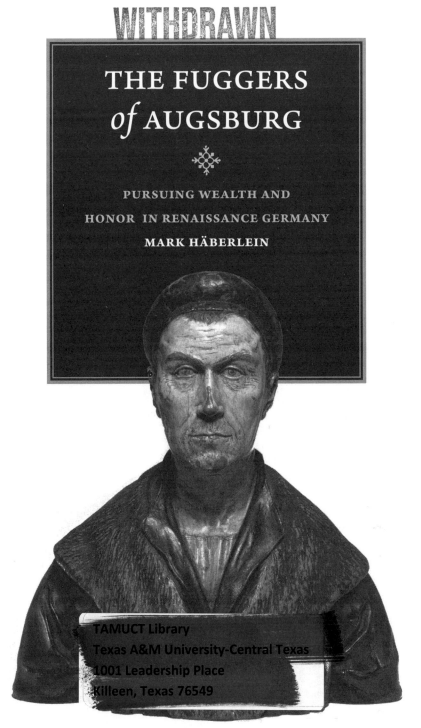

THE FUGGERS
of AUGSBURG

❖

PURSUING WEALTH AND

HONOR IN RENAISSANCE GERMANY

MARK HÄBERLEIN

UNIVERSITY *of* VIRGINIA PRESS CHARLOTTESVILLE *&* LONDON

Originally published in German as
Die Fugger: Geschichte einer Augsburger Familie, 1367–1650,
© 2006 W. Kohlhammer GmbH, Stuttgart

University of Virginia Press
Translation © 2012 by the Rector and Visitors
of the University of Virginia
Printed in the United States of America on acid-free paper
First published 2012

1 3 5 7 9 8 6 4 2

Library of Congress Cataloging-in-Publication Data

Häberlein, Mark.
  [Fugger. English]
  The Fuggers of Augsburg : pursuing wealth and honor in Renaissance Germany / Mark Haberlein.
      p.   cm. — (Studies in early modern German history)
  "Originally published in German as Die Fugger : Geschichte einer Augsburger Familie, 1367–1650,
c2006"—T.p. verso.
  Includes bibliographical references and indexes
  ISBN 978-0-8139-3244-6 (cloth : alk. paper) — ISBN 978-0-8139-3258-3 (e-book)
  1. Fugger family. 2. Augsburg (Germany)—Biography. 3. Renaissance—Germany—Augsburg.
4. Capitalists and financiers—Germany—Augsburg—Biography. 5. Wealth—Germany—Augsburg—
History. 6. Honor—Germany—Augsburg—History. 7. Augsburg (Germany)—Social conditions.
8. Augsburg (Germany)—Economic conditions. 9. Europe—Commerce—History—To 1500. 10. Europe—
Commerce—History—16th century. I. Title.
  DD901.A92H2513 2012
  929.20943—dc23

                                                                                      2011028911

Frontispiece: Bust of Jakob Fugger the Rich by Conrad Meit.
(Bayerisches Nationalmuseum, Munich, loaned by Ernst von Siemens Kunststiftung;
L 2006/208; photo by Walter Haberland)
Maps adapted by Michael Wobring from the German edition.
Genealogy adapted from a genealogical table conceived by Franz Karg (Fugger archives, Dillingen)
and designed by Peter Palm (Berlin).

CONTENTS

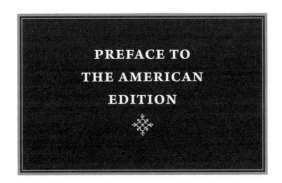

**PREFACE TO
THE AMERICAN
EDITION**

This book is an English translation of my work *Die Fugger: Geschichte einer Augsburger Kaufmannsfamilie (1367–1650)*, originally published in Germany in 2006. As the wealthiest and most prominent German merchant family of the sixteenth century, the Fuggers have attracted wide scholarly attention, and most textbooks and general accounts of the period refer to them. In striking contrast to the other famous merchant family of the period, the Medici of Florence, however, there is no English-language work on the subject currently available. The present book intends to fill this gap by offering a concise overview that builds on the latest scholarly literature, printed primary sources, and the author's own prior work on sixteenth-century merchant capitalism. In comparison with the German edition, the text and bibliography have been updated to include several titles that have appeared since 2006.

In eight chapters, the book traces the history of the Fugger family from the immigration of the weaver Hans Fugger to the imperial city of Augsburg in 1367 to the end of the Thirty Years' War. The first four chapters focus on the Fuggers' business activities and place them in the context of general economic and political developments. Under the forceful leadership of Jakob Fugger the Rich, the family ventured beyond the traditional long-distance trade in cotton and fustian from the 1480s onward and engaged in the marketing of Tyrolian and Slovakian silver and copper. In this field, the Fuggers profited immensely from the Habsburg rulers' need for credit as well as the rising demand for precious metals on European and overseas markets. The Fuggers became the preeminent financiers of Emperor Maximilian I and his successor Charles V, served as papal bankers, and granted substantial loans to European monarchs such as Henry VIII of England. During the reign of Charles V, the focus of their operations shifted to Spain, where the Fuggers leased the lands of the Spanish chivalric orders and exploited the mercury mines of Almadén. In contrast to the old view that the family firm declined after the death of Jakob Fugger's nephew Anton in 1560, chapter 4 shows that Anton's successors managed to restructure the firm and keep it profitable until the Thirty Years' War. As the Fuggers' business operations involved long-distance trade, mining, state finance, and overseas ventures, their history exemplifies the meanings of globalization at the beginning of the modern age.

Chapters 5 to 8 address the political, social, and cultural roles of the Fuggers: their patronage of Renaissance artists such as Albrecht Dürer and Christoph Amberger, the founding of the largest social housing project of its time (the Fuggerei in Augsburg), their support of Catholicism in an imperial city that largely turned Protestant during the Reformation, and their rise from urban merchants to imperial counts and feudal lords. By 1618, the various branches of the family ruled over more than one hundred Swabian villages. While some scholars have treated the ennoblement of the Fuggers, their marriage alliances with the Bavarian and Austrian nobility, and their accumulation of real estate in the countryside as evidence of the family's "feudalization," the book shows that this is only partly true. Until the seventeenth century, the Fuggers remained closely integrated into urban society and culture. I argue that the Fuggers organized their social ascent in a way that allowed them to be merchants and feudal landholders, burghers and noblemen at the same time. This observation ties in with another central argument of the book: Far from being mere profit-maximizing capitalists, the Fuggers were careful to present their economic success in terms that were acceptable within early modern estate society. They styled themselves as loyal servants of the emperor and emphasized familial honor and reputation, as well as their contributions to the general welfare. In sum, the case of the Fuggers provides a window on larger issues of social mobility, cultural patronage, confessionalization, and social values in the age of the Renaissance and the Reformation.

The idea of writing a new history of the Fugger family was originally suggested to me by the current scholarly director of the Fugger archives, Johannes Burkhardt. I am grateful to him for his confidence that a younger colleague, who had mainly worked on the Fuggers' south German competitors before, was capable of writing this survey. Monica Wejwar of Kohlhammer Verlag in Stuttgart was in charge of seeing the original German manuscript to publication. Numerous conversations with Peter Geffcken have helped to clarify problems of sixteenth-century economic and social history for me. Erik Midelfort, series editor of the Studies in Early Modern German History, and Richard Holway, editor at the University of Virginia Press, kindly accepted this translation for publication in their series. I am grateful to Erik Midelfort for his careful revision of my translation, Raennah Mitchell for steering the manuscript through the publication process, Christian Kuhn for obtaining the images and permissions, Michael Wobring for preparing the maps for this publication, and Susan Deeks for the final copyediting. As always, my wife, Michaela Schmölz-Häberlein, has been my main source of scholarly and emotional support.

FUGGER ("VON DER LILIE") GENEALOGY
FIFTEENTH TO SEVENTEENTH CENTURIES

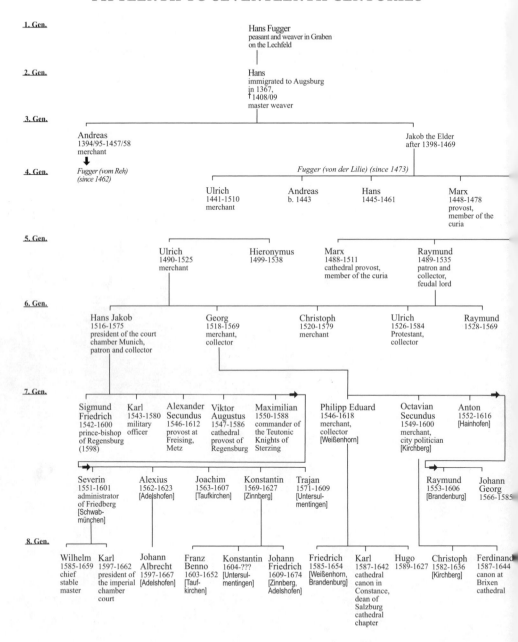

1. Gen.

Hans Fugger
peasant and weaver in Graben
on the Lechfeld

2. Gen.

Hans
immigrated to Augsburg
in 1367,
† 1408/09
master weaver

3. Gen.

Andreas
1394/95-1457/58
merchant

Jakob the Elder
after 1398-1469

4. Gen.

Fugger (vom Reh)
(since 1462)

Fugger (von der Lilie) (since 1473)

Ulrich
1441-1510
merchant

Andreas
b. 1443

Hans
1445-1461

Marx
1448-1478
provost,
member of the
curia

5. Gen.

Ulrich
1490-1525
merchant

Hieronymus
1499-1538

Marx
1488-1511
cathedral provost,
member of the curia

Raymund
1489-1535
patron and
collector,
feudal lord

6. Gen.

Hans Jakob
1516-1575
president of the court
chamber Munich,
patron and collector

Georg
1518-1569
merchant,
collector

Christoph
1520-1579
merchant

Ulrich
1526-1584
Protestant,
collector

Raymund
1528-1569

7. Gen.

Sigmund
Friedrich
1542-1600
prince-bishop
of Regensburg
(1598)

Karl
1543-1580
military
officer

Alexander
Secundus
1546-1612
provost at
Freising,
Metz

Viktor
Augustus
1547-1586
cathedral
provost of
Regensburg

Maximilian
1550-1588
commander of
the Teutonic
Knights of
Sterzing

Philipp Eduard
1546-1618
merchant,
collector
[Weißenhorn]

Octavian
Secundus
1549-1600
merchant,
city politician
[Kirchberg]

Anton
1552-1616
[Hainhofen]

Severin
1551-1601
administrator
of Friedberg
[Schwab-
münchen]

Alexius
1562-1623
[Adelshofen]

Joachim
1563-1607
[Taufkirchen]

Konstantin
1569-1627
[Zinnberg]

Trajan
1571-1609
[Untersul-
mentingen]

Raymund
1553-1606
[Brandenberg]

Johann
Georg
1566-1585

8. Gen.

Wilhelm
1585-1659
chief
stable
master

Karl
1597-1662
president of
the imperial
chamber
court

Johann
Albrecht
1597-1667
[Adelshofen]

Franz
Benno
1603-1652
[Tauf-
kirchen]

Konstantin
1604-???
[Untersul-
mentingen]

Johann
Friedrich
1609-1674
[Zinnberg,
Adelshofen]

Friedrich
1585-1654
[Weißenhorn,
Brandenburg]

Karl
1587-1642
cathedral
canon in
Constance,
dean of
Salzburg
cathedral
chapter

Hugo
1589-1627

Christoph
1582-1636
[Kirchberg]

Ferdinand
1587-1644
canon at
Brixen
cathedral

The place names set in squared brackets indicate territories and feudal estates
[Babenhausen] = Lord of Babenhausen

1. Gen.

2. Gen.

3. Gen.

4. Gen.

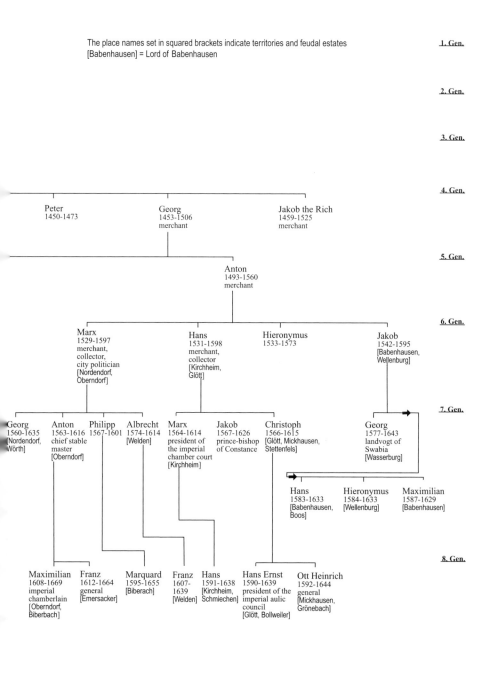

5. Gen.

6. Gen.

7. Gen.

8. Gen.

THE
FUGGERS
of
AUGSBURG

The name Fugger (pronounced Fooger), at least in German, has a good ring to it. Travelers arriving at Augsburg's main train station are welcomed in the "Fugger city," and tourists visiting Augsburg can follow in the footsteps of the city's most famous family in the Fuggerei, the world's oldest social settlement still in existence; in the Fugger chapel in the church of St Anna; and in front of Albrecht Dürer's impressive portrait of Jakob Fugger the Rich in Augsburg's state gallery. The Fuggers show up as literary figures in popular historical novels, and they have even become the subject of a card game in which the players can distinguish themselves by clever speculation in commercial goods.

For a long time the family's history has also been the subject of historical research. The beginnings of Fugger historiography date back to the sixteenth century, when the *Book of Honors* and the "Fugger Chronicles" were composed for the purposes of establishing a family tradition and remembering earlier generations. Of decisive importance for further scholarly research, however, was the establishment of the Fugger family and foundation archives (Fürstlich und Gräflich Fugger'sches Familien- und Stiftungsarchiv) in 1877. By commissioning a scholarly director in 1902 as well as a full-time archivist in 1949 and by setting up a special book series, the Studies in Fugger History (Studien zur Fuggergeschichte), the house of Fugger made a substantial contribution to the scholarly investigation of its own family history. Founded in 1907, the Studies in Fugger History now includes forty-two volumes.[1]

Research on the Fuggers, which has been pursued intensively since the late nineteenth century, has gradually expanded factual knowledge about the family's economic activities and social position, patronage, and charitable foundations. But beyond that, research always reflects the interests, worldviews, and prejudices of the researchers and their times. The scholars who examined the history of the Fuggers between the 1870s and the 1920s were primarily interested in the family's phenomenal economic rise. "How attractive it is," Max Jansen wrote in 1907, "to pursue the development of a family

1

from a weavers' workshop through the world-encompassing counting-house of two merchants up to the prince's palace."[2] Richard Ehrenberg and Jakob Strieder characterized the sixteenth century as one of the great eras of German economic history and mainly saw the Fuggers as forerunners of the "great business leaders" and "captains of industry" of their own times. In the "age of early capitalism" at the end of the Middle Ages, they detected the roots of industrial capitalism. "During the fifteenth and sixteenth centuries the spirit of capitalism spread rapidly," Jakob Strieder wrote in 1925, "the spirit of a persistent, restless, unbridled striving for profit, never satisfied with its success, among a broader, economically active elite stratum of the German people."[3] Jakob Fugger was seen as a protagonist of this "restless, unbridled" striving for gain; Strieder viewed him as the representative of a new, liberal-capitalist cast of mind which had first emerged in Italy. Fugger's remark that he "wished to make a profit as long as he could" was detached from its original historical context (the specific situation of the Fuggers' Hungarian trade at the beginning of the 1520s) and stylized as the life motto of a merchant for whom the earning of money had allegedly become an end in itself. Up to the present day, the image of the Fuggers, and especially of Jakob Fugger the Rich, is strongly shaped by this perspective of the Wilhelminic Age and the era of high industrialization.[4] The view of the Fuggers as unscrupulous large-scale capitalists and political manipulators, which was popularized by the economic journalist Günter Ogger in the 1970s and is widely current, is basically nothing more than a negative inversion of this image of the great business leaders.[5]

From the 1930s to the 1960s, one man above all has shaped Fugger historiography: Baron Götz von Pölnitz, the long-term scholarly director of the Fugger Archives and later professor of economic and social history at the University of Erlangen-Nuremberg. Pölnitz's merits in Fugger research can hardly be overestimated: Besides Jakob Fugger, who had been the main focus of historical interest until then, he also discovered his nephew and successor Anton Fugger as a subject worthy of study and exhaustively researched his life. Pölnitz based his voluminous biographies of Jakob and Anton Fugger not only on the entire body of extant literature but also on archival sources from all over Europe, which no other historian has mined so completely. Finally, he transcended the dominant economic historical perspective in favor of an integral view of sixteenth-century politics, society, and culture.

But Pölnitz has left Fugger historiography not only with a rich legacy but also with a problematic one. As a scholar, he was shaped by the historicist tradition of nineteenth- and early twentieth-century historiography. By writing the biographies of great men, he intended to elucidate the formative historical forces and ideas of their period, in Jakob Fugger's case especially the "double-edged struggle of a strife-torn generation." For Pölnitz, this conflict was expressed in the contrast between Emperor Maximilian I, whom he characterized as a "prince of dreams" and a "scheming dreamer on the imperial throne,"[6] and Jakob Fugger, whom he regarded as the embodiment of mercantile rationality. Pölnitz portrayed Jakob Fugger as a "merchant in every fiber of his being," who was "infused with a transparent, cool clarity" and loved "his figures with the same intensity . . . as others loved their classical texts." This man "knew to calculate his own economic and political world and build with them [the figures of his business accounts] as ingeniously as any real master among the great architects." For Pölnitz, a "substantial part of this mercantile ingenuity" rested on "rational penetration of the world and mastery of its problems by sober insight." As Jakob Fugger has left little testimony about himself, however, Pölnitz had no choice but to read his character into scattered remarks, visual representations, and actions documented in the sources. Modern historical researchers view such an identification of actions and representations with individual character and personality traits with great skepticism.

But Pölnitz's approach not only appears problematic from a methodological point of view, but also with regard to the underlying "national" categories which he employed. For him Jakob Fugger embodied the "cool spirit of the Romanic rationalists" which, "irreverent to tradition and belief, dominated Italian counting houses." As a representative of this "Italian" spirit, Jakob Fugger was in danger of losing sight of "certain imponderable values of life . . . which were otherwise lovingly treasured within the communities of Germany's imperial cities." Fugger thus imported a new, foreign attitude into the "tender world" of the old German gothic, which became more radical and eventually turned into a "spirit of restless activism and fighting" by the end of the great merchant's life. Shortly after the end of the Second World War, which in the preface to his biography Pölnitz describes as a traumatic life experience, this line of argument was obviously meant to provide psychological relief.[7] That it tells us more about the author than about his subject is confirmed by the essay "The Fuggers and the Medici," which Pölnitz published in the leading German-language historical journal, the *Historische Zeitschrift*, in 1942. In the article, which originated in a lecture tour of fascist Italy, the cooperation of the two famous merchant houses had been appropriated for the invention of a common historical tradition of the two Axis powers.[8] It was only under the impression of the military defeat of National

Socialist Germany that Pölnitz apparently arrived at a more critical appraisal of the "Italian" shaping of Jakob Fugger. It would be a rewarding task to trace this process of transformation in more detail.

There is a third respect in which Pölnitz has left a problematic legacy to Fugger research: his focus on two generations of the family's and firm's history. Like Ehrenberg and Strieder before him, Pölnitz regarded the times of Jakob and Anton Fugger as the family's era of greatness, when their rise was closely intertwined with the demand of European princes, and particularly the Habsburg emperors Maximilian I and Charles V, for money. Anton Fugger's descendants, however, who allegedly took no interest in their forefathers' enterprise and cultivated a "seigniorial" lifestyle on the basis of their inherited wealth, were regarded by him as mere epigones of a dynasty distinguished "more by its fame than by new deeds." In Pölnitz's history of the Fugger family, which first appeared in the 1950s and is still in print, less than twenty of more than three hundred pages of text are devoted to the generations after Anton Fugger.[9] A lack of interest in the family's history during the late sixteenth century also characterizes the work of the economic historian Hermann Kellenbenz, who rarely went beyond 1560, the year in which Anton Fugger died, in his numerous publications on the Fuggers' Spanish business affairs.[10] So far, this imbalance has been rectified only partially by more recent studies.

During the 1960s and 1970s, the hitherto dominant historicist perspective on great men, formative events, and guiding ideas was gradually replaced by a structural historical approach that was less interested in the individuality of people and families than in processes of economic and social development. Research on the Fuggers has benefited from this changing perspective. Thus, the French historian Robert Mandrou examined the role of the Fuggers as landed proprietors in Swabia and critically reevaluated the hypothesis that the Fuggers withdrew from urban life in the late sixteenth century to become part of the landed nobility. In the study of Georg Fugger's heirs—a family line that separated from the Fugger trading company in 1578 to run its own firm—Reinhard Hildebrandt pursued the question how changing social norms influenced the family's entrepreneurial activities and social status. Finally, Katarina Sieh-Burens interpreted the Fuggers as a distinct type of urban elite in her study of political leadership in the imperial city of Augsburg.[11]

Nowadays, however, many historians regard neither the historicist nor the structural historical perspective as satisfactory, and the problem of relating actors and structures, individual personalities and long-term economic, social, and cultural developments in meaningful ways is receiving increasing attention. To meet this challenge, social scientists and cultural anthropologists have developed new interpretive approaches, emphasizing that individuals never act autonomously. Instead, their actions always reflect social role models and cultural norms. According to the French sociologist Pierre Bourdieu, the individual reception and appropriation of social structures and expectations are expressed in a person's habit and practices.[12]

Several recent dissertations, which view the Fuggers neither as great individuals nor as mere representatives of a particular social type but examine their fields of activity and practices, demonstrate that such an approach can open up new perspectives on the family's history. Benjamin Scheller's study of Jakob Fugger's foundations explores the connections and tensions between the founder's motives, the foundations' recipients, and the parties involved in their administration. In a study of the Fuggers' "Secret Book of Honors," Gregor Rohmann shows how the family interpreted its own rise and established a family tradition. In her biography of Anton Fugger's great-grandson Ott Heinrich Fugger, Stephanie Haberer points out how Fugger acted in different fields and various social roles—as princely servant, military officer, manager of the trading company, landed proprietor, and patron of the arts. Regina Dauser analyzes the transfer of goods, information, and favors within the correspondence network of Hans Fugger. Most recently, Sylvia Wölfle explores the links between the Fuggers' social rise, their building of a family tradition, and their reception of innovative artistic styles and trends from Italy in her study of the family's art patronage between 1560 and 1618.[13]

For a new history of the Fugger family from its first appearance in the imperial city of Augsburg in 1367 to the end of the Thirty Years' War, which marks an important caesura as it coincides with the dissolution of the Fugger company, several conclusions can be drawn from these developments in scholarship. First, this history cannot focus too exclusively the two great leaders of the firm, Jakob and Anton Fugger, but has to pay more attention to the succeeding generations, their personal relations, and social environment. Anton Fugger's sons, nephews, and grandsons, who continued the enterprise under changing economic and social circumstances, as well as the large group of employees, who provided the firm's personnel infrastructure, have to be taken into account adequately. Second, it is important to avoid a teleological perspective: In the Fuggers' case, there was no linear progression from the guild weavers' craft to commercial enterprise and on to the imperial nobility. Rather, it is remarkable that family members *simultaneously* pursued different activities—long-distance commerce, urban and imperial politics, court service, the management of landed estates, patronage of the arts, ecclesiastical and military careers—during the sixteenth and early seventeenth centuries.

Third, a history of the Fuggers should be sensitive to the social norms that were of fundamental importance to late medieval and early modern estate society and that remained an important guideline for the family. Unbridled striving for profit most certainly was not one of these norms. Instead, this book argues that the Fuggers engaged in commerce, built up a great European enterprise, collected works of art, established foundations, acquired manorial estates, and obtained noble privileges to increase the family's benefit and reputation. Within estate society, it was legitimate for individuals and families to promote their own welfare—to acquire wealth by hard work and honest commerce with God's blessing and to pass on this wealth to their descendants. In this society's normative system, however, the individual's and his family's benefit—their self-interest (*Eigennutz*)—was always subject to the common good (*Gemeiner Nutz*); that is, the general welfare of the public. Time and again, the Fuggers were accused of pursuing their commercial interests and accumulating wealth at the expense of the common good. Conversely, the Fuggers went to great lengths to prove the compatibility of their business affairs with the common good, commissioning reports from legal and theological experts, establishing large charitable foundations, and supporting artisans and scholars.

Like the common good, honor was a fundamental value of late medieval and early modern society. A certain amount of honor, conceived as a form of symbolic and social capital, was ascribed to a person in accordance with his or her rank, sex, wealth, education, and character. The reputation of families, groups, corporations, and communities depended on that of its members. The ascription of honor, however, was neither fixed nor unchanging. Instead, honor could be increased through rising wealth, charitable activities, representation, and political office or it could be lost through business failure, deviant behavior, and personal failings. In this society, honor thus was a field of unceasing conflicts over matters of rank.[14] A case study of the Fugger family can demonstrate how the family's prestige and reputation were acquired, increased, and secured within very different fields of activity. If we take these norms and values guiding individuals' and families' actions and behavior seriously, I am convinced that we can arrive at a better understanding of the Fuggers' economic, social, and cultural activities than if we project modern conceptions of capitalist entrepreneurs and social climbers on them. At the same time, I also remain conscious of the fact that every historical account reflects the author's personal viewpoints and his perception of his own times.

A NOTE ON WEIGHTS AND CURRENCIES

Early modern Europe knew a bewildering amount of currencies, weights, and measures. In the Holy Roman Empire, the standard currency during the period covered here was the Rhenish florin. One florin equaled 60 kreuzer. In Hungary, the (Hungarian) florin was used at the beginning of the sixteenth century but was replaced by the (Hungarian) ducat in the 1530s. In Italy, scudi (Italian crowns) and Venetian ducats were the most common currencies in sixteenth-century long-distance trade. Ducats were also used in Spain and Portugal; the Portuguese ducats were sometimes referred to as cruzado ducats or cruzados. Flemish pounds were the standard currency in Antwerp, the commercial metropolis of the Netherlands; some loans on the Antwerp money market in the middle of the sixteenth century were also transacted in Carolus florins, a currency named after Emperor Charles V. While exchange rates fluctuated considerably, the following rates provide a rough indicator of the relative value of the most common currencies around 1550:

100 Venetian ducats	140 Rhenish florins
100 scudi (Italian crowns)	150 Rhenish florins
100 Portuguese ducats (cruzados)	167 Rhenish florins
100 Spanish/Hungarian ducats	167 Rhenish florins
100 Flemish pounds	420 Rhenish florins
100 Flemish pounds	600 Carolus florins

The weight unit for silver was the Mark, with one hundred Mark equaling 28.1 kilograms. The standard weight unit for copper was the (Vienna) hundred-weight (56.13 kilograms).

1

THE
FUGGER FAMILY
IN LATE MEDIEVAL
AUGSBURG

FUCKER ADVENIT

In 1367, the tax book of the city of Augsburg recorded the arrival of the weaver Hans Fugger. The immigrant paid a property tax of 44 pennies, which indicates a considerable estate worth 22 pounds. Hans Fugger initially lived as a renter in a house near the Church of the Holy Cross but was able to buy the house no later than 1378. One year after Hans's arrival, Augsburg's *Achtbuch*, a record of criminal investigations, mentions his brother Ulin (Ulrich) Fugger as a weaver's manservant. From 1382 onward, Ulin also lived in his own house. According to the sixteenth-century Fugger family chronicle, the brothers came from Graben, a village situated on the Lechfeld to the south of the imperial city.[1] After Ulin had died from an assault in 1394, his descendants can be traced in Augsburg for some fifty years before they disappear from the records. Hans Fugger's descendants, by contrast, would come to play an important role in the imperial city over a much longer run.[2]

The plain first entry in the tax book—*Fucker advenit*—marks the beginning of the history of the family in the metropolis on the Lech River, and Fugger historiography has transformed Hans Fugger, the ancestor of the generations that would eventually become so successful, into a quasi-mythical figure who set a new course for the family's history. Actually, however, the move from the countryside to the city was anything but unusual. The textile trades and long-distance commerce of Augsburg were flourishing at the time, and the favorable economic development attracted numerous rural weavers. As early as 1276, Augsburg's city law code shows that cloth production for export was firmly established. This textile production probably included the city's rural environs, for the Augsburg office of the linen inspectors (*Leinwandschau*), an institution for the quality control of cloth, also monitored the quality of textiles that had been produced in the countryside.[3]

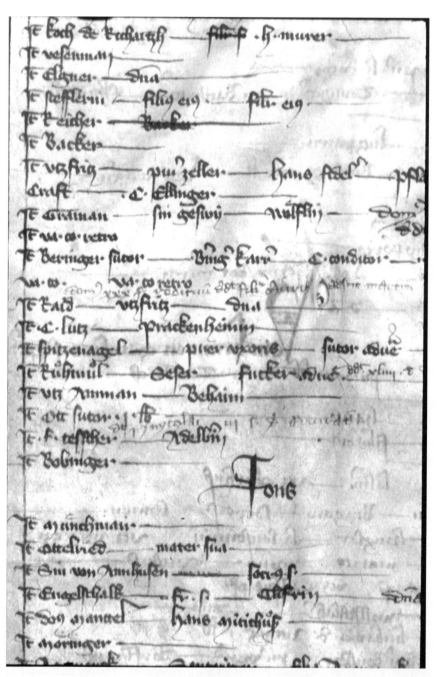

FIGURE 1

Fucker advenit. *Entry for the weaver Hans Fugger in the Augsburg tax register of 1367.*
(Stadtarchiv Augsburg, Reichsstadt, Steuerbuch 1367)

Important hints at Hans Fugger's further career can be drawn from the family tradition, especially from the so-called *Book of Honors* (*Ehrenbuch*) of the Fuggers, a work commissioned by Hans Jakob Fugger and written by Clemens Jäger, an employee of the Augsburg city council, in the 1540s, as well as the "Fugger Chronicles" from the second half of the sixteenth century. According to the sources, Hans Fugger married Klara Widolf in 1370 and had two daughters with her. Klara may have been a daughter of Oswald Widolf, who became guild master of the weavers in 1371. With this marriage, if not earlier, he should have obtained the legal status of Augsburg citizen. Archival sources confirm that Hans Fugger was married to Elisabeth Gefattermann, a weaver's daughter, in 1380. His father-in-law became guild master of the weavers in 1386, and Hans Fugger was elected to the Twelve—the guild's leadership committee—in the same year. The Twelve were automatic members of the imperial city's Grand Council, as well. Hans Fugger's growing social status is also indicated by the fact that he became a guardian of the merchant Konrad Meuting's children in 1389. In January 1397, Hans and Elisabeth Fugger purchased a house in the centrally located Augsburg tax district "vom Ror" from Heinrich Grau and his wife for the substantial sum of 500 Hungarian florins. A few years later, the couple also acquired rural property: In 1403, they spent 200 florins on a farmstead and adjoining land in the village of Scheppach to the west of Augsburg, and two years later they purchased a farmstead, four smallholdings (*Sölden*), and a plot of land in the village of Burtenbach. The house of his deceased brother Ulin in Augsburg's Klebsattelgasse apparently became Hans Fugger's property, as well.[4]

Augsburg's tax books, which have been preserved in a virtually uninterrupted series from 1389 onward and which constitute an extraordinarily important source for urban social history in the late Middle Ages, allow us to trace the evolution of Hans Fugger's wealth in more detail. To be sure, late medieval tax records are brittle and difficult sources, but thanks to the painstaking work of social historians, we know how they operated. Basically, every citizen of Augsburg had to declare his property. The tax system distinguished between *liegend gut* (real estate, as well as eternal and life annuities) and *fahrend gut* (the movable property, excluding the tax-exempt items of daily use). Real estate was taxed at half the rate of movable property. Citizens who did not own substantial property—always a large group in late medieval cities—paid the so-called Have-Nots tax (*Habnit-Steuer*). Before 1472, the tax rate, which was fixed annually by the imperial city's Grand Council, usually oscillated between 1/60 and 1/240 of the declared property; afterward, it ranged between .5 and 1 percent. Citizens were not required to make a new property declaration each year, however; they only had to make a declaration every three to seven years in the so-called sworn tax years. Therefore, the commercial success of merchants manifests itself not in a gradual rise of their property tax but in marked leaps from one "sworn tax year" to the next. As the tax books record the payments only summarily, whereas real estate and movable property were taxed at different rates, moreover, the actual payments allow only a rough estimate of the actual property value. Researchers have found, however, that the city's tax collectors calculated a "property assessment" (*Anschlagvermögen*) by adding the value of the movable property to half the value of the real estate. This property assessment provides the most important indicator for the reconstruction of the economic rise of the Fuggers.[5] Clemens Jäger used the tax books as a source for his *Book of Honors* of the Fugger family as early as the mid-sixteenth century. "And it is true that we find in old tax books on many occasions," Jäger wrote about Hans Fugger, the immigrant from Graben, "that he was rich above three thousand florins, which at that time was regarded as a really large amount of property."[6]

The findings of modern historical research approximate Jäger's estimate rather closely. They show that Hans Fugger had substantially increased his starting capital within less than three decades after his first appearance in Augsburg. According to the 1396 tax book, his property was assessed at 1,806 florins at that time, putting him in position 40 within the hierarchy of the city's taxpayers. While he was still worlds apart from the richest citizen, the widow Dachs, who paid taxes on more than 20,000 florins, the immigrant weaver was already among the wealthiest 1 percent of Augsburg's taxpayers and on equal economic terms with members of long-established patrician families such as the Portners, Langenmantels, and Ilsungs.[7]

How did Hans Fugger acquire this wealth? A century ago, the economist Werner Sombart expressed the opinion that he already came to the city with "considerable property" from the countryside. The economic historian Jakob Strieder emphatically disagreed with Sombart, however. In his view, Hans Fugger's wealth only saw "a very substantial increase" after his immigration to Augsburg. This rise could only be caused by successful commercial activities.[8] We do not have any hard evidence for Hans Fugger's activities in long-distance trade, but it appears unthinkable that he earned his fortune at his own loom. In the years up to his death in 1408–9, Fugger's economic career proceeded in an unspectacular way. His property assessment sank to 1,560 florins in 1399 before rising again to 2,020 florins in 1408.[9]

After 1408 Hans Fugger's widow, Elisabeth, paid the property taxes. According to the older literature, she "held the property, and therefore the business, together until 1436."[10] This is a blatant understatement, however, for the tax books demonstrate that her property assessment continuously increased

TABLE 1

Wealth of Hans Fugger's widow, Elisabeth, 1413–1434

Year	Property assessment[1]
1413	2,860 florins
1418	3,240 florins
1422	3,960 florins
1428	4,200 florins
1434	4,980 florins

Source: Geffcken, "Soziale Schichtung," appendix, 42 (table 6), 49 (table 7), 57 (table 8), 66 (table 9), 73 (table 10).

1. See also Jansen, *Anfänge,* 21–23; Pölnitz, *Jakob Fugger,* 1:8.

from one sworn tax year to the next (see table 1). By 1434, Elisabeth Gefattermann had more than doubled the wealth of her deceased husband and had reached position 27 in Augsburg's wealth hierarchy. Even though precise information about her economic activities is lacking and the grown sons Andreas (Endres) and Jakob, who were assessed together with their mother in 1434, actively assisted her, Hans Fugger's widow must have been a remarkably business-minded woman. She thus exemplifies a frequently observable, though long neglected, phenomenon: In late medieval and early modern trade, women were well able to hold their own.[11]

In 1441, the first sworn tax year after their mother's death, the brothers Andreas and Jakob, who had initially been apprenticed to a goldsmith, paid taxes on a combined property of 7,260 florins. The joint property assessment is a certain indicator that the brothers were engaged in business cooperation. From the fact that the tax books repeatedly recorded Jakob's absence, we may further conclude that he represented the firm at other places. The brothers' engagement in long-distance trade can be inferred from the fact that they belonged to a group of merchants to whom the city council issued a warning in 1442 for having bypassed a road leading through the territory of Duke Otto of Bavaria and having thereby evaded toll payments. Their tax assessments show, moreover, that their business was doing well. In 1448, the brothers owned 10,800 florins, the fifth-largest estate in the imperial city at the time. Only the powerful Peter von Argon, the heirs of Hans Meuting, and the widows of Hans Lauginger and Ulrich Meuting had more capital.[12] But afterward the brothers parted ways: In the 1455 tax book they were assessed separately for the first time, Andreas at 4,440 florins and Jakob at 5,697 florins. This separation marks the beginning of the two family lines: the Fuggers "vom Reh," named after a coat of arms showing a roe deer that, according to tradition, was conferred on the line in 1462, and the Fuggers "von der Lilie," named after the lily on their coat of arms.[13]

THE RISE AND FALL OF THE FUGGERS "VOM REH"

Andreas Fugger died as early as 1457, and his widow, Barbara, a daughter of the merchant Ulrich Stammler, was able to preserve, though not increase, the family's wealth during the following decade.[14] Peter Geffcken, the leading expert on Augsburg's economic history during this time period, assumes that Barbara Fugger invested in the trading company of her son-in-law Thoman Grander and that her son Lukas worked for the Grander firm. This assumption is mainly based on the fact that Lukas Fugger is first documented as an independent merchant in 1469, shortly after the death of his brother-in-law in 1467–68. Perhaps it was Lukas Fugger who continued the operations of the Grander company. Thoman Grander had begun his mercantile career as an employee of the important Meuting company and had gained admission to the Augsburg merchants' guild with his marriage to a daughter of Hans Meuting the Younger in 1449. After the death of his first wife, he had married Barbara Fugger, a daughter of Andreas Fugger, in 1453–54. By 1460, Thoman Grander's firm had a branch office in Nuremberg. According to the Fugger *Book of Honors*, he was "an eminent merchant of Augsburg."[15] Grander's brother-in-law and presumable successor, Lukas Fugger, first appears as an independent taxpayer in the Augsburg tax book of 1472. Over the following two decades, his wealth steadily increased.

The rise of Lukas Fugger's wealth (see table 2) mirrors the success of his trading company, whose associates were his younger brothers Matthäus, Hans, and Jakob. The Fuggers' *Book of Honors* states that he had an "enormous trade . . . with spices, silks, and woollen cloth".[16] The mainstay of this "enormous trade" was the textile business. The protocols of the Augsburg city court (*Stadtgericht*) record numerous lawsuits that Fugger's representatives Stephan Krumbein, Bernhard Kag, and Hans Stauch filed against weavers who had received cotton or wool and had failed to deliver the finished cloth on time. Commercial ties with Italy were also of great importance to the firm. In 1475, the brothers Lukas and Matthäus Fugger obtained a ducal letter of safe conduct for their trade with Milan, a center for the production of and commerce in high-quality fabrics and luxury items. According to the sixteenth-century "Fugger Chronicles," Matthäus died on a journey to Milan in 1490. In Venice, the most important distribution center for cotton from the eastern Mediterranean, the sons of Lukas Fugger's uncle Jakob represented his firm for some time. According to Max Jansen, Lukas Fugger and

TABLE 2

Wealth of Lukas Fugger, 1472–1492

Year	Property assessment[1]
1472	2,588 florins
1475	3,748 florins
1480	7,733 florins
1486	8,638 florins
1492	17,200 florins

Source: Geffcken, "Soziale Schichtung,"
appendix, 130 (table 16), 138, 140 (table 17),
147 (table 18), 157 (table 19), 166 (table 20).
1. See also Jansen, *Anfänge,* 43; Rohmann,
Ehrenbuch, 1:95.

his brothers practiced "a division of labor of sorts" in which Lukas "was the hub of the whole business" in Augsburg, Matthäus took charge of relations with Milan, Markus cultivated the connection to Venice, and Hans worked on the axis from Nuremberg to Frankfurt on the Oder far to the northeast. Lukas Fugger's son-in-law Christoph Müller took care of the firm's interests in the Netherlands.[17] Hans Fugger "vom Reh" moved to Nuremberg in 1481 and purchased a house there three years later. In 1485, he lent 8,000 Rhenish florins to a councilor of Archduke Sigismund of Tyrol—probably by order of the family trading company. For this loan he received payment in the form of Tyrolean silver. Business connections to Frankfurt on the Oder are documented for 1486. The suit that one "Thomann Tonnstedt from Lunden in Engelland" filed against Lukas Fugger before the Augsburg city court in 1495 underscores the geographical extent of his business relations.[18]

Family and kinship ties formed the backbone of this far-flung trade network. Thus, Lukas Fugger's son-in-law Christoph Müller worked for the firm in Antwerp; Lukas also cooperated closely with his brother-in-law Gastel Haug, a rich Augsburg merchant and city councilor. In 1484, the two merchants issued general powers-of-attorney to each other "on account of their company." In addition, Fugger maintained close ties to the Stammler brothers, who were close kinsmen.[19] In 1490, a wagon train of Lukas Fugger, Ulrich Stammler, Balthasar Wolf of Augsburg, and a merchant from Cologne was robbed in the Valsugana, a valley in the northern Italian prince-bishopric of Trent.[20] Kinship ties also constituted an advantage when it came to raising outside capital for the financing of business ventures. Lukas Fugger and Gastel Haug invested 2,705 florins, which they had administered as guardians for the children of the rich patrician Bernhard Rehlinger since 1488, in Lukas Fugger's firm.[21]

In the 1480s, the company supplemented its commerce in goods with financial operations. The city of Augsburg commissioned Lukas Fugger for the transfer of 1,000 ducats to Venice in 1482, and money transfers to Rome, which Fugger handled during a lawsuit between the city of Augsburg and the local cathedral chapter, are documented for 1484–85. In the late 1480s, the Netherlands, where Maximilian, as king, was fighting for the Burgundian inheritance of his first wife, became the focus of the financial activities of the Fuggers "vom Reh." Lukas Fugger's company transferred funds for the payment of Maximilian's soldiers, and in 1489 he transmitted the sum of 6,700 florins for the king from Antwerp to Innsbruck. The military conflict over the Burgundian inheritance also formed the background to a loan of 9,600 gold florins guaranteed by the city of Leuven and the province of Brabant. This loan turned out to be Lukas Fugger's undoing when the city, which had pawned its income as security, refused to pay it back. The Fuggers "vom Reh" filed suit against Leuven before the Council of Brabant and, later, before the imperial chamber court, as well. Although the imperial chamber court supported their claim in 1497, no payment was made. Even the imperial ban on Leuven in 1499 did not produce results. In 1504, when King Maximilian finally ended the lawsuit, the Fuggers "vom Reh" were already bankrupt.[22]

Faced with massive payment problems, Lukas Fugger's son Markus fled Venice in 1494. After twenty-five of the thirty Venetian creditors had indicated that they were willing to negotiate with their debtors, Lukas and Markus Fugger were promised safe conduct for a period of three months. This enabled them to negotiate with their creditors without fear of imprisonment for debt. The safe conduct was renewed in 1497–98, and Lukas and Markus managed to reach a settlement with their creditors. In Augsburg, where two of the Fuggers' brothers-in-law, Andreas Lang and Georg Mülich, acted as mediators, the chances for a compromise initially did not look too bad, either. The situation deteriorated, however, when the trading firm of Martin Winter and Gotthard Stammler had to swear an oath of disclosure, for Lukas Fugger was still in debt to that firm, and its creditors now addressed their claims to him. In 1501, these conflicts escalated. Christoph Scheurl of Nuremberg summoned the Augsburg city council to sequester the property of the Fuggers "vom Reh," while Georg Mülich threatened Lukas Fugger with a knife as he was on the way home from Augsburg's central square, the Perlach; Mülich called Fugger a "villain" whose head he would like to cut off. Now even family members and close relatives filed claims in court. The children from Lukas Fugger's first marriage demanded the payment of their maternal inheritance, and his second wife, Klara Konzelmann, could claim 1,500 florins according to her marriage contract. Matthäus Fugger's widow, Helena Mülich, also presented claims through her brother. Pressed by his creditors, Lukas Fugger withdrew to Graben, the village on the Lechfeld from which his ancestors had come to Augsburg long ago. In 1504, a group of creditors that included the brothers Bernhard, Hans, and Christoph Rehlinger obtained all rights to Fugger's assets. Lukas's cousin Jakob Fugger, who had risen to become the richest man in Augsburg in the meantime, took over Lukas's properties in Graben and Burtenbach in 1511–12 and paid his children's inheritance in return. Lukas died shortly afterward.[23]

For a fifteenth- and sixteenth-century merchant, bankruptcy not only constituted economic failure. It had grave social consequences, as well. Bankrupts lost the right of access to the socially exclusive drinking halls of the patricians and merchants and thus faced a considerable loss of prestige. Bankrupts such as Lukas Fugger forfeited "faith and trust"; they were deprived of the credit of other merchants and therefore found it very difficult to reenter the field of commerce. With Lukas's failure, the Fuggers "vom Reh" had played out their role as independent merchants in Augsburg. Instead, they went to work as goldsmiths, artisans, or commercial employees of their rich cousins. Finally, bankruptcy cast a shadow on the family name. This was still evident in the mid-sixteenth century, when the *Book of Honors* of the Fuggers "von der Lilie" tried to justify the failure of their impoverished cousins. Lukas Fugger, the *Book of Honors* claims, had suffered "a grave accident" when the city of Leuven refused to pay back the loan. In addition, various people had "pressed him too hard, and schemed for his ruin,"[24] and his son and collaborator had drowned in Lake Garda in northern Italy. What makes this justification interesting is the fact that bankruptcy proceedings in the fifteenth and sixteenth centuries carefully distinguished between inadvertent failures caused by accidents and ill fortune and deliberate, possibly even fraudulent, bankruptcies.[25] Whereas it exempted Lukas Fugger from criticism, the *Book of Honors* charged his brother Matthäus with having been "a negligent merchant" who become "impoverished in trade" through his own fault.[26]

Moreover, scholars have assumed that the Fuggers "vom Reh" engaged in "all too daring ventures," and Lukas, who also occupied numerous offices in the imperial city's government, may have lost control over his business affairs.[27] As we will see, however, his cousins, the Fuggers "von der Lilie," also took high risks. However, a decisive weakness in Lukas Fugger's company seems to have been the lopsided balance of company capital to outside capital. Lukas appears to have financed the expansion of his firm's business ventures mainly with capital deposited by wealthy citizens of Augsburg and Nuremberg at fixed interest rates. Apart from Christoph Scheurl and the Rehlinger brothers, the sources also mention the widows Wieland and Wägeler. The property of Lukas Fugger's wives had been invested in the firm. During the crisis that began in 1494, Lukas Fugger was obviously unable to persuade his creditors to sit still and wait until his situation improved. During the boom period of Augsburg's economy in the sixteenth century, numerous prominent firms faced similar problems.[28]

THE ECONOMIC RISE AND SOCIAL NETWORK
OF THE FUGGERS "VON DER LILIE"

In 1441, Jakob Fugger the Elder, who founded the line of the Fuggers "von der Lilie," married Barbara Bäsinger, a daughter of the goldsmith and mint master Franz Bäsinger. Bäsinger had become one of the richest inhabitants of Augsburg through long-distance trade and minting but had incurred high debts in the process; the chronicler Burkhard Zink put his liabilities at 24,000 florins. In 1444, he defaulted on his payments and, according to the chronicler, thereby caused "great clamoring and grumbling" in the city. Although Bäsinger approached the emperor to obtain a moratorium on his payments, the Augsburg city council had him imprisoned—the first known bankruptcy in the circle of the Fuggers' relatives. Bäsinger's creditors canceled some of his debts, however, and a group of relatives, which apparently included Jakob Fugger, guaranteed the payment of the rest. The former mint master later went to Schwaz in Tyrol. Some scholars have speculated about a possible connection between this move and the Fuggers' later involvement in the Tyrolean mining business, but hard evidence for this is lacking.[29]

The reconstruction of Jakob Fugger's career has to rely on the brittle data of the Augsburg tax books, on the one hand, and a few sentences in the Fugger family's *Book of Honors,* on the other. According to the *Book of Honors,* he was a "rich and wealthy man, and a leader of the honorable weavers' guild, as well as a merchant." There were "numerous stories about the fortunes of his mercantile business in wartime," but, unfortunately, they remained unrecorded. Instead, the *Book of Honors* sketches a general character portrait of the man in broad strokes: "He was upright, honest, mild and friendly towards everyone but very hard and severe on those who despised fairness and behaved haughtily towards him." Moreover, he had "preserved the Fuggers' properties well."[30]

The tax books enable us to add to this rough sketch. Above all, they show that not only Jakob, but also his widow, "preserved the Fuggers' properties

TABLE 3

Wealth of Jakob Fugger the Elder and his widow, Barbara, 1462–1492

Year	Property assessment	Rank[1]
1462	6,600 florins	10
1466	7,350 florins	7
1472 widow	6,471 florins	16
1475	7,971 florins	13
1480	10,000 florins	11
1486	13,200 florins	13
1492	15,971 florins	12

Source: Geffcken, "Soziale Schichtung," appendix, 110 (table 14), 120 (table 15), 128 (table 17), 136 (table 17), 147 (table 18), 156 (table 19), 166 (table 20).
1. Rank among the wealthiest taxpayers of Augsburg.

well" and even increased them substantially. Between 1472 and 1486, Barbara Bäsinger doubled her taxable wealth, and when she died in 1497, she left an estate of 23,293 florins (see table 3).[31]

The 1480 tax book also records Ulrich Fugger, the eldest son of Jakob Fugger and Barbara Bäsinger born in 1441, with a property assessment of 5,067 florins. Six years later, his taxable wealth had increased to 9,300 florins. In 1492, finally, we encounter the three brothers Ulrich, Georg, und Jakob Fugger in the tax book, with Ulrich assessed at 16,971 florins; Georg at 13,971 florins; and Jakob at 11,971 florins.[32] These figures show two things. On the one hand, they demonstrate that the line of the Fuggers "von der Lilie" commanded greater wealth than the family line "vom Reh" even before Lukas Fugger's bankruptcy. Thus, the statement in the Fuggers' *Book of Honors* that Lukas and his brothers were "claimed to be the richest Fuggers by many" is not to be taken literally.[33] On the other hand, the tax books show that the elder Jakob's widow retained control over a large part of the family's assets long after her sons had grown to maturity. The sons undoubtedly helped her to continue the family business. According to family tradition, it was Ulrich on whom Emperor Friedrich III conferred the lily coat of arms during his stay in Augsburg in 1473, after Ulrich had provided the emperor's entourage with cloth and silk fabric. The brothers also became members of the Augsburg merchants' guild and acquired real estate. In 1488, Ulrich and Jakob purchased a house on the Rindermarkt (cattle market) for 2,032 florins.[34] Nevertheless, the brothers obtained full rights of disposal over the family property only after their mother's death in 1497. The *Book of Honors* from the 1540s, however, remains silent about the crucial role of Barbara Bäsinger—probably a deliberate omission. Since the Fugger women were categorically excluded from the management of the trading company in the sixteenth century, there was no place for business-minded women in the family tradition.[35]

Like their cousins, the Fuggers "von der Lilie" initially focused on the traditional long-distance trade in goods. A preliminary version of the *Book of Honors* states that Ulrich Fugger had "associated himself with his brothers in a company for conducting their commerce, and they began to trade in silken and woolen cloths, that being the most considerable commerce at the time." Like his cousin Lukas, Ulrich Fugger in the 1480s repeatedly filed suits before the Augsburg city court against weavers who failed to deliver fustian—a fabric made from native linen yarn and imported cotton—according to prior agreement.[36] As in the case of Lukas Fugger and his brothers, an intrafamilial division of labor can be observed in the trading company of Jakob Fugger's sons. While Ulrich Fugger coordinated business activities from the Augsburg headquarters, his brother Georg took care of commercial relations with the central and eastern German regions in Nuremberg. Until 1486, the brothers closely collaborated with the Nuremberg merchant Hans Kramer; in 1493, the Fuggers purchased their own house in the Franconian imperial city. The Augsburg–Innsbruck–Venice axis, finally, was the domain of Jakob Fugger. In 1484, the Fugger company obtained a chamber in the house of the German merchants in Venice, the Fondaco dei Tedeschi, which had belonged to the town of Judenburg (Styria). Six years later, a letter of safe conduct for trade with Milan was issued to the brothers.[37] For the early 1490s, we also know the names of several commercial employees: Hans Suiter and Konrad Meuting represented the firm in Tyrol; Hans Mairhofer, in Salzburg; Wolfgang Hofmann, in Nuremberg; Sebastian Rem and Hans Keller, in Venice; Onophrius Varnbühl, in Antwerp; and Otto Russwurm and Hans Metzler, in Wrocław.[38]

Besides commerce in goods, financial transactions became increasingly important. A first money transfer of 706 florins to the curia in Rome is documented for 1476.[39] The establishment of business ties with Rome especially benefited from the fact that Marx Fugger (b. 1448), a brother of Ulrich, Georg, and Jakob, occupied a position as recorder in the papal registrar's office, where petitions to the curia were recorded. From this position he could effectively promote the Roman business interests of his family. Moreover, Marx collected clerical benefices and obtained the position of provost in Regensburg (1475) and Freising (1477). In 1474, a position on the Augsburg cathedral chapter had already been conferred on him, but the chapter, which was dominated by noblemen, refused to accept him, citing a papal privilege that excluded the sons of Augsburg citizens. Although the Fuggers were supported by the city council in their conflict with the cathedral chapter, the pope confirmed the chapter's privilege. The early death of Marx Fugger in 1478 ended the legal conflict, but it flared up again in similar cases during the following decades.[40] Despite Marx's death, the brothers were able to intensify their business relations with the curia even further. Thus, in 1485–86 the archbishop of Mainz refunded Ulrich Fugger several sums that Fugger had lent to him. From 1485 to 1489, Ulrich Fugger also transferred money to Rome on the order of the imperial city of Augsburg, and in 1490, the bishop of Kammin (Pomerania) owed him 1,675 florins.[41]

As in the case of the Fuggers "vom Reh," a steadily intensifying integration into the kinship network of the Augsburg elite accompanied the economic rise of the Fuggers "von der Lilie." Commercial activities, social status, and the choice of marriage partners were mutually dependent and reinforced one another. In 1479, Ulrich Fugger married Veronika Lauginger, a daughter of Hans Lauginger, the veteran guild master of the salt traders (*Salzfertiger*), and Margaretha Riedler.[42] In 1486, Georg Fugger married Regina Imhof, a daughter of the successful merchant Peter Imhof and his wife, Regina Walther. Their sisters also married into prestigious families. Anna became the wife of Hektor Mülich in 1468; Barbara married Konrad Meuting; and Walburga married Wilhelm Rem in 1484.[43] Through these marriages the Fuggers forged alliances with politically influential and highly respected families. In addition to their social prestige, these alliances increased the Fuggers' economic capital, for Ulrich and Georg Fugger could invest their wives' fortunes in the family company, and their brothers-in-law Konrad Meuting and Wilhelm Rem worked for the firm for some time. Last but not least, the families who concluded marriage alliances with the Fuggers made significant contributions to the city's cultural life. The merchant Hektor Mülich, whose second wife was Anna Fugger, not only played a role in urban politics as long-term guild master of the shopkeepers (*Kramer*). He was also a well-traveled man who had undertaken a pilgrimage to the Holy Land in 1450 and an important contributor to the imperial city's historiography. After he initially continued the older chronicle of Sigmund Meisterlin, he wrote his own chronicle of the city for the years 1348–1487. In contrast to the imperial and world chronicles of the fifteenth century, Mülich's chronicle focused on the city's internal development.[44] In later times, when members of the Fugger family cultivated literary and scholarly interests and supported authors and historiographers, well-educated fellow citizens and kinsmen such as Hektor Mülich may well have served as role models.

The rise of the two lines of the Fugger family and of their trading companies in the fifteenth century took place in the context of general demographic and economic expansion. The population of Augsburg, which had been decimated after the great plague epidemic of the mid-fourteenth century, began to rise again in the first half of the fifteenth century. The number of taxpayers rose from 2,957 in 1408 to 4,798 in 1461. Following a period of stagnation that lasted into the 1480s, the late fifteenth century witnessed the beginnings of a spectacular growth period. In 1498, the city counted 5,351 taxpayers. The population of the imperial city rose from roughly 12,000 inhabitants at the beginning of the fifteenth century to an estimated 19,000 around 1500.[45]

The textile sector, especially the production of fustian, was the engine of Augsburg's economy. Historians regard the introduction of fustian weaving as a "fundamental process of innovation in the second half of the fourteenth century." Merchants in the Swabian imperial cities of Nördlingen, Ulm, Ravensburg, Memmingen, Biberach, Constance, and Kaufbeuren used their commercial relations with Venice to import cotton, and they organized regional textile production by selling raw materials, providing credit, and marketing the finished product. In the late Middle Ages, one of the great European regions of craft production extended from Lake Constance to the Danube and Lech rivers. In the course of the fifteenth century, however, Augsburg and Ulm emerged out of the plethora of cities as the leading centers of textile production and long-distance commerce. The breakthrough of the fustian industry in Augsburg can be dated to the 1370s. On the basis of the *Ungeld,* the indirect taxes collected by the city, an annual production figure of 12,000 pieces of cloth can be calculated as early as 1385, and more than 85,000 pieces were produced in 1410. The fact that the weavers' guild purchased its own guild house in 1389 may be regarded as an indicator of a favorable economic situation. From 1395 onward, Augsburg fustian was marketed at the Frankfurt fairs, and at the turn of the century it also found markets in Cologne, Prague, Wrocław, Krakow, and Vienna. Meanwhile, the so-called *Ungeld* riots of 1397–98, in which poor weavers protested against an indirect tax, also show that the fustian boom coincided with growing social tension between successful long-distance merchants and poor craftsmen.[46]

Nor was the textile sector immune to crises in the fifteenth century. During 1412, 1418–28, and 1431–33, trade bans proclaimed by Emperor Sigismund against the Republic of Venice impeded cotton imports. The so-called Second City War of 1449–50 and the empire's war against Duke Ludwig of Bavaria-Landshut in 1462–66 once again affected the Swabian economy,

FIGURE 2

Oldest view of the city of Augsburg from the chronicle of Sigismund Meisterlin, 1457.
(Staats- und Stadtbibliothek Augsburg)

and the development of indirect tax revenues in Augsburg indicates a severe crisis of the urban crafts that lasted from 1450 to 1480. This difficult period also witnessed the *Ungeld* riots of 1466–67, in which the populace vented its anger over the high tax burden. In 1475, still in the middle of the economic crisis, 550 weavers brought 43,400 pieces of fustian to the urban bleachery. Including the inferior types of cloth, which were not bleached but dyed, total production may have come to 65,000 pieces of cloth. A quarter of Augsburg's guild members were engaged in fustian production at that time.[47]

Crises and boom periods of craft production are also reflected in the admission of new citizens. While Augsburg's book of new citizens (*Bürgerbuch*) recorded a growing number of foreign weavers who obtained citizenship after 1390, the number of new citizen weavers declined after the proclamation of the trade ban against Venice in 1410. Beginning in the 1430s, the number of admissions moved sharply upward. In addition to immigrants from Augsburg's rural environs, weavers from towns such as Günzburg and Weissenburg were now received as citizens. At the peak of the economic crisis in the 1460s, no new citizens were recorded at all, but in the 1480s, the migration of weavers to Augsburg began to rise substantially again.[48]

The ebb and flow of new citizens also provides evidence that economic development was shaped by dynamic interactions between urban and rural textile crafts. By 1400, a putting-out system had developed in eastern Swabia, in which urban merchants delivered cotton to rural weavers and received the finished cloth from them. Augsburg merchants are also documented as participants in the putting-out system in Nördlingen and in the area around Memmingen. After urban weavers protested against competition from the countryside, Augsburg in 1411 prohibited the putting-out system in the textile sector within a radius of three German miles (about 20 kilometers) around the city. This prohibition was repeated several times during the following decades.[49] The production of flax yarn and *Wepfen* (a semi-finished product) in the countryside, however, continued to be of great importance to urban fustian production. In 1443, a *Wepfenschau*, an institution for monitoring the quality of this semi-finished product, was founded in the imperial city. While the institution was prohibited again after a short time and all intermediate trade in yarn was forbidden, the importation of yarn and *Wepfen* from the countryside was an established practice in the second half of the fifteenth century. The yarn-trading area of the city of Augsburg extended as far as the Allgäu and Bavaria. Yarn imports from central Germany and Silesia, which are documented from the mid-1480s onward, once again led to massive conflicts that lasted from 1494 to 1501. Poor weavers who depended entirely on their craft emphasized that yarn imports would render them more dependent on the merchants. Moreover, they feared a decline of cloth prices due to intensifying competition among the producers and negative consequences for flax production and yarn spinning in Augsburg's rural environs. The proponents of the yarn imports—who included Lukas Fugger, among other long-distance merchants—countered these criticisms by pointing to a shortage of raw materials in the textile sector, the higher quality of yarn from central Germany, and the prospects of increasing production, which would also lead to higher indirect tax collection. The city council initially heeded the arguments of the merchants but then restricted yarn imports in 1501 and issued a detailed ordinance on quality control.[50]

Many of the richest families in Augsburg of the fifteenth century were active in the putting out of fustian. Some families, such as the Artzts, Hämmerlins, and Kramers, were social climbers from the weavers' guild themselves. In addition, the ranks of Augsburg's merchants were augmented by immigrants from other Swabian textile towns, such as Lauingen, Nördlingen, and Donauwörth.[51] At the Nördlingen Pentecost fair, an important distribution center for southern German long-distance traders, a total number of thirty-six Augsburg merchants are documented between 1393 and 1440; nearly all of them were engaged in the textile trade. In the 1390s, Karl Egen, Hans Rem, and Hans Prun went to Nördlingen with cloth to sell; in 1434, Hans Meuting took white fustian to the fairs; and in 1468–69, the brothers Ulrich und Wolfgang Stammler, in-laws of the Fuggers "vom Reh," did business there. Hektor Mülich, who married Anna Fugger as his second wife, is also documented as a cloth trader in Nördlingen.[52] The earliest documented fustian transaction of a "Füker from Augsburg"—who is not identified by his first name—dates from January 1440. This "Füker" sold 102 pieces of black fustian to the son of the Nuremberg merchant Marquard II Mendel for 137 gold florins. This transaction also marks the earliest appearance of the Fuggers' trademark, the trident, on an archival document.[53]

The economic competitiveness of the imperial city of Augsburg, however, relied not merely on the production of fustians. As early as the mid-fifteenth century, the urban craft sector was characterized by a highly developed textile-finishing branch. Furriers and leather-working trades were important, as well, and by the end of the fifteenth century, a differentiated metalworking sector had developed.[54] The financial sector was still dominated by Nuremberg firms around 1400, but Augsburg companies were already transacting financial business with the courts of Bavaria and France and handled money transfers from German dioceses to Rome. The most dynamic Augsburg merchant firm of the mid-fifteenth century undoubtedly was the Meuting company. It maintained close business ties with Venice, Genoa, and Bruges, and in 1456, it granted Duke Sigismund of Tyrol a loan of 35,000 florins, for which it was assigned silver from the Tyrolean mines.[55] Three decades later, this combination of credit and trade in precious metals became a mainstay of the Fuggers' commerce. The rise of Augsburg's long-distance trade was accompanied by a substantial concentration of wealth. The twenty-two persons who paid taxes on estates of more than 10,000 florins in 1492 owned 30 percent of the city's total wealth.[56]

Knowledge of these economic interdependencies and contexts is important for understanding the rise of the Fuggers. When Hans Fugger made the move from Graben to Augsburg, the fustian boom was just beginning. Thanks to a certain amount of starting capital and two advantageous marriages, he was able to profit from the favorable economic circumstances of the late fourteenth century and early fifteenth century. The lawsuits of Lukas and Ulrich Fugger against Augsburg weavers before the city court and their intensive commercial relations with Venice in the late fifteenth century indicate that they were active in the textile putting-out system. At the same time, the upward trend of the family's wealth during the crisis periods from 1410 to 1430 and again from 1450 to 1480 demonstrates the ability of the first generations of the Fuggers of Augsburg to weather troubled economic times. When a new economic upswing started at the end of the fifteenth century, the Fuggers were prepared for it in terms of personnel, financial means, and business organization.

POLITICAL OFFICE AND SOCIAL STATUS

Since the uprising of dissatisfied artisans in October 1368, Augsburg's civic constitution had been dominated by the guilds. The original eighteen, and later seventeen, guilds—associations of craftsmen and traders—were the "basic units of the citizens' political participation." The most important political institution was the forty-four-member Small Council, which was composed of seventeen guild masters, twelve additional leaders of large and prestigious guilds, and fifteen *Herren,* or members of the urban patriciate. The patriciate, which had governed the city exclusively until 1368, refused to accept new members after 1383. By the end of the fifteenth century, the makeup of the Small Council had evolved further. It now had forty-two members and consisted of two representatives of each of the seventeen guilds, as well as eight patricians. The Grand Council included the seventeen guild masters, the twelve members of the leadership committee of each guild, and eight *Herren,* thus consisting of 229 members at the end of the fifteenth century. This institution played hardly any role in day-to-day civic affairs; nevertheless, its significance as a forum where public opinion was formed and the interests of city government and citizenry were balanced against each other should not be underestimated. Two burgomasters—one patrician and one guild master—stood at the top of the government hierarchy. Together with three *Baumeister,* who were in charge of the city's expenditures; three receivers (*Einnehmer*); two keepers of the seal (*Siegler*); and three more councilors, they formed the Committee of Thirteen, which had emerged as the real center of political decision making by the end of the fifteenth century. The Committee of Thirteen prepared council decisions and handled most of the city's day-to-day political business. The gradual expansion of the city's administration had created some forty additional offices by 1500, which were all occupied by members of the Small Council. They included the head guardians of widows, orphans, and charitable endowments (*Oberpfleger*); the masters in charge of the quality control of textiles (*Schaumeister*); the wedding masters (*Hochzeitsmeister*); and the judges sitting on the city court.[57]

In the fifteenth-century imperial city, political influence was closely tied to economic standing. Between 1396 and 1516, 94 percent of the holders of the four most important civic offices came from the ranks of the top 3 percent of Augsburg's taxpayers. Thus, the mercantile elite's dominance of the most important offices was virtually unchallenged. An important reason for this predominance of the elite lay in the fact that council members did not receive a salary; rather, they received merely a small allowance for their expenses. They had to be available and financially able to afford the exercise of political office. Moreover, the political culture of the imperial city was shaped by the conviction that council offices should be filled by the most virtuous and prestigious men, and the great merchants and most successful craftsmen were generally thought to possess these qualities. Therefore, the annual elections were not democratic polls but acts of confirmation in which the incumbents were almost invariably reelected.[58]

So what was the role of the early Fuggers, whose economic success had propelled them into the ranks of Augsburg's richest citizens, within this oligarchic city government? Hans Fugger, the immigrant from Graben, sat on the Grand Council as a member of the twelve of the weavers' guild, and for the year 1398 he is documented as a collector of the *Weinungeld,* the indirect tax on wine.[59] For the first half of the fifteenth century, there is no evidence whatsoever that the Fuggers were politically active. By midcentury, Jakob Fugger the Elder emerges as one of the twelve of the weavers' guild and a member of the Grand Council. Moreover, he held the offices of collector of the tax on linens (*Leinwandungelter*), member of the monitoring board for linen products (*Leinwandschauer*), and judge on the city court. These offices testify to a certain reputation within Augsburg's citizenry, but they were not among the highest civic offices that were the exclusive domain of members of the inner circle of power.[60] Jakob Fugger's nephew Lukas Fugger "vom Reh" rose higher in the hierarchy of civic offices than his uncle. He sat on the Grand Council as a member of the twelve of the weavers' guild in 1474 and held a plethora of civic offices in the 1480s — *Seelhauspfleger,* or guardian of a charitable institution; *Findelhauspfleger,* or guardian of the foundling home; *Einunger,* in charge of settling petty quarrels; *Wollschauer* and *Heringsschauer,* commissioned to monitor the quality of wool and herrings; *Barchentungelter* and *Weinungelter,* or collector of the taxes on fustians and wine. Between 1484 and 1494, he filled the important office of tax master, and from 1490 to 1494, he sat on the Council of Thirteen as one of the receivers (*Einnehmer*). He became involved as a mediator in the lengthy quarrel between the city council and the cathedral chapter about the acceptance of Augsburg citizens into the chapter in 1485, and four years later he took part in the reception of King Maximilian outside the city gates as guild master of the weavers. Through his second wife, Klara Konzelmann, and his daughter-in-law Justina Riedler, Lukas Fugger was also connected by family ties to other influential families in urban politics. It is quite possible that only his bankruptcy prevented his election to the office of burgomaster.[61]

Even though Lukas Fugger made it almost to the top of the hierarchy of civic offices, the Fugger family as a whole clearly played a secondary role in fifteenth-century urban politics compared not only with patrician families such as the Rehlingers, Langenmantels, and Welsers, but also with merchant families such as the Riedlers, Walthers, and Hörnlins.[62] What was more important than political office holding was the fact that the family systematically increased its prestige — or, to use modern terminology, it accumulated social capital. Family alliances were certainly important in this process. Lukas Fugger's sons Matthäus and Jakob gained access to the Gentlemen's Drinking Hall (*Herrentrinkstube*), the exclusive association of patricians and prestigious guild members, through their marriages, respectively, to Helena Mülich in 1478 and Ursula Rem in 1480. The right to participate in meetings and festivities in the drinking hall could be obtained only by virtue of birth or marriage into a family that held drinking-hall privileges.[63] The Gentlemen's Drinking Hall functioned as the "social center of gravity of the economic and political elite" and simultaneously as the "economic center of communication" for the rich merchants.[64] In 1488, Lukas Fugger also gained access to it by virtue of his second marriage, to Klara Konzelmann.[65] At that time, the Fuggers "von der Lilie" had already been accepted into this prestigious circle through their marriage alliances with the Lauginger, Imhof, Rem, and Mülich families. The importance that the family attached to access to the drinking hall is underscored by an entry in the Fuggers' *Book of Honors* stating that Jakob Fugger had offered at his own cost to rebuild the house on Augsburg's Perlach Square in which the Gentlemen's Drinking Hall was located. In return, Fugger asked the drinking-hall society for permission to attach "the Fuggers' lily coat of arms" to it "out of gratefulness and to honor the Fuggers' name." The drinking-hall society reportedly denied the request, but the decision gave them "ample cause for regret on later occasions."[66]

In addition to the city council as the central political institution and the drinking hall as the pivotal social institution, the parish churches functioned as important forums for the allocation of social prestige. In the late fifteenth century, the Fugger family made deliberate use of this forum, as well. In 1479, the widow of Jakob the Elder purchased a pew in the collegiate church of St. Moritz, whose parish included numerous members of the urban elite, and in 1485, her son Ulrich did the same. The focus of the Fuggers' activity at the time, however, was the abbey church of St. Ulrich and Afra, which was being remodeled in the late gothic style. In 1478, the brothers Ulrich, Georg, and Jakob Fugger paid for two new arches for the vault and announced their intention to commission an altar painting and a stained-glass window. In return, they obtained the right to attach their coat of arms to the altar. Two years later, they had the seating for two chapels made and their coat of arms attached to one of them. In 1485, the sculptor Michel Erhart of Ulm received the commission to produce "a raw, carved wooden altarpiece" that was to cost between 40 and 60 florins. The painter Gumpold Gültlinger was to paint the altar in 1490 for up to 200 florins.[67] Although the Fuggers' foundations and art patronage would take on altogether different dimensions in the sixteenth century, even these early activities show that the family strove to increase its social prestige by contributing to the decoration of public spaces.

THE BEGINNINGS OF JAKOB FUGGER THE RICH

Among the recurring commonplaces of the Fuggers' history is the claim that their most important merchant, Jakob Fugger, who was born on March 6, 1459, as the tenth of eleven children of Jakob Fugger the Elder and Barbara Bäsinger in Augsburg, was initially destined to become a cleric. According to Max Jansen, "Jakob had already received the minor orders and was a canon in Herrieden [when] Ulrich won his brother Jakob back for the secular life in 1478, and with him the most ingenious representative of the Fuggers' trade."[68] "The theologian became a merchant," Jakob Strieder wrote. Baron Götz von Pölnitz also claimed that "the youngest son was not needed in the trade," and therefore it seemed logical to "destine him for a clerical career."[69] A chain of misfortunes—the death of his father in 1469; the early demise of his brothers Hans and Andreas during their commercial apprenticeship in Venice; the death of his brother Peter in Nuremberg in 1473; and, finally, Marx's demise in Rome in 1478—apparently left the surviving brothers Ulrich and Georg with no option other than to take the youngest brother into the business and send him to Venice as the family firm's representative.[70] This version is supported by the family's *Book of Honors,* which states: "But when, by divine providence, the Fuggers' commerce had increased and prospered, and their four brothers had expired, the two brothers Ulrich and Georg made this man, Jakob Fugger, renounce and give up his benefice as a canon, and called on him to conduct their commerce, which he did in obedience to them."[71]

There is no doubt that the family had acquired a canonical benefice for Jakob in Herrieden when he was still young. In 1479, Jakob Fugger personally resigned this benefice in Rome. Max Jansen discovered one hundred years ago, however, that Jakob Fugger apparently never attended a university—an observation that hardly fits the notion of systematic preparation for a clerical career. Pölnitz even came to the remarkable conclusion that Jakob's stay in Herrieden seems to have lasted only a few months. He stated that Jakob Fugger was "never a clergyman" but "remained close to the business from his youth."[72] Moreover, Peter Geffcken has recently found evidence that Jakob was staying in Venice as early as 1473. This implies that he started his mercantile apprenticeship at about the same age as other south German merchants' sons.[73] We may conclude from this that the Fugger family pursued several options from the very beginning. The youngest son was provided with a clerical benefice in case he was not needed in the trading company, but the acquisition of such a benefice was by no means understood as excluding other alternatives. Given the uncertainty of life and the omnipresence of death in the late Middle Ages, it was indispensable for merchant families to have such alternatives.

THE ORGANIZATION OF COMMERCE

On August 18, 1494, the brothers Ulrich, Georg, and Jakob Fugger signed a contract in which they proclaimed their willingness to continue their existing "common brotherly trade." The company contract of the firm Ulrich Fugger and Brothers of Augsburg was valid for a period of six years. During this period, the capital that the associates had invested and the profits earned were to remain in the company, and the brothers obliged themselves to conduct no trade on their own account during the contract period. Each associate was equally entitled to represent the company in its external affairs, to do business for it, and to hire or fire employees. Furthermore, the contract established rules for the withdrawal of capital for personal use and for the mediation of differences by majority vote. If one of the associates died within the six-year period, his capital investment was to remain in the company for three more years before it had to be paid out to his heirs in installments.[1] While the older historiography discerned a "merciless neglect of all the heirs" in this contract, which allegedly testified to the "inner greatness, the lordly, even domineering character of this fundamental law of the Fuggers' commerce,"[2] comparative research demonstrates that the terms of the 1494 agreement were hardly unusual. Most southern German trading companies around 1500 were combinations of a small number of kinsmen; like the Fugger firm, other companies also drew a clear distinction between associates, who voted in company affairs and shared in the profits, and other family members, who could merely invest their money as deposits at fixed interest rates. And as in the Fuggers' case, other company contracts set definite rules for the event of the death of one or more associates to ensure the survival of the firm.[3]

That the company was named after Ulrich Fugger in the 1494 company

FIGURE 3

Portrait of Jakob Fugger the Rich (1459–1525), Albrecht Dürer and workshop, 1518/20.
(Bayerische Staatsgemaeldesammlungen—Staatsgalerie Augsburg)

TABLE 4
Tax payments of the Fuggers "von der Lilie" (in florins)

	1486	1492	1498	1504	1510
Ulrich	9,300	16,971	22,771 ⎫		
Georg	—	13,971	18,971 ⎬ 100,000		258,400
Jakob	—	11,971	15,971 ⎭		
Jakob's widow	13,200	15,971	22,971 (estate)		
Total	22,500	58,884	80,684	100,000	258,400

Source: Geffcken, "Soziale Schichtung," appendix, 156–57 (table 19), 166–67 (table 20), 176–77 (table 21), 186 (table 22).

contract indicates, on the one hand, that he was the oldest brother. The fact that the youngest brother had been largely responsible for the firm's expansion was less important in this context than the principle of seniority.[4] On the other hand, the naming of the firm may also reflect the fact that Ulrich, according to the city tax books, owned a larger estate at the time than Georg and the still unmarried Jakob. The tax data assembled in table 4 also show that the assessed property value of the three brothers and their widowed mother had sharply risen since 1486. Together, the Fuggers "von der Lilie" were assessed at more than 20,000 florins above the richest person in late-fifteenth-century Augsburg, the widow of Lukas Herwart. In 1504, the brothers' estate was summarily valued at 100,000 florins, and six years later, after Georg had died in 1506 and Ulrich in 1510, Jakob paid taxes on an estate of 258,400 florins for himself and his relatives. Although the Fuggers' tax payments had increased more than tenfold within twenty-four years, these payments reflect the actual development of their estate only partially, for the assessments certainly took into account only a small part of their investments beyond the city walls of Augsburg. Moreover, Jakob Fugger came to an agreement with the city of Augsburg in 1516 that absolved him and his family from disclosing their fortune if they annually paid a lump sum. This precedent for the special treatment of a rich family in matters of taxation ensured that the true wealth of the Fuggers would remain unknown to the city's tax collectors in the future.[5]

Although the 1494 contract expired in 1500, a new contract was signed only on December 23, 1502. Once again, it was to run for a period of six years but should tacitly continue if none of the associates terminated it. This document essentially confirmed the terms agreed on in 1494. At the same time, however, a separate contract was drawn up for the Hungarian trade (*Ungarischer Handel*), which the Fuggers operated jointly with Hans Thurzo and his sons. The mining and trading activities of this separate venture were to be conducted at joint profit and loss. This special contract explicitly stipulated that female descendants and family members who had become clerics were to be excluded from the mining and smelting properties; these should remain "with our legitimate male heirs and with our own name and lineage as an advance portion." In the event that one of the brothers died, the survivors were to continue the trade, pay off the female and clerical descendants of the deceased, and prepare the most capable among his sons for future participation in the management of the firm. As a rule, responsibility for the operations of the Hungarian trade was to rest with two managers. In an additional contract, the brothers established guidelines for the administration of their joint property and for the transfer of their real estate in and near Augsburg and their valuables to their heirs.[6]

The deaths of Georg Fugger on March 14, 1506, and Ulrich Fugger on April 19, 1510, left Jakob Fugger as the sole surviving associate. According to the 1502 contracts, he was entitled to run the company alone. On August 3, 1510, his nephews Ulrich the Younger and Hieronymus, sons of Ulrich Fugger, as well as Marx, Raymund, and Anton, sons of Georg Fugger, formally agreed to the continuation of the company under the directorship of their uncle, who had married in 1498 but had remained childless. Jakob Fugger then drew up a general balance and paid off his brothers' daughters, as well as Marx Fugger, who had become a clergyman. Moreover, he issued a document in 1512 proclaiming his intention to continue the company with his nephews Ulrich, Hieronymus, Raymund, and Anton Fugger under the name of "Jacob Fugger and his Brothers' Sons." The nephews left their entire estates in the firm and committed themselves to unconditional obedience to their uncle's orders, as well as to absolute discretion about the company's affairs. Jakob Fugger now styled himself "principal lord of this, my own trade," and reserved for himself the right to fix profit shares, exclude associates, and dissolve the firm. In the event of Jakob's death, Ulrich and Raymund were to take over the management of the firm; in addition, one of them besides Jakob was to manage the Hungarian trade. In additional clauses, Jakob Fugger settled the inheritance of common real estate and the usufruct rights of his wife, Sibylla, during her widowhood.[7]

Taken together, the contracts of 1494, 1502, and 1512 document the shifting balance of power within the company from three formally equal brothers to the sole leadership and control of Jakob Fugger. Moreover, they reveal the tendency to restrict the circle of associates to the male descendants. The 1502 contract on the Hungarian trade for the first time explicitly states the aim to maintain "our name and lineage and our male heirs and descendants in more prosperous circumstances." In the declarations he issued on the future of the Hungarian trade and the real-estate holdings in 1512, Jakob Fugger referred to the "honor, utility, and prosperity in particular of our legitimate, secular male name and lineage."[8] Although most other contemporary trading companies were made up of male associates, the explicit restriction to the male lineage of the family was actually something novel. With this new policy, the Fuggers also broke with their own family history, for in the fifteenth century, it had been the women who ensured the continuity of the Fuggers' commerce.

MINING AND METAL TRADE IN TYROL AND HUNGARY

A decisive turning point in the development of the Fugger enterprise came in 1485 when the brothers Ulrich, Georg, and Jakob Fugger lent 3,000 florins to Archduke Sigismund of Tyrol, who was perennially short of funds. This did not yet make them large creditors of the archduke, who owed 10,000 florins to the trading and mining firm of the Baumgartners of Kufstein and more than 60,000 florins to Antonio Cavalli, or Anton vom Ross, a courtier, mining entrepreneur, and director of Tyrol's financial administration at the time. But this first loan of 3,000 florins already shows the typical characteristics of the Fuggers' business in Tyrol, for the loans bore no interest but were paid back in silver. Tyrol's mining entrepreneurs—the so-called *Gewerken*—were obliged to sell the metal that they had extracted to the territorial lord at a fixed price, and the lord ceded his option of purchase to his creditors, who also took over the silver at fixed prices. As the mines in the Inn Valley, and especially those in the district of Schwaz, were then the richest in all of Europe, these contracts allowed the Fuggers to enter the large-scale trade in metals. Thus, the Tyrolean mining operator Christian Tänzl received an order in 1485 to supply the Fuggers with 1,000 Marks, or 281 kilograms, of silver.[9]

The Fuggers' relations with Sigismund were strengthened by the war between the archduke and the Republic of Venice in 1487–88. On the one hand, this war led to the removal of Venetian merchants and investors from Tyrol; on the other hand, the Fuggers and Antonio Cavalli advanced some of the funds that Sigismund had to pay to Venice after the conclusion of peace. Once again, silver was assigned to them in return, and the Tyrolean estates guaranteed the repayment of the loans. In the fall of 1487, the Fuggers advanced the archduke a total of 14,500 florins on several occasions, and in the following spring they supplied him with an additional 8,000 florins. On June 9, 1488, these loans were followed up by a transaction that took on an entirely different dimension. In return for an advance of 150,000 florins, which was to be paid out in monthly installments, the Fuggers secured the entire output of the Schwaz silver mines for themselves at a price of 8 florins. Five of these 8 florins were to be paid to the smelter, while the archduke's "advantage," amounting to 3 florins, served to pay back the loan. The Fuggers committed themselves to supplying the territorial lord's mint in the town of Hall with 200 Marks of silver per week. In 1489, the Fuggers paid Sigismund 122,000 florins and delivered 12,785 Marks of silver to the mint in Hall. If any surplus of silver was left over, the firm was permitted to sell it on the open market. The firm's profits mainly lay in the difference between the fixed purchase price they paid in Tyrol and the silver's real market value. By extending further credit, the Fuggers were able to secure silver from the territorial smelting works in Innsbruck, from the mint in Hall, and from Primör (Fiera di Primiero), in addition to the silver from Schwaz. By the end of 1489, the loans to Sigismund added up to more than 268,000 florins. Within the span of a few years, the Augsburg firm had thus replaced the Baumgartners of Kufstein as the archduke's most important business partners. As the town of Kufstein was then part of the duchy of Bavaria-Landshut, and as a takeover of Tyrol by its Bavarian neighbor after the death of the childless Sigismund seemed a real possibility, the Tyrolean estates initially welcomed the Kufstein firm's replacement.[10]

When the heavily indebted Tyrolean archduke yielded to pressure from the estates in March 1490 and abdicated his throne in favor of his relative, King Maximilian, who became the new sovereign of Tyrol and Outer Austria, the Fuggers benefited from the fact that they had already established close relations with the new ruler and had transferred money to Flanders for him. Maximilian recognized the current contracts with the Fuggers and assumed his predecessor's liabilities to the amount of 46,000 florins, which were to be paid back by weekly deliveries of 125 Marks of silver from the mint in Hall. In March 1491, Maximilian took his first substantial loan from the Fuggers. In return for an advance of 120,000 florins, the firm received almost 30,000 Marks of silver in that year. In 1492, the Augsburg firm again advanced 10,000 florins per month to the king and received more than 44,000 Marks of silver in return.[11]

During these years, the Fuggers were always prepared to supply the king with money when he needed it, and their financial services rendered them virtually indispensable. They redeemed the margravate of Burgau, a Habsburg territory extending between the cities of Augsburg and Ulm, which the House of Habsburg had pawned for its debts. They paid off Maximilian's liabilities, financed diplomatic embassies, and paid the salaries of bureaucrats and military officers. When Maximilian went to war against King

Charles VIII of France over the Burgundian inheritance of his first wife in 1493, the Fuggers made payments to the delegates negotiating the Peace of Senlis on behalf of Maximilian. When the Habsburg ruler married his second wife, Bianca Maria Sforza, the niece of the Milanese ruler Lodovico il Moro, the Italian branches of the Fugger firm supported the wedding preparations by providing credit and delivering valuable velvet cloth. The transfer of the bride's substantial dowry to her husband was likewise handled by the Fuggers. In 1494, the firm granted Maximilian three large loans amounting to 80,000 florins and paid him monthly advances of 6,600 florins. For 1495, Tyrol's account books, the *Raitbücher,* record Fugger loans totaling 101,213 florins, for which the Fuggers received 41,503 Marks of silver. According to Max Jansen, the Fuggers' advances to Archduke Sigismund and King Maximilian from 1485 to 1494 added up to more than 624,000 florins. Jansen calculated the amount of silver that the firm received in return at 200,000 Marks and estimated the profits the Augsburg firm drew from these transactions at 400,000 florins. Jansen's estimate is probably too high, but it clearly shows the large quantities of precious metal that the European markets absorbed within only a few years.[12]

The Fuggers initially focused their attention on the silver business but expanded their field of activity to trade in copper, which was increasingly needed for the production of a variety of commodities, including weapons and cannon, after 1490. When King Maximilian summoned the Baumgartners of Kufstein in 1492 to sell a part of their copper stores to him, the Fuggers resold the copper for the king's account in Venice at a profit. In May 1494, the firm made its first purchase of Tyrolean copper for its own account; at that time, however, it received only a small portion of total copper production.[13] Beyond that, the Fuggers also invested in the Salzburg mining districts of Gastein und Rauris, where they acquired their own shares in mines, and in Styria, but these activities were on a smaller scale than their Tyrolean business affairs.[14]

Subsequently the relations between the Fuggers and the Tyrolean government were not always cordial, and temporarily the firm hesitated to grant new loans. In the long run, however, the government in Innsbruck was unable to cope without the Fuggers' credit. Whatever the issue—representation at imperial diets, the financing of military actions in the Swiss War of 1499, Maximilian's wars against France and Venice, his proclamation as Holy Roman Emperor at Trent in 1508, payment for diplomatic embassies, or the salaries of members of his court and government—the Fuggers were asked for new advances over and over again.[15] Apart from numerous smaller loans, the silver and copper purchases remained the backbone of the financial relations between the crown and the firm. In October 1508, for example, a metal contract was concluded in which the Fuggers agreed to purchase 30,000 Marks of silver from the mint in Hall and 15,000 hundredweight of copper in return for an advance of 300,000 florins.[16]

How do we account for this meteoric rise of an enterprise that had certainly counted among the successful southern German commercial houses before 1485 but by no means had been in a dominant position? The answer that Jakob Fugger's biographers gave to this question is unequivocal: It was the genius of the great merchant, his enormous energy, and his feel for new business opportunities. But it also needs to be emphasized that the overall economic constellations and developments in the final decades of the fifteenth century were uniquely favorable. One important precondition was the upswing of Tyrolean mining, which is evident from silver output in the most important production region, Falkenstein near Schwaz (see map 1). Between 1470 and 1490, output tripled from 73,113 Marks in 1470–74 to 173,260 Marks in 1480–84 and 226,691 Marks in the late 1480s.[17] This upswing in silver production, which has to be viewed in the context of a general demographic and economic expansion accompanied by rising demand in the European economy for precious metals, went hand in hand with a growing demand for capital by mining entrepreneurs, the *Gewerken*. Shafts and tunnels needed to be deepened and maintained at greater cost, and technical innovations such as the introduction of new smelting processes required investments that the Tyrolean entrepreneurs were unable to make on their own. This provided well-capitalized southern German merchant houses with the opportunity to enter the lucrative trade in precious metals by combining the provision of credit with the marketing of the mines' output.[18]

In addition, the southern German merchant companies, whose activities had been strongly oriented toward Italy in the late Middle Ages, traditionally cultivated their connections to Tyrol. In the 1480s and 1490s, the Herwart and Gossembrot firms of Augsburg, as well as the Vöhlin company of Memmingen, invested in the Tyrolean metal trade.[19] In 1477, Georg Gossembrot, who came from a commercially active patrician family in Augsburg, had become the administrator (*Pfleger*) of the manor of Ehrenberg, which was located on the road from Augsburg to Innsbruck. In 1483, he had signed his first contract with Archduke Sigismund for the delivery of 1,000 hundredweight of copper. Later, Gossembrot entered the service of the Innsbruck court, and in the 1490s he was a leading member of Tyrol's financial administration as councilor of the Hofkammer, the central financial administration. Further steps marking his social ascent were the purchase of the manor of Hohenfreiberg, the marriage of his daughter into the noble Freiberg family,

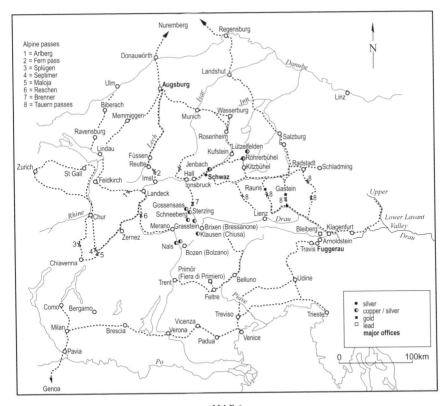

Within the image the following labels appear:

Alpine passes
1 = Arlberg
2 = Fern pass
3 = Splügen
4 = Septimer
5 = Maloja
6 = Reschen
7 = Brenner
8 = Tauern passes

Nuremberg, Regensburg, Danube, N, Donauwörth, Landshut, Ulm, Augsburg, Linz, Biberach, Memmingen, Munich, Wasserburg, Ravensburg, Lindau, Rosenheim, Salzburg, Zurich, Füssen, Reutte, Kufstein, Lützelfelden, Röhrerbühel, Radstadt, Schladming, St Gall, Feldkirch, Imst, Jenbach, Hall, Kitzbühel, Schwaz, Innsbruck, Rauris, Gastein, Upper, Landeck, Lienz, Lower Lavant Valley, Rhine, Chur, Gossensass, Schneeberg, Sterzing, Drau, Zernez, Merano, Grasstein, Brixen (Bressanone), Bleiberg, Klagenfurt, Klausen (Chiusa), Arnoldstein, Chiavenna, Nals, Bozen (Bolzano), Travis Fuggerau, Primör (Fiera di Primiero), Belluno, Udine, Trent, Feltre, Como, Bergamo, Treviso, Trieste, Milan, Vicenza, Brescia, Verona, Padua, Venice, Pavia, Po, Genoa, Piave, Inn, Isar, Lech, Drau

silver
copper / silver
gold
lead
major offices

0   100km

MAP 1

Major mining districts and company offices in the Alpine region at the time of Jakob and
Anton Fugger.
(Adapted from Pölnitz, Anton Fugger, *3:2:685)*

the construction of a house and funerary chapel near the monastery of St. Mang in Füssen, and his elevation to the nobility in 1500. In 1501, Gossembrot launched an ambitious project to lease the entire revenues of the hereditary lands of Austria, but he died in the following year.[20] As a member of the Tyrolean government, Gossembrot naturally promoted the interests of the commercial company that he ran with his brother Sigmund. In December 1492, however, he also negotiated a loan contract between the Fugger firm and the Tyrolean government, and in the following years he handled a number of transactions with the Fuggers. In 1495, the Fugger, Gossembrot, and Herwart firms jointly granted King Maximilian a loan of 64,000 florins for a military operation and received 48,000 Marks of Tyrolean silver in return. In 1496–97, the three firms purchased Tyrolean silver together with the Baumgartner company of Kufstein.[21] The Augsburg citizen Hans von Stetten, who represented the Baumgartners' interests in Tyrol, was also among the Fuggers' regular business partners during these years.[22]

Despite these strong connections between Augsburg and Tyrol, the Fuggers hardly would have been able to provide the enormous amounts of money requested by their princely business partners on their own. Instead, they had to raise a large portion of the sums they advanced to Sigismund and Maximilian as outside capital at fixed interest rates. The 1494 company contract made explicit provisions for this option. Unfortunately, we have little information about the Fuggers' raising of capital during this phase of expansion. In 1488, they accepted a deposit of 4,607 florins from the children of the Augsburg patrician Bernhard Rehlinger, and in 1495, the merchant Georg Grander and his wife invested capital in the Fugger firm.[23] Moreover, we know that Augsburg merchant companies preferred to take deposits from family members and relatives. Thus, we can assume that additional capital was mobilized through the marriage alliances with the rich Lauginger, Imhof, Meuting, Mülich, and Rem families. Possibly, the Fuggers also accepted sums from influential bureaucrats and councilors at the Innsbruck court even at this early stage. Melchior von Meckau, the prince-bishop of Bressanone (Brixen) who was also a councilor in Innsbruck, later became one of their most important creditors. In any case, the Fuggers probably benefited from the fact that interest rates on urban life annuities and eternal annuities, in which many wealthy citizens had invested their capital, had fallen during the second half of the fifteenth century. In Augsburg, they stood at merely 4 percent. This made deposits in merchant companies an attractive form of investment and allowed firms to expand their business operations.[24]

November 15, 1494, marked another watershed: the founding of the common Hungarian trade (*Gemeiner Ungarischer Handel*). On that day, Kilian

Auer, a citizen of Wrocław, signed a contract with the mining engineer Hans Thurzo of Krakow and his son Georg in the Fuggers' name. Thurzo had leased the mines in Neusohl (Banská Bystrica) in present-day Slovakia only shortly before. The Fuggers and the Thurzos agreed on the joint operation of the mines for a period of sixteen years and on the construction of a smelting works. While Thurzo brought his mining properties and technical know-how into the partnership, the Fuggers consented to finance all business activities. The agreement was made under favorable political circumstances, for King Maximilian was pursuing a dynastic rapprochement with the new Hungarian king, Władisław II, after the Peace of Pressburg (Bratislava) between the Holy Roman Empire and Hungary was concluded in 1491. Władisław recognized the Habsburgs as co-rulers of his kingdom and as successors in the event of his childless death. The bishop of Pécs, who pushed his own claims to the Neusohl mines, was pressured by Maximilian and signed a contract in late December in which he leased his Neusohl properties to Hans Thurzo for a period of ten years. In March 1495, King Władisław also gave his assent, and the Fuggers and Thurzos renewed the contract that they had concluded the year before. The ore extracted by the Neusohl mining entrepreneurs was submitted to a *Saiger* process—a separation of silver and copper by adding lead—in the smelting works Hans Thurzo built in Neusohl. In April 1496, the Hungarian king gave the Thurzos permission to construct additional smelting works and granted them the right to sell a portion of the silver they extracted on the open market.[25]

This opened up enormous opportunities for profit. As early as 1495, the company acquired a lead mine near Villach in Carinthia and constructed the *Saiger* works of Fuggerau on the territory of the monastery of Arnoldstein, which was part of the Carinthian possessions of the prince-bishop of Bamberg. Most of the copper was marketed in Venice. Shortly afterward, the company built a *Saiger* works at Hohenkirchen in Thuringia, which was also situated on the territory of a monastery, in this case the Cistercian convent of St. Georgenthal. Hohenkirchen mainly served to supply the German market with copper via Nuremberg and Frankfurt on the Main. Because Hohenkirchen, in contrast to Carinthia, did not have a local supply of lead, the metal was brought in from Goslar in Lower Saxony and from the Rhineland. With the help of technical experts from Tyrol and Slovakia, Fuggerau and Hohenkirchen were turned into highly productive enterprises. From 1495 to 1504, Fuggerau delivered about 50,000 hundredweight of copper and almost 22,000 Marks of silver to the Venetian market alone, while Hohenkirchen processed 54,000 hundredweight of copper and extracted more than 30,000 Marks of silver during the same time span. A third *Saiger* works was built in Moschnitz (Moštenice), 30 kilometers northwest of Neusohl. In Neusohl, the company also constructed smelting works and hammer mills. Step by step, the real estate, mines, and industrial holdings in Neusohl were expanded. By providing credit to the Hungarian royal couple, the Fuggers secured additional rights and privileges for themselves. By 1504, the investments in the Hungarian trade added up to more than 1 million Hungarian florins (see map 2).[26]

To market the Slovakian copper, the Fuggers built an elaborate European distribution network. They constructed a road from Neusohl to Teschen (Cieszyn) via the Jablonka Pass, which was used to transport more than 40,000 hundredweight of copper between 1500 and 1504 alone, and another pass road to Rosenberg (Ružomberok).[27] In addition, they established a string of new offices. Wrocław, where the firm was initially represented by its business partner Kilian Auer but where it had its own representatives no later than 1498, functioned as the distribution center for the northeastern parts of central Europe. The major portion of the copper transports arriving in Wrocław went on to Leipzig and Hohenkirchen. From Wrocław, the company also entered the gold-mining district on the Reichenstein in 1502. Within ten years, the firm had extracted 1,138 Marks of gold there, which yielded a return of 66,000 Hungarian florins. The office in Leipzig, which had been established in 1496, received about 200,000 hundredweight of Hungarian copper from 1507 to 1526, most of which was sent on to Hohenkirchen. In the kingdom of Poland, the company set up an office in Krakow, and no later than 1504 it also had a branch in the Hungarian city of Ofen (present-day Budapest). Through this network of offices, the Fuggers organized the transport of Hungarian copper to the Baltic seaports of Gdansk (Danzig), Szczecin (Stettin), and Lübeck, from where the metal was shipped through the Danish Sound to Antwerp. The Venetian copper market was supplied on the land route via Wiener Neustadt, as well as on the sea route via the Adriatic ports of Trieste and Zengg (Senj). A system of toll and safe-conduct agreements secured the major transport routes and limited the duties the company had to pay.[28]

According to Léon Schick's calculations, the three *Saiger* works of the Hungarian trade had a total output of 316,832 Marks of silver, with a market value of 2 million florins, from 1494 to 1526. Some 174,907 Marks were produced in Moschnitz; 116,192 Marks, in Hohenkirchen; and 25,643 Marks, in Fuggerau. After King Maximilian issued a prohibition of the *Saiger* process in 1504 to protect Tyrolean silver production, Fuggerau was transformed into a brass works.[29] During the same period, more than 800,000 hundredweight of copper were extracted in the Neusohl district. The Fuggers prob-

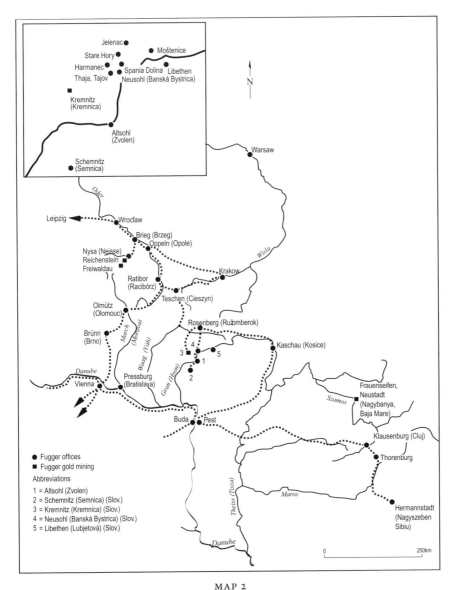

Inset map labels:
Jelenac
Moštenice
Stare Hory
Harmanec
Spania Dolina   Libethen
Thaja, Tajov   Neusohl (Banská Bystrica)
Kremnitz (Kremnica)
Altsohl (Zvolen)
Schemnitz (Semnica)

N

Main map labels:
Odra
Leipzig
Wrocław
Warsaw
Brieg (Brzeg)
Oppeln (Opole)
Nysa (Neisse)
Reichenstein
Freiwaldau
Wisła
Ratibor (Racibórz)
Krakow
Teschen (Cieszyn)
Olmütz (Olomouc)
Brünn (Brno)
Rosenberg (Ružomberok)
March (Morava)
Waag (Váh)
4
3   5
1
Kaschau (Kosice)
Danube
Pressburg (Bratislava)
Vienna
Gran (Hron)
2
Szamos
Frauenseifen, Neustadt (Nagybanya, Baja Mare)
Buda   Pest
Klausenburg (Cluj)
Thorenburg
Theiss (Tisza)
Maros
Hermannstadt (Nagyszeben Sibiu)
Danube

● Fugger offices
■ Fugger gold mining
Abbreviations
1 = Altsohl (Zvolen)
2 = Schemnitz (Semnica) (Slov.)
3 = Kremnitz (Kremnica) (Slov.)
4 = Neusohl (Banská Bystrica) (Slov.)
5 = Libethen (Lubjetová) (Slov.)

0   250km

MAP 2

Major mining regions of the Fuggers in Silesia, Slovakia, and Transylvania.
(Adapted from Pölnitz, Anton Fugger, 3:2:686)

ably marketed about 700,000 hundredweight for their own account. Based on Reinhard Hildebrandt's calculations, the Slovakian output accounted for 37 percent of total European copper production in the first decade of the sixteenth century and 40 percent in the second decade. If we consider the role of the Fuggers in the Alpine copper trade, which made up about 40 percent of European production during the same period, the dominant position of the firm on the European copper market becomes obvious.[30] A calculation of the profits that the Fuggers made from the Hungarian copper trade is difficult because of the nature of the sources. Whereas some researchers have estimated a net profit of 1.5 million–2 million florins from 1494 to 1525, others have pointed out that the firm did not make any deductions during this period.[31]

The great upswing of the Hungarian trade, however, put copper prices on the international markets under pressure. To sustain the price of Tyrolean copper on the Venetian market, the Fuggers and three other firms—the Gossembrot and Herwart companies of Augsburg and the Baumgartners of Kufstein—formed a syndicate for which the Fuggers' factor handled the sale of copper on the Rialto. But Jakob Fugger dismantled the syndicate by selling Hungarian copper under the Thurzos' name as early as the fall of 1499. The resentment this measure caused among his competitors manifested itself in the strongly anti-Fugger policy that Georg Gossembrot subsequently pursued at the Innsbruck court.[32] A legal opinion on the copper syndicate written by the Augsburg city recorder Dr. Conrad Peutinger on behalf the Fuggers' competitors saw no contradiction in principle between this kind of combination and the ideal of the common good; still, it sharply criticized Fugger for violating trust and good faith. In Peutinger's opinion, "Such a company has to be regarded as a kind of fraternity, and [its members] should act in love and faithfulness toward one another like brothers." By linking business activities to ethical norms, Peutinger touched on a theme that would continue to occupy the Fuggers during the following decades.[33]

Meanwhile, the presence of the Fuggers in the Baltic Sea ports of Gdansk and Szczecin aroused the resistance of the cities of the Hanseatic League. Lübeck in particular feared the commercial expansion of its southern German competitors to Riga and Novgorod and the displacement of the Hanseatic merchants from the important markets in the Baltic states and Russia. Lübeck's capturing of a ship laden with Hungarian copper initiated a lengthy conflict in which Jakob Fugger mobilized the support of the emperor and the curia in Rome. Maximilian threatened Lübeck with the imperial ban and rejected the Hanseatic cities' claim that the Fuggers were conducting a monopolistic trade in copper. The conflict was eventually resolved on a contractual basis, but relations between the Hanseatic city and the southern German merchant company remained tense.[34]

The large-scale organization of mining in the Neusohl district also led to conflicts with the local population, especially the privileged inhabitants of the mining towns (the so-called *Waldbürger*), who feared the loss of their economic position. Previously independent mining entrepreneurs now became dependent on the Fuggers and Thurzos, and native traders regarded the company's commerce in supplies for the miners and smelters (*Pfennwerthandel*) as unwelcome competition. The Hungarian trade's high demand for wood led to arguments about the right to exploit the forests, and the Fuggers' and Thurzos' exemption from communal duties contributed to the financial crisis of the mining towns. The years around 1500 witnessed the first disputes between Hans Thurzo and the *Waldbürger* about the quality of silver supplies and their payment. In 1508, a man named Hieronymus Tischler, who was indebted to the Thurzos, apparently tried to incite an uprising and was sentenced to death as an instigator. Dissatisfaction with Thurzo's administration of the office of count of the chamber (*Kammergraf*), which implied far-reaching control of Slovakian mining production, manifested itself in refusals to pay duties in 1515. After King Władisław's death in 1516, moreover, the noble opposition, which rejected the succession of the Habsburg dynasty to the throne and viewed the close connection between the Fuggers and the House of Habsburg, as well as the crown's growing indebtedness to the associates of the Hungarian trade, with suspicion, gained influence at the Hungarian court. The decision of new Hungarian King Ludwig II to transfer the Slovakian mining towns to his wife, Maria, in 1522 and the appointment of Maria's confidant Bernhard Behaim as count of the chamber in 1524 signaled a shift in power that was detrimental to the Fuggers and the Thurzos, for Behaim supported the complaints of the mining towns against the Hungarian trade.[35] In 1525, the year of Jakob Fugger's death, the accumulated anger exploded into an open uprising that will be treated in more detail in the next chapter.

BUSINESS WITH THE ROMAN CURIA

In the late medieval church, the assignment of offices and benefices was heavily dependent on the beneficiaries' ability to pay for them; the resulting flow of ecclesiastical funds turned Rome into an important European financial center. The bankers transferred especially the *servitia*, which were due at the pope's confirmation of each newly elected bishop or prelate, and the *annates*, duties on offices or benefices conferred by the curia. Moreover, there were crusade taxes, funds from the sale of indulgences, and, in some regions, the so-called Peter's pence. During the fourteenth and fifteenth centuries, the transfer of these funds to the curia initially was handled largely by Lucchese bankers before it was taken over by Florentine and other Tuscan bankers. The Fuggers' earliest involvement in the transfer of *servitia* from Scandinavia to Rome dates back to 1476, and in 1488 the Fuggers and their partner Kilian Auer of Wrocław participated in transfers from Silesia to Rome. In 1495, they transferred the *servitium* of the newly elected bishop of Würzburg, Lorenz von Bibra, to the curia. Nevertheless, they still played a secondary role within the curial payment system of the time compared with the Medici, Strozzi, and other Florentine banking houses. Over the next two years, however, the volume of the Fuggers' Roman financial transactions increased sharply. During the accounting period 1496–97, the Fuggers handled more than 7,000 florins, including the *servitia* of five dioceses: Bremen, Münster, Osnabrück, Samland (East Prussia), and Utrecht.[36]

Subsequently, the Fuggers temporarily transferred funds from several French bishoprics. More important, however, they strengthened their connections to northern and eastern Europe (Sweden, Denmark, Poland, and Hungary). The transactions of the accounting period 1502–3 added up to a total of 9,370 florins. In addition to payments from a number of central European dioceses, they included transfers from Glasgow, Krakow, and Gran in Hungary. At the same time, the Fuggers handled their first transfer of funds from the sale of indulgences in Lothringia. Moreover, they established themselves as creditors of the curia. After the pope formed an alliance with Hungary and Venice against the Ottomans in 1501 and promised the Hungarian king annual subsidies of 40,000 ducats, the Fuggers took over the payment of these subsidies through their Venetian office and offered considerable advances on them. While Georg Schwab, a native of Eichstätt, had played a significant role in the establishment of the firm's Roman office,[37] Johann Zink coordinated the expansion of its business with the curia at the turn of the century. Zink, a native of Augsburg who headed the Fugger office in Rome from 1501 onward, promoted the interests not only of his employers but also his own. After he became a cleric, he accumulated at least thirty-two benefices in various German dioceses, as well as the curial offices and honors of count palatine, knight, notary, recorder, and papal *familiar*.[38]

Baron Götz von Pölnitz has emphasized that the economic importance of the Fuggers' transactions with the curia should not be exaggerated. Compared with the profits from the firm's Tyrolean and Hungarian mining activities, the income from favorable exchange transactions, the fees and commissions from money transfers, and the interest on loans (which partly had to be declared as "gifts" from the pope because of the prohibition of interest in canon law) would indeed have been merely of subsidiary importance.[39] But these profits hardly exhausted the advantages the family could derive from close business ties with the curia. As one of the most powerful central Italian states, with a highly developed administrative apparatus by the standards of the time, the papacy was also an important purchaser of the Fuggers' copper and silver. As an actor on the European political stage, the papacy made decisions that affected the firm's business interests—for example, commerce between Milan and Venice. Finally, as the center of the ecclesiastical system of benefices, Rome provided members of the Fugger family with opportunities for reward and social advancement that could be promoted by cultivating business ties with the curia. Georg Fugger's son Marx Fugger the Younger, who was born in 1488, collected ecclesiastical benefices at an early age. In 1503, his family purchased a canon's position in Würzburg and a provostship at the cathedral in Passau for him, and at the time of his early death in 1511, he held provostships in Passau, Speyer, Bamberg, Regensburg, and Augsburg, an archdeaconate in Legnica in the bishopric of Wrocław, and the papal offices of protonotary and recorder.[40]

After the death of Pope Alexander VI in August 1503 and the pontificate of Pius III, which lasted only a few weeks, Johann Zink continued to work energetically and successfully to strengthen the Fuggers' position at the curia under Pope Julius II (1503–13). The firm kept transferring the *servitia* and *annates* of numerous German, Polish, Hungarian, Dutch, and Scandinavian bishoprics. Moreover, it financed papal diplomatic embassies and the recruitment of 150 Swiss soldiers. The soldiers, who arrived in Rome in January 1506 and received their first monthly salary from the Fuggers, mark the origins of the pope's Swiss Guard, which still exists. The firm supplied the papacy with copper and tin, which was delivered to Civitavecchia, and in 1509 it was able to lease the *zecca*, or papal mint. Subsequently, the *zecca* minted a number of coins bearing the Fuggers' trademark, the trident and ring. The business in papal sales of indulgences also gained in importance during this time. The Fuggers transferred a portion of the funds that Raymond Peraudi, Cardinal of Gurk, had collected in the empire for a projected crusade against the Ottomans (which never materialized) up to his death in 1505. When Pope Julius II proclaimed an indulgence in 1507 to finance the construction of St. Peter's cathedral in Rome, the Fuggers took over the collection of indulgence moneys in Bohemia, Silesia, Hungary, and Poland.[41]

Under Julius's successor, Leo X (1513–21), a scion of the house of Medici, the business of indulgences moved to the center of the Fuggers' Roman affairs. Basically, an indulgence is the papally authorized replacement of an ecclesiastical penance by other pious and charitable works. The medieval church had developed the doctrine of purgatory as a "third space" between heaven and hell to alleviate the harsh alternative between salvation and damnation for the faithful. To shorten the time in purgatory, people might engage in good works such as pilgrimages and charitable donations, or they might purchase letters of indulgence that the popes issued on special occasions such as ecclesiastical jubilees. This practice was supported by the notion that the church administered a treasure of grace because of Christ's and the saints' merit; this treasure enabled the church to waive penances for sins the faithful had committed. From the fifteenth century onward, the people's growing desire to save their souls led to a rising demand for letters of indulgence while the church regarded them as a welcome means of financing charitable institutions, the building of churches, and other tasks. In 1516, for example, the city of Nuremberg asked Engelhard Schauer, who represented the Fuggers' interests in Rome beside Johann Zink, to provide it with a papal indulgence for the new city hospital. In the following year, the Fuggers guaranteed that one-third of the revenues from the sale of an indulgence, which was to finance the completion of the church in the Saxon mining town of Annaberg, would be transferred to the curia. The firm was also involved in organizing indulgences for the cathedral church in Constance, which had been badly damaged in a fire in 1511, and for the Dominican church in Augsburg.[42]

To finance the building of St. Peter's cathedral, Pope Leo X issued a new indulgence in 1514 for the ecclesiastical provinces of Mainz and Regensburg; the prince-bishoprics of Mainz, Magdeburg, and Halberstadt; and the margravate of Brandenburg. The initiative for this indulgence came from Albrecht von Brandenburg, who was also entrusted with its administration and was to keep half of the revenues. Albrecht, a brother of the elector of Brandenburg, had been elected archbishop of Magdeburg and administrator of Halberstadt in 1513; a year later, he had also been elected archbishop of Mainz. As these offices required not only papal confirmation but also dispensations for the accumulation of several bishoprics and for the youthful age of the Hohenzollern prince (who was born in 1490), Albrecht had to raise substantial sums and borrowed 21,000 ducats (about 28,000 florins) from the Fuggers. In the course of the lengthy negotiations in Rome, his debts increased to more than 48,000 florins. The indulgence was supposed to help him defray his debts, and by 1518 he was able to pay back 42,000 florins.[43] The sermons delivered by the Dominican monk Johann Tetzel to propagate this indulgence were the direct cause of the ninety-five theses that Martin Luther, professor of theology at the University of Wittenberg, published in October 1517. As the business ties between the archbishop and the commercial firm were unknown to him, Luther was primarily interested in a clarification of whether such sales of indulgences were theologically legitimate. They seemed questionable, especially because obtaining indulgences for deceased people had become more and more common.[44]

Apart from the sale of indulgences, the Fuggers continued to transfer a large portion of the *servitia* from German and Scandinavian dioceses during the pontificate of Leo X and granted loans to the curia. They paid out the curia's pensions to Swiss cantons and cardinals and supplied the papal artillery with copper. Leo X terminated the lease of the papal mint in 1515, but the Fuggers appear as leaseholders again from 1519 to 1521. When emperor and pope went to war against France in 1521, the Fuggers advanced considerable sums for the recruitment of Swiss soldiers. When Leo X died in the same year, he owed the firm 27,684 ducats. Pope Hadrian VI (1522–23) granted the Fugger factor Engelhard Schauer another minting monopoly for fifteen years, but the grant was repealed as early as September 1524 by his successor, the Medici Pope Clemens VII. Under Clemens, the close ties between the Fuggers and the curia gradually dissolved.[45]

THE FUGGERS IN THE CENTERS
OF EARLY MODERN WORLD TRADE

To market large quantities of Tyrolean and Hungarian copper and silver, it was indispensable for the Fuggers to maintain a presence at the most important European distribution centers. Around 1500, three economic centers were playing a crucial role. Venice was the traditional hub of southern German trade with Italy, as well as the center for imports of goods from the eastern Mediterranean and Asia—cotton, exotic fruits, silk, spices, and all kinds of luxury items. Lisbon was the starting point for Portugal's overseas expansion, first to the western coast of Africa, then, from 1498 onward, to the riches of East India. Finally, Antwerp replaced Bruges at this time as the commercial metropolis of northwestern Europe.[46] At these gateways of commerce, which can be characterized as early centers of world trade because of their significance for commercial exchange with the extra-European world, the Fuggers did not confine themselves to marketing certain products but also handled financial transactions of growing complexity.

For a long time, Venice had been a central point of reference for Augsburg's trade. Both the Fuggers "vom Reh" and their cousins "von der Lilie" are known to have traded on the Rialto in the 1470s, at the latest. Jakob Fugger had spent the time of his commercial apprenticeship there and had become familiar with the Venetian merchants' highly developed commercial and accounting techniques. On November 30, 1489, the state council of Venice confirmed the Fuggers' permanent possession of their chamber in the Fondaco dei Tedeschi, on whose maintenance and decoration they had spent large sums. During the following years, "Ulrich Fugger and Brothers" transacted Venetian letters of exchange with the Blum company of Frankfurt, and the sources frequently mention the firm's branch on the Rialto as an outlet for copper and silver from Tyrol and Slovakia, a center for the purchase of luxury goods, and a clearing station for transfers to the Roman curia.[47]

At the turn of the century. Venice had to cope with a series of setbacks. The expansion of the Ottomans in the eastern Mediterranean imperiled Venetian commercial and territorial interests; the Portuguese discovery of the sea route to India broke Venice's monopoly on the importation of Asian spices; the Fondaco dei Tedeschi was devastated by fire in 1505; and Emperor Maximilian repeatedly went to war against the republic from 1508 to 1516 and forbade his subjects to trade with Venice. Nevertheless, the Fuggers held on to their Venetian office. They contributed money to reconstruct the Fondaco after the disastrous fire, and, in close coordination with other commercial companies from Augsburg, they worked to keep the trade with Venice alive during the military offensives of Maximilian and the League of Cambrai against the republic. Both the emperor and the republic granted them special privileges for this purpose.[48] When the Venetian merchant-banking house of Agostini went bankrupt, the Fuggers, to whom the insolvent firm still owed payment for 500,000 pounds of copper, purchased a diamond with an estimated value of 20,000 ducats from the Agostini estate in 1509. The diamond was subsequently sold to the pope for 18,000 ducats. This transaction, which at first glance appears to have ended in loss, in fact had several advantages for the Fuggers. They disposed of a large amount of copper just before it could be confiscated after the outbreak of war between Maximilian and the republic of Venice; they safely transferred capital out of the danger zone; and they recommended themselves to the pope as suppliers of cherished luxury goods.[49]

The most detailed information we have for Jakob Fugger's Venetian trade comes from 1516. In that year, Matthäus Schwarz returned to his native city of Augsburg after a commercial apprenticeship in Venice and was hired by Jakob Fugger as a bookkeeper in the firm's Augsburg head office. In 1518, Schwarz wrote a model tract on bookkeeping in which he demonstrated his knowledge of mercantile accounting techniques. As Alfred Weitnauer has plausibly argued, Schwarz based his tract on the 1516 accounts of the Fuggers' Venetian office.[50] According to Weitnauer, the Fuggers' commerce in goods at the time focused on the sale of Tyrolean silver and copper, as well as the purchase of high-quality textiles (velvet, damask, sateen, camelhair) and precious stones.

The model tract does not offer any hints, however, about the purchase of cotton and spices. Whereas the turnover of goods documented in this source amounted to 225,000 ducats, the Venetian office's financial transactions during the same period had a volume of roughly 600,000 ducats. The transfer of letters of exchange between Venice and Antwerp alone had a volume of 100,000 ducats, and the office also handled numerous financial transactions with Lyons, Nuremberg, and Rome.[51]

When reports of the success of Vasco da Gama's expedition to India reached Augsburg in 1499, they were greeted with lively interest there and directed the attention of the imperial city's merchants toward Lisbon. The Augsburg city recorder Dr. Conrad Peutinger, who was interested in cosmography, collected news of Portuguese expeditions and translated a text on East India into German together with his brother-in-law Christoph Welser. Handwritten reports about Vasco da Gama's second expedition in 1502 as well as early news about the India trade in a collection of "merchant practices" preserved in the archives of the Augsburg merchant family of Baumgartner have fueled speculations that Germans participated in this East India voyage. The arrival of the first Portuguese spice transports in the port of Antwerp bolstered the news about the sea route to the riches of Asia.[52] The first southern German firm to seize the initiative and established direct relations with Portugal was Anton Welser, Konrad Vöhlin, and Associates of Augsburg in the fall of 1502. Three of its representatives traveled to Lisbon, where Simon Seitz concluded a commercial contract with King Manuel I of Portugal in February 1503 while Lucas Rem set up an office. Like other southern German firms, the Fuggers now rushed to establish their own office on the Tejo River. After some initial difficulties, an agreement was signed in August 1504 about the participation of Italian and southern German merchants in the Indian fleet of Francisco de Almeida, which was to set sail the following year.[53]

On the Portuguese side, the need to raise capital for the financing and outfitting of the expensive East India fleets, whose voyages lasted many months before the return freight arrived and any profits could be realized, provided the chief motivation for the crown's readiness to permit foreign merchants to participate directly in the India trade. Because copper and silver turned out to be the European trade goods that were most in demand in commercial exchanges with India, and because the southern German merchants held a dominant position in the marketing of Alpine and Hungarian metal products, they were particularly attractive contractual partners for the Portuguese crown. Apart from the news about the profits of the first East India fleets, the competition of Genoese and Florentine merchants, who invested in trade with Asia as early as 1501, may have been an important stimulus for the southern Germans. Moreover, the Fuggers and their southern German competitors had firsthand experience of the political and economic problems that conflicts with the Ottomans and the emperor had caused in Venice. From this perspective, too, the development of an alternative market for copper and silver and a new place to purchase spices and other Oriental goods made sense.[54]

The share of the Augsburg and Nuremberg merchants, who outfitted three vessels of Almeida's fleet together with the Italians, amounted to 36,000 Portuguese ducats, with the Welser-Vöhlin company raising the lion's share of 20,000 ducats. The Fuggers contributed 4,000 ducats, and the remaining 12,000 ducats came from the Augsburg houses of Gossembrot and Höchstetter and from the Imhof and Hirschvogel firms of Nuremberg. In contrast to the Welser-Vöhlins and Imhofs, the Fuggers apparently did not send their own agent to India. After the return of the ships in 1506, King Manuel I, fearing a glut of Portuguese pepper on European markets and falling prices, initially barred the foreign merchants from selling their freight, thereby causing lengthy legal disputes. When the imported goods were finally released, the Germans realized a profit of 150 percent to 175 percent on their sale, according to contemporary sources.[55]

After the king had declared the Portuguese India trade a crown monopoly in 1506, however, further direct participation of Augsburg and Nuremberg merchants became impossible. In addition, the 1506 fleet, in which the Welser-Vöhlin company had invested 3,430 ducats, turned out to be a costly failure. Despite these setbacks and high mortality among the Germans in Lisbon, the Welser-Vöhlins as well as the Fuggers held on to their Lisbon offices. When the Fuggers sent Hans von Schüren to Lisbon as their new representative in 1511, his arrogant demeanor caused severe conflicts within the Fuggers' office on the Tejo River, as well as within the German fraternity of St. Bartholomew.[56]

For Jakob Fugger, however, the significance of the Portuguese spice trade waned after 1510. When the agents of the Portuguese crown in Antwerp, Tomé Lopes and Rui Fernandes, came to Augsburg in 1515 and 1519, respectively, to negotiate with him about supply contracts for copper and pepper, the demand for copper for the India trade clearly was the central issue. Considering their dominant position in the European copper market, the Fuggers appeared to be the only firm capable of supplying the desired quantities, and the stagnation of the Venetian trade due to Emperor Maximilian's wars against the Republic of Venice made the development of a secure new outlet attractive from the Fuggers' perspective. Consequently, the negotiations between Lopes and Fugger in 1515 faltered not because of the conditions of the copper trade but because of Jakob Fugger's refusal to accept the quantities of pepper offered by the Portuguese crown. Rui Fernandes, however, was eventually able to conclude a three-year supply contract for copper with the Fuggers in 1521.[57]

The decline of Jakob Fugger's interest in Lisbon was not only due to the difficulties on the spot; it also reflected the fact that the city of Antwerp in the Netherlands, not Lisbon, rose to become western Europe's commercial metropolis as a consequence of Portugal's overseas expansion. In the fifteenth century, Antwerp, which had about 40,000 inhabitants by 1500, had emerged as a distribution center for English woolen cloth on the European continent. The woolen cloth trade, as well as the transit trade in Dutch goods, lured a growing number of Italian, Spanish, and German merchants to Antwerp. From about 1480 onward, the presence of the Meuting, Höchstetter, and Fugger "vom Reh" companies of Augsburg is recorded. But the real boom period of the city began when the Portuguese crown decided to bring the pepper imported from Asia to the markets of western Europe via Antwerp. In August 1501, the first caravels laden with pepper arrived in the port, and in 1508, a royal Portuguese trading post, the Feitoria de Flandres, was established. As the Portuguese needed mostly silver and copper for their trade with Africa and Asia, the southern German merchants became their most important commercial partners. For their part, the Augsburg and Nuremberg firms delivering silver and copper to Antwerp could make purchases of spices and English cloth there. As a consequence, Antwerp became the central market of northwestern Europe.[58]

A branch office of the Fugger firm on the Scheldt River is first documented in 1493. The firm was initially represented by Konrad Meuting, a Fugger relative, and from 1494 onward by Onofrius Varnbühl, who paid out a sum to King Maximilian in that year.[59] Antwerp's significance for the company grew with the city's role as a distribution center for copper from the Hungarian trade. As early as 1503, forty-one ships laden with copper arrived in the port of Antwerp from Gdansk. Between 1507 and 1526, about half of the Hungarian copper was placed on the Antwerp market.[60] The firm's position on the Scheldt was highlighted by the purchase and lavish decoration of a house in the Steenhouwersveste, a central location in the city of Antwerp, which the Fuggers acquired from the merchant Nicolaus (Claus) von Richterghem in 1508. The painter Albrecht Dürer, who visited the Fugger trading post during his stay in Antwerp in 1520, wrote that it had been "constructed altogether new and at great expense, with a particular tower, wide and large, and with a beautiful garden."[61]

Inasmuch as the most important goods for Antwerp's commerce, Hungarian copper and Portuguese pepper, were transported by sea, the firm's representatives repeatedly confronted the risks of maritime trade. Attacks by corsairs and maritime warfare posed dangers to their transports. In 1507, the Fuggers and some of their southern German competitors—the Imhof, Hirschvogel, Rehlinger, Höchstetter, and Welser-Vöhlin firms—jointly lobbied for the restoration of a shipload that a French corsair had captured en route from Antwerp to Lisbon.[62] In 1510 and 1513, ships laden with pepper for the Fuggers were on the way from Lisbon to Antwerp when they fell into the hands of pirates.[63] The commerce in luxury goods is exemplified by the Fuggers' relations with the tapestry weaver Pieter van Aelst of Brussels, who owed them 2,686 Flemish pounds in 1522. Van Aelst was able to pay back part of the sum at the Antwerp Pentecost market in 1523; for the remainder, he pawned seven valuable tapestries to the Fuggers. Since he was unable to pay back the remaining debt, the Fuggers were entitled to export the tapestries to Spain in 1525 and offer them for purchase by Emperor Charles V.[64]

Apart from its function as a distribution center for goods, Antwerp emerged as an important financial market in the early sixteenth century. Its rise as a financial metropolis is also reflected in the business affairs of the Fugger trading post. After Maximilian I had concluded an alliance with King Henry VIII of England, the Fuggers' trading post in Antwerp transferred English subsidies to the emperor in 1516. Moreover, it paid imperial troops in the Netherlands and became involved in the emperor's financial relations with Spain and the Swiss Confederacy. In the same year, Bernhard Stecher, the Fugger's representative in Antwerp, also granted the court in Brussels a loan of 27,000 Flemish pounds, which was guaranteed by the city of Antwerp. In 1518, the loans that had been granted in the Netherlands amounted to 38,000 pounds.[65] During the following decades, Antwerp's importance as a center of banking and finance continued to increase for the European economy in general and for the Fuggers in particular.

PARTNERS AND COMPETITORS

The Fuggers' ascent to a preeminent position among the southern German merchant companies around 1500 took place in the context of a general upswing of long-distance trade. Up to this point, we have encountered a number of firms that competed with the Fuggers on international markets but also cooperated with them time and again: the Gossembrots, Baumgartners, Welsers, Vöhlins, Höchstetters, Rehlingers, Imhofs, and Hirschvogels. In the pages that follow, a few particularly striking examples will illustrate the role of these firms in international commerce and their relations with the Fuggers.

Founded in 1496, the Welser-Vöhlin company, which would emerge as one the most important competitors of the Fugger firm, was the successor of the Vöhlin company of Memmingen. The Augsburg patrician Anton Welser (1451–1518) had married into the Vöhlin family of Memmingen in 1479 and had gradually taken over the position of junior director in the firm of his father-in-law, Hans Vöhlin. As his brother-in-law Konrad Vöhlin had married a Welser, the alliance between the two families was particularly intimate. In 1498, the Welser-Vöhlin company moved its headquarters from Memmingen to Augsburg, a decision that also reflects the growing superiority of the economic metropolis of Augsburg over the other Swabian imperial cities.[66] Whereas in the Fuggers' case, the circle of associates was restricted to the small group of male family members, the Welser-Vöhlin company had no fewer than eighteen associates in 1508. All of them were related, and fourteen were residents of Augsburg, while two lived in Nuremberg, one in Memmingen, and one in Antwerp. On the one hand, this large pool of associates broadened the capital base of the Welser-Vöhlin firm, but on the other hand, it made business decisions more difficult because the members sometimes had different interests. In 1517, several associates left the firm in a dispute over the distribution of profits; one of them was Anton Welser's brother Jakob, who subsequently founded an independent firm in Nuremberg.[67]

Another aspect that set the Welser-Vöhlins apart from the Fuggers was the fact that the former did not play a comparable role in the trade of mining products; instead, they relied more heavily on traditional commerce in items of mass consumption such as textiles, silken wares, spices, and dyestuffs. In contrast to the Fuggers, the Welser-Vöhlin company was strongly anchored by a number of trading posts in southern Germany and Switzerland. In Kaufbeuren, Mindelheim, Ulm, and Biberach they purchased linen and fustians, the production of which they partly organized in a putting-out system. In the Swiss town of Fribourg they purchased the entire urban cloth production for more than three decades, and on Lake Como and Lake Lugano they organized the production of woolen cloth. Their important office in Nuremberg handled their relations with Bohemia, Silesia, and Poland. The firm acquired Italian luxury textiles, as well as gold and silver thread, in Milan and imported Spanish wool via Genoa. In the French city of Lyons, important for its four annual fairs, the company purchased fine textiles, wool, saffron, and pastel dyes. For the acquisition of saffron, the Welser-Vöhlin company also maintained branch offices in the Italian town of Aquila, in the city of Toulouse in southern France, and in Saragossa, Spain. Pepper and other exotic spices were obtained in both Venice and Lisbon, where the Welser-Vöhlin company had been the first southern German merchant firm to establish its own office. The firm also had its own office in Venice; its representatives regularly visited the Frankfurt and Leipzig fairs, and in 1506 it purchased its own office building in Antwerp. Transport of goods from Antwerp to southern Germany included pepper, English cloth, and herring. After Bartholomäus Welser had taken over the management of the firm, it became more actively involved in mining and the metal trade during the 1520s, focusing on the mining of copper and tin in Saxony and Bohemia. Finally, the company's heavy investment in the Portuguese East India fleet of 1505 indicates its strong interest in commercial opportunities outside Europe. By 1510, the Welser-Vöhlins had an office on the island of Madeira and owned a sugar plantation on La Palma, one of the Canary Islands.[68]

The different orientation of the two firms minimized rivalry between them—the Fuggers and the Welsers appear as direct competitors mainly in their relations with the Roman curia—and encouraged sporadic cooperation in new business ventures, such as the Portuguese expeditions to Asia.[69] Matters were different when firms were strongly involved in the commerce in Tyrolean mining products and in loans to the Innsbruck government. When Jakob Fugger broke up the copper syndicate with the Gossembrot, Herwart, and Baumgartner firms in 1499, he clearly demonstrated that he was not interested in permanent forms of cooperation in that field. Nevertheless, some firms successfully weathered the Fuggers' competition on the Tyrolean metal and financial markets. One example is Philipp Adler, a native of Speyer who had moved to Augsburg in the mid-1480s. Adler was active in trade with Venice by 1490, and by 1500, he was one of the ten biggest taxpayers in the imperial city. As a longtime guild master of the salt traders, he also commanded some political influence within the city. In 1509, the emperor owed him more than 26,000 florins. His activities in the Tyrolean mining sector certainly benefited from the fact that his daughter had married Maximilian's treasurer, Jakob Villinger, in 1511. When he negotiated new loans in Augsburg, Villinger preferred to turn to his father-in-law.[70]

The Fuggers' strongest rivals in Tyrol at this time, however, were undoubtedly the Höchstetters. The brothers Georg, Ambrosius, and Hans Höchstetter came from the ranks of the cloth traders—their father Ulrich had been involved in the business as a *Gewandschneider*—and had accumulated a considerable fortune in their long-distance commerce, which extended to Antwerp as early as 1486 but also to Venice, Milan, Lyons, and Lisbon. As in the case of the Welser-Vöhlin company, the Höchstetter company included other relatives in addition to members of the Höchstetter family. To finance its extensive commercial activities and its entry into Tyrolean, Bohemian, and Saxon mining, the firm accepted outside capital on a large scale. In 1509, the Höchstetters obtained an imperial privilege for the establishment of a brass works on the Stainenberg in Pflach near Reutte, and by providing credit to the Tyrolean government, they secured a supply of copper from Taufers in the Ahrntal from 1511 onward. An important figure in the building of the Höchstetters' Tyrolean enterprise was their factor in Nuremberg, Stefan Gabler—a former Fugger employee who had resided in Lisbon for several years before returning to his native city of Nuremberg. It appears plausible that Portuguese demand for copper and brass for the African and Indian trades, about which Gabler was able to collect information in Lisbon, provided a strong impulse—perhaps even the decisive impulse—for the establishment of the Tyrolean brass works.[71] By entering the Tyrolean business area, the Höchstetters competed with the Fuggers on the Fuggers' original terrain, but since the Habsburg emperor, who was perennially short of money, ultimately needed both creditors, the two competitors had no choice but to cooperate. In 1515, Jakob Fugger once again had to advance 40,000 florins to the emperor, even though his claims already added up to 300,000 florins at the time and the entire copper production of the 1515–19 period had already been pawned to him. The Höchstetters participated in the new loan; in turn, the Tyrolean copper output of the 1520–23 period was assigned to them and the Fuggers. Moreover, from 1516 on, the Fuggers annually supplied 2,500 hundredweight of copper from Schwaz to the brass works in Pflach. To prevent ruinous price competition, Jakob Fugger and Ambrosius Höchstetter agreed to divide up the European markets for Tyrolean and Hungarian copper. While only Tyrolean copper was to be sold in southern Germany and Italy, the Netherlands and northern Germany were reserved for copper from Neusohl. In the history of the European economy, this agreement has become known as the first territorial cartel for copper.[72] As the next chapter will show, however, this cooperation was a temporary phenomenon. After Jakob Fugger's death, the competing interests of the Fuggers and the Höchstetters clashed sharply.

EXERCISING CONTROL, GIFT GIVING, AND NEGOTIATING: JAKOB FUGGER'S MANAGEMENT OF SOCIAL RELATIONS

Late medieval and early modern merchants were expected to handle their business affairs diligently and carefully, to work hard, and to keep their books and accounts accurately. In his autobiography, Lukas Rem, who represented the Welser-Vöhlin company in Lisbon and Antwerp, among other places, repeatedly stressed his exertions for the firm: "Day and night I had neither rest nor peace." Rem contrasted his commitment with the negligence and easy living of other members of the firm, and he bitterly complained how poorly the company rewarded him for the work he had done.[73] Jakob Fugger, however, apparently conformed to the ideal of the hardworking merchant to a large degree. This is not only supported by the famous miniature in the book-keeper Matthäus Schwarz's "costume book," which shows Schwarz and Jakob Fugger working together in the counting house, but also by the fact that Fugger frequently traveled on behalf of the company. On the occasion of the founding of the Hungarian trade, Ulrich and Jakob Fugger made a journey to Vienna in 1494, and Jakob subsequently rode to Füssen, Landshut, Innsbruck, Hall, and Frankfurt to settle business affairs. A projected journey to Hungary in 1502 did not materialize, but in 1515, Fugger, who was then fifty-six years old, undertook another trip to Vienna on the occasion of the dual marriage alliance between the house of Habsburg and the Hungarian royal family.[74] By personally auditing the accounts of the Hungarian trade regularly, the firm's director retained a large measure of control over its affairs.[75]

In a society that was largely structured around personal relations, the management of social relations, especially contacts with people of influence, was of crucial importance. For the Fuggers' business affairs, it was particularly important to cultivate close connections to the elites at the courts of the Habsburg monarchy, the Hungarian court, the Roman curia, and the German princely courts. The presents that Jakob Fugger gave to ecclesiastical and secular dignitaries on numerous occasions should be viewed in this context. These gifts were not merely a means of bribery; in the late medieval and early modern periods, they were a central means of social interaction that established, strengthened, and renewed relationships and that increased the prestige of the gift giver, as well as of the receiver.[76]

Jakob Fugger employed this means very effectively. According to the accounts of the Hungarian trade for 1494–1500, almost 10,000 florins were spent on presents to Hungarian prelates and diplomats. Cash, fine cloth shot with gold thread, furs, and valuable objects helped to overcome resistance to the Augsburg firm's lease of the Slovakian mines. After the bishop of Pécs had initially attempted to thwart the Neusohl enterprise of the Fuggers and Thurzos, the Fuggers' representatives followed him and made him change his mind with presents worth almost 700 ducats. The Neusohl accounts for the 1500–4 period register more than 2,000 ducats spent on gifts in furs and an additional 1,800 ducats for presents to ecclesiastical and secular officials, as well as to top Hungarian bureaucrats. One of the Fuggers' earliest Spanish transactions was the conveyance of presents that King Maximilian gave to his daughter-in-law Juana on the occasions of her wedding with Philip the Fair and the birth of her son and heir Charles. A Hungarian embassy arriving in Augsburg in the fall of 1510 included six richly decorated horses as prestigious presents for Jakob Fugger and Georg Thurzo. The ambassadors were not only hosted lavishly but also received valuable gifts in return. Finally, on the occasion of the congress that sealed the dual marriage alliance between the houses of Habsburg and Hungary in 1515, Jakob Fugger made the journey to Vienna with chests full of valuable goods and presents for high-ranking people whose protection was important to the firm. The account of the Hungarian trade recorded 9,946 florins for "the expenditure and gift-giving of Herr Jacob Fugger at Vienna, i.e. to the bishops of Olmütz and Pécs, to the Herren Jörg and Alexis Thurzo, to Duke Karl von Münsterberg, to Dietrichstain on the occasion of his marriage, to the king of Poland's daughter, and sent to Herren Hans Ernst and his wife at Zackaturn (Chaktornya), that is a number of golden rings with precious stones, rubies, diamonds, sapphires, turquoises, necklaces, pearls, silk garments, damask, camel hair, and other gems."[77]

In addition to gifts, other transactions and favors tied influential people to the firm. From the 1490s on, the Fuggers are regularly mentioned as court factors who supplied the Innsbruck court with spices, furs, fine textiles, jewels, and other luxury goods. When the ruler of Tyrol was so short of funds that he could no longer pay the salaries of his servants and bureaucrats, the firm helped out. Moreover, it recovered pawned objects and settled open accounts with artisans and innkeepers.[78] A loan of 10,000 florins that the Fuggers granted to the emperor in March 1511, for example, was made up of 6,331 florins in Hungarian gold; 2,000 florins in English cloth; 1,000 florins in velvet, silk, and camelhair; and diverse payments to court officials and artisans. In January 1518, the firm promised the emperor 15,000 florins in cash, as well as the delivery of woolen, silken, damask, sateen, and brocade cloth worth 8,000 florins.[79] In an age when warfare was an integral element of dynastic politics, the Fuggers supported the king not only by providing loans and paying troops but also by supplying weapons.[80]

Among the valuable services the firm could provide to its princely and noble clients was the transmission of news. Cities such as Venice and Antwerp were centers of information, as well as economic metropolises,[81] and the Fuggers used both the existing imperial and urban messenger systems and their own messengers to build up an effective communication system that always kept them well informed about political developments, military operations, and dynastic events. The firm transmitted information to the emperor, the pope, and the Republic of Venice, thereby increasing its value for princely clients.[82] In the final years of his life, Jakob Fugger frequently sent newsletters (neue Zeitungen) to Duke Georg of Saxony.[83] In addition, the company accepted deposits from ecclesiastical dignitaries such as the bishop of Schleswig, the Italian Cardinal Fazio Santori, and the archbishop of Gran, Thomas Bakosz. As the depositaries had a strong interest in keeping these transactions secret because of the prohibition of interest in canon law and public criticism of the ecclesiastical system of benefices, absolute discretion was guaranteed in these cases.[84]

Their management of social relations enabled the Fuggers to establish long-term ties with numerous people whose importance can hardly be exaggerated in a society in which personal influence, patronage, clientelism, and mutual trust were crucial and in which technical and administrative knowledge were a scarce resource. The Fuggers' involvement in the mining business, on the one hand, required strong connections to the territorial administrations in Tyrol and Hungary; on the other hand, it required technical and organizational knowledge. Therefore, it was of central importance for the Fuggers to cultivate relations with brokers who established contacts and set up business agreements and with experts with relevant experience and know-how in the extraction and processing of mining products who also had legal and administrative knowledge. The Fuggers could rely on a number of these brokers and experts, but particular significance may be attached to their relationships with their financier Melchior von Meckau, their Tyrolean middleman Paul von Liechtenstein, and their partner in the Hungarian trade, Hans Thurzo.

Melchior von Meckau, born circa 1440 as the scion of a Saxon noble family, had embarked on a fast-rising ecclesiastical and administrative career after studying in Leipzig and Bologna. Around 1471, he replaced the dean of the Bressanone Cathedral during his stay in Rome, and the following year he was elected to the cathedral chapter himself. In 1473, Archduke Sigismund of Tyrol accepted him as a councilor and servant. Meckau mostly lived in Rome until 1480 and rose to become apostolic privy councilor and recorder in the papal chancellery. In these functions, he gained deep insights into the ecclesiastical system of benefices and managed to use it to his own advantage. He secured benefices in the bishoprics of Meissen, Bressanone, Freising, and Magdeburg; in Rome, he kept an extravagant household with more than one hundred servants. In 1481, he is mentioned as chancellor of the Innsbruck government, and the following year he was elected coadjutor of the diocese of Bressanone. In that position he was the designated successor to the prince-bishop of Bressanone, a title he acquired in 1488. After Archduke Sigismund stepped down from his throne in 1490, Meckau took over the direction of Tyrolean government affairs as governor, and in 1498, he became president of the newly formed Hofkammer, Tyrol's central financial administration.[85] Thus, the Saxon nobleman made an impressive "dual career" as ecclesiastical dignitary and member of the Tyrolean government; in both functions, he was an important partner of the Fuggers. Moreover, as a successful collector of benefices and imperial lord, Meckau was also a wealthy man. We do not know when he first made Jakob Fugger's acquaintance, but the two men apparently intensified their relations around 1490. In December 1492, Meckau guaranteed financial obligations of the Tyrolean government to the Fuggers for the first time, and the next year, the Fuggers reimbursed Meckau for a sum of 2,100 florins that the bishop had advanced to the king. But at that time, the bishop of Bressanone also transacted some of his financial affairs with other companies, such as the Hirschvogels of Nuremberg and a Venetian firm. This changed in 1496 when a loan of 20,000 florins, which Meckau had advanced to the Tyrolean government, was transformed into a deposit with the Fugger company. A year later, Meckau guaranteed the loan that was part of the Fuggers' Tyrolean silver purchase contract.[86] Thus, the Fuggers and Meckau moved beyond the role of partners in negotiations about Tyrolean financial affairs and became intimately tied up in each other's financial matters.

Subsequently, the ties between Meckau, who also obtained the title of cardinal in 1503, and the Fuggers further intensified. When the repayment of the bishop's loans to King Maximilian became due in 1506, Jakob Fugger paid back the outstanding sum by concluding a new contract for the purchase of silver and copper. In the course of this transaction, a sum of 19,000 florins was turned into a deposit by Meckau with the Fugger firm. At the end of 1507, Meckau invested another 25,000 florins in the company. When he died in 1509, Meckau's investments in the Fugger firm added up to more than 150,000 florins; this equaled about three-quarters of the firm's capital at the time.[87]

Georg Gossembrot, the most important financier of the Innsbruck court around 1500, kept his distance from the Fuggers, despite his Augsburg origins. Jakob Fugger, however, found another reliable middleman in Paul von Liechtenstein, a south Tyrolean who became responsible for Tyrol court and government finances after Gossembrot's death in 1502. Liechtenstein had entered the service of the Innsbruck court through the mediation of influential relatives during Archduke Sigismund's time, and he had been appointed marshal probably as early as 1486 but certainly no later than 1490. His close relationship with Maximilian is reflected in the fact that the monarch became the godfather of one of his sons in 1498. Thus, Liechtenstein had extensive experience in court affairs, and by 1512 he belonged to the innermost circle of the Innsbruck government, along with his brother-in-law Zyprian von Serntein and Cardinal Matthäus Lang, another native of Augsburg.[88] During his career at the Innsbruck court, a relationship of mutual trust developed between Liechtenstein and Jakob Fugger, who repeatedly paid Liechtenstein's salary from his own cashbox. In countless negotiations for loans that he conducted with Jakob Fugger in the emperor's name, Liechtenstein time and again gave personal guarantees for the repayment of the loans. Shortly before his death, the imperial debts he had guaranteed amounted to 16,000 florins. It is telling that Liechtenstein's death in 1513 occurred in Augsburg, where he had once again gone for negotiations. His last will was witnessed by Jakob Fugger and two of his Augsburg competitors, Hans Baumgartner and Ambrosius Höchstetter.[89]

From 1502 to 1512, Liechtenstein was not only the most important middle-man between the Tyrolean government and Jakob Fugger in negotiations for loans and metal contracts. He also played a key role when the death of Melchior von Meckau threw the Fugger firm into an existential crisis. When both the Roman curia and the bishopric of Bressanone claimed rights of in-heritance to Meckau's estate, the firm was threatened with bankruptcy, be-cause it would not have been able to pay back the deceased bishop's enor-mous investments all at once. Faced with this critical situation, Jakob Fugger managed to bring about the emperor's intervention. That it was Liechten-stein who entered the negotiations as a mediator was particularly fortunate for the Fuggers, since he was also a brother-in-law of Meckau's successor, Christoph von Schrofenstein.[90] Jakob Fugger weathered the crisis caused by the cardinal's death both by drawing influential advocates into the affair and through his ability to delay negotiations until the desired result had been ob-tained. The curia finally left Meckau's estate to Maximilian, and the emperor permitted the Fuggers to satisfy their obligations with deliveries of cloth in-stead of interest payments.[91]

Maximilian also relied on Liechtenstein as a middleman to Jakob Fugger when he embarked on what was arguably his most ambitious project. When Pope Julius II became fatally ill in 1511, the monarch considered having him-self elected pope while still holding his imperial office, and he sent Liech-tenstein to Augsburg to negotiate a loan of up to 300,000 florins. In turn, Maximilian offered to pawn the entire revenues of the Holy Roman Empire and the hereditary Austrian lands, as well as the Spanish subsidies, and to appoint a Fugger confidant to the directorship of the apostolic chamber in Rome. Once again, Jakob Fugger delayed negotiations, and once again this strategy turned out to be successful, for Julius II recovered, making Maxi-milian's plans obsolete.[92]

The most important broker and expert who cooperated with Jakob Fug-ger, however, was undoubtedly Hans Thurzo. Born in Leutschau in the Zips (Spiš) in 1437, he was the son of a merchant. He studied at the University of Padua and initially pursued a clerical career but returned to the world of business after his father's death. In 1463, he took up residence in Krakow and became a citizen. While operating a smelting works near Krakow and participating in lead and copper mining in the Goslar region, Thurzo gained important experience in the mining sector. In 1475, Hungary's King Matthias Corvinus entrusted him with the overhaul and improvement of the mines in the Slovakian mountain towns, which were technologically and economically in poor shape. Although Thurzo managed to obtain the financial support of Krakow citizens, the overhaul of the Slovakian mines at first proceeded slowly. From 1491 onward, Thurzo purchased shares in mines at Neusohl, and in 1493, he obtained royal privileges for his mining operations. A few years earlier, he may already have come into contact with Jakob Fugger through Fugger's partner in Wrocław, Kilian Auer, and Auer's son-in-law Hans Metzler. The forming of this business relationship may have benefited from friendly relations between Georg Fugger and Georg Thurzo, who were both living in Nuremberg for some time. In any case, it is likely that the Fuggers took part in Thurzo's investments in Neusohl even before the contractual agreements on the Hungarian trade were made in the fall of 1494.[93]

According to Pölnitz, the Thurzos were pushed aside by the Fuggers after a few years and subsequently "were merely taken in tow" by their powerful Augsburg partners. This assessment overlooks the fact, however, that the Thurzos remained important for the Hungarian trade not only as mining experts but also as mediators who cultivated ties with the Polish and Hungarian royal courts and to the nobility in both realms. In 1498, Hans Thurzo obtained the title Kammergraf—count of the chamber—at Kremnitz, which gave him the power to control Slovakian mining production. By agreement with the Fuggers, the business of the Kremnitz chamber was integrated into the Hungarian trade. Around 1500, Thurzo obtained further privileges for the Hungarian trade. The presence of his son Alexi in the Hungarian king's encampment near Ofen is documented as early as 1496.[94] For the most part, the Thurzos also managed the relations between the kingdoms of Poland and Hungary and the curia in Rome. Hans Thurzo the Younger became collector of papal revenues in Poland, cathedral dean and coadjutor in Wrocław, and, eventually, prince-bishop. Moreover, he temporarily acted as chief administrator (*Oberlandeshauptmann*) of Silesia. His brother Stanislaus became the bishop of Olomouc in 1497, while Alexi Thurzo, who took up residence in Ofen, entered the service of the Hungarian crown and made a career as count of the chamber, treasurer, court judge, and, finally, royal governor. The Hungarian king and the curia appointed Hans and Stanislaus Thurzo as commissioners for the collection of indulgence fees in Bohemia, Moravia, and Silesia.[95] Last but not least, marriage alliances strengthened the bonds between the two families. Ulrich Fugger's daughter Anna became the wife of Georg Thurzo in 1497, and Hans Thurzo's daughter Katharina was married to Raymund Fugger in 1513. Georg Thurzo moved to Augsburg as administrator of the Hungarian trade.[96] The Fugger family's Book of Honors emphasized that the Thurzos had "greatly assisted" the Fuggers' commerce "at imperial and royal courts with their strong support."[97]

Viewed against this background, the Fugger-Thurzo relationship should be seen as a tight symbiosis into which both families invested a great deal of networking and that also paved the way for the Thurzos' steep social ascent. The balance between the two families began to shift only after Georg Thurzo's death and as a consequence of the Thurzo brothers' growing indebtedness to the Hungarian trade. In a contract in 1521, the Thurzos formally had to accept the Fuggers' leading role, as well.[98]

NEW DEPARTURES, 1519–1525

Since the 1480s, the rise of the Fuggers had been closely intertwined with the dynastic policies of the House of Habsburg. In 1518, the total debt that Emperor Maximilian I had incurred in silver and copper purchases amounted to almost 350,000 florins, more than half of which was owed to the Fuggers.[99] When Maximilian died in January 1519, it was natural for Jakob Fugger to support the candidacy of his grandson Charles, Duke of Burgundy and King of Spain, for the throne—all the more so, as the Fuggers had already handled substantial transactions with the Spanish crown during the preceding years.[100] When King Francis I of France and King Henry VIII of England announced their candidacies and Francis I obtained promises from the electors of Trier and the Palatinate to vote for him, Charles had to go to great lengths to obtain a majority in the college of the seven electors. Above all, this meant that he had to pay large sums to the electors, who succeeded in extorting higher and higher prices. Finally, the sum that Charles had to pay for his election rose to an enormous 851,918 florins. In the tight atmosphere of electoral negotiations during the Augsburg Diet of 1518, Jakob Fugger may briefly have considered supporting the French king, but eventually he threw his financial weight into the balance on behalf of the Habsburg candidate. He himself advanced 543,585 florins, or about two-thirds of the money necessary for the election, while the remaining third came from the Welsers of Augsburg and three Italian firms. The letters of exchange that these firms had sent from Spain were cashed by Jakob Fugger in Frankfurt on the Main. On this basis, Charles was unanimously elected Roman king and emperor on June 28, 1519, and was subsequently crowned at Aachen in 1520.[101] In the same year, the Fuggers raised 77,000 florins for the Swabian League's military offensive against Duke Ulrich of Württemberg, which forced the duke into exile while his territory was placed under Habsburg administration.[102]

After Charles had personally come to the Holy Roman Empire, a contractual agreement about the redemption of the imperial debts, which then amounted to about 600,000 florins, was signed on May 4, 1521. The Fuggers were assigned the Tyrolean silver and copper production for about two-thirds of the sum, or 415,000 florins. Charles's brother Archduke Ferdinand, on whom Charles had conferred authority over the Austrian hereditary lands in 1521–22, recognized these claims at the Diet of Nuremberg in 1522.[103] This constituted a landmark for the Fuggers, for it meant that they remained major players in the commerce in Alpine mining products. As a gradual decline of Tyrolean copper production had already become apparent at this time, however, it made sense to secure the firm's interests by directly entering the field of production, as well. This entry came when a longstanding competitor, the Baumgartner firm in Kufstein, went bankrupt. Together with the Tyrolean entrepreneur Hans Stöckl, the Fuggers acquired shares in Tyrolean mines at Schwaz, Rattenberg, and Lienz and a smelting works in Kundl from the bankrupt firm's estate. This signified the transformation of the Fugger firm, which had confined itself to banking and metal trade in Tyrol for more than thirty years, into a mining and smelting enterprise; subsequently, the firm deliberately expanded its mining holdings.[104] By providing further loans and concluding more contracts for copper and silver purchases, Jakob Fugger strengthened his relations with the new ruler of the Austrian hereditary lands. He helped Archduke Ferdinand pay off his debts to Duke Georg of Saxony, and in 1525, he supported Ferdinand and the Swabian League with substantial sums during the great uprising of peasants and miners in Tyrol and southern Germany.[105]

The Fuggers' agreement with Charles in May 1521 constituted a landmark in other respects, for the firm was assigned to the emperor's Spanish revenues for the remainder of the debt (i.e., they were entitled to receive payments out of the revenues of the Spanish crown as reimbursements of their loan). Above all, these included the revenues of the Spanish chivalric orders, which had fallen to the crown during the preceding years. After lengthy negotiations, in the course of which Jakob Fugger self-consciously reminded the emperor that it was he who had helped Charles win the throne, the Fuggers were able to lease these revenues, the so-called Maestrazgos, for the first time in 1525. They will be considered more extensively in subsequent chapters.[106] The growing significance of Spain for the Fuggers also became manifest in their participation in the preparations for Garcia de Loaysa's expedition to the Moluccan Islands. After the circumnavigation of the globe by Fernando

Magellan's fleet (1519–22) had proved the existence of a western route to the Spice Islands, Loaysa's expedition was designed to bolster Spanish claims to the Moluccas. The connection to the Fuggers was probably mediated by Cristóbal de Haro, a merchant from Burgos who had played a leading role in the preparations for Magellan's expedition and who was a business partner of the Fuggers in Lisbon, as well as in the Netherlands. Jakob Fugger invested 10,000 ducats in the venture, raising 4,600 ducats from his own funds and the remainder from the Augsburg and Nuremberg merchants Christoph Herwart, Konrad Rehlinger, Jörg Imhof, Hans Baumgartner, and Hans Manlich. The high expectations remained unfulfilled, however, for the expedition ended in a disastrous failure. None of the seven ships that had set sail in the port of La Coruña in July 1525 ever returned to Spain.[107]

The alliance between the emperor and his southern German bankers turned out to be momentous in yet another respect. During the reign of Charles's predecessor, Maximilian, the business practices of the large merchant companies had been criticized time after time at imperial diets and sessions of the Tyrolean estates. The "usury" and "engrossment" of the commercial firms and their monopolistic practices were blamed for high prices and the impoverishment of large segments of the population. This anti-monopoly movement, which was also fueled by the ethical writings of Martin Luther and other early Protestant reformers on economic matters, received particularly strong support not only from the imperial knights but also from some members of the high nobility. During the Nuremberg Diet of 1522–23, the imperial estates debated whether to limit the capital stock of commercial companies to a maximum of 50,000 florins and whether to prohibit the acceptance of outside capital. For firms as large as the Fugger company, this effectively would have meant total suppression. Augsburg's city recorder, Dr. Conrad Peutinger, who distinguished himself as an advocate of the large commercial companies during that time, argued that such a measure would only benefit foreign merchants. The activities of the large companies in the mining sector had brought about the mining boom in the first place, and competition among trading firms resulted in lower prices for the "common man." Therefore, he said, "By nature every commercial activity, where it is carried out faithfully, [should] be free." According to Peutinger's argument, the private gain of merchant firms was thus compatible with the public good. The diet refrained from putting a ceiling on the capital stock of merchant companies but passed a 4 percent import duty, which would also have constituted a heavy burden on the companies. Moreover, in 1523 the imperial prosecutor filed suit against the Fuggers, Welsers, Höchstetters, and three other Augsburg firms for violating the laws against monopolies.

The imperial cities reacted by sending a delegation to the emperor in Spain, and the delegate from Augsburg prevailed on Charles V to repeal the import duty and dismiss the monopoly suits. In an edict in 1525 in which he decided the monopoly issue in favor of the merchant companies, Charles V explicitly followed their argument that private interest and the common good were compatible. The edict declared that mining was the "greatest gift and benefit" to the Holy Roman Empire and that the large companies' activities were providing employment and sustenance to hundreds of thousands of people. Stable prices for precious metals therefore were in the public interest.[108]

Finally, in the two wills that he wrote in 1521 and 1525, the aging Jakob Fugger set the course for his succession in the firm. In his declaration of 1512, examined at the beginning of this chapter, Fugger had already envisioned that the trade would be directed by two managers after his demise. In 1521, he appointed his nephews Ulrich the Younger and Raymund as executors of his last will. But because Ulrich died in 1525 and his brother Hieronymus had "not been particularly useful in commercial matters up to this point, nor taken a great interest in it," the second will promoted Raymund's brother Anton to the positions of executor and manager. Moreover, since Raymund "was not really capable of traveling or otherwise investing great effort and labor on account of his bodily condition," Anton was to direct the Fuggers' commerce "alone, albeit with the advice of his brother Raymund and his cousin Hieronymus." To carry out this task, Anton was to have the same "power and authority" that Jakob Fugger had commanded. After the death of the long-term "governor," the entire "burden, effort, and labor," as well as the responsibility for the firm's future, were to rest on Anton's shoulders.[109]

On Christmas Eve of 1525, when Jakob Fugger lay dying in his house on the Augsburg wine market, the chronicler Clemens Sender wrote that many of the city's inhabitants saw a black rainbow over St. Anna's Church, which housed the Fuggers' funerary chapel. Like most of his contemporaries, Sender, a pious Benedictine monk, believed that God revealed his will through signs of providence. The impending death of the greatest merchant of his time, whose commerce extended "to the four corners of the whole world," was a momentous event for the imperial city of Augsburg and for European commerce and finance.[110]

3

ANTON FUGGER,
THE HOUSE OF
HABSBURG, AND THE
EUROPEAN WORLD
ECONOMY, 1525–1560

THE NEW "GOVERNOR," 1525–1532

While Jakob Fugger's name is intimately linked to the establishment of the great enterprise, that of Anton Fugger, who managed the firm from 1525 to 1560, stands for the preservation of his uncle's heritage. Writing on the occasion of Anton Fugger's five-hundredth anniversary in 1993, the Augsburg historian Johannes Burkhardt emphasized his contributions to the continuity of the family and firm. In the economic realm, Burkhardt views the "institutionalization of financial policy" and "growing autonomy of the idea of the firm" as Anton Fugger's major achievements. By cultivating close ties to the House of Habsburg, which regularly called on his services, Anton Fugger became a "semi-official imperial factor of sorts," and his business strategy, which separated the issue of the firm's future from the individual person of the manager, virtually institutionalized the Fugger firm. As we will see in the course of this chapter, however, these achievements reached their limits in the final decade of Anton Fugger's life and came to be questioned by Fugger himself.[1]

According to the family chronicle, Anton Fugger, the son of Georg Fugger and Regina Imhof, was educated "in all good, virtuous, and honorable arts" from childhood and early youth and spent some time in France and Italy. From 1506, the year of his father's death, onward, he is documented at the most important places where the family firm did business: first in Venice, where he stayed with his cousin Ulrich, then in Nuremberg in 1510; in Wrocław from 1512 to 1514; in Ofen, where he was in charge of a Fugger trading office for the first time; and in Rome since late 1517. A first will, which the twenty-four-year-old Anton Fugger wrote on the eve of his journey to Rome, reflects the pre-Reformation piety of the later head of the firm, as well as the dominant influence of his uncle Jakob, whom Anton named as exec-

68

FIGURE 4

Portrait of Anton Fugger (1493–1560) by Hans Maler von Schwaz.
(Vereinigung der Freunde der Staatlichen Kunsthalle Karlsruhe e. V.)

utor. Alms and masses were meant to promote the salvation of the young merchant's soul, and if he died in Augsburg, he wished to be buried in the burial chapel that his father and his uncles had built there. In Rome, Anton Fugger lobbied for the foundation of his uncle's preachership, to which I will return later.[2] Furthermore, he was involved in the business of handling letters of indulgence and other financial affairs with the curia and was made a papal knight and count palatine in 1519. In 1523–24, he stayed in Tyrol, from where he made another journey to Rome in late 1524 before heading for Nuremberg the following year. These stations of his early career indicate a solid preparation for and familiarity with the most important fields of business of the Fugger enterprise. Still, Jakob Fugger, the leader of the firm, long set his hopes on his nephew Ulrich's succeeding him. Only Ulrich's death in May 1525, months before his uncle, forced Jakob to change his mind.[3]

Immediately after taking over the firm's management, Anton Fugger had to weather several difficulties that had grown dramatically during the final months of his uncle's life. The most severe one was the crisis of the Hungarian trade, which manifested itself in the early summer of 1525 in a revolt of the miners in the Slovakian mining towns and in the Hungarian crown's decision to expropriate the Fuggers. These two spatially and thematically separate issues had common roots in a currency devaluation that began around 1521 and led to rising prices. While the miners feared for their livelihood and demanded higher wages, the noble opposition in Hungary blamed the Fuggers and Thurzos for the price increases. Unrest in the mining towns began to stir in early 1525, and an armed uprising of miners forced the Fugger agent Hans Ploss to yield to the demand for double wages in early June and pay the miners in newly minted coins. In the same month, the employee Hans Alber was imprisoned in Ofen, and the firm's property was confiscated. The cashier Hans Dernschwam, however, had been able to arrange for the transport of the trading post's cash and valuables to Neusohl just in time. A messenger on horseback sent by Dernschwam warned the Neusohl office, which promptly sent its cash holdings to Krakow. Alexi Thurzo, who was a partner in the Hungarian trade as well as a member of the Hungarian court—and therefore fell between two stools in this conflict—agreed to the dissolution of the lease contract for the Slovakian mines. Bernhard Behaim, a trusted adviser of Hungary's Queen Maria, count of the chamber of Kremnitz, and a fierce opponent of the Fuggers, now assumed control over the mining and smelting operations. But when Behaim was unable to pay the workers because of his empty coffers, unrest in the Neusohl region flared up again. The emigration of the Fuggers' mining specialists and ongoing strikes—which were directed not at the disowned Fuggers but at the new administration and the local elite of the "forest burghers" (*Waldbürger*)—led to a dramatic decline in production. In February 1526, revolting miners held Bernhard Behaim captive for nine days. The deployment of troops in the rebellious area and a legal investigation of the incidents temporarily calmed the situation, but when outstanding wages remained unpaid, a radicalized minority among the miners revolted once again, pillaging the Neusohl parish court and a number of houses and setting them on fire.[4]

Meanwhile, Jakob Fugger had taken energetic countermeasures in July 1525 to obtain the restitution of the Hungarian trade. Activating his close ties to the House of Habsburg, the duke of Saxony, and the Roman curia, he mobilized political support. Copper transports were blocked, and leaders of the Hungarian noble opposition such as Johann Zápolya were lavished with gifts.[5] In the final days of 1525, Anton Fugger, the new leader of the firm, journeyed to Vienna, from where he coordinated the negotiations with the Hungarian crown. In February 1526, the members of the Thurzo family released their shares in the Hungarian trade to the Fuggers, and two months later, all punitive measures against the firm were suspended. The Hungarian crown, which desperately needed money to ward off advancing Ottoman troops, leased the Slovakian mines to the Fuggers for another fifteen years, for which the firm agreed to pay 20,000 florins per annum and deliver 7,500 Marks of silver to the royal treasury for a fixed price. Moreover, the crown accepted the Fuggers' demand for compensation for the damage caused by the disowning of the firm and assumed responsibility for a debt of 206,741 florins.[6]

In 1525, the miners revolted not only in Slovakia but also in Tyrol. Whereas higher wages were the main issue in the Neusohl region, the Tyrolean uprising has to be seen in the larger context of the rebellion of the "common man," which is often referred to (somewhat imprecisely) as the Peasants' War. Demands for religious renewal mingled with economic and social grievances. In addition to the nobility, the clergy, the ruler Archduke Ferdinand, and his adviser Gabriel Salamanca, the rebels' criticism targeted the "usurious" and "monopolistic" practices of the large trading companies. In the articles that they passed in the town of Merano on Pentecost of 1525, the peasants of South Tyrol demanded "that such companies, be they small or large, . . . be abolished" to bring the prices of basic goods down. More particularly, "The Fuggers, Höchstetters, Welsers, and other companies are not to be permitted any more silver purchases, but the same [companies must be] dissolved." The meeting of the Tyrolean estates (*Landtag*) also voiced grievances against the Fuggers. The firm's trading post in Hall was pillaged, and in South Tyrol, the important transit routes to Italy were blocked.[7] The complaints of the miners—the social group most directly affected by the large trading companies—were aimed not so much at the "capitalists," however, as at the local supply trades.[8]

For the Fuggers' Roman affairs, finally, the Sacco di Roma—the pillaging of the eternal city by imperial troops in 1527—constituted a decisive break.

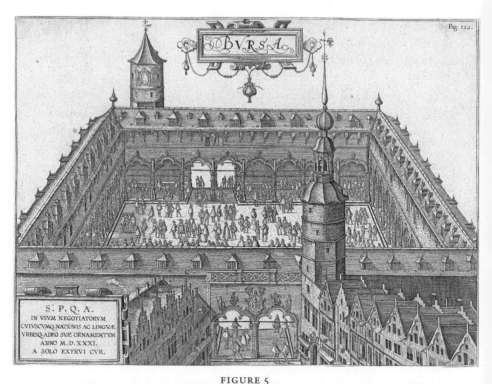

FIGURE 5
The Antwerp exchange. Copper engraving by Petrus von der Borcht, 1581.
(Museum Plantin-Moretus/Prentenkabinet, Antwerp—UNESCO World Heritage)

Although the Roman office not only remained undamaged but actually earned money by transferring soldiers' booty to Germany, the unstable situation in Italy and the advance of the Reformation in Germany made banking transactions with the curia less lucrative. For these reasons, the Roman office was closed in the late 1520s; the remaining financial operations were subsequently handled by the offices in Venice and Naples.[9]

Apart from political and social unrest and military conflicts, the unstable situation on the European markets caused problems for the large trading companies in the 1520s. The rising commercial metropolis of Antwerp experienced a severe setback when the Venetian spice market recovered and Portuguese and Venetian spice suppliers competed for shares of the market (see fig. 5). The European copper markets were likewise affected by an oversupply of the metal, which led to declining prices. Among the large firms that failed under these difficult economic circumstances was the Höchstetter company of Augsburg, for some time the closest rival of the Fuggers in the mining and metal sectors. In 1525, Ambrosius Höchstetter the Elder had leased the mercury output of the Idria mines in Slovenia for four years, and in 1527, he managed to obtain control of Bohemian mercury production. To secure his dominance of the European market, he needed only the Spanish mines at Almadén, but in the attempt to bring them under his control, he overstretched his means and had to throw his mercury stocks on the market at a heavy loss to satisfy his creditors. Besides this failed attempt to establish a mercury monopoly, the firm's limited capital stock, losses incurred in other fields of business, and the behavior of their competitors contributed to the Höchstetters' downfall. In the spring of 1528, the Fuggers spread rumors about their rivals' financial difficulties in Antwerp and Lyons. At the same time, they took over obligations of the struggling company and paid out some of the Höchstetters' creditors, a strategy that evidently caused additional unease among those creditors who had not been satisfied. When a run of creditors on the Höchstetter family's assets finally started in 1529, Ambrosius Höchstetter's urgent plea for help from his "dear cousin" Anton Fugger fell on deaf ears. The once powerful merchant, his son Ambrosius the Younger, and his nephew Joseph were jailed in Augsburg while Anton Fugger picked up several prime pieces from the bankrupts' estate: the castle and estate of Burgwalden, the Höchstetter house in Schwaz, and the Jenbach smelting works.[10]

In the midst of this turbulent period, the Fugger firm drew up its first balance sheet under Anton's direction. This document provides with the best general view of the company's situation in the 1520s. The balance for December 31, 1527, reveals assets of roughly 3 million florins and liabilities of 870,000 florins. Among the assets, the mining holdings were assessed at 270,000 florins—the Slovakian mines and smelting works at 210,000 and the Tyrolean ones at 60,000 florins—and real estate at 150,000 florins. Houses and other properties in and near Augsburg were estimated at 57,000 florins; the landed estates acquired by Jakob Fugger, at 70,000 florins; the Antwerp trading office, at 15,000 florins; and the Roman office, at 6,000 florins. The inventoried goods, the major portion consisting of unsold copper and silver and a minor portion of textiles, were assessed at 380,000 florins, and cash reserves stood at 50,000 florins. The largest part of the firm's assets, however, consisted of outstanding debts. King Ferdinand owed the Fuggers some 651,000 florins; for repayment of this sum, the firm was assigned the production of the Hall salt works, Tyrolean silver and copper, and Ferdinand's income from rents in the kingdom of Naples. Outstanding debts in Spain amounted to more than half a million florins; in Antwerp, the king of Portugal owed more than 18,000 Flemish pounds; and in Rome, the viceroy of Naples was indebted to almost 15,000 ducats. Moreover, the firm had lent 10,000 florins each to the imperial cities of Augsburg and Ulm and almost 2,000 florins to Margrave Kasimir of Brandenburg. Several outstanding loans were considered doubtful, including the debt incurred by the Hungarian crown when it disowned the Fuggers in 1525 (206,741 florins), Alexi Thurzo's liabilities (113,122 florins), and debts incurred by the deceased Pope Leo X (20,958 florins).

Regarding the firm's liabilities, roughly 340,000 florins of debt had been incurred in Spain, and deposits at fixed interest rates accounted for another 290,000 florins. A large part of these deposits came from the Fuggers' relatives and employees. Georg Fugger's widow, Anna Thurzo, for example, had invested almost 80,000 florins in the firm, which entitled her to more than 2,000 florins in interest payments. The children of Hans Marx von Bubenhofen and Sibylla Fugger held about 30,000 florins in capital and interest; the agent Gastel Fugger "vom Reh" held 5,000 florins; and even Anton Fugger's domestic servant Martin Schmid had invested 160 florins. After deducting liabilities, the firm was worth roughly 2 million florins. Considering that the capital stock in 1511 had merely amounted to 197,000 florins, the company's assets had increased by 1.8 million florins within sixteen years. The company's operations were continued with a capital stock of 1.6 million florins.[11]

Almost seven years passed after the death of their uncle Jakob, however, before Raymund, Anton, and Hieronymus Fugger signed a new company contract for a period of six years in September 1532. In this document, the partners explicitly confirmed the tradition established by Jakob Fugger, with whom they had traded in "such good brotherly and friendly unity" that by "grace of God" they had acquired a large fortune and an "honorable estate." In his will, Jakob Fugger had left them a sizable inheritance and had admonished them to "further maintain their worldly family stem and name in a good and honorable manner." Furthermore, he had entrusted his nephew Anton with the sole management of the firm and relegated Anton's brother Raymund and his cousin Hieronymus to merely advisory positions. According to this last will, Anton Fugger had also drawn up the general balance in 1527. The company's future name was set as "Raymundus, Antonius and Hieronymus the Fugger Brothers," but Raymund and Hieronymus explicitly acknowledged that it was Anton who functioned as "the supreme administrator and manager of this, our common company trade." Documents that Anton Fugger drew up on behalf of the company were binding for the other two partners, as well. He alone could hire or fire commercial employees, and Raymund and Hieronymus could do business on behalf of the firm only with Anton's explicit consent. The company contract also set rules for the withdrawal of capital from the firm, as well as for the continuation of business and the payment of inheritances in the event of the death of one or two partners. If Raymund and Hieronymus survived Anton, they should run the company with the help of one or two experienced commercial employees.[12]

In fact, it was Raymund Fugger who was the first of the three partners to die, in 1535. A new general balance was drawn up in 1536, which provided Anton Fugger with an up-to-date overview of the company's situation. The assets now amounted to 3.8 million florins, of which 2.35 million florins consisted of the firm's outstanding loans. These included more than 1 million florins due in Spain alone. "The growth of the Spanish business," Richard Ehrenberg wrote more than a century ago, constituted "the most important fact of the whole time period" since the death of Jakob Fugger. The liabilities now stood at 1.77 million florins, showing a considerable increase since 1527. Liabilities from deposits and letters of exchange added up to roughly 700,000 florins. The "growth of business since 1527," Ehrenberg wrote, was thus "made possible only by outside capital."[13]

After Anton Fugger had paid off his cousin Hieronymus in October 1537, he followed the example of his uncle Jakob and accepted his brother Raymund's four sons—Hans Jakob, Christoph, Georg, and Raymund—into the firm as junior partners "upon their diligent pleading." In a declaration signed on February 5, 1538, however, Anton Fugger retained exclusive authority in all business matters. His nephews were to keep their inherited fortune in the company; they had to acknowledge their uncle's position as head of the firm and faithfully carry out all of his orders. If one of the nephews behaved "disorderly," Anton Fugger had the right to dismiss him. The calculation and disbursement of profits were the exclusive domains of the firm's head. Should he die during the six-year contract period, his nephew Hans Jakob was to take over the management together with a senior employee, since he was still young and "not properly informed and experienced" in commercial matters.[14] Like his uncle Jakob before him, Anton Fugger thus reserved supreme authority in all company affairs for himself. As the following survey of the company's most important fields of activity will demonstrate, his business strategies were likewise marked by a strong element of continuity.

EMPEROR CHARLES V, SPAIN, AND THE NEW WORLD

By financing the election of Charles V in 1519, Jakob Fugger had set the course for close ties between the Fugger firm and the emperor and Spanish king to continue; this relationship remained crucially important for both the monarch and the company until the 1550s. In a monumental scholarly work, the Spanish historian Ramón Carande has assembled all loan contracts (*asientos*) of the Spanish crown between 1521 and 1555 for which the Kingdom of Castile guaranteed repayment. Although it is difficult to construct a general

TABLE 5

Loans to the Spanish crown (payable by the Castilian treasury), 1521–1555 (in Spanish ducats)

Creditor	Total amount lent	Number of individual loans	Share (%) of total owed by the crown
Augsburg			
Fugger	5,499,516	74	19.54
Welser	4,223,822	41	15.01
Others	491,490	12	1.74
Subtotal	10,214,828	127	36.30
Genoa	9,649,790	285	34.29
Antwerp	2,985,315	46	10.61
Spain	5,048,432	150	17.94
Others	240,001	13	0.85
Total	28,138,393	621	100

Source: James D. Tracy, *Emperor Charles V, Impresario of War,* 101. (Copyright © 2002 James D. Tracy; reprinted with the permission of Cambridge University Press)

picture from these contracts, as new credit agreements often served to cancel older obligations, table 5 still indicates the relative importance of the monarchy's individual creditors. According to table 5, the Spanish crown borrowed roughly 28 million ducats during the reign of Charles V. More than 10 million ducats, or 36 percent of the total, came from Augsburg merchant bankers, including 5.5 million ducats from the Fuggers and 4.2 million from the Welsers. The Fuggers therefore accounted for almost one-fifth of the total credit provided to the crown. The Genoese bankers raised sums comparable to those of their Augsburg counterparts: They lent the Spanish crown more than 9.6 million ducats, accounting for more than a third of the total volume of credit. From the middle of the sixteenth century onward, they were in fact considerably more important as suppliers of credit to the Spanish monarchy than the southern Germans. Antwerp merchants and Spanish financiers also lent the crown substantial sums, but on the whole they were less important than the Augsburgers and the Genoese. Seven merchant-banking houses supplied the emperor with almost two-thirds of all loans that he received between 1521 and 1555: the Fuggers and Welsers; the Genoese firms Grimaldi, Spinola, Gentile, and Centurione; and the Schetzes of Antwerp.[15]

From 1527 on, Anton Fugger and his firm concluded a long series of asientos with the emperor, providing him with money for his travels and embassies, for Habsburg marriage projects, for the wars against France in Italy and the Netherlands, and for support of his brother Ferdinand's struggle against the Turks. In these transactions, the firm cooperated time and again not only with the Welser firms of Nuremberg and Augsburg and the brothers Rem from Augsburg, but also with Genoese merchants and bankers from Burgos. Of this string of loans, only a few of the most important can be singled out here. Prior to Charles's coronation as emperor in Bologna, representatives of the Fugger and Welser companies signed an asiento in Spain in February 1530 to the amount of 1.5 million ducats. Additional loans came forward during Charles's stays at the Diet of Augsburg in 1530, in the Netherlands during the following year, and at the Regensburg Diet in 1532. An asiento concluded in Madrid in 1535 supplied the crown with 600,000 ducats to defray current government expenses, as well as to maintain Spanish fortresses in Roussillon and North Africa. In March 1539, representatives of the Fuggers and Welsers negotiated a loan of 150,000 ducats in Toledo, which was to be paid out in the Holy Roman Empire. Another loan to which the two Augsburg firms agreed in Madrid during the same year provided for the payment of 156,000 ducats in the Netherlands and an additional 100,000 scudi in Milan. Anton Fugger's nephew Christoph, who had been staying in Spain since 1539, negotiated an asiento of 200,000 ducats in Valladolid in February 1544. Prior to the War of the Schmalkaldic League in 1546–47, the crown borrowed more than half a million florins from the Fuggers. When the war reached its climax, the government of the Netherlands borrowed 100,000 ducats from the Fuggers in October 1546, and in January 1547, Anton Fugger once again provided the emperor with substantial sums in the form of Dutch letters of exchange. In addition, the firm handled papal subsidies for the emperor's struggle against the German Protestants. The culmination of this series of loans, however, was the Villach asiento of May 28, 1552, when Anton Fugger lent the emperor 100,000 ducats and 300,000 Italian scudi on his own account—that is, apart from his nephews. This loan came at a time when Charles V was in dire straits because of the rebellion of the princes in the Holy Roman Empire.[16]

To repay these loans, the Spanish crown could mainly draw on its income from the Castilian lands. These included the *servicio* granted by the estates (*cortes*) of Castile; the *alcabalas* and *tercias* (rents split among the individual towns and communities); the *cruzada*, a crusading indulgence granted by the pope during Spain's wars with the Moors, which had gradually been transformed into a regular source of crown income after the end of the *reconquista*; and the *quarta*, which was levied on ecclesiastical incomes. From the 1530s onward, precious metals, which the Spanish fleet brought to Europe from the New World and one-fifth of which was reserved for the

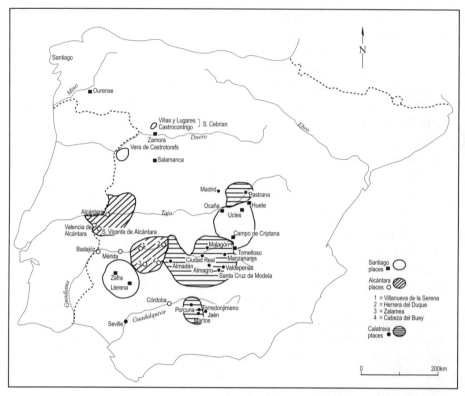

MAP 3
Major territories of the Spanish chivalric orders (Maestrazgos).
(Adapted from Kellenbenz, Die Fuggersche Maestrazgopacht [1525–1542], *403)*

crown, became increasingly important as means of repayment. From 1530 to 1533, the Fuggers and Welsers collected the cruzada, and for the huge loans they gave in 1539, the two firms were assigned servicios, the cruzada, and precious metals from America. During the 1550s, Spanish silver transports to the Netherlands were repeatedly transferred to the Fuggers. The sale of royal rents, so-called *juros*, constituted another source of income. Since 1524, the Fuggers had acquired these rents time and again and resold them in small portions to ecclesiastical institutions, royal officers, and private individuals. In these transactions, the firm's Spanish employees also cooperated with the Welsers' representatives. Finally, the Maestrazgos—the estates of the Spanish knightly orders of Santiago, Alcántara, and Calatrava—were particularly significant in the company's financial dealings with the crown. After the conclusion of the reconquista, the administration of these extensive landholdings had reverted to the crown, which leased them in return for financial advances. The income from these Maestrazgos consisted of ground rents and tithes, which were collected either in cash or in kind (grain, wine, olive oil).[17]

The Fuggers had obtained the lease of the Maestrazgos for the first time in 1524, when Jakob Fugger was still alive, for the period from 1525 to 1527. During this period, the firm paid an annual sum of 135,000 ducats for the lease. During the following lease periods from 1528 to 1537, the Welsers of Augsburg and a group of Italian merchants led by Maffeo de Taxis and Giovanni Battista Grimaldi administered the Maestrazgos. For the 1538–42 period, the Fuggers once again obtained the lease and paid an annual sum of 150,000 ducats. After a group of Spanish investors had secured the lease for the five-year period starting in 1542, the Fuggers once again became administrators of the Maestrazgos from 1547 to 1550. The lease contract was attractive for two reasons. First, the leaseholders were able to export grain surpluses from the orders' estates; and second, the landholdings of the order of Calatrava included the mercury mines of Almadén. The metal was used in the production of mirror glass, in the processing of gold, and for medical uses, among other things. As mercury and vermilion production were confined to only a few locations besides Almadén in sixteenth-century Europe—especially Idria, in present-day Slovenia, and in Bohemia—the operation of the mines constituted a lucrative source of revenue until a fire devastated them in November 1550. During the 1547–50 period, the Fuggers sold 3,761 hundredweight of mercury and 653 hundredweight of sublimate—a mercury product used to separate gold and silver—at Almadén. For the lease period from 1538 to 1542, the firm's head office in Augsburg calculated annual revenues of roughly 224,000 ducats and expenses of 152,000 ducats, indicating a profit of close to 52 percent on the money invested. Profits for the 1547–50 period were calculated at 24 percent. For the administration of the Maestrazgos, the Fuggers established a trading post at Almagro, which was subordinate to the head office at the Spanish court.[18] The special relationship between the firm and the town of Almagro is reflected in the history of the local church of San Salvador. In the 1520s, the firm financed the construction and decoration of a chapel, which was enlarged and supplied with its own foundation for religious services at Anton Fugger's behest from 1550 onward.[19]

As the Fuggers repeatedly depended on gold and silver shipments from America to recover their loans to the crown, it appeared logical for them to set their eyes on the New World, as well. Moreover, the fact that their Augsburg competitor, the firm of Bartholomäus Welser, had established a trading post in Santo Domingo in 1526 and had signed contracts with the Spanish crown for the colonization of Venezuela and the shipment of 4,000 African slaves to America in 1528 may have heightened the Fuggers' propensity to invest in the New World. In addition, the financial relations between the Augsburg merchant house and the crown reached a climax in 1530 with the asiento of 1.5 million ducats and the Fuggers' financing of Ferdinand's election as Roman king. It was against this background that the Fugger agent Veit Hörl negotiated a contract with the Spanish Council of the Indies in 1530 for the conquest and colonization of the western coastal region of South America from Chincha in Peru to the Straits of Magellan. This region included present-day southern Peru and all of Chile. After Charles V had signaled his agreement with the conclusion of the contract in January 1531, Veit Hörl signed the respective document the following June. For unknown reasons, however, the emperor failed to ratify the treaty, and after the loss of a ship that had been sent to South America on a reconnaissance mission, the Fuggers did not pursue the project. Considering that the Welsers' Venezuela project degenerated into a mere slave-raiding and booty enterprise and ended in substantial losses, Anton Fugger's abandonment of this undertaking may well have been a wise decision.[20]

Although the Fuggers' direct participation in overseas ventures was sporadic, Seville, the monopoly port for Spain's trade with America, became an important commercial center for them. The Fugger trading post on the Guadalquivir River, which had been established in the 1520s, received precious metals and pearls from America in repayment of royal loans. It also handled letters of exchange between Seville and the Castilian fairs; sold juros; carried out financial transactions in the context of the Maestrazgo lease; and marketed Swabian fustian, Tyrolean and Slovakian copper, and mercury and vermilion from the mines of Almadén. Fustian produced on the Fuggers' manorial estate of Weißenhorn was sold to customers on the

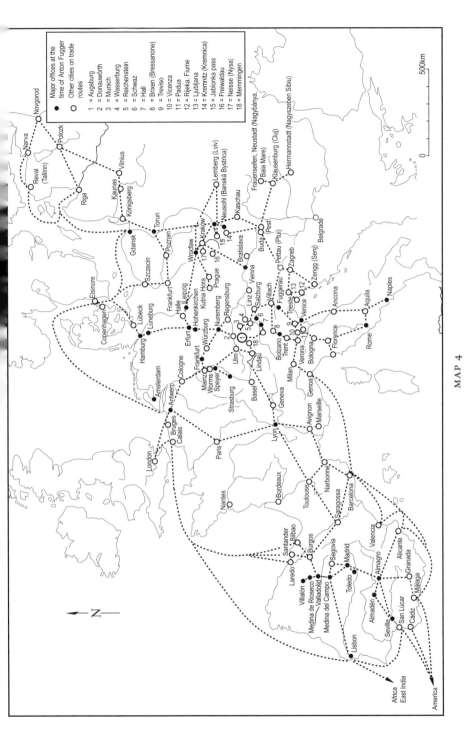

● Major offices at the time of Anton Fugger
○ Other cities on trade routes

1 = Augsburg
2 = Donauwörth
3 = Munich
4 = Wasserburg
5 = Reichenstein
6 = Schwaz
7 = Hall
8 = Brixen (Bressanone)
9 = Treviso
10 = Vicenza
11 = Padua
12 = Rijeka, Fiume
13 = Ljubljana
14 = Kremnitz (Kremnica)
15 = Jablonka pass
16 = Freiwaldau
17 = Neisse (Nysa)
18 = Memmingen

MAP 4

Offices and transportation routes in Anton Fugger's company.
(Adapted from Pölnitz, Anton Fugger, 3:2:683)

Iberian Peninsula and in the New World.[21] Alpine and Hungarian copper that was marketed via Antwerp was another important item of overseas commerce, entering the American trade via Seville and the African trade via Lisbon. In a remarkable contract dated January 20, 1548, the Fuggers' Antwerp agent Christoph Wolff promised to supply the representative of the Portuguese crown, João Rebello, with 7,500 hundredweight of brass rings, 24,000 pots, 1,800 broad-rimmed bowls, 4,500 barber's basins, and 10,500 kettles within three years. The contract explicitly stipulated that these brass items were to be used in the Guinea trade, and they were to be delivered to the Casa da India e Mina in Lisbon, which coordinated Portuguese overseas trade.[22]

In addition to precious metals, pearls, and gems, the goods from the New World that the Fuggers exported from Spain included guaiacum wood, a remedy against syphilis, which had been rampant in Europe since the 1490s. The guaiacum cure had become known in central Europe as a therapy for the venereal disease circa 1515; in 1521, the Fuggers established a "wood house" for the treatment of the ill in their social housing project in Augsburg. The young physician Theophrastus of Hohenheim, known as Paracelsus, who favored the treatment of syphilis with mercury, accused the Fuggers of promoting the guaiacum therapy out of economic self-interest in two treatises published in 1528–29. Although the Fuggers are known to have traded in guaiacum wood in Seville and their Antwerp office shipped "Indian wood" to Hungary in the 1520s, however, the notion that the firm held a monopoly in guaiacum commerce has been unequivocally disproved by recent scholarly research.[23]

FERDINAND I, TYROL, AND NAPLES

Like Emperor Charles V, Ferdinand I, his brother and successor, depended on loans time and again, as the administration of the Austrian and Bohemian lands, the defense against the Turks, the struggles for the crown of Hungary, and imperial politics required enormous financial means. Moreover, Ferdinand had taken over a substantial part of the liabilities that had resulted from the imperial election of his brother. However, the Fuggers also needed to remain on good terms with the ruler of the Austrian, Bohemian, and Hungarian lands, as their Tyrolean and Hungarian mining ventures, as well as a large part of their Swabian landholdings, were located in his realm. Therefore, the relations between the firm and the Habsburg ruler remained very close during the entire period in which Anton Fugger ran the company, although they were not devoid of conflict. With a sum of 651,000 florins, Ferdinand was the firm's largest debtor, according to the general balance of 1527, and the following year the Augsburg companies of Anton Fugger, the brothers Anton and Hans Bimmel, and Christoph Herwart lent the ruler 45,000 florins—25,000 in cash and the remainder in linen and fine cloth. Ferdinand's election as Roman king in 1530 was supported by the Fuggers with an advance of 275,333 florins and a lifelong rent of 7,000 florins for the elector of Mainz. Including interest and an extra commission of 40,000 florins, the debt that Ferdinand had incurred for his election amounted to 356,845 florins.[24] The Fuggers' general balance of 1533 showed that the king's liabilities amounted to roughly 1 million florins, and Ferdinand subsequently continued to need money. In 1537, he borrowed 83,000 florins from the company, and in 1541, Anton Fugger, Hans Baumgartner, and Matthias Manlich of Augsburg advanced him 110,000 florins against Tyrolean silver.[25] According to the general balance of 1546, the king's debts with the Fuggers amounted to 443,000 florins; seven years later, they still stood at 380,000 florins.[26]

Under Anton Fugger's leadership, the Tyrolean mining and metal trade remained an important pillar of the firm's business. The general balance of 1527 lists shares in mines at Klausen in the Eisack Valley, at Gossensass and the Schneeberg, at Lienz in the Puster Valley, in the vicinity of Rattenberg, and in the Schwaz mining district, where the Fuggers held shares in forty-five mines at Falkenstein Mountain alone. The ores extracted from these mines were processed in smelting works at Schwaz, Jenbach, and Rattenberg, the Jenbach works being the most important. In 1527 and 1528, Jenbach produced about 13,500 Marks of silver and 5,500 hundredweight of copper. After the bankruptcy of the Höchstetter company, the Fuggers also took over the smelting works at Jenbach. The head of the Schwaz trading post, Georg Hörmann, acquired further shares in mines near Klausen around 1530 and had a smelting works erected there. In early 1526, the Fuggers, Christoph Herwart, the brothers Anton and Hans Bimmel, and Benedikt Burkhart founded the Schwazer Berg-, Schmelz- und Pfennwert-Handel, a joint venture for the operation of mines and smelting works and the supply of miners with foodstuffs and other necessities. Each of the three Augsburg firms invested 24,000 Hungarian florins in the venture, while Burkhart, who commanded less capital, contributed 12,000 florins. Burkhart sold his share to the Bimmels and Fuggers as early as 1527.[27]

The lists of silver production at Falkenstein near Schwaz, where the richest mines were, illustrate the development of Tyrolean mining during the 1530s and 1540s (see table 6). The years from 1525, when Jakob Fugger died, to 1530 witnessed a process of concentration. Whereas the lists recorded eleven mining entrepreneurs in 1525, their number had shrunk to six by 1530. Apart from the Höchstetters of Augsburg, who had gone bankrupt in

TABLE 6

Silver production at Falkenstein near Schwaz, 1530–1549

Time period	Mean annual production	Fugger production	Fugger share (%)
1530–34	38,602	8,011	20.8
1535–39	29,909	5,654	18.9
1540–44	28,208	6,060	21.5
1545–49	27,049	5,238	19.4

Source: Westermann, Die Listen der Brandsilberproduktion, 102–9.

Note: Production figures in Marks silver; 1,000 Marks = 281 kilograms.

1529, several indigenous entrepreneurs had quit the business. Three of the six remaining were Tyroleans (the Tänzls, Reiffs, and Stöckls) and three were Augsburg firms (the Fuggers, Hans Baumgartner, and a joint venture of Anton and Hans Bimmel and the heirs of Christoph Herwart). After the death of the Bimmel brothers in 1531, their heirs formed the company Anton Haug, Hans Langnauer, Ulrich Linck and Associates, and Christoph Herwart's son-in-law Sebastian Neidhart took the lead among Herwart's heirs. Consequently, the Bimmel-Herwart company became the Haug-Neidhart company in the 1540s. The shares of the Reiff family's heir, Jakob Gratt, were finally taken over by the brothers Hans Paul and Hans Heinrich Herwart of Augsburg in 1546.[28] The lists of silver production show that output at Falkenstein declined significantly during the 1530s but stabilized afterward.[29] From 1535 to 1549, the Fuggers, on average, produced 5,000–6,000 Marks of silver per annum, roughly one-fifth of total production there.

As in Jakob Fugger's time, the credit contracts of Augsburg firms with the king and the Tyrolean government of the 1530s und 1540s were frequently linked with metal transactions.[30] In February 1540, for example, King Ferdinand signed a document in Innsbruck affirming that the Fugger, Baumgartner, and Haug-Neidhart companies had advanced him 30,000 florins "for our needs and our projected journey to visit our dear lord and brother, the Roman Emperor, in the Netherlands." In exchange for this loan, the firms were promised a total of 20,000 Marks of silver, which they had produced in Schwaz and which were originally designed to be delivered to the mint at Hall, for the price of 9 florins and 12 kreuzer per Mark. They had the option to sell this silver on the open market or deliver it to the mint at a higher price of 10 florins and 30 kreuzer. In another contract, concluded in the town of Linz in November 1541, the Fugger, Baumgartner, and Haug-Neidhart companies granted the king a loan of 120,000 florins all together and were promised 54,545 Marks of silver at a price of 9 florins and 26 kreuzer per Mark. Three years later, the same firms advanced King Ferdinand 100,000 florins in Vienna in exchange for 45,454 Marks of Tyrolean silver, which they purchased for the same price as in 1541. The Haug-Neidhart company also held a one-third share in the contract signed at Hohenfurt in November 1541, in which the Fuggers obtained 30,000 Marks of silver and 12,500 hundred-weight of copper in return for a loan of 80,000 florins. The debt Ferdinand incurred in this contract remained unpaid a late as 1554. Anton Fugger himself estimated the profits that his firm drew from this single contract at more than 60,000 florins.[31]

Whereas the firm's Tyrolean affairs had been supervised by the Innsbruck office in Jakob Fugger's time, the center of gravity shifted during the 1520s to Hall, seat of the Tyrolean mint and salt office, as well as an important loading place for copper and silver transports, and to Schwaz, the center of metal production. The mines and smelting works were managed from these two central locations, with Schwaz mainly responsible for the technical side and Hall for the financial side of Tyrolean business. The office at Innsbruck was retained but merely in a subsidiary function. The office at Bolzano (Bozen) formed a kind of extension of the firm's Tyrolean commerce and linked it to the Italian trading posts. The commercial centers Venice and Nuremberg were the main outlets for the sale of Tyrolean copper.[32]

In the course of a distribution of assets and restructuring of the firm that he undertook in 1548, Anton Fugger separated the Tyrolean and Carinthian enterprise from the family firm. Hermann Kellenbenz has characterized this new, specialized company as "a combined mining, smelting, metal trade, and supply trade enterprise," which sold its products to the family firm. The Tyrolean Trade Company, with estimated assets of 461,410 florins, became a debtor to the Fugger firm. At the time of the separation it included shares in thirty-nine mines at Falkenstein and twelve at Ringenwechsel in the Schwaz mining district; eleven mines at Röhrerbühel in the mining district of Kitz-bühel; smaller holdings at Gossensass, Terlan, Klausen, Nals, and Schnee-berg; and smelting works at Jenbach and Grasstein. Activities in Carinthia focused on the production of lead and on gold mining in the Lavant Valley. According to the first balance of the Tyrolean Trade Company for 1548–49, the firm made an annual net profit of 73,686 florins, or 8 percent on the capital invested. By the end of 1555, however, profits had declined to 33,893 florins, or 3.9 percent per annum on the capital stock, which was estimated at 472,327 florins at the time. Moreover, Anton Fugger made annual deductions of 2,000 florins during the 1550s.[33]

As the productivity of the "old" mines in the Schwaz district continued to decline, the Fuggers invested in new mines from 1548 onward. They also had a new building constructed for the Lützelfelden smelting works and built hammer works at Falkenstein and Bleiberg (Lead Mountain) in Carinthia. At the same time, they closed down older operations or reduced their workforce. After 1548, the company temporarily proved very reluctant to engage in new loan contracts with the Tyrolean government. A loan of 56,000 florins for the dowry of Ferdinand's daughter Katharina in 1549, the guaranteeing of a loan of 40,000 florins that the cardinal of Trent granted to the Innsbruck Hofkammer in 1552, and another advance of 56,000 florins in 1555 were among the largest business transactions during this period. Meanwhile, the declining output of the mines and difficulties in supplying the miners caused significant tension between the mine owners and the Tyrolean bureaucracy. Subsidies for the mining sector and the price of silver delivered to the mint at Hall became subjects of extended negotiations. To ensure the supply of its own mint, the government prohibited the export of silver. When illegal silver exports to Venice caused a severe conflict between the company, on the one hand, and Emperor Ferdinand and the Tyrolean government, on the other, Anton Fugger even offered his entire mining holding to the government for sale. This offer, which the Tyrolean government turned down, should not only be interpreted as the threatening gesture of an aging merchant banker. It was also part of Anton Fugger's efforts to liquidate all commercial activities, to which I will return later.[34]

The close financial ties with Ferdinand I also led to extensive activities of Anton Fugger's firm in the kingdom of Naples. King Ferdinand of Aragon had willed an annual rent of 50,000 ducats from his Neapolitan revenues to his grandson of the same name in his testament, and Charles V had raised the sum to 60,000 ducats per annum in the context of the partition treaties for the Habsburg lands to which the brothers agreed in 1522. In December 1524—and hence still in Jakob Fugger's lifetime—Ferdinand had assigned these revenues to his Augsburg creditors for the first time. Debts amounting to 200,000 ducats were to be paid from the Neapolitan rent. Subsequent Fugger loans were also assigned to Naples, and by the end of 1527, Ferdinand's liabilities amounted to roughly 650,000 florins, of which more than 240,000 were to be recovered from his revenues in southern Italy. The Fuggers had initially entrusted the collection of these moneys to their Roman office, but its closure and the growing importance of their southern Italian business affairs induced them to send their own agent to Naples.[35]

When southern Italy became a theater of war in the struggle between Charles V and Francis I of France in 1528, Charles's governor Hugo de

Moncada stopped the rent payments to Ferdinand. After the French troops had withdrawn, however, the Fugger agent Georg Hörmann was able to negotiate a new agreement with Ferdinand that provided for repayment of the ruler's debts to the amount of 182,740 ducats at 8 percent interest from the Neapolitan revenues. The loans Anton Fugger granted to finance Ferdinand's election as Roman king in 1530 were also linked to rents from Naples. In exchange for a loan of 173,300 florins, the king sold annual rent incomes totaling 16,000 ducats to the Fuggers. With a total debt of nearly half a million florins and assignments on Naples amounting to 249,000 florins, Ferdinand proved unable by the end of 1530 to meet his regular payment obligations and therefore handed over the administration of the receiver's office at Naples to the firm; from the beginning of 1532, this office was headed by the Fugger agent Christoph Mülich. The receiver's salary and the Neapolitan pensions of Ferdinand's favorites and trusted advisers were subsequently paid by the Fuggers. In the years that followed, the collection of the rents and the payment of pensions were the main tasks of the Naples office. Furthermore, it marketed Tyrolean copper and extended credit to southern German firms that purchased saffron at the market of Aquila in the Abruzze Mountains. Following up on a report sent by the agent Leonhard Vogel, Anton Fugger's confidants Sebastian Kurz and Georg Hörmann journeyed to Naples in 1540 to inspect southern Italian ore deposits together with two mining experts. The results of this inspection trip were negative, however. Another loan of 110,000 florins to Ferdinand, in exchange for which the firm was granted the Neapolitan revenues, is documented for May 1546, and the ruler repeatedly transferred rents to the Fuggers as repayment for outstanding debts. After midcentury, however, the importance of this branch of business declined, and the office in southern Italy was closed. The firm's business interests in Naples were subsequently handled by freelance agents.[36]

THE HUNGARIAN TRADE

After the crisis of 1525–26 had been resolved, the Fuggers remained the sole owners of the Hungarian trade, which Jakob Fugger had built up with Hans Thurzo since 1494. The Thurzo family had been completely paid off by 1528, but Alexi Thurzo remained the Fuggers' agent at the Hungarian court and received an annual salary until his death in 1543. Under Anton Fugger's leadership, the Hungarian trade continued to focus on the Neusohl mining district and the smelting works constructed under Jakob Fugger. Around 1530, the company also acquired mines in Libethen (Lubietová) south of Neusohl, but they remained of relatively little significance. The marketing and distribution organization was largely maintained intact, including the smelting works at Fuggerau and Hohenkirchen; the offices at Wrocław and Krakow as coordinating centers in Silesia and Poland; offices in Gdansk, Leipzig, Nuremberg, Lüneburg, and Vienna as distribution centers in central Europe; and Venice and Antwerp as the most important markets in southern and western Europe. Only the trading post in Ofen was given up, in 1533, because of the Ottoman threat.[37]

In the late 1520s and the 1530s, the development of the Hungarian trade was shaped by two factors: the unstable political situation in the realm of Hungary and the gradual decline of mining output. Amid the struggles between Ferdinand I of Habsburg and Johann Zápolya, who had been crowned as rival king, it was Anton Fugger's main aim to continue production and trade undisturbed. This meant that he had to come to terms with both competitors for the Hungarian crown. Zápolya's troops occupied the Slovakian mining towns near the end of 1526; Anton Fugger concluded a lease contract with him in March 1527 and paid the amounts due to him. At the same time, however, he retained his close ties with Ferdinand I because of his Tyrolean and Neapolitan interests and supported him with additional loans. Moreover, the Fuggers had their commercial privileges confirmed by King Sigismund of Poland, thereby securing their supply of Polish lead, as well as their transport routes through Sigismund's realm. After Ferdinand had regained the upper hand by the end of 1527, the Fuggers' lease payments for the years 1528 and 1529 went to the Habsburgs. Subsequently, Zápolya's supporters again took control of the Neusohl region, so the lease payments from 1530 to 1532 went to the king who had been crowned by the Hungarian noble opposition. Ferdinand I, who depended on the Fuggers' loans for the defense against the Turks, for the financing of his election as Roman king, and for the Habsburg dynasty's imperial politics, accepted these payments to his rival and elevated Anton, Raymund, and Hieronymus Fugger to the ranks of the Hungarian nobility in 1535.[38]

In the meantime, the productivity of the Slovakian mines gradually declined. According to Reinhard Hildebrandt's calculations, annual production fell from 37,000 hundredweight in the 1510s to 29,000 hundredweight in the 1520s and 23,000 hundredweight in the 1530s. All together, the Fuggers brought 267,000 hundredweight of copper to market between 1526 and 1539, of which 163,000 hundredweight were shipped to Antwerp; 43,000 were distributed via Lüneburg; and 35,000 were sold in Wrocław. Some 112,125 Marks of silver were produced during the same period, 97,500 Marks being delivered to the Hungarian mint and the rest minted in Krakow and Kremnitz or sold in Nuremberg and Leipzig. Meanwhile, a boom of the Mansfeld copper district in central Germany during the 1520s and 1530s put pressure on copper prices, and the large supply on the copper market led to growing stocks of unsold metals.[39] Nevertheless, a balance compiled in December 1533 shows that the company had made respectable profits. Discounting old expenses and uncertain claims, the period from 1527 to 1533 had yielded a profit of roughly 325,000 Hungarian florins, or 54,000 Hungarian florins per annum. The general account for the period from September 1536 to September 1539, by contrast, reveals a profit of merely 18,000 florins. Apart from ongoing political instability and the military threat of the Ottomans, conflicts with the Slovakian mining towns over the use of resources and administrative matters, as well as rising transport costs, strained the Hungarian trade and gave Anton Fugger cause to think about its liquidation as early as 1537. It was with grave doubts that he agreed to another extension of the lease contract in 1541.[40]

In March 1545, Anton Fugger terminated the lease as of April 1546, and in the fall of 1545 he sent his agents Hans Dernschwam and Sebastian Saurzapf to Vienna to take care of the details. Although the Hungarian trade still had outstanding claims totaling more than 115,000 florins, a large amount of which had to be written off as irrecoverable with the firm's withdrawal from Neusohl, Fugger was unwilling to negotiate a new lease. He merely agreed to a loan of 30,000 florins to secure the continuation of mining production. In 1548, the Augsburg merchant Matthias Manlich took over the Neusohl copper contract, and Manlich and Fugger signed a cartel contract for the distribution of Slovakian and Tyrolean copper on European markets. According to the terms of the contract, Manlich's exclusive field of distribution was to include Poland, Silesia, northern Germany, and France, while southern Germany, Italy, and the French Mediterranean ports were to be considered the domain of the Fuggers. The important Antwerp market and the Iberian Peninsula were to remain open to both companies.[41]

The termination of the Hungarian trade also affected the smelting works in Hohenkirchen and Fuggerau. Hohenkirchen had already lost much of its attractiveness in the mid-1530s when the elector of Saxony secularized the monastery of Georgenthal, on whose territory the smelting works was located, in the course of the Protestant Reformation. Moreover, a fire in 1543 heavily damaged the works, and Hohenkirchen was sold six years later. By contrast, the works at Fuggerau in Carinthia, which processed Tyrolean and Slovakian copper and had obtained lead from the nearby Bleiberg (Lead Mountain), was expanded in the 1540s and incorporated into the Tyrolean enterprise. At midcentury, the Carinthian works delivered brass and lead to Venice.[42]

The firm's gold-mining activities near Reichenstein and Freiwaldau in Silesia, in which Jakob Fugger had invested since the turn of the century, were purposefully expanded under his nephew Anton. By 1529, the company controlled half of the mines and smelting works there. Gold production reached its peak at midcentury: From 1540 to 1547, the average annual output came to 237 Marks of gold, part of which was minted at Kremnitz, and the remainder was sold via Wrocław, Nuremberg, and Augsburg.[43] Finally, the obligations that the Hungarian crown had incurred when it restored the Slovakian mines and smelting works to the Fuggers in 1526 opened up a new avenue of commerce, for the debts of more than 200,000 Hungarian florins were to be defrayed by revenues from the Transylvanian salt mines. After the agent Hans Dernschwam found the mines in poor condition in 1528, the Fuggers invested another 40,000 florins. Dernschwam's ambitious plans for the organization of a new production and distribution chain, however, went up in smoke as Zápolya's troops occupied Transylvania. The salt business had to be liquidated, with heavy losses.[44]

BEYOND THE HABSBURG EMPIRE:
RELATIONS WITH EUROPEAN PRINCELY COURTS

Although financial relations with Charles V and Ferdinand I were at the heart of Anton Fugger's business strategy, his firm also extended credit to a number of other European princes, including the kings of Portugal, England, and Denmark and the grand duke of Tuscany. These loans highlight the firm's increasingly westward orientation and the importance of Antwerp as the financial center of Europe. Although they did not lead to the kind of close and durable relationship that connected the Fuggers to the House of Habsburg, they underscore that Anton Fugger was not merely a "semi-official imperial factor" (in the words of Johannes Burkhardt) at midcentury but a merchant banker operating on a truly international scale.

As mentioned earlier,[45] Portugal was chiefly important for the Fugger firm as a major purchaser of copper and brass. Antwerp, the preeminent western European distribution center for Hungarian copper, was also the place where business between the company and the Portuguese crown was transacted. The general balance of 1527 recorded the king of Portugal among the firm's Antwerp debtors, owing a sum of 18,450 Flemish pounds. Six years later, he owed 12,500 Flemish pounds, and in 1539, he owed 22,000 pounds. According to the general balance of 1546, the firm's claims against the Portuguese king in Antwerp still stood at 6,252 Flemish pounds.[46] While financial relations with the Portuguese crown extended over a longer time period, loans to the English crown acquired larger dimensions in the mid-1540s, when the Fuggers began to dissolve the Hungarian trade and were looking for new investment opportunities. The fact that the English king was temporarily allied to the Habsburg rulers in their struggle against the French crown made these loans appear politically opportune, as well. In 1545, the firm granted King Henry VIII a loan of 100,000 Flemish pounds and sold jewels to him from the Burgundian treasury, which Jakob Fugger had acquired from the city of Basel four decades earlier, for 60,000 pounds. At one point, the claims against the English crown from loans and sales of textiles, copper, and jewelry added up to more than 1 million florins. In the fall of 1549, Henry's successor, Edward VI, received a loan of 54,800 Flemish pounds, or 328,000 Carolus florins, and the following June, he received another 127,000 Carolus florins; substantial loans are also recorded for 1552. But these relations with the English crown were soon pared down again. By 1553, Thomas Gresham, the royal financial agent in the Low Countries, had paid back debts on the amount of 123,000 Flemish pounds. In light of the bloody religious conflicts in England during the reign of Mary Tudor (1553–58), the business in English crown loans may have appeared too risky, and the enormous demands of the Habsburg rulers for credit during these years pressed the Fugger firm to the limit of its financial abilities. From 1554 onward, a substantial part of the English debt was paid back. A new loan of 10,000 Flemish pounds that Anton Fugger's son Hans granted to the young Queen Elizabeth I of England in Antwerp in 1559 did not result in lasting ties between the Protestant ruler and the Catholic merchant house.[47]

To secure its copper transports from the Baltic ports to the Low Countries, the Fugger company consistently cultivated its relations with the Danish crown. The volume of credit transactions with Denmark was not very significant, however. In the course of negotiations about a contract for the passage of ships through the sound, King Christian III received a loan of 20,000 florins in 1541.[48] Cosimo I, Grand Duke of Tuscany from the House of Medici, appears among the company's major customers for a few years around midcentury. In 1548, the Fugger firm granted a loan of 100,000 scudi to Cosimo, a close political ally of the House of Habsburg, and a series of large credit transactions followed until 1553. In 1551, the company sold a piece of jewelry to the grand duke for 12,000 scudi, and in 1554, Cosimo borrowed 75,000 ducats and bought another piece of jewelry for 23,600 gold scudi. All together, the Fuggers' loans to Cosimo amounted to 420,000 scudi between 1548 and 1554, making the Augsburgers the grand duke's largest creditors at midcentury. For some time, the firm took over part of the grand duke's Neapolitan revenues, and in the year of Anton Fugger's death (1560), it still held claims of 58,000 scudi against him.[49]

By 1546, Anton Fugger's company had reached the peak of its expansion. The general balance drawn up in that year showed assets of 7.1 million florins; since 1539, assets had increased by a phenomenal 2.9 million. The liabilities stood at roughly 2 million florins; thus, the company had a capital stock of 5 million florins.[50] At the same time, Anton Fugger restructured his enterprise: The Hungarian trade was abandoned, and the Tyrolean and Carinthian mining and metal trading ventures were separated from the company. By the time the next general balance was drawn up in 1553, more than 2 million florins had been distributed to the partners; therefore, the company's assets shrank to 3.25 million florins.[51] Moreover, the firm increasingly borrowed money to finance its loan transactions. In 1546, it had borrowed a total of 110,000 Flemish pounds (equaling 460,000 florins) from thirty-five business partners in Antwerp on letters of exchange—for example, 14,570 pounds from Sebastian Neidhart of Augsburg, 12,600 pounds from Bartholomäus Welser's company, about 4,000 pounds from the Haug-Langnauer-Linck company, and about 6,500 pounds from the Ligsalz company of Munich. While the firm paid 8–10 percent interest on these exchange loans, it received 12 percent interest on debt certificates issued by the rent masters of the Netherlands and 13–14 percent interest on its advances to European monarchs.[52] The firm also borrowed on the Augsburg capital market. On the evidence of the so-called *Unterkaufbücher*, which record exchange and credit transactions witnessed by the city's official brokers from 1551 to 1558, the Fuggers received loans totaling about 70,000 florins in the second half of 1552 alone.[53] In February 1554, Anton Fugger urgently needed 30,000 florins from Antwerp to pay back his own obligations; as he wrote, "My credit depends on it."[54] For a long time, this kind of borrowing did not appear worrisome in light of the firm's excellent reputation on international financial markets. Considering that a large part of the assets consisted of claims against the House of Habsburg and other princes, the liabilities would turn out to be problematic, however, if these princely debtors no longer met their obligations. This is exactly what happened on Antwerp's financial market in the 1550s.

After Emperor Charles V and his son Philip moved to the Netherlands in 1553, the focus of the Fuggers' credit transactions with the Habsburg rulers shifted to Antwerp. Philip's marriage to Queen Mary Tudor of England and renewed warfare between Habsburg and France once again called for large loans, and the imperial secretary Francisco de Erasso promised deliveries of American precious metals from Spain to the firm in return. After Spanish silver worth 200,000 ducats arrived in Antwerp in 1553, the Fugger agent on the spot, Matthäus Örtel, proved willing to grant further loans. In May and September 1555, he lent the Spanish crown 320,000 ducats all together, followed by 540,000 ducats in 1556. The duke of Savoy, who fought against the French king on the side of Spain, likewise received considerable sums. In addition, Örtel invested large sums of money in the already mentioned debt certificates of the Dutch rent masters. Finally, on New Year's Day of 1557, Örtel gave the Spanish king a loan of 430,000 ducats, which was to be paid back from the next shipments of gold and silver from America.[55]

A few months later, however, in June 1557, King Philip II issued a decree that voided his creditors' assignments on revenues of the Spanish crown and exchanged their claims for royal rents (*juros*) that carried merely 5 percent interest. This so-called Spanish state bankruptcy was actually an effort at debt conversion by which the crown tried to free itself from its crushing interest obligations. In the case of the Fuggers, however, a second crown measure dramatically worsened the situation, for in 1557 the crown also had all Spanish silver shipments from America, which had already been assigned to the Fuggers, confiscated in Antwerp to pay its troops in Spain's ongoing military conflict with France. At one stroke, the Fuggers thus incurred losses of 570,000 ducats. To master this crisis, Anton Fugger sent his son Hans and his senior trusted adviser Sebastian Kurz to Antwerp and withdrew Örtel's power of attorney. Confronted with enormous outstanding debts from Spanish state loans and rent masters' debt certificates in the Low Countries, the crisis managers were faced with two major tasks: They needed to get an overview of the business situation, and they had to attempt to ward off new demands for loans and recover at least part of the company's claims. Hans Jakob Fugger, the nephew and designated successor of the firm's head, traveled to Spain in 1560 to protect the firm's interests there.[56]

Despite the difficult financial situation in the Netherlands, however, the firm had no choice but to grant new loans to preserve its creditworthiness and reputation. Besides the already mentioned loan to the English queen, Hans Fugger advanced almost 12,000 Flemish pounds to the duke of Alba in Antwerp in 1559.[57] The firm's relations with Emperor Ferdinand I had been strained since 1558 because of charges that the company had illegally exported silver to Venice — charges against which Anton Fugger had to defend himself at the imperial Diet of Augsburg in 1559. Yet despite these tensions, Anton Fugger retained his position as financier to the Austrian branch of the House of Habsburg until his death on September 14, 1560. A few months before he died, he advanced Ferdinand another 40,000 florins, for which his firm was granted the revenues from the salt offices at Vienna and Aussee. Ferdinand's son, the Roman king and later Emperor Maximilian II, also borrowed 30,000 florins from him in the same year. Thus, the course had been set for an enduring cooperation between the firm and the imperial dynasty in the following generation.[58]

Long before the financial crisis in the Netherlands broke, Anton Fugger had given serious thoughts to dissolving the firm. In the will he dictated in 1550, he stated that he had "governed and administered" the company after the death of his brother Raymund and the paying off of his cousin Hieronymus "with great effort and labor, also with sickening and weakening my body and with losing my health, alone and single-handed up to the present day." Contrary to his hopes that his nephews would follow in his footsteps, none of them had turned out to have "pleasure or inclination" toward the merchant's profession. As no successor was available, he had abandoned the Hungarian trade and begun "to withdraw from all our common Fugger trading ventures and undertakings." If the dissolution of the business and the distribution of the capital stock had not been completed by the time of his death, they should be finished as soon as possible thereafter.

Due to the company's strong involvement in Tyrol, Spain, and the Netherlands, however, these plans could not be realized, and the codicil Anton Fugger added to his will on July 11, 1560, about two months before his death, was marked by deep concern about the fate of the company. Fugger wrote that he had "seriously talked" to his nephew Hans Jakob that he should take over the management of the firm together with one of Anton's own sons, but Hans Jakob had "refused this," referring to his political activities and private business. His nephew Georg had "completely turned down" the offer to become part of the company's management, claiming that he "was unable to do the work and would much rather remain in peace and quiet." And even Christoph Fugger—the one among his nephews who had been "employed the most in commerce in his youth, to wit in the Tyrol, Antwerp, and Spain"—was not prepared to succeed his uncle under any circumstances. Because Raymund, the fourth nephew, was clearly unable to take over business affairs because of his weak constitution, Anton Fugger appointed the unwilling Hans Jakob, his eldest and most competent nephew, manager of the firm. Together with Anton's eldest son Marx Fugger, Hans Jakob was to continue the company "until everything will be recovered and until trading runs out and comes to an end."[59] From Anton Fugger's perspective, the company that his father and his uncles had founded, and that he himself had continued, clearly had no future. That almost another century would pass before the Fugger company would actually go out of business was beyond his wildest dreams.

The period from 1485 to 1560, in which Jakob Fugger turned the trading company into the leading southern German enterprise of his day and his nephew successfully continued the firm, has often been called the "age of the Fuggers," a term coined by Richard Ehrenberg's classic study published in 1896. The name implies, on the one hand, that the Fuggers held such a predominant position in international commerce and finance that all other firms remained in their shadow. On the other hand, the term "age of the Fuggers" is linked to the notion that the history of the family is of exemplary significance for the history of sixteenth-century trade. The historian Horst Rabe, for example, has characterized Jakob Fugger as "the most important, but at the same time a very typical, representative of this upper German merchant capitalism."[60] Both notions, however—that of the Fuggers' predominance and that of the firm's exemplary character for the phenomenon termed "upper German merchant capitalism"—are only partly true.[61]

To be sure, the Fugger firm was the single most important financier of the Holy Roman Emperor and Spanish King Charles V. But the data compiled by Ramón Carande and summarized earlier clearly show that Charles V also needed other bankers and merchant companies to finance his military and political ventures: upper German companies such as the Welsers, along with Genoese, Dutch, and Spanish financiers. The Fuggers accounted for only one-fifth of the royal loans. Regarding the second domain of the Fuggers' business, Tyrolean mining, a number of other Augsburg merchant firms entered the field during the first half of the sixteenth century: the companies of Hans Baumgartner, Ambrosius Höchstetter, the Bimmel brothers, Matthias Manlich, and Christoph Herwart. Available production figures do not indicate that the Fuggers predominated. At Falkenstein in the Schwaz district, they controlled about one-fifth of the total output between 1530 and 1550. Among the creditors of Ferdinand I, other Augsburg firms came to the fore during the 1550s at the expense of the Fuggers. They included the Haug-Langnauer-Linck company, Joachim Jenisch, and Wolfgang Paler.[62] The third domain, Slovakian mining, was actually under the control of the Fuggers until 1546, but when Anton Fugger gave up the Hungarian trade, other Augsburg firms filled the void. Matthias Manlich leased the Slovakian mines from 1548 onward, while Wolfgang Paler and the heirs of Leonhard Weiß controlled the Neusohl mining district from 1569 until the early 1620s.[63]

The cases of Tyrolean and Slovakian mining demonstrate that other Augsburg firms besides the Fuggers had accumulated sufficient capital since the close of the fifteenth century to engage in large-scale mining ventures. The mercury produced in the mines of Idria in present-day Slovenia was likewise marketed by Augsburg firms for several decades, at first by the Höchstetters, and then by the Baumgartner, Herwart, and Haug-Langnauer-Linck companies. The Haug-Langnauer-Linck company also became involved in English mining ventures in the 1560s. The Wieland family was active in the Salzburg mining region, while the Welsers were engaged in Saxon and Thuringian districts.[64] On the Augsburg financial market of the 1550s, which is well documented in the records of the city's official brokers, the Fuggers certainly played a prominent, but hardly a predominant, role. The exchange and credit transactions of the firms of Hans Paul and Hans Heinrich Herwart, Hieronymus Imhof, and the Kraffter brothers, for example, reached comparable dimensions.[65]

The notion that the Fuggers can be taken to represent the while history of the southern German merchant companies *pars pro toto* is also misleading because few other firms were so strongly focused on the lands of the Habsburg monarchy and on mining and the provision of credit. Most merchant companies from the German imperial cities remained much more heavily involved in the traditional commerce in goods such as textiles, spices, metal wares, and luxury items, and many of them directed their trade toward different areas. A telling case is the French market, where the Fuggers were only sporadically active because of their close ties with the House of Habsburg. The Fugger company did not even maintain a trading post of its own in Lyons, the leading commercial and banking center within the French monarchy in the first half of the sixteenth century; it was merely represented by agents. As Lyons was an important market for southern German textiles and Alpine copper, as well as a place where saffron and pastel dyes from southern France along with wool, silk fabrics, leather, books, and numerous other goods could be conveniently purchased, other Augsburg firms saw significant opportunities there—even more so because the French kings granted special privileges to the southern German merchants. The Welser company was already present in Lyons by 1500; the Manlich and Zangmeister firms made their appearance in the 1510s; the Höchstetters marketed mercury there in the 1520s; and the brothers Hans and David Weyer, who conducted their own long-distance trade in goods, also looked after the business interests of the Fuggers and Baumgartners in Lyons in the 1530s. Loans from Augsburg, Nuremberg, and Strasbourg merchants to the French crown, which are sporadically documented from the 1520s on, became more and more frequent after 1540. The high interest rates promised by the crown led several firms into risky credit ventures. The Weyer brothers; Hieronymus and David Zangmeister; Hans Paul and Hans Heinrich Herwart; Bernhard and Philipp Meuting; and Sebastian Neidhart and Hieronymus Sailer, a son-in-law of

Bartholomäus Welser, advanced large sums to the crown at midcentury. After King Henry II suspended payments in 1557, the Weyer, Zangmeister, and Meuting firms went bankrupt.[66]

Lyons is only one among several examples of commercial and financial centers in which other merchant companies from the imperial cities were much more deeply involved than the Fuggers. A number of firms focused on trade with Italy, which was traditionally important for the city of Augsburg. These firms were regularly present at the Bolzano fairs; they purchased cotton and luxury goods in Venice; they traded in Spanish wool, central European linen, velvet, and coral in Genoa; they purchased high-quality fabrics in Florence, Lucca, and Bologna; and they acquired yarn made of gold in Milan.[67] A large number of Augsburg merchants were active at the Frankfurt and Leipzig fairs, as well. The Ulstett and Österreicher companies were important actors in the linen-weaving districts of east-central Germany, and the demand of Lutheran and Reformed German princes for credit was met by Protestant merchants such as Jakob Herbrot, the sometime burgomaster of Augsburg.[68]

In addition to Augsburg, Nuremberg remained an important economic center in southern Germany, and the great Franconian merchant families, including the Tuchers and Behaims and the Nuremberg branches of the Welser and Imhof families, had different priorities from those of their Augsburg counterparts. They were more reluctant to engage in speculative credit transactions and to accept large amounts of outside capital, and they mostly left the Alpine and Slovakian mining regions to the Augsburg firms. However, they were deeply involved in the central German mining and metal trade, in iron production in the Upper Palatinate, in textile production using the putting-out system, and in the "classic" long-distance commerce in metal wares, textiles, luxury items, and other goods.[69] Augsburg and Nuremberg companies were both present in the most important commercial centers of Europe—Antwerp, Lyons, Venice, and Lisbon. And although the mercantile communities in other southern German cities were neither as numerous nor as well supplied with capital as the Augsburg and Nuremberg firms, important long-distance merchants also came from the cities of Ulm, Strasbourg, Memmingen, and Munich.

The rise of the Fuggers, therefore, should be viewed in the context of a general boom of southern German long-distance trade in the sixteenth century, which was supported by dozens of firms from the two commercial metropolises of Augsburg and Nuremberg, as well as from a number of secondary centers of trade. This commercial boom is a significant symptom of the growing integration of Europe's economic regions at the beginning of the modern age. The long-distance trade and credit activities of merchant companies connected east-central Europe (Poland, Bohemia, and Hungary), the Netherlands, northern Italy, and Spain ever more closely to the German-speaking lands in central Europe. The fact that most of these regions were ruled by a single dynasty, the House of Habsburg, in the sixteenth century undoubtedly helped this process of integration.[70] While some of the firms that conducted long-distance trade in the sixteenth century competed with the Fuggers in their favorite business domains—Alpine mining, commerce with Spain, and the Antwerp market—others set different priorities. The internal structures of these companies and their organization of business also differed significantly. Whereas the Fugger company and most other southern German firms were combinations of a few close relatives, others, such as the Welser-Vöhlin and Haug-Langnauer-Linck companies, comprised a much larger circle of associates.[71]

Finally, it should be noted that the composition of the elite group of southern German merchant-bankers was not static but subject to dynamic processes of change. While a number of firms—for example, the Höchstetter, Hirschvogel, Manlich, Zangmeister, and Haug-Langnauer-Linck companies—went out of business because of bankruptcy or lack of competent successors, others, such as the Paler-Weiß, Österreicher, Zobel, and Hainhofer companies in Augsburg and the Viatis-Peller firm in Nuremberg, replaced them.[72] By 1600, some 300–400 merchants and trading companies were active in each of the two southern German commercial metropolises. Apart from the large family firms, which maintained permanent offices in important commercial centers, there were numerous specialized agents and commissioners, transport firms, and middling merchants. They benefited from technical and organizational innovations in the fields of banking, insurance, and information supply, and they were able to respond flexibly to economic fluctuations, as well as to occupy market niches. For these reasons, it is inappropriate to identify the fortunes of individual firms with the general development of southern German long-distance trade—let alone the southern German economy—as a whole.[73] Therefore, we should speak not of the "age of the Fuggers" but, rather, of the "age of the southern German family trading companies"—a phenomenon that characterizes the long sixteenth century between 1470 and 1620. This shift in terminology will help understand the fate of the Fugger company after 1560.

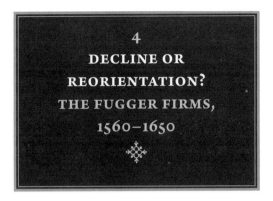

4

DECLINE OR
REORIENTATION?
THE FUGGER FIRMS,
1560–1650

CRISES AND THEIR RESOLUTION

For a long time, researchers held the generations that followed Anton Fugger in low esteem. Richard Ehrenberg characterized the history of the Fugger firm after 1560 as a "time of decay," and in Baron Götz von Pölnitz's view, the generations of the "founders" and "rulers" were followed by a generation of "epigons and Diadochi"—that is, unworthy successors who had neither the will nor the capability to master the challenges of their time. Allegedly, these "epigons" increasingly withdrew from active involvement in commercial affairs and used the wealth their ancestors had accumulated for other goals and interests—art collections, libraries, and personal hobbies.[1]

The view that the firm declined in the generation following Anton Fugger has not been without its critics, however, for an adequate assessment of its development in the late sixteenth century has to take into account both the course set by Anton Fugger and the changing economic circumstances. As was pointed out at the end of the preceding chapter, Anton Fugger planned to dissolve the family trading company, and this decision was very much present in the minds of his descendants. In 1580, Anton's son Marx spoke of our "common trade, dissolved way back in the year of 1548, but not yet completely distributed so far," and a year later he used the term "*tacita continuatio societatis* (the tacit continuation of the company)." Legally, Marx Fugger thus conceived of himself as the head of a firm that already had been dissolved but whose liquidation was not yet feasible.[2]

Anton and Raymund Fugger had provided a broad humanist and learned education to their sons and thereby had infused them with new social norms and values. In 1546, Anton Fugger declared that the schooling of the next generation should aim at educating "men of means, who excelled by their adherence to the old faith." In the will he dictated in 1550, he commanded that his sons should "continue to study and travel with learned men as tutors as well as experience and learn foreign languages." Afterward, they should be "placed at the courts of his Roman imperial and royal majesties, so that they might be promoted to and employed in offices and honorable services in due time." Anton Fugger's sons Marx (b. 1529), Hans (b. 1531), Hieronymus (b. 1533), and Jakob (b. 1542) were initially educated by private tutors who had received a humanist education themselves. In 1537, the jurist Dr. Johann Planta was employed as a tutor in the Fugger household; two years later, Dr. Georg Sigmund Seld, later the imperial vice-chancellor, probably held the same position; and in 1540, the Latinist Johannes Pinicianus and the philologist Dr. Laurentius Sifanus, who later became a university professor in Ingolstadt, taught Fugger's sons. After a brief sojourn in Vienna, the three elder brothers came "in contact with almost all the countries of Catholic Europe" during the extended travels and visits to universities they undertook beginning in 1542. They spent four years in Italy, including an extended period in Padua, and in the late 1540s, Marx and Hans Fugger studied at the University of Leuven in the Low Countries, where Marx primarily occupied himself with ancient languages and philosophy. In addition, two trips to France are documented in the years 1546 and 1549–50. In 1552, the brothers, accompanied by their tutor Johannes Tonner, went on a journey to Spain. Apparently, this journey, which led them to Seville via Almagro and Cordoba, was not only meant to prepare them for future employment in the Fugger company but was primarily taken up with scholarly studies. After a sojourn at Genoa, Marx Fugger worked in the Fuggers' Antwerp office in 1553 before returning to Augsburg the following year. His brother Hans seems to have remained at court in Vienna until 1557 before his father sent him to Antwerp, where a difficult situation for the firm's business had ensued after the Spanish crown and the regency in the Netherlands had stopped making payments.[3]

Like Marx and Hans Fugger, Hans Jakob and Georg Fugger, their older cousins, had been prepared for future employment in the trading company but also enjoyed a broad learned and humanist education. They had studied at the universities of Bourges, Padua, and Bologna beginning in 1531 and had received a commercial education in the Antwerp trading office in 1536 and 1537, respectively. In 1538, the Fugger representative in Schwaz, Georg Hörmann, introduced Hans Jakob Fugger to the secrets of the firm's Tyrolean affairs, and in 1550, Anton Fugger entrusted him with the management of the Maestrazgos in Spain. Therefore, Hans Jakob Fugger was well prepared to take over the management of the firm; at the same time, his studies, travels, and political activities in Augsburg had opened up manifold possibilities for him to pursue other interests and inclinations.[4]

FIGURE 6
Portrait of Marx Fugger (1529–1597)
from Fuggerorum and Fuggerarum . . . imagines, *1618.*
(Bayerische Staatsbibliothek München [Rar. 643, Bl. 74a])

Moreover, it has to be kept in mind that Anton Fugger left a problematic heritage to his nephew Hans Jakob and his son Marx, whom he appointed managers of the trading company. The Spanish crown's debts, which already amounted to 2.3 million ducats in 1557, had risen to 3 million ducats by 1563. Although the factor Christoph Hörmann was able to negotiate a relatively favorable contract in which the crown recognized a large part of these claims, the repayment of the debts continued to be fraught with difficulties. Hans Jakob Fugger, who was increasingly pressed by these high outstanding debts, implored Emperor Ferdinand I and Emperor Maximilian II to intercede with their Spanish cousin Philip II regarding repayment of the loans. In 1563, Maximilian instructed the imperial ambassador to the Spanish court, Adam von Dietrichstein, to support Fugger's cause. As Fugger's "reputation and trust . . . depended on it so very much," Dietrichstein should commit himself "as if it were our own business and affair." Yet the intervention proved unsuccessful: Dietrichstein reported to Vienna in April 1564 that Philip II was prepared to pay back at least part of the loans, but two months later, he had to write that he had "but poor hopes," for the Spanish crown was obviously attempting to force its creditors to give up part of their claims rather than lose everything.[5]

When the general balance for 1563 was compiled, the firm had total assets of 5.66 million florins, including a capital stock of 663,299 florins. Almost two-thirds of this stock—422,000 florins—belonged to Anton Fugger's heirs, and the remainder belonged to other family members. Liabilities in the amount of 5.40 million florins demonstrate that the company was now heavily dependent on outside capital. Debt certificates issued by the rent masters in the Low Countries, which had been bought in Anton Fugger's time at a nominal value of 95,000 Flemish pounds, the equivalent of 430,000 florins, were meanwhile considered so doubtful that they were not listed among the assets. Considering that a large part of the assets consisted of Spanish and Dutch debt claims that were difficult to collect, the ratio of capital stock to outside capital was highly unfavorable. To be sure, a significant part of the deposit capital came from family members who had invested in the company not at "gain or loss"—that is, with full rights to share in profits and full responsibilities for losses—but as deposits at fixed interest rates. But even with non-family members, the Fuggers had incurred deposit liabilities amounting to 2.7 million florins, including almost 2 million florins borrowed in Antwerp.[6]

The problems were larger than just the Fugger company, for a whole series of bankruptcies shook Augsburg's financial world after 1557. While some firms had to suspend their payments because they had invested too heavily in French, Dutch, Spanish, and Portuguese state loans, others had incurred heavy losses from their mining shares or had miscalculated elsewhere. A common feature of all these firms, however, was that they had relied too much on outside capital and were therefore unable to satisfy their creditors when pressed for repayment. The older scholarly literature has viewed these bankruptcies as nothing less than the "breakdown of early southern and central European capitalism," but this is a gross exaggeration of their significance for the economy as a whole. In fact, the Augsburg tax records for the period from 1558 to 1604 reflect sizable growth in the number of wealthy merchants within the city. Bankrupt trading companies were replaced by new firms that were well equipped with capital but reluctant to become involved in risky financial transactions.[7] Still, the financial crisis that began around 1557 did undoubtedly cause much uncertainty within the city's business community, and the wave of bankruptcies hit two members of the Fugger family. In 1562, Hans Jakob Fugger's brother Ulrich went bankrupt with debts amounting to 160,000 florins; a few years later, he moved to the court of the elector-palatine at Heidelberg. In the following year, Hans Jakob Fugger himself had to suspend his payments; reportedly, he had incurred debts of no less than 1 million florins. Hans Jakob's indebtedness, however, does not imply that the Fugger company as a whole failed, for it appears that most of his liabilities resulted from business transacted on his own account; his extravagant expenditures for his scholarly interests and public display also may have contributed to it. In any case, a bankrupt was unacceptable as the head of the trading company, so Hans Jakob Fugger left the firm in 1564 and entered the services of the Bavarian court.[8]

Hans Jakob Fugger's separation from the company was anything but smooth. In particular, the calculation of Anton and Raymund Fugger's respective shares in the firm's assets in the general balance of 1563 was highly contentious. In February 1564, a settlement was reached with the help of Duke Albrecht V of Bavaria, who was personally close to Hans Jakob Fugger. Anton Fugger's heirs agreed to assume the liabilities of their cousin Hans Jakob to the amount of 35,000 florins, and in the following year, they paid him 230,000 florins for his remaining claims against the company. This sum enabled Hans Jakob Fugger to satisfy a number of his creditors. As the Dutch and Spanish debt claims of the Fugger firm were excluded from these settlements, however, the legal conflicts continued for years. The lawsuits, which were carried on with growing bitterness on both sides, were eventually appealed to the imperial chamber court.[9] When Hans Jakob Fugger stayed at the emperor's court in 1567, his cousin Hans suspected that he would "practice and act against us in every way" and "cause us much trouble with his falsehoods and unfounded claims." Later, Hans Fugger characterized his cousin as "lying, impudent, and malicious" and regarded him as a man who possessed "no honor or decency whatsoever."[10]

Subsequently, the firm's capital stock was further diminished when even more partners had to be paid off. The unmarried Christoph Fugger left the firm in 1572 after falling out with his cousin Marx and received several hundred thousand florins as his share. Although he retained deposits of about 1 million florins in the company, a large part of his inheritance had to be paid out after his death. In 1578, the heirs of Georg Fugger, who had managed the family firm together with Marx Fugger from 1563 until his death in 1569, also left the company and founded their own firm. Apparently, the most important reason for this step was Marx's refusal to let his cousins participate in the company's management. After bitter conflicts over the size of their shares, Georg's heirs eventually received a total of 756,000 florins, paid out in installments until 1584.[11] This left only Anton Fugger's sons Marx, Hans, and Jakob as partners in the family firm. While Marx acted as administrator, his brother Hans helped with the management, cultivated ties with royal and noble clients, and stood in for the firm's head during his illnesses and business trips. Recent researchers consider his role in the management of the trading company more important than do older works, which viewed Hans Fugger primarily as a rich man of independent means and patron of the arts.[12] The third brother, Jakob, however, seems to have played merely a passive role. As Hans Fugger wrote to the Spanish factor Christoph Hörmann in 1569, the older brothers seldom had been able to "bring him to the office." Jakob got up late in the morning, seemed more interested in sleigh rides, and spent his time in loose company.[13]

The merchants' bankruptcies and economic crises of the 1560s and 1570s put a strain on the company headed by Marx Fugger for several reasons. To begin with, the insolvencies of business partners repeatedly resulted in financial losses. When the firm David Haug, Hans Langnauer, and Associates defaulted in 1574, it owed the Fuggers more than 280,000 florins. In compensation, the Fuggers took over shares in a joint mining venture in Tyrol, the Jenbach company, and debts of the Portuguese crown. The failure of Hans Paul Herwart in 1576 caused further losses, and when the merchant Konrad Roth failed in 1580, he owed Marx Fugger and his brothers 86,000 florins.[14] Moreover, the bankruptcies contributed to a general credit scarcity. As early as 1566, Hans Fugger turned down a request for a loan, claiming that, under the circumstances, "the money [could not] be obtained at fair Christian or even at un-Christian interest rates." When the widow Regina Artzt wrote to Hans Fugger two years later about a debt that "we Fuggers owe you in com-

FIGURE 7
Portrait of Hans Fugger (1531–1598)
from Fuggerorum and Fuggerarum . . . imagines, *1618.*
(Bayerische Staatsbibliothek München [Rar. 643, Bl. 76a])

mon," he had to admit that "all transactions are blocked" because of current political unrest; therefore, the firm had difficulties paying back the "load of debt with which we find ourselves burdened."[15] An Austrian nobleman's request for a loan was denied in 1570 as there was "no money among the people" because of the unfavorable business situation. And in 1573, Hans Fugger remarked that there was "no money available at interest" in these times.[16] The war in the Netherlands especially caused ongoing problems for the firm: After the looting of Antwerp in 1576, the trading office had to by removed to Cologne—temporarily at first, but eventually for good.[17]

Irrecoverable claims from loan transactions that had been carried out under Anton Fugger's leadership, the costly payments to partners who left the company, a difficult situation on the financial markets, and warfare in the Netherlands added up to a task of truly Herculean proportions for the administrator Marx Fugger. But where Pölnitz saw only decline and decay, an important essay by Georg Lutz reaches exactly the opposite conclusion. According to Lutz, the general balance compiled in 1577 documents nothing less than "a brilliant restoration of the internal solidity of the Fugger firm, a return to the best times under Anton—a development which was to continue in the same favorable direction." The general balance records total assets of 6.54 million florins and a capital stock of 1.27 million. An additional 3.4 million had been invested by family members as deposits at fixed interest. The deposit capital invested by "friends," employees, and others in the firm had been reduced to 590,000 florins. Consequently the firm's dependence on outside capital was significantly lower than it had been fourteen years earlier. Marx Fugger's strategy of concentrating on a few selected areas of business, raising the firm's capital stock, and reducing the dependence on outside capital clearly made sense under difficult circumstances. "The ability to secure the very existence of the firm under these conditions may be taken as proof of a mercantile competence comparable to that of his ancestors with their extraordinary profits."[18]

The differing assessments by these historians also reflect the perceptions of their own times. Authors writing in the late nineteenth century and early twentieth century, for whom entrepreneurial achievement equaled expansion and the building up of new productive and commercial capacities, had little sympathy for Marx Fugger's policy of consolidation and consequently interpreted it as a case of decline. At the beginning of the twenty-first century, when not merely the expansion of production but lasting competitiveness is considered the key to the future of enterprises, such a perspective has become questionable. Restructuring, cutting costs, separating or shutting down unproductive segments of an enterprise, and concentrating on core fields of business are now regarded as important strategies for securing a firm's future, and the firm Marx Fugger and Brothers actually pursued a very similar strategy.

But Marx Fugger's leadership of the company was distinguished by more than his ability to consolidate, for his firm was still capable of carrying out transactions on a grand scale and remained an important actor on European financial markets. Moreover, a large variety of works of art, luxury items, and consumer goods for princely and noble households were acquired through the network of Fugger offices. Finally, Anton and Raymund Fugger's heirs also played a prominent role in the area of communication in the late sixteenth century. The handwritten news reports (*Zeitungen*) about political and military events, as well as economic and social developments, that Philipp Eduard and Octavian Secundus Fugger received from employees and other correspondents between 1568 and 1605, preserved in the Austrian National Library in Vienna, have long been considered a pivotal source for the history of communication in the sixteenth century.[19] In addition, recent research has shown that Hans Fugger, too, played a comparable role as a "news broker" who supplied his correspondence partners with current information on the Dutch revolt against the Spanish crown, the French Wars of Religion, and developments on the Habsburg–Ottoman front.[20] In sum, the generation after Anton Fugger was able to move a lot of things forward, and their economic activities deserve more attention than they have received for a long time.

THE BUSINESS AFFAIRS OF ANTON FUGGER'S HEIRS

The abandonment of the Hungarian trade in the late 1540s had resulted in the closing of numerous trading posts, and under Marx Fugger's leadership, the network of offices was consolidated still further. In Italy, the company had not retained any offices of its own since the 1560s but entrusted commissioned agents in Rome, Venice, and Genoa with its business affairs. These commissioned agents were independent firms that carried out specific orders for the Fuggers. During the 1560s and 1570s, David Ott, a native of Ulm, in Venice and Christoph Rem in Genoa handled most of the Fuggers' money and exchange transactions in Italy, but they also purchased citrus and tropical fruit, wine, and fish; delivered high-quality cloth, coral, glassware, and perfume; and acquired paintings, books, statues, coins, and antiques for the art galleries of the Fuggers and the dukes of Bavaria. When David Ott died in 1579, his sons Hieronymus and Christoph followed in his footsteps and retained close ties with the Fuggers; in Genoa, Christoph Furtenbach replaced Rem. The Madrid office looked after the interests of the firm in Spain;

the Nuremberg office remained the hub for business transactions with east-central and eastern Europe; Antwerp—succeeded by Cologne after 1576—was the central office in northwestern Europe; and the branches in Vienna and Prague primarily cultivated the contacts with the imperial court.[21]

The all-important key to the successful consolidation of the enterprise was located in Spain. Marx Fugger himself commented in the late 1570s that "virtually all our profits flow from" the Spanish business.[22] After an interruption of a dozen years, the Fuggers took over the lease of the Maestrazgos—the administration of the lands of the Spanish knightly orders—once again in 1562. Crucially, the mines of Almadén, which had been shut down after a fire in 1550 and had been administered by the state, were again included in the lease contract. In the mid-1550s, the amalgamation process, which separated silver from the ore by adding mercury, had been successfully tried in the Central American and South American mining regions. With the help of the amalgamation method, which was highly damaging to the environment and the health of the workers but enormously effective from an economic point of view, unheard-of amounts of silver could be extracted from the mines of Potosí in Peru and New Spain (Mexico). Consequently, the demand for mercury soared, and as the royal mining administration did not command the necessary capital and know-how, the mines of Almadén were once again handed over to the Fuggers. The company promised to put the mines into working order and deliver a minimum of 1,000 hundredweight of mercury per annum; in turn, the Spanish government agreed to purchase the mercury at a fixed price of 25 ducats per hundredweight during the first five years and 20 ducats afterward. Gold and silver shipments from the New World were to serve as payment. To put the mines to work as quickly as possible, several dozen experts from Germany were recruited. In 1567, the Fuggers succeeded in raising the sale price to 26 ducats and agreed in turn to deliver 1,200 hundredweight annually. Digging a second shaft made it possible to raise production to 1,500 hundredweight and the price to 29 ducats within a few years. As production costs did not exceed 14–15 ducats per hundredweight, the profit margin was in the range of 100 percent.[23]

The other components of the Maestrazgos—the collection of ground rents and the marketing of grain and other agrarian products—had become somewhat less lucrative because some of the orders' lands had been sold off, but they were still profitable enough. From 1562 to 1567, the profits recorded in the company's books amounted to 200,000 ducats, and in the following five-year-period they even rose to 570,000 ducats. Actually, however, these profits were reduced by considerable sums of outstanding payments. As the lease of the Maestrazgos developed favorably, the Fuggers agreed to a new lease contract in December 1571, which was to run for ten years starting on New Year's Day in 1573. The firm now promised to deliver 1,700 hundredweight of mercury, for which it received a fixed price of 30 ducats per hundredweight. As an advance on the lease payments, the Fuggers granted a loan of 1 million ducats. The use of new reverberation furnaces improved the technical process of extracting mercury, and the lack of workers in Almadén was filled by the forcible recruitment of Moriscos (Moors who had converted to Christianity) from neighboring communities and the employment of slave labor.[24] Meanwhile, the network of Spanish offices had been concentrated in Madrid, which King Philip II had made the permanent capital city, and Almagro, the administrative center of the Maestrazgos, by the 1570s. The branch office in Seville, which in its final stages had been occupied almost exclusively with the collection of repayments from the silver fleets returning from America, was abandoned when the senior employee Jobst Hurter left the firm.[25]

In the lease period from 1573 to 1582, the Fuggers once again made high net profits—490,000 ducats in the first and 167,000 ducats in the second five-year period. In addition, they produced almost 24,000 hundredweight of mercury, which they sold for more than 700,000 ducats. The production costs, by contrast, amounted to merely 346,000 ducats; thus, the profit margin once again lay in the range of 100 percent. When the Spanish crown stopped its payments for a second time in 1575, the Fuggers were explicitly exempted from the royal decree because of their importance as mercury producers. However, they were increasingly called on to transfer money to the Netherlands, where the revolt against the Spanish crown had grown into an all-out civil war. When Spanish troops mutinied in the Low Countries, the Madrid office lent King Philip II 200,000 ducats.[26] In the fall of 1576, Hans Fugger voiced his concern to his brother Marx that the firm had to serve the king financially "from day to day"; it was feared "that the Spaniards will want to use us to all eternity, suck us dry and manipulate us." In March 1579, he wrote to a correspondence partner that the firm would soon have to pay Spanish letters of exchange in the amount of 279,000 florins in Augsburg and Frankfurt.[27]

Nevertheless, the subsequent lease periods once again yielded handsome profits. From 1582 to 1594, the mines at Almadén produced almost 38,000 hundredweight of mercury, from which the company made a profit of 636,000 ducats, and in the lease period from 1595 to 1604, the net profits from the Maestrazgos came to 300,000 ducats while the mercury contract yielded almost twice this amount. There were two structural impediments, however: the ever higher demand of the crown for credit—in 1586, for example, the

Fuggers had to raise a loan of a million ducats in addition to the million they had advanced for the current lease of the Maestrazgos—and the growing arrears in payments. On the whole, however, the lease of the Maestrazgos and the mercury contract appear to have been splendid business investments in the era of Marx Fugger. After the death of Philip II in 1598, Marx Fugger's son Albrecht, who was traveling to Spain at the time, could offer the new monarch, Philip III, a "gift" of 250,000 ducats, in addition to declaring that he was willing to deliver silver worth a million ducats to Milan for the Spanish government.[28]

The high revenues of the Spanish trade also enabled the Fuggers to continue to play a prominent role within the circle of major international financiers and advance large sums to the emperor, other European princes, and important business partners. In March 1566, the firm transferred 100,000 scudi out of the "Spanish subsidy and exchange money," which were to be employed toward the defense against the Turks to Georg Ilsung, the imperial master of finance (*Reichspfennigmeister*) for Emperor Maximilian II.[29] Adam von Dietrichstein, imperial ambassador at the court of Madrid and chief steward (*Obersthofmeister*) of the archdukes Rudolf und Ernst, received a loan of 50,000 florins in May 1568.[30] In May 1569 and February 1570, the Spanish Fugger employee Christoph Hörmann paid Dietrichstein 140,000 florins in total; in addition, the firm granted a loan of 60,000 florins on the occasion of Archduchess Anna's wedding with King Philip II in December 1569. Including interest, the claims of the firm Marx Fugger and Brothers against the imperial household from these credit transactions, which had been guaranteed by the imperial master of finance, Georg Ilsung, and the Paler-Weiß company of Augsburg, amounted to 225,320 florins in 1573. In return, the firm was assigned annual revenues of the territories of the Bohemian chamber to the amount of 30,000 florins. In addition, the Fuggers had transferred more than 70,000 scudi for Emperor Maximilian II from Naples to Augsburg in 1570, and Silesian revenues had been assigned to them for the remainder of a further loan of 50,000 florins.[31] In the fall of 1575, the Fuggers advanced 134,500 florins to the emperor in Augsburg, Nuremberg, Prague, and Vienna, and in 1578–79, they handled payments of Spanish pensions to Archduke Ferdinand.[32] During the Diet of Augsburg in 1582, Emperor Rudolf II had to borrow money from the Fuggers to pay his debts.[33] Finally, in 1594 the Fuggers granted the emperor the enormous sum of 300,000 florins for the war against the Ottomans, thereby demonstrating the firm's undiminished competitiveness and capability at the end of the sixteenth century.[34]

In addition to these advances to members of the House of Habsburg, credit was extended time and again to the dukes of Bavaria, Albrecht V and

Wilhelm V. In return for a loan of 100,000 florins to Duke Albrecht, the manorial estate of Mering was pawned to Marx and Hans Fugger in 1572, and the next year, the firm advanced 80,000 florins to the hereditary Prince Wilhelm. At the beginning of 1575, when Wilhelm's debts amounted to 300,000 florins, about one-third of this sum was claimed by the Fuggers. These liabilities temporarily caused considerable ill feeling between the firm and the dukes. The Fuggers neither heeded Duke Albrecht's demands to assume the entire debt nor could they realize their plans to defray Wilhelm's obligations through a loan that the grand duke of Tuscany would have granted to Bavaria. During the Cologne War (1583–85), a military struggle for the throne of the archbishop of Cologne, Marx and Hans Fugger granted several large loans to the house of Wittelsbach—the dynasty from which the dukes of Bavaria came—totaling 39,000 florins from 1583 to 1585. To cover wartime expenses, Hans Fugger raised an additional 15,000 florins from his private funds.[35] Moreover, Hans handled innumerable purchases for the Bavarian dukes, ranging from antiquities and works of art to foodstuffs, precious cloth, riding horses, and even young "moors," who were obtained for the hereditary Prince Wilhelm's court at Landshut in 1573. These purchases, for which the firm apparently did not charge fees, primarily served to cultivate cordial relations with the ducal household and bolster the Fugger family's reputation.[36]

As late as 1574, only two years before warfare in the Netherlands forced them to close their office, the Fuggers brokered a loan of 20,000 florins to the city of Antwerp in which two dozen merchants from southern Germany participated.[37] In Venice, the firm likewise played a prominent role as creditor. In 1597, Hieronymus and Christoph Ott, the Fuggers' longstanding business partners and agents on the Rialto, had great difficulties meeting their payments after the rejection of letters of exchange. The Fuggers initially had Hieronymus Ott imprisoned in Augsburg, as he was suspected of having embezzled funds that he should have transferred to Archduke Ferdinand on their instruction. He was apparently cleared of this suspicion, however, for in the same year the firm Marx Fugger and Brothers saved the Ott brothers with a loan of almost 260,000 ducats, for which the Venetians pawned their entire estate. After 1600, additional large loans by the Fuggers to Ferdinand II were paid to the archduke's Venetian representatives via the Ott brothers: 175,000 ducats to 1603 and 35,000 ducats in 1604.[38]

In an age of nearly permanent warfare in the Netherlands, France, the Balkans, and the Mediterranean, officers and military entrepreneurs were also among the Fuggers' regular customers.[39] In 1566, Marx Fugger lent 4,000 scudi for the recruitment of a Spanish regiment in southern Germany. The next year, the Antwerp office advanced 11,000 florins to Count Albrecht von

Lodron for the mustering of a regiment.[40] In 1568, Wolfgang Jörger received an advance of 900 florins to recruit mercenary soldiers in Transylvania.[41] When Albrecht von Lodron mustered a new regiment in 1572, Hans Fugger purchased several hundred suits of armor for it in Augsburg and Nuremberg. The acquisition of suits of armor for 551 mercenaries alone cost more than 3,000 florins.[42] When Hans Ferenberger, an officer in Spanish service, purchased military supplies, Hans Fugger guaranteed more than 13,000 florins in 1573.[43] The advances to officers often proved difficult to recover, because the debtors had to wait for a long time until they were paid by their princely superiors or because they turned out to be unreliable individuals. Don Juan Manrique de Lara, with whom Hans Fugger corresponded for several years and to whom he advanced 10,000 florins for the purchase of suits of armor, aroused his creditor's suspicion in 1576 when Fugger learned that Manrique had collected money without paying him. But neither the dispatch of the Fugger employee Matthäus Recheisen to Manrique de Lara nor a lawsuit against Manrique proved successful.[44]

The Fuggers also pursued a policy of consolidation in the Tyrolean mining sector, which had to contend with declining output from the mid-sixteenth century onward. After the indigenous Stöckl and Tänzl companies went bankrupt in 1552 and the Baumgartners of Augsburg sold their shares in the following year, the firm of the brothers Hans Paul und Hans Heinrich Herwart also sold its holdings to the territorial lord. The Haug-Langnauer-Linck company of Augsburg likewise made a sales offer to the archduke, but he refused. After Christoph Manlich and his brothers had also dropped from the ranks of the mining entrepreneurs because of their bankruptcy in 1564, only three Augsburg firms remained among the large Tyrolean mining enterprises: the Fuggers, the Haug-Langnauer-Lincks, and the heirs of Matthias Manlich, who cooperated with the brothers Abraham and Michael Katzbeck. To concentrate their resources and counter the growing influence of the territorial lord, the Fuggers, Haug-Langnauer-Lincks, and Manlich-Katzbecks formed a joint venture, the Jenbach company, for a period of five years starting on March 3, 1565. The purpose of the consortium was the joint smelting and marketing of Tyrolean ores. The Fuggers brought their mines and mining shares valued at roughly 114,000 florins—at Falkenstein and Ringenwechsel in the Schwaz district, in the Ahrn Valley, at Schneeberg and Gossensass Mountain, as well as at Klausen, Grasstein, Terlan, and Nals—into the new company. The shares of the Haug-Langnauer-Linck company were estimated at 109,000 florins, and those of the Manlich-Katzbeck group were assessed at 92,000 florins. The equipment of the works and the real estate remained the property of the individual partners but were leased to the Jenbach company. In the Fuggers' case, the value of their houses, ore deposits, and smelting works was assessed at 15,950 florins; that of the Haug-Langnauer-Lincks, at 15,300 florins; and that of the Manlich-Katzbecks, at 21,133 florins. The goods the three companies held in stock were jointly estimated at almost 175,000 florins, and the company's total capital stock was valued at roughly 490,000 florins. Differences in the value of the partners' shares were equalized by cash investments. Marx Fugger, Hans Langnauer, and Abraham Katzbeck assumed the management of the enterprise; they met for weekly conferences in Augsburg and were to inspect the Tyrolean works twice a year. The Fugger employee Heinrich Ruedl was appointed as the company's administrator in Tyrol. The Jenbach company, however, constituted only part of the Fuggers' Tyrolean and Carinthian investments and holdings. Important parts such as the smelting works at Lützelfelden and the holdings in the Kitzbühel mining district were retained as the Schwazer Propriohandel (lit., Schwaz Proper Trade, or the trade at Schwaz belonging exclusively to the Fuggers), in which Raymund Fugger's heirs participated along with Anton's.[45]

Initially, the Jenbach company's affairs developed favorably. The fusion lowered operating costs, and the participating firms had a stronger position vis-à-vis the territorial lord. In 1566, the company lent the Tyrolean government 13,410 florins, followed by another loan of 24,000 florins three years later. In 1570, the company contract was extended for five more years. Subsequently, however, the effects of a general crisis of the European economy began to show on a massive scale, and the conflicts of interest between the merchant companies and the government, which had been softened by interest-free loans to territorial officeholders in earlier years, intensified. Silver production at Falkenstein, which had been maintained at 10,000–12,000 Marks per annum between 1566 and 1569, fell to 8,000 Marks after 1570. Copper output also had declined sharply since 1571. The number of miners at Falkenstein declined from almost 7,000 in 1556 to about 4,000 in 1582. The Jenbach company's profits evaporated, and it had to subsidize the *Pfennwerthandel,* the trade that supplied the miners with the most important items of consumption, because of a steep rise in food prices. In 1571, the Jenbach company offered to sell its entire holdings to the archduke, but he refused. After the Haug-Langnauer-Linck company went bankrupt in 1574, the Fuggers took over its shares. As the Haugs had pawned their Tyrolean property to the archduke before these transactions, however, legal conflicts about the creditors' rights ensued that went on for decades. In 1577, the Fuggers also took over the shares of the Manlich-Katzbeck company, which made them the sole remaining major Tyrolean mining entrepreneurs besides

the territorial lord himself. As the price of silver had declined sharply because of the growing imports of American silver, the copper trade became
progressively more important than the silver business. The Fuggers either
sold the copper produced in the smelting works at Jenbach, Achenrain, and
Lützelfelden to intermediary traders or processing works or they marketed it
via Nuremberg, Venice, and Genoa. In Venice, it was the Ott brothers and in
Genoa, Christoph Furtenbach, who handled the sales as the Fuggers' commissioned agents. Apart from the declining ore output, the lack of supply
materials, such as wood for construction and fuel, along with water damage
in the mines and the government's raising of customs duties made the Tyrolean trade ever more difficult. In 1583, therefore, the Fuggers once again offered their shares to the territorial lord. By the end of the sixteenth century,
it had become increasingly clear that the Fuggers were trying to reduce their
involvement in Tyrol. Even when they took over the shares of another competitor, the Dreyling firm, in 1590, this marked not a change in policy but
merely a stopgap measure. From 1598 onward, a number of mines at Schwaz,
Sterzing, Klausen, and Terlan were abandoned.[46]

In sum, Marx Fugger's business strategy aimed at a concentration on core
areas without loosening the close ties with the House of Habsburg. The
Spanish trade above all yielded high profits because of the mercury boom,
whereas in Tyrol, the course had been set toward reduced involvement and
the winding up of mining activities and the metal trade. This business strategy was an expression of changing priorities and inclinations: Marx Fugger
devoted himself to scholarly and literary interests to a much greater extent
than had his father. But it also constituted a sensible adaptation to changing circumstances. In the context of economic crises, a growing number of
bankruptcies, and wartime interruptions of trade, Marx Fugger permanently
secured the family's property. Therefore, it comes as no surprise that in the
will he dictated in 1595, Marx Fugger distanced himself from his father's
plans to dissolve the company as soon as possible. On the contrary, commerce should, "as has happened hitherto with advantageous benefits ...,
[be] maintained in common and continued into the future." After the death
of Marx and Hans Fugger, their sons were to continue the firm undivided for
at least fifteen years.[47]

However, the conflicts over the management of the family firm, which had
been solved by paying off several partners in the 1570s, flared up again when
Marx Fugger was incapacitated by a stroke in 1595 and died two years later.
The management was now taken over by his brother Hans, who had already
replaced Marx on many earlier occasions and was well informed about the
company's affairs. But Marx and Jakob Fugger's sons challenged the lead-

ership of their uncle, and Marx's son Anton in particular demanded to be acknowledged as second administrator. On a journey that the young Anton Fugger undertook to Spain, these divisions erupted openly among the Spanish employees, who had already been fighting one another. Even before Hans Fugger's death in 1598, the conflict could be resolved thanks to the mediating role of Octavian Secundus Fugger, who will be considered in more detail shortly. The joint commercial company of Marx, Hans, and Jakob Fugger's heirs was thus preserved while the management was to rotate among representatives of the three family lines. Between 1598 and 1614, Hans Fugger's son Marx headed the firm that his uncle of the same name had successfully consolidated. His cousins Georg and Anton supported him as "adjuncts."[48]

GEORG FUGGER'S HEIRS

After Georg Fugger's sons Octavian Secundus and Philipp Eduard Fugger had left the family company and had been paid off, a second, independent firm bearing the name of the great merchant house came into being under the name Georg Fugger's Heirs. The existence of this firm is a telling sign of the family's breakup into several lines, which had already become apparent at midcentury. These lines wished not to pursue their interests within the framework of the "common trade" that Jakob Fugger had founded but to go their separate ways. The affairs of Georg Fugger's Heirs, which have been much better researched than those of Marx Fugger and Brothers, thanks to the work of Reinhard Hildebrandt, partly concentrated on similar fields of business as their cousin's firm. Like their cousins Marx and Hans Fugger, Philipp Eduard and Octavian Secundus focused on Spain and relations with the Habsburg and Wittelsbach dynasties. By becoming involved in the Portuguese spice trade, however, they also ventured into a new field of business from 1585 onward.[49]

Like other family members, Philipp Eduard Fugger, who was born in 1546, and his brother Octavian Secundus, who was three years younger, had enjoyed a broad humanist education that centered on travel, the learning of languages, artistic and scientific pursuits, and the acquisition of a genteel lifestyle that followed the example of the nobility. Since 1555–56, the brothers had been privately tutored in Ingolstadt. Philipp Eduard had registered at the universities of Dôle and Basel in 1556–57 and attended the University of Padua from 1560 on. A year later, Octavian Secundus matriculated in Bologna, where the brothers pursued their studies together from 1562 forward. These studies aimed not merely at an academic education, however, but also—and primarily—at the shaping of noble virtues and styles of behavior. Philipp Eduard, for example, not only learned Italian in Padua but was also instructed in fencing and playing the lute. In the spring of 1565, Georg Fugger's sons traveled to Rome to complete their education at the Collegium Germanicum. The essentials of mercantile practice were transmitted to Philipp Eduard during a stay in the Fugger office in Antwerp in 1568–69. After his sojourn in Italy ended in 1568, and after a subsequent period of study in Leuven, Octavian Secundus was also employed in the Antwerp office for some time. The contacts with southern German and Austrian noblemen that had already been established during their travels abroad were further cultivated in Augsburg, where the two brothers mostly resided after 1573. According to Hildebrandt, their education, family traditions, and social environment also shaped the business aims of Philipp Eduard und Octavian Secundus Fugger when they decided to form their own merchant company in 1578: "Control over a private economic empire of European dimensions was no longer the goal; instead, the aim was the profitable use and increase of the fortune they had inherited. In this context the sought-after profits were not an end in itself; [the brothers rather aimed at] a way of life befitting their rank and the realization of personal inclinations and passions."[50]

After their separation from the "common trade," Georg Fugger's sons controlled a fortune estimated at 1.1 million florins, which constituted a solid foundation for their own business initiatives. One of the brothers, however—Anton Fugger the Younger—was paid off with more than 200,000 florins in 1580 and separated from the community of heirs. Excluding real estate, the company's capital stock amounted to almost 800,000 florins in 1589. Individual partners' private withdrawals reduced the capital stock to slightly more than 300,000 florins in 1600, the year Octavian Secundus died. While Philipp Eduard and Octavian Secundus Fugger jointly ran the company Georg Fugger's Heirs, their brother Raymund, who was mentally retarded, remained a silent partner, his property being administered by his brothers. The youngest brother, Hans Georg, died on a journey to Spain in 1585.[51]

Apart from its head office in Augsburg, Georg Fugger's Heirs maintained its own trading offices in Madrid and Lisbon and, together with the Welsers, for a few years in Goa, India. In Hamburg, Cologne, Frankfurt on the Main, and Venice, they were represented by commissioned agents. The small number of permanent offices corresponds with the firm's field of activity, for its focus clearly was on banking and credit, and the handling of financial transactions could be entrusted to commissioned agents. Like their relatives Marx and Hans Fugger, Philipp Eduard and Octavian Secundus primarily granted loans to Catholic princes whose confessional and political orientation they shared. Their close financial relations with the dukes of Bavaria dated back to their uncle Christoph Fugger, who had advanced 150,000 florins to Duke

Albrecht V. One-third of this sum was still outstanding when Georg Fugger's Heirs inherited the fortune of their childless uncle in 1579. From 1581 to 1590, Philipp Eduard and Octavian Secundus Fugger lent Duke Wilhelm V another 36,000 florins in several installments. On the one hand, these loans bear witness to the brothers' high liquidity after their separation from the family firm; on the other hand, they demonstrate the Bavarian dukes' demand for money at the time of the Cologne War, money used to enforce militarily the claims of Duke Wilhelm's brother, Ernst of Bavaria, to the throne of the elector of Cologne. By granting loans to the imperial master of finance, Zacharias Geizkofler, for the Habsburgs' war against the Turks in 1596–97, Georg Fugger's Heirs secured the company's rights to the manorial estates of Kirchberg and Weißenhorn. Archduke Ferdinand of Tyrol received a loan of 14,000 florins in 1580 and another of 16,000 florins two years later. In 1587, Ferdinand's outstanding debts, which by then amounted to 34,000 florins, were converted into eternal annuities at 5 percent interest, and three years later, the brothers granted the archduke another loan of 5,000 florins. It appears that the provision of credit to the archduke primarily served to extend their seigneurial rights in Outer Austria, for the brothers' involvement in mining in the Montafon region remained sporadic. Along with their uncle Christoph's inheritance, moreover, Philipp Eduard und Octavian Secundus Fugger had taken over financial claims against the southern German monasteries of Roggenburg, Zwiefalten, and Wiblingen.[52]

Like their financial relations within the Holy Roman Empire, the brothers' activities on the Iberian Peninsula originated in Christoph Fugger's financial activities, for Christoph had substantial claims against the family firm's Spanish trade and King Philip II. From the 1580s on, Georg Fugger's Heirs invested large sums in juros—the royal debt certificates on which pensions or life annuities were paid—and *censos,* a form of mortgaged credit. Until 1587, the factor in Madrid, Philipp Krell, had invested more than 50,000 ducats in juros and 63,500 ducats in censos. When these rent certificates were to be resold in the wake of the brothers' involvement in the Asia contract with the Portuguese crown, however, the sale process proved rather cumbersome.[53]

The interest of Augsburg companies in the Portuguese spice trade with Asia was aroused by a risky project of the merchant Konrad Roth. In 1576, the Portuguese crown, which had great difficulties meeting its payment obligations, had offered the so-called Europe contract to its southern German creditors to settle its debts and obtain new financial means. This contract included the purchase of all the pepper imported to Lisbon from India for a period of several years and its marketing in Europe. When the creditors—including the heirs of Anton Fugger, Sebastian Neidhart, and Matthias Manlich—turned down the offer, Konrad Roth stepped into the breach and took over the Europe contract for five years. Roth promised to purchase a total of 92,000 *quintales* of Indian pepper at a fixed price of 34 Portuguese ducats per quintal. In addition, he was to supply materials for the construction and outfitting of ships worth 60,000 ducats; to provide credit for Portuguese grain purchases; and to take care of the settlement of the southern German creditors' debt claims against the crown. As these conditions far exceeded Roth's own financial means, he had to try to win wealthy investors for his venture. After the Fuggers declined to participate, Roth found an investor in the Italian Bardi firm, which took over three-eighths of the contract. In the context of this venture, Roth pursued a cleverly conceived plan: He wanted to take over the debt certificates of the southern German creditors at 50 percent of their nominal value but claim the full amount of the debt against the crown. Moreover, he intended to satisfy his creditors not in cash but with pepper shipments and thus profit a second time from the difference between the purchase price and the sale price. In addition, this would have secured Roth a fixed circle of customers. Roth's business partners in Augsburg saw through the scheme, however, and refused to go along. Therefore, he was forced to throw part of the pepper on the market at discount prices as early as 1576.[54]

After King Sebastian of Portugal died, Roth once again raised the stakes when he also obtained the Asia contract in 1578, which was extended from a financial contract into a monopoly contract for the purchase of spices in India at the time, and he agreed to raise the annual purchase quota by one-third. To finance the new venture, Roth divided the Asia contract into thirty shares, keeping twelve and a half shares for himself and leaving ten shares to the Portuguese firm of Ximenes, as well as seven and a half shares to the Italian company of Giacomo Battista Litti. Furthermore, he interested Elector August of Saxony in the founding of a company that was to turn Leipzig into the sole distribution center for pepper in central Europe. The final step in Roth's plan was the division of the European pepper market: The Portuguese participants were to market their pepper on the Iberian Peninsula and in France and England; the rest of the Mediterranean was to be the exclusive domain of the Italians; and the Thuringian company initiated by Roth was to organize the sale of pepper in Germany, east-central Europe, and the Netherlands. Although Roth had already promised this last distribution area to the Thuringian company, he did not inform his other partners, and the Ximenes and Litti firms objected to the agreement. Further, the proposed regional cartel proved impracticable because Asian pepper continued to be imported via the Levant and Venice. Faced with imminent bankruptcy in the spring of 1580, Roth fled Augsburg and feigned suicide. (Actually, he survived the alleged attempt by three decades and managed to rise to the rank of consul of the German merchants in Lisbon, where he reappeared some time later.) His Augsburg creditors attempted to recover their losses by confiscating his pepper stores.[55]

Despite Roth's failure, the interest that the southern German business community took in the riches of Asia did not die. In the summer of 1582, for example, news about the arrival of a new spice fleet from India reached Augsburg via Lisbon.[56] Three years later, Marx and Matthäus Welser decided to participate in the Asia contract for the years 1586–91 and won the brothers Philipp Eduard and Octavian Secundus Fugger over as partners. Originally, Georg Fugger's Heirs held a 25 percent investment with the Welsers, who had taken over five-twelfths of the contract but whose creditworthiness had already been damaged, according to internal Fugger correspondence of the time. The remaining seven-twelfths of the contract were held by a merchant from Milan named Rovelasca. In 1588, the Fuggers' position as subcontractors of the Welsers was converted into a partnership with equal rights and obligations. In India, both firms were represented by Ferdinand Cron, a native of Augsburg, from 1586 onward. Later, the Fuggers supplemented Cron with Christoph Schneeberger and, after Schneeberger fell severely ill, with Sebastian Zangmeister and Gabriel Holzschuher.

In the years 1586–90, the partners in the Asia contract sent five ships per year to India; in 1591, the fleet comprised six ships. The results of the first voyage proved rather disappointing because of a difficult situation on the Indian spice market and high losses at sea. Only two ships carrying merely a third of the anticipated quantity of pepper reached the port of embarkation, Lisbon. Eight of the ten ships sent out in 1588 and 1589 returned to Lisbon with large shipments of pepper, but the Venetian pepper market was so well stocked at the time that oversupply threatened to cause a slump in pepper prices. Therefore, the Portuguese crown started to pay the partners in the Asia contract with pepper instead of cash. According to Hildebrandt, this forced the Fuggers, who initially had viewed the Asia contract mainly as a form of capital investment, to take care of the marketing of the imported pepper in Europe against their will. Consequently, the Fuggers and the Welsers also participated in the Europe contract in partnership with the Portuguese Ximenes firm and Italian companies from 1591 onward. Pepper sales were primarily carried out via Amsterdam, Lübeck, and Hamburg. Five of the six ships out of the last India fleet that sailed under the Asia contract of the Fuggers and Welsers in 1591 were lost in storms at sea or in attacks by English corsairs. Hildebrandt assumes, however, that the Fuggers made a small overall profit from the pepper trade, despite all of the problems involved—difficult conditions of transport and communications, hostile attacks, and a corrupt Portuguese administration. On the whole, however, the venture turned out to be much more hazardous and less lucrative than the firm's heads in Augsburg had hoped. Within the decidedly conservative business strategy of Georg Fugger's Heirs, which was primarily geared toward revenues from interest payments and the collection of rents, participation in the Portuguese spice trade clearly constituted a special case.[57]

THE TRADING COMPANY IN THE FIRST HALF
OF THE SEVENTEENTH CENTURY

Up to the beginning of the seventeenth century, it is hardly justified to speak of a decline of the Fuggers' trade in view of the successful consolidation of the family firm and the activities of Georg Fugger's Heirs. The family firm's two most important areas of business, the Tyrolean trade and the "common trade" that focused on Spain, continued, and the hierarchical company structure established in the sixteenth century, with one or two "governors" at the top, remained intact. Above all, the profits from mercury mining in Almadén, Spain, secured the firm's liquidity, and production was increased until the 1620s. As late as 1623, Hans Ernst Fugger was able to raise a loan of 1.2 million florins with Italian bankers for the Catholic League, which fought on the side of the emperor against Bohemian rebels in the early stages of the Thirty Years' War. Fugger also advanced tens of thousands of florins to this religious military alliance out of his own funds.[58]

For internal as well as external reasons, however, the firm's Spanish trade entered a grave crisis in the early seventeenth century. Declining silver imports from America, a severe agrarian depression, and a difficult situation in the textile sector contributed to a deep structural crisis of the Spanish economy. The crown was forced to go more and more deeply into debt, and the initiatives that the leading minister, Olivares, took from 1621 onward to reform the public administration, army, and state finances and restore Spain's prior imperial greatness were doomed to failure. An important factor affecting the firm's internal structure was that none of the managers who ran the company in the seventeenth century had enjoyed a mercantile education: "The management of the trading company became more and more difficult on account of a lack of specialized knowledge and changing interests of the partners and administrators."[59]

When the Spanish crown once again suspended its payments in 1607, the Fuggers had to accept lower interest rates on a large portion of their claims to the amount of 3 million ducats and were granted crown revenues from rents and the crusading tax (*cruzada*). The conditions under which the Fuggers continued the lease of the Maestrazgos also took an increasingly unfavorable turn, as part of the revenues were already pawned to other creditors of the crown. Therefore, the lease period from 1604 to 1614 was the first one to end in losses. Meanwhile, a drastic reduction of the capital stock and growing dependence on deposit investments marked the firm's internal development. Between 1600 and 1610, the capital stock dwindled from about 5 million florins to 767,000 florins because of massive withdrawals by the heirs of Marx, Hans, and Jakob Fugger. When the lease of the Maestrazgos was extended in 1624, the lease payments already had been reduced considerably because of declining revenues, but in 1627, the Fuggers had to agree to aid the crown with large sums of money once again to avert the consequences of another suspension of payments.

The employees' high degree of independence, which resulted from their geographical distance from the head office in Augsburg, constituted another structural problem, for the firm's management was hardly able to exert effective control over them. In 1626, the firm accepted responsibility for the monthly payments to Spanish courtiers and bureaucrats, the so-called *mesadas*, without the prior knowledge of the Augsburg head office. It was especially this obligation, which amounted to 50,000 ducats per month, that forced the Fuggers to take large loans from Genoese bankers such as Bartolomeo and Francisco Spinola, as well as from Christoph and Paul Furtenbach, who were of German origin. In 1630, the company already had great difficulties in meeting these liabilities. A visitation undertaken by the employee Hans Christoph Eberlin and the jurist Dr. Johann Jakob Holzapfel came to the conclusion that the firm had incurred deposit debts amounting to 2.5 million ducats and exchange debts amounting to almost 1 million ducats. Moreover, it was in arrears on its payments of the mesadas. When they signed the last lease contracts for the Maestrazgos and the mines at Almadén, the Fuggers also took over the once rich silver mines at Guadalcanal, Spain, but the attempt to put the mines back to work turned out to be a disastrous failure that only increased the losses. Among the Fuggers' creditors, Bartolomeo Spinola was in a particularly strong position because he was also a member of the Spanish financial councils. It was primarily due to Spinola's influence that a royal commission took the unprecedented step in 1637 of ousting the Fuggers' agent Eberlin and handing control over the business affairs over to Vicente Squarcafigo. The new administrator gradually replaced the firm's personnel, and the administration of the Spanish trade took on the character of bankruptcy proceedings. In a letter he wrote to Spain in 1641, Ott Heinrich Fugger, who was then the head of the firm, expressed his opinion that the "honor and reputation" of the house of Fugger could be rescued only by a total withdrawal from Spain. Four years later, the Spanish trade was completely abandoned; the lease of the Maestrazgos, which the Fuggers had held uninterruptedly for more than eight decades, went to a Genoese consortium in 1647.[60]

Spain was not the only place that the Fuggers became increasingly dependent on other financiers. With regard to the Ott family of Venice, relations between creditors and debtors underwent a complete reversal. After gradually defraying the large loan they had received from the Fuggers in 1597, the Otts appear among the Fuggers' creditors from the 1620s onward. In 1639, Hans Ernst, Ott Heinrich, and Johann Eusebius Fugger had to issue a debt certificate to Pietro Paolo Ott in the amount of roughly 330,000 ducats. When the Otts demanded payment of this debt because of problems with their own liquidity in the second half of the 1640s, the Fuggers proved unable to pay. This resulted in a drawn-out lawsuit until a settlement was reached in 1651 that "gave the Ott[s] possession of Tyrolean mining shares of Hans Fugger's line, customs revenues at Zirl, and the manorial estate of Irmatzhofen."[61]

In Tyrol, where the Fugger firm had been contending with production and supply problems, as well as declining prices on the European copper markets, for a long time, difficulties mounted from the 1620s onward as output continued to fall and the Thirty Years' War gravely affected transport routes to markets. A summary survey of the state of affairs in 1629 revealed that annual expenses exceeded revenues by 15,000 florins. Since 1623, a number of mines at Falkenstein had been abandoned, and miners were laid off. Output also declined steadily in the old mines (*Erbstollen*) in the Schwaz district and in the mines at Gossensass, Ringenwechsel, and the Rattenberg district. The workforce at the Jenbach smelting works fell from 125 in 1631 to 78 in 1634. Mining at Terlan was terminated in 1630, and attempts to establish new mines at Hall and Schwaz met with little success. Only the development of new mines in Palleiten in the Sterzing district brought temporary relief. The output of the Carinthian lead mines also declined, and the entrepreneurs became indebted to the Rambser family of Villach, who supplied the miners with food and extended credit. The Rambsers took over shares in several mines and seized control of the lead trade. During the 1630s and 1640s, reports about the hopeless situation of Carinthian mining and the general lack of credit multiplied. According to a report compiled by the factors Ulrich Truefer and Adam Trestendorffer in October 1649, the Tyrolean ventures incurred annual losses of 15,600 florins. For the year 1650 they even anticipated losses of almost 24,000 florins. Meanwhile, the indebtedness of the Jenbach company amounted to 43,455 florins, and the family firm's remaining holdings in Tyrol—the Tiroler Propriohandel—were also showing a deficit. They were also dissolved in 1657.[62]

In this period of growing economic difficulties in the Alpine region and on the Iberian Peninsula, reports about conflicts within the Fugger family and about the irresponsible behavior of individual partners also became more numerous. As early as 1623, the heirs of Marx and Jakob Fugger had left the family company. The Spanish business was subsequently continued by Hans Fugger's grandsons Hans Ernst and Ott Heinrich and their cousin Hans, who had to pay 550,000 Reichsthaler (825.000 florins) to their relatives, the descendents of Marx and Jakob. To raise this amount, Hans Fugger's heirs had to borrow a large sum from the city of Augsburg. As Marx's and Jakob's heirs still had substantial claims to interest payments after this initial payment, massive conflicts broke out in 1624 that culminated in "representatives of the Marx and Jakob lines breaking into the Fugger office and violently forcing the handover of account books." By that time, the brothers Hieronymus, Maximilian, and Hans Fugger, who were heirs of Jakob Fugger, founded their own trading company with their cousin Marquard. This company, named Hieronymus Fugger Brothers and Cousin, carried out business transactions with the Spanish crown on its own account and leased the cruzada for some time in return for a loan of 1 million ducats. The administrators of the family firm filed suit in the Augsburg city court against this competition from within their own family. From 1628 onward, an imperial commission tried to deal with the conflict between the two lines.[63]

Meanwhile, the partners in the Tyrolean trade, which after a series of inheritances and takeovers consisted of a complex web of shareholdings of Anton and Raymund Fugger's descendants, withdrew more and more cash in anticipation of future business profits. By 1645, these anticipatory withdrawals amounted to nearly 164,000 florins. The firm's difficulties were augmented by conflicts over management, and a number of partners expressed their wish to leave the company. The internal struggles culminated in 1636 when Ott Heinrich Fugger used his position as commanding officer of Augsburg's city guard to prevent his cousin Hans from leaving the city, ordering him to be arrested and his baggage to be searched for business documents. As in the case of Spain, the termination of business in Tyrol eventually seemed to be the only remaining option to preserve the Fuggers' "reputation and credit."[64]

The repeated statements that honor and reputation could be maintained only through a withdrawal from loss-making business activities alert us to an important fact: While "the firm and the bearers of the Fugger name still enjoyed a reputation for limitless wealth and high creditworthiness, their actual economic situation at the time had already deteriorated substantially," so they had to finance their business transactions mainly with outside capital. "Therefore," Stephanie Haberer points out, "the continuation of business in the 'common' and Tyrolean trades primarily depended on the investment of symbolic and social capital."[65] Whereas the economic success of family members in the sixteenth century had been primarily responsible for the honor and prestige of the Fuggers, the relationship between wealth and honor had been inverted by the mid-seventeenth century. The Fuggers' reputation now seemed to demand withdrawal from the very areas of business that had once made the family great.

5
SERVANTS AND MASTERS
THE PERSONNEL OF THE
FUGGER COMPANIES

THE EMPLOYEES: LEGAL POSITION,
ECONOMIC SITUATION, AND SOCIAL MOBILITY

A commercial, mining, and financial enterprise like the Fugger firm was highly dependent on a reliable and competent workforce. The far-flung distribution network of the Tyrolean and Hungarian trades; the extensive financial transactions in Antwerp, Rome, and Venice; the complex business affairs in Spain; and the multifaceted trade in goods had to be handled by skilled and experienced employees who were permanently present at important commercial centers. With their solid knowledge of foreign languages and legal codes, business organization and bookkeeping, these employees were the "actual backbone of commercial houses."[1]

As a rule, the factors of the large trading companies acquired their skills at a young age in the course of a commercial education that often took place in Italy. Researchers have pointed out that the trading firms' workforce underwent a process of professionalization during the sixteenth century, which manifested itself in the institutionalization of training and "a new form of knowledge management within commercial enterprises" in the form of handbooks and manuals on commercial practices. In this context, the commercial employee "increasingly [became part of] a profession, which was also publicly known and esteemed."[2] At the same time, the group of commercial employees was also marked by a process of differentiation. The manager of the Fugger enterprise stood at the top of a hierarchy that included the main bookkeeper, subaltern bookkeepers, cashiers, and scribes in the Augsburg headquarters, as well as factors, bookkeepers, cashiers, and scribes in the external trading posts. In the second half of the sixteenth century, an additional differentiation between the mercantile company's employees and the administrative personnel of the Fuggers' real estate, landed territories, and foundations became evident.[3]

The tasks of the factors and other commercial employees were fixed in their employment contracts. An early example is Hans Metzler's contract, dated 1499. Metzler, who had already been in the Fuggers' service in Wrocław and now worked in Neusohl, thereby committed himself to serve the company for eight years, keep accurate accounts throughout, not work for competing firms or on his own account, and maintain secrecy on all business affairs. Only the employer could terminate the contract before it expired. Metzler received an annual salary of 400 florins in addition to free food and lodging, thus earning twice as much as high-ranking members of the Tyrolean government. According to Baron Götz von Pölnitz, the factors in Hohenkirchen likewise received "about double or triple the average of a professor's salary at the University of Ingolstadt at the same time." This income could be supplemented by gifts or special gratuities given for exceptional service. Matthäus Lachenbeck, who worked in Hohenkirchen around 1500, was presented with a gift of 150 florins and a silver dish on his tenth anniversary of service. Older factors occasionally received old-age benefits or testamentary bequests. Finally, factors usually had the option to invest capital in the firm as deposits at fixed interest rates.[4]

At the same time, however, the headquarters strictly controlled the factors' accounts. In 1503, for example, Jakob Fugger criticized the high personal expenses of the Neusohl factor Stenzel Beck, remarking, "I don't know what is going on here."[5] Reinhard Hildebrandt has noted a growing tendency to regulate employees' lives according to ethical norms in the course of the sixteenth century: The employees had "to commit themselves to a God-fearing and honorable way of life, to diligence, faithfulness, and obedience to the firm's management, and to keeping all business matters secret. They were neither allowed to stand surety for anyone, even in private, nor to gamble for money, and they were liable with their entire private property for possible damage to the firm caused by their decisions and behavior."[6]

Moreover, the factors needed to be highly mobile. From 1517 onward, Hans Lenz represented the Fuggers in Leipzig, Gdansk, Hohenkirchen, Nuremberg, Lüneburg, and Hamburg. Jakob Hünlein was active in Leipzig from 1522 onward, later moving to Ofen and eventually to Vienna.[7] Sebastian Kurz from Lindau was especially well traveled: Anton Fugger sent the young commercial employee to Spain in 1527, and he journeyed to the New World in 1530, apparently to investigate commercial opportunities on the Yucatán Peninsula. During the following years, Kurz seems primarily to have stayed at the courts of Emperor Charles V and King Ferdinand. In 1536–37, we find him in Wrocław und Neusohl. In 1537, he was at the Spanish court and subsequently in Prague, where he negotiated with King Ferdinand, then back again in Spain by the summer of 1538. After a stay in Augsburg, Kurz traveled to Naples on company business in the spring of 1540. Although Anton Fugger's trusted friend Georg Hörmann, who had made the journey to southern Italy with Kurz, complained to the management about the latter's gaudy appearance and arrogant demeanor, Kurz remained an important man for the firm. As Anton Fugger's special representative of sorts, he subsequently reappears in Spain, Naples, and Slovakia, but also in Genoa and the Holy Roman Empire, where he attended the Diet of Regensburg in 1541 and the Diet of Speyer in 1544. During the War of the Schmalkaldic League, he remained in the imperial army camp, and during the "armored Diet" of Augsburg in 1547–48, he engaged in loan negotiations with the emperor. In October 1554, Kurz became head of the office in Schwaz, but in 1557, he was sent to the Netherlands to investigate the situation after the state bankruptcy declared by King Philip II. After Anton Fugger's death, Kurz left the firm for which he had been on the road for more than three decades. In financial and social terms, his activities had been eminently successful: Kurz had been elevated to noble rank together with three other members of his family as early as 1536, and he was able to purchase the castle and estate of Senftenau within the territory of Bregenz for slightly over 4,000 florins in 1551. In 1558, he invested 24,000 florins in the Fugger firm at 8 percent interest.[8]

The permanently employed factor must be distinguished from the commissioned agent, who was merely commissioned for particular business transactions, worked for several firms at once, and did business on his own account besides.[9] The Fuggers made use of such commissioned agents in locations where they did not maintain their own trading post but still had occasional transactions to handle. In Strasbourg, for example, the Prechters served as the Fuggers' agents for decades. They were active on Jakob Fugger's behalf even before 1508 and were still being entrusted with business matters by his grandson Hans Fugger in the 1570s.[10] In Lyons, where the Fuggers chose not to open a permanent office for political reasons, Italian and southern German correspondents handled their affairs.[11] When the firm abandoned its offices in Italy during Marx Fugger's tenure, commissioned agents such as David Ott and Christoph Rem represented them in Venice and Genoa.[12]

To show off the Fugger company's economic status and financial means effectively to business partners and customers, important trading posts were lavishly decorated. Johann Zink, Jakob Fugger's factor in Rome, had a triumphal arch erected on the occasion of a festival procession marking the beginning of the pontificate of Pope Leo X in 1513. Subsequently, the trading office was redecorated by the Renaissance artist Perino del Vaga.[13] In the 1530s and

1540s, the rooms of the Venice office were furnished with gold-ornamented leather chairs and richly decorated with tapestries, paintings, statues, maps, and mirrors. Paintings, rugs, and mirrors also embellished the Naples trading post, and the Antwerp office had a house chapel, a parrot house, and musical instruments, along with numerous paintings, tapestries, and silver dishes. When a son of the imperial adviser Granvelle married a sister of the countess of Mansfeld in Antwerp in September 1549, Emperor Charles V himself, his son Philip, the queen of France, and the Dutch regent Mary of Hungary were guests at the Fugger house, and Philip, the future king of Spain, held a great banquet there at the expense of the city of Antwerp.[14] As the company office at the Spanish court was traveling with the court, it was housed in rented rooms and not as lavishly decorated as the Venetian and Antwerp offices. But leather wall coverings, paintings, and a large assortment of silver and copper dishes could also be found there.[15]

Who were the firm's representatives at these commercial places? When he built the firm, Jakob Fugger frequently relied on factors from the family's circle of relatives. Thus, members of the Fugger "vom Reh" line were in the service of their relatives "von der Lilie" around 1500. After the bankruptcy of the trading company headed by his brother Lukas, Hans Fugger "vom Reh" entered the services of the firm Ulrich Fugger and Brothers in Nuremberg in 1496. From 1499 until his death in 1501, he was active on behalf of the Hungarian trade in Fuggerau. Jakob Fugger "vom Reh" worked for the same venture in Hohenkirchen around 1500. Gastel Fugger "vom Reh" was active for the Fuggers in Hungary in 1503 and Venice in 1506; his son of the same name served Anton Fugger in Nuremberg from 1528 to 1535 and Fuggerau in 1536. Marriages into the families of other Fugger employees and capital investments in the trading company strengthened the ties between the "poor" Fuggers "vom Reh" and the rich Fuggers "von der Lilie."[16] Jobst Zeller of Nuremberg, for example, who worked for the Hungarian trade in Fuggerau from 1504 to 1512, was married to a Fugger "vom Reh."[17] Jakob Fugger also employed several members of the Meuting family, which was related to the Fuggers by marriage. The offices in Innsbruck and Antwerp were established by Konrad Meuting in the 1490s, and Jörg Meuting took care of Antwerp in 1507. Lukas Meuting worked for the Fuggers from 1511 onward, at the latest.[18] Wilhelm Rem, who was married to a sister of Ulrich, Georg, and Jakob Fugger, represented the brothers in Milan in 1493.[19] Jörg Reihing, one of the earliest Fugger factors in Spain, was the son of Veronika Imhof, whose sister was Georg Fugger's wife.[20]

In the process of building up the Tyrolean and Hungarian trades, moreover, members of the social elite of these regions played important roles. The

Innsbruck factor Hans Suiter doubled as mayor of Innsbruck from 1499 to 1508, and in this capacity he also sat in the assembly of the Tyrolean estates, the Landtag. His son-in-law Wendel Iphofer, a long-time Fugger employee in Tyrol, is also documented as mayor of Innsbruck between 1514 and 1520. Substantial real estate in Innsbruck testifies to the wealth of those two factors. Apart from the numerous negotiations that he conducted on the company's behalf, the fact that Iphofer deposited his will with Jakob Fugger testifies to the bonds of trust that connected the two men.[21] Andreas Mattstedt, who headed the Leipzig office of the Hungarian trade from 1498 to about 1525, was a city councilor and one of Leipzig's richest men. In 1520, his capital investment in the firm stood at 8,000 florins.[22] The esteem enjoyed by these factors in their respective locations undoubtedly bolstered the social prestige of the firm they represented. According to Reinhard Hildebrandt's research, however, individuals from the mercantile elite became less important within the group of commercial employees in the course of the sixteenth century. Instead, the firm increasingly recruited men from craft guild backgrounds or sons of commercial employees. Only a handful of employees in the second half of the sixteenth century successfully took the step into an independent mercantile existence—if they aspired to it at all.[23]

The two Fugger employees Konrad Mair and Hans Bechler, both natives of the imperial city of Memmingen, are telling examples of the opportunities for advancement in urban society that service in a trading company could provide. Konrad Mair is documented as Jakob Fugger's employee in Innsbruck from 1512 onward. After stints as factor in Hall (from 1520) and Vienna (from 1527), he went to Augsburg, where he married Euphrosina Walther in 1531. He continued to work for the Fuggers as "private secretary" (*Gehaim secretarius*) but could also transact business on his own account. His wife's social status gave him access to the exclusive drinking hall of the patricians and related families, and when the ranks of Augsburg's patriciate were extended in 1538, Mair benefited from the measure along with his masters, the Fuggers. After Emperor Charles V abolished the guild constitution of Augsburg and established a patrician city government in 1548, Mair also made a career in urban politics. He became a member of the Small Council, served as burgomaster from 1550 to 1561,[24] and was a member of the imperial city's innermost leadership circle, the Privy Council, from 1561 until his death four years later. From 1562 onward, he also sat on the city court.[25]

When Mair became involved in Bohemian tin mining in 1549 and took over the entire production of tin at Schlackenwald and Schönfeld, he probably acted as a mere agent for the Fuggers, who supported the venture with large loans. But at the time of his death in 1565, Mair's net wealth was estimated at almost 36,000 florins. In addition to mines in the Montafon, a house in Augsburg, and the landed estate of Bergheim, his property included debt claims against the emperor; against Hans Jakob Fugger and his wife, Ursula von Harrach; and against the counts of Ortenburg. His heirs transferred Hans Jakob Fugger's debt certificate and the Bergheim estate to the Fuggers in compensation for the latter's claims from the Bohemian tin venture.[26]

It is highly likely that Mair brokered the entry of his nephew Hans Bechler (b. 1529), whose father was a member of the Memmingen tailor's guild, into Fugger service. In 1544, Anton Fugger sent Bechler and Christoph Hurter, who also hailed from Memmingen, via Antwerp to Spain, where Bechler initially worked as a bookkeeper in the Fugger company's office at the Spanish court. During the main factor's absence in 1548, Bechler handled business transactions as his replacement. He then appears in Lisbon in 1551 and in a leading position in Madrid shortly afterward.[27] In the year of his uncle Konrad Mair's death, he married the daughter of an Augsburg citizen, thus acquiring citizenship himself. In 1569, he accompanied Georg Fugger's son Octavian Secundus on a journey to the Netherlands, and when Georg Fugger's heirs separated from their relatives, the descendants of Anton Fugger, Hans Bechler entered the services of their trading company and held a special position of trust there as main bookkeeper. At the same time, he occupied important municipal offices: In 1572, he became a member of the Small Council, and from 1576 until his death in 1589, he served as burgomaster. His son Hans Ulrich worked for Georg Fugger's Heirs in Lisbon, while Hans Ulrich's brother Friedrich Bechler joined the firm Marx Fugger and Brothers after a period of study in Siena, serving the company as cashier and bookkeeper in Madrid from 1600 to 1602. Friedrich Bechler was taxed for one of the fifty largest property assessments in Augsburg in 1618 and was elected burgomaster five years later.[28] For both Konrad Mair and Hans Bechler, several decades of work at external trading posts—at first in subaltern positions, then in positions of leadership—were the precondition of their social and political ascent within the imperial city of Augsburg. Social mobility in the service of a large mercantile company thus was a real possibility, but also a lengthy process.[29]

Besides social advancement in the imperial city, many years of service as a factor could lead to social integration in the host country. Jobst Walther, the son of the Augsburg Welser company's representative in Leipzig, was employed in the Fugger office in Seville from 1537 on and headed the company office at the Spanish court from 1544 to 1557. During this period, he married the daughter of a knight of the Order of Santiago named Rodrigo Zapata, thus gaining excellent connections to Spanish court circles.[30] Like Walther,

Hans von Schüren and his son-in-law Hans Schedler, long-term factors in Almagro, assimilated into Spanish society. Hans Fugger wrote to the Cologne factor Hans Frick in 1583 that Schedler was "an old Andalusian." One of Schedler's sons became chief overseer of the Spanish mines, a second obtained a position at the royal court, and a third became chaplain to the cardinal infant. Finally, one of Schedler's daughters married the Fugger employee Magnus Lutzenberger.[31]

The brothers Philipp und Daniel Krell illustrate rather different career patterns. Philipp initially worked for Marx Fugger and Brothers as a bookkeeper in Spain but was fired in 1578 after squabbles with the main factor, Thomas Miller, who chastised Krell for his "Junker-like, lazy, and lethargic" way of life. Subsequently, Krell continued to be employed by Christoph Fugger, then by Georg Fugger's Heirs, whom he served in Madrid from 1580 until his death in 1595. Like Jobst Walther, Philipp Krell was married to a Spanish wife and left his sons a substantial inheritance worth 90,000 ducats.[32] His brother Daniel, who worked in Hans Jakob Fugger's service until 1572, later embarked on a career as an independent merchant. From 1579 on, he issued powers of attorney for commercial transactions in Bolzano, Hamburg, Middelburg in the Netherlands, London, and Toulouse. With a property tax assessment of 384 florins and 15 kreuzer in 1604, he was in the top bracket of Augsburg's taxpayers. In addition, he represented the merchants in the imperial city's Small Council from 1598 until his death in 1613.[33]

Like Hans Bechler, who was accepted into the Fugger firm on the recommendation of his uncle Konrad Mair, other factors and leading employees managed to get their sons and sons-in-law into the company. Georg Hörmann, for example, who came from the ranks of the patriciate in the imperial city of Kaufbeuren, founded a genuine "dynasty of factors." Hörmann had attended a Latin school and the University of Tübingen; his later correspondence with Erasmus of Rotterdam und Philipp Melanchthon bears witness to his humanist interests. In 1512, he married Anton Fugger's cousin Barbara Reihing. A few years later, he joined Jakob Fugger's enterprise, which initially employed him in the Antwerp office. When the Fuggers ventured into mining in the Schwaz district on their own in 1522, Hörmann became head of the Schwaz office. In this position, he was in close contact with King Ferdinand I and the Tyrolean government, with whom he negotiated numerous loan contracts. In 1528, the emperor elevated him to noble rank. As one of Anton Fugger's closest collaborators and trusted friends, he trained Fugger's nephews Hans Jakob and Christoph in Tyrol, and during the War of the Schmalkaldic League, he acted as the manager's replacement for several months. Together with Hans Jakob Fugger, Hörmann was the guardian of

Fugger's brothers during their minority in 1548. Following the example of his master, Hörmann pursued a conscious family strategy: In his will of 1545, he ordered that his family's real estate—a house in Kaufbeuren, the rural estate of Gutenberg northeast of the city, and a farm in Untergermaringen—were to remain undivided in the possession of his male heirs.[34]

From 1529 on, Hörmann's son Hans Georg worked for the Fuggers in Augsburg, where he married a woman from the patrician Herwart family in 1538.[35] After a commercial education in Antwerp in 1528 and a period of study in Leuven, Hans Georg Hörmann's brother Christoph went to Spain in 1538. Anton Fugger instructed the twenty-four-year-old Christoph to report to him "whenever he found anything improper or detrimental, for example when a servant was not doing what his masters expected of him." Christoph Hörmann, who initially administered the cashbox of the company office at the Spanish court, rose to the position of head factor after twenty years of service. From 1557, when the management of Spanish affairs was handed over to him, until his return to Augsburg in 1576, he was a main pillar of the Fuggers' trade.[36] A third brother, Ludwig, worked for Anton Fugger in Naples before becoming a son-in-law of the merchant Anton Haug and a partner in the Haug-Langnauer-Linck company in 1543.[37] Another Christoph Hörmann, probably a nephew of the Spanish factor of the same name, was bookkeeper in the Augsburg headquarters from 1566 to 1574, where he was occupied with the administration of the family's manorial estates in Swabia, and subsequently became a factor in Tyrol.[38]

Apart from the formation of "dynasties of factors" like the Hörmann family, the emergence of social networks can be observed among the Fugger employees who were living in Augsburg and working for the headquarters or the administration of landed estates and foundations in the late sixteenth century. Sebastian Zech, who represented Anton Fugger's company in Venice in the mid-1550s,[39] married in Augsburg in 1560 and was subsequently active there as a bookkeeper for Marx Fugger and Brothers. His wealth progressively increased during the following decades, and in 1604 his widow paid taxes on at least 25,000 florins. Zech witnessed Georg Fugger's testament in 1563 and Marx Fugger's will in 1589. When he dictated his own will in 1577, all seven witnesses were Fugger employees. In 1601, his son Hieronymus married Katharina Geizkofler from another "dynasty" of Fugger factors.[40]

Like Sebastian Zech, Georg Stegmann, who worked for Anton Fugger from 1548 on, was among the witnesses of Georg Fugger's will in 1563; in 1569, he acted as guardian of the children of Melchior Griesstetter, a long-term Fugger employee.[41] Philipp Wanner, who was in Marx Fugger's service in the 1570s, was married to Christina Stegmann, presumably Georg Stegmann's daughter. Upon the death of the Fugger employee Philipp Stürtzel in 1606, Wanner was appointed legal adviser to Stürtzel's widow.[42] When Michael Leonhard Mair was sent to Italy by the Fuggers to handle business and family matters in 1568, he made his will prior to the journey and called on his colleague Georg Stegmann as witness. When Mair dictated a new will in 1582, Christoph Hörmann and Anton Bidermann, among others, acted as witnesses. A close relationship of trust apparently developed between the unmarried Mair and Hans Fugger, who called him "father Michl" in his correspondence.[43] Finally, Lukas Geizkofler, who acted as lawyer for the Fuggers, wrote in his autobiographical account that the Fuggers had "presented" the niece of their Spanish factor Christoph Hörmann to him as a prospective bride. Six of Marx Fugger's seven testamentary witnesses in 1589 were trusted friends and long-term employees.[44] Besides their common ties and loyalty to the house of Fugger, the fact that most of them were Catholic may have also been responsible for the close relationships the employees formed among themselves; the Fuggers attached great importance to the Catholic religion of their employees at the time,[45] and as members of the "old faith" they constituted a minority within the predominantly Protestant imperial city.

EXEMPLARY CAREERS

Among the Fugger firm's employees in the sixteenth century there were literally dozens who gained the management's trust during decades of work in positions of responsibility and who possessed linguistic skills, organizational ability, and mercantile competence and thus contributed to the firm's profits while increasing their own prosperity, honor, and reputation. A few individuals, however, stand out from the ranks of the Fuggers' leading employees and trusted advisers because of the range and varied nature of their activities. Matthäus Schwarz, Hans Dernschwam, and Pompejus Occo, who will be presented as representative examples of this group, accumulated cultural and social capital in the course of their work for the Fuggers—capital that reflected not only their own reputation but that of the Fugger family, as well.

Matthäus Schwarz

Like Konrad Mair, Hans Bechler, and Sebastian Kurz, Matthäus Schwarz successfully advanced in the ranks of urban society during his long tenure with the Fuggers. He was born in Augsburg on February 20, 1497, the son of an innkeeper and wine trader. His father Ulrich Schwarz's progeny were incredibly numerous. A votive picture painted in 1508 shows the young Matthäus in the company of sixteen brothers and fourteen sisters! After attending the Latin school of St. Moritz in Augsburg in 1509–10, Matthäus worked in his father's wine business for a few years and made journeys to Munich, Lindau, and Constance on his behalf. In 1514, his father sent him to Italy for a commercial education. After stays in Milan and Genoa, Schwarz received training in Venice until 1516, learning the techniques of double-entry bookkeeping. Although he would later make disparaging remarks about the quality of his education, his sojourn in Italy was undoubtedly an important stage in Schwarz's career, for Jakob Fugger hired him as a bookkeeper immediately after his return in the fall of 1516—initially on a trial basis, but then permanently at the beginning of 1517. Schwarz visited the Frankfurt fairs around 1520 and accompanied Fugger transports of gold and silver in Tyrol during the Peasants' War of 1525–26. He retained his close ties with the firm after Jakob Fugger's death, and as main bookkeeper of the Augsburg headquarters, he held the strings of the company's accounting system together. At the time of Anton Fugger's death in 1560, he was still in charge of the firm's bookkeeping. According to Augsburg's tax books, his wealth steadily increased during his decades of work in the Fuggers' counting house, and in 1552, he purchased a house fronting the Obstmarkt, Augsburg's fruit market. In 1541, Matthäus Schwarz and his brothers Lukas, guild master of Augsburg's salt traders, and Kaspar were elevated to noble rank by Emperor Charles V.[46]

Like many of his colleagues in the Fugger firm, Matthäus Schwarz was part of the network of employees. When he married in 1538 at the advanced age of forty-one, his wife, Barbara Mangold, was a daughter of the factor Anton Mangold; his sons were also employed by the company later on. Matthäus Ulrich Schwarz, born in 1539, can be found in the Fuggers' service in Italy around 1555 but joined the Haug-Langnauer-Linck company by 1560 and later became a knight of the Order of St. John. Another son, Veit Konrad (b. 1541), by contrast, remained attached to the firm for decades after his education in Verona in 1555–56. In the wake of the conflicts within the company Marx Fugger and Brothers, he joined the firm Georg Fugger's Heirs in 1578.[47]

As main bookkeeper of the Augsburg headquarters, Matthäus Schwarz held a responsible but not very exciting position within the firm, so researchers have focused their attention on him for two other reasons. First, Schwarz strove to synthesize and document his knowledge of commercial accounting in a systematic way. As early as 1518, when he was still a young man, he wrote a model treatise on bookkeeping that he amended in later years. In that work. he outlined the basics of his profession under the heading "What Bookkeeping Is" and explained different accounting techniques in the section "Of Three Forms of Bookkeeping." Moreover, he described the procedure of completing an account by using the trading office in Venice as an example; in this respect, however, it appears that he simply copied or excerpted large portions of the actual office account. It is not quite clear whether Schwarz was merely compiling a pragmatic instruction manual and reference work for internal use within the company; whether he wanted to present himself to Jakob Fugger as an accounting expert and recommend himself for more important tasks within the firm; or whether he even intended to have the model treatise on accounting printed. In the last case, it is highly likely that Jakob Fugger prohibited publication, as the explication of the important Venice office's business affairs to curious readers clearly would have been contrary to his interests. The model treatise on accounting was printed only in the twentieth century.[48] A different work that was certainly restricted to internal usage was a manual concerning mercantile practices that had been compiled by 1548. Matthäus Schwarz has been identified as the author of the work, which today is preserved in the Austrian National Library in Vienna. The manuscript, which appears to be based on reports of the Fugger trading posts, systematically summarizes information on money, weights and measures, transport routes and freight costs, business practices, and modes of payment in important centers of European commerce.[49]

Art and cultural historians have intensively studied Matthäus Schwarz's "costume book." This work, which was begun in 1519 and continued for more than forty years, is preserved in the Herzog Anton Ulrich Museum in Brunswick. It comprises 137 portrait miniatures with comments in Schwarz's own hand, the majority of which were executed by the Augsburg artist Narziss Renner from 1521 to 1536. A few portraits from the years 1538–46 have been attributed to Christoph Amberger's workshop, while the final picture, which shows the aging Matthäus Schwarz in mourning dress after Anton Fugger's death, was drawn by Jeremias Schemel. The costume book repeatedly refers to an autobiographical work by Schwarz, also begun in 1519 and titled *Der Wellt lauff* (The way of the world), which has not been preserved. As the term "costume book" indicates, the work focuses on the clothes worn by Schwarz on different festive occasions and social events. The portraits depict him sporting extravagant and colorful outfits at carnivals, hunting parties, target-shooting competitions, sleigh rides, weddings, and imperial diets. Frequently he noted the expensive fabrics from which the clothes were made—sateen, taffeta, damask, or silk—in his own handwriting.[50] As an apprentice in Italy, for example, Schwarz dressed in southern fashion and wore a hooded Spanish cape, a Genoese biretta, a Lombardian coat, and a vest made of taffeta. At the wedding of his master Anton Fugger in 1527, Schwarz wore a biretta made of velvet and sateen, a red coat adorned with silk threads, trousers lined with taffeta and leather stripes, and a taffeta vest. As he notes, this extravagant outfit was a gift of the bridegroom.[51]

But what was the purpose of such a costume book? Scholars sometimes refer to Schwarz as a "fool for clothes," a man with an inflated tendency to present himself and demonstrate his wealth and status in urban society through his lavish clothing. The portraits undoubtedly testify to their patron's strong sense of himself: the best-known miniature depicts the main book-keeper in intimate conversation with Jakob Fugger in the counting house. But this interpretation does not exhaust the costume book's significance. Some scholars have pointed out that Schwarz consistently ascribed precise dates to the images and attached great importance to the exact rendition of his looks, his *gestalt*. When he found the portraits of himself or other people well exe-cuted, he repeatedly noted so in his handwritten remarks. As the images chronicle Schwarz's entire life, from his childhood in Augsburg through his apprenticeship in Italy and his young manhood to his old age, they also re-flect the passing of time and historical change—changing fashions in urban society, as well as the changing appearance of the clothes' bearer. This aspect is particularly evident in the two miniatures that show Schwarz naked after Jakob Fugger's death. Facing the reality of death, Schwarz, who was nearly thirty years old at the time, appeared conscious of the transitory character of life on earth and had his body portrayed in a manner typical of contempo-rary depictions of the Last Judgment and purgatory.[52]

In addition, a brilliant study by Valentin Groebner has recently pointed out the connections between the costume book and Schwarz's activities as bookkeeper for a large mercantile company. Like no other branch of the urban economy, long-distance commerce was fraught with risk—armed robbery, transport accidents, military conflicts, reluctant debtors, unreliable business partners, and bankruptcies. In this context, Groebner argues, the costume book as well as the model treatise on accounting served as media of self-control and self-reassurance in a world that was marked by uncertainty.[53]

A number of other images that Schwarz commissioned testify to his abid-ing interest in his bodily appearance. In 1521, he began a prayer book that, like the costume book, he had illustrated by the Augsburg painter Narziss Renner. It also contains a series of portraits of its patron. In addition, it includes several impressive depictions of jesters with whom Schwarz was personally acquainted. These images, which are highly unusual for a prayer book, can be taken as further references to the transitory and trivial character of human life—and, perhaps, as self-critical comments on personal vanity.[54] Around the year 1522, Schwarz also commissioned a painting from Renner showing thirty pairs of Augsburg patricians and wealthy citizens at a round dance in a lavish garden. This patrician dance (*Geschlechtertanz*), which Renner executed fol-lowing an older model, does not depict a real scene but shows Augsburgers

FIGURE 8

Jakob Fugger and his bookkeeper Matthäus Schwarz in the Fugger counting house, from the costume book of Matthäus Schwarz. (Herzog Anton Ulrich-Museum Braunschweig, Kunstmuseum des Landes Niedersachsen)

who had already died in the company of others still living—including Jakob Fugger, who appears twice. The clothing worn by the dancers also chronicles the development from late medieval fashions up to the 1520s. The patrician dance can thus be read as a family and costume history connecting the past and present of the imperial city and its social elite.[55] In addition, Schwarz had himself portrayed by Hans Maler of Schwaz in 1526 and Christoph Amberger of Augsburg in 1542. Friedrich Hagenauer as well as Hans Kels and his workshop executed several portrait medallions of him. Finally, Schwarz prompted his son Veit Konrad to compose a costume book on his father's model.[56] All of these works demonstrate Schwarz's position as an important patron of the visual arts in sixteenth-century Augsburg, an outstanding example of bourgeois identity and representation, and a self-conscious and perhaps vain, but also attentive and sensitive, chronicler of his life and times.

Hans Dernschwam

Like Matthäus Schwarz, Hans Dernschwam was an important employee of the Fugger firm, as well as a man of many interests who actively participated in the cultural life of his times and put his mark on them. Dernschwam, who was born on March 23, 1494, in the Bohemian mining town of Brüx (Most), came from a wealthy family and attended the universities of Vienna and Leipzig. In 1510, he obtained his baccalaureate degree in Leipzig. After travels through Germany and Italy and a longer sojourn in Rome in 1513, he entered the service of the humanist Hieronymus Balbi, who worked as a tutor at the Hungarian court in Ofen and became provost of Pressburg (Bratislava) in 1515. As Balbi's servant, Dernschwam attended the Vienna Congress of 1515, which marked the conclusion of the Habsburg–Hungarian treaty of succession and for which Jakob Fugger had also made the journey from Augsburg. It is not known whether the two men met on this occasion, but Dernschwam later reported that he became acquainted with Georg Thurzo at that time. In 1517, he went into the Thurzo family's service, and when the crises of the Hungarian trade broke out in 1525, he was working in the Ofen trading post as a cashier. When the factors were imprisoned and the post was looted by rebellious citizens, Dernschwam proved to be an able crisis manager and negotiator, thus recommending himself for more important tasks. Together with Heinrich Rybisch, he conducted the negotiations with the Hungarian crown that led to the granting of a new lease contract for the Slovakian mines to the Fuggers in April 1526. After King Ferdinand assigned the revenues from the Transylvanian salt mines to the Fuggers in compensation for the losses they had incurred in Hungary in 1525–26 and additional loans, the Fuggers sent Dernschwam to Transylvania to represent their interests there. When the troops of Johann Zápolya, who had been crowned king of Hungary by the Hungarian noble opposition to Ferdinand of Habsburg, occupied the Slovakian mining towns, Dernschwam negotiated with him on the Fuggers' behalf. Subsequently, he continued to be entrusted with special commissions in Neusohl; it was not before 1536 that he became the head of the office there. Dernschwam regularly supplied the headquarters in Augsburg with news on political circumstances in Hungary and on the Habsburg–Ottoman military frontier. After the Fuggers abandoned the Hungarian trade in 1546, he remained in their service until early 1549. From 1553 to 1555, he took part in a Habsburg embassy that took him to Constantinople and through Anatolia to Amasya and wrote a travel report about it. Between 1558 and 1567, he worked for the mint office in Kremnitz. He probably died at the end of 1568 on his Schattmannsdorf estate in the Slovakian Fugger territory of Bibersburg.[57]

Besides his activities as a special representative and factor of the Fugger firm, the university-educated and multilingual Dernschwam—who was fluent not only in German and Latin but also in Hungarian and Slovakian—cultivated literary and scientific interests. During his travels, he collected Roman inscriptions, and when he inventoried his library in 1552, it contained more than 2,000 works in 1,162 volumes. After Johannes Sambucus's library, this was probably the second-largest private collection of books within the Hungarian realm. Loans of books and correspondence with men such as Joachim Camerarius the Elder, Johannes Cuspinianus, and Hieronymus Wolf testify to his integration into the networks of central European humanism.[58] His travelogue on the Ottoman Empire, which has been characterized as a "pilgrimage to the places of ancient tradition," likewise reflects his learned interests. The richness of the Greco-Roman heritage contrasts with his experience of the Ottoman present, which Dernschwam viewed as a legal and political tyranny, as well as a "poor, rudely boorish society."[59]

Meanwhile, researchers continue to be puzzled about the motivation for this journey into the Ottoman Empire. In his report, Dernschwam claimed that he merely traveled as a private individual, and there is little evidence that he made the trip as an agent of the Fuggers. Notes on mining or the metal and salt trades, which had been the subject of his earlier reports to the Fuggers, are only marginal, and the anti-Catholic invectives that run through the travelogue would certainly not have pleased the Fuggers. But there have also been doubts that this was really a merely private journey of education and pleasure, for conditions of travel were difficult, travelers' freedom of movement was severely restricted, and the discovery of antique monuments and inscriptions was more a matter of chance than the result of systematic exploration. Instead, Dernschwam demonstrated a striking interest in Hungarian prisoners of war within the Ottoman Empire. Does this indicate that Dern-schwam took the journey as an informer to a high-ranking member of the Hungarian government, as Marianna Birnbaum has assumed?[60] Was the collector of antiques and observer of Ottoman everyday life actually a political spy? Although such questions are hard to answer because we lack direct evidence, they point to the multilayered character of Dernschwam's travelogue, which calls for further attention as scholarly interest in the relations between the Ottoman Empire and Western Europe has revived in recent years.

Pompejus Occo

Pompejus Occo, a native Frisian, represented the Fuggers in Amsterdam from about 1510 onward. At that time, the Dutch port city was not yet the radiant center of commerce with worldwide connections that it became during the seventeenth century. But it was already an important distribution center for goods from the Baltic region, including shipments of Slovakian copper from Gdansk and Szczecin to the Netherlands. It was Occo's task to organize copper shipments, receive them, and secure the ships' free passage through the sound. In this respect, relations with Denmark were of pivotal importance, for the kingdom controlled the sound, charging tolls on all ships traveling between the North Sea and the Baltic. Owing to his background, Occo was probably familiar with both the Low Countries and Scandinavia. He came in contact with the Fuggers through his uncle, the Augsburg city physician Adolph Occo, who took his nephew into his house around 1494 and educated him. Jakob Fugger was one of Adolph Occo's patients. In addition, Pompejus Occo had acquired the basics of an academic education during a period of studies in Cologne in 1504.[61]

To secure the passage of Fugger copper transports through the sound, Occo cultivated close ties with King Christian II of Denmark, whom he lavishly hosted in his house during the monarch's sojourn in Amsterdam in 1521 and for whom he worked as a financial agent. In 1520, Occo played a major role in negotiations between Danish ambassadors, the Brussels court, and the estates of the Netherlands concerning payment of the dowry of Isabella, the sister of Emperor Charles V, to her husband, King Christian. A substantial portion of the dowry—about 100,000 florins—was paid to Occo, who supplied the Danish king with weapons, gunpowder, and a variety of other goods in return. Moreover, he recruited Dutch specialists and settlers for Denmark. A completely new situation ensued in 1523, however, when Christian II had to flee Denmark after a political coup and sought exile in the Netherlands. The Fuggers' representative subsequently had to walk a precarious tightrope. On one hand, the emperor and the Dutch regency govern-

FIGURE 9
Portrait of Pompejus Occo by Dirck Jacobsz, 1531.
(Rijksmuseum Amsterdam)

ment sought the restoration of the exiled monarch—who was the emperor's brother-in-law, after all—and Occo could not possibly withhold his support of these endeavors if he wished to maintain the goodwill of the Dutch government toward the Fuggers and himself. On the other hand, the Fuggers were dependent on cordial relations with Christian's successor, Frederick I from the dynasty of Holstein, because of their shipments through the sound.

Occo mastered this balancing act between the emperor's interests and those of the Fuggers with considerable skill, thus helping to keep the all-important passage from the Baltic to the Netherlands open. It was only in the last years before Occo's death in 1537 that his ties with the Fugger firm seem to have weakened.

Occo was not only an effective political agent but also a successful merchant. He exported large amounts of English cloth to Scandinavia and the Baltic region and transferred money collected from the sale of letters of indulgence from the northern European bishoprics to the Roman curia. Although Dutch sources refer to him as the Fuggers' "factor," he also handled business transactions for other firms, such as the Welsers, and on his own account. Therefore, it makes more sense to call him a commissioned agent. This sketch of Occo would be incomplete, however, if it did not mention his role in the social and cultural life of Amsterdam. Although Occo did not sit on the city council, he was a church master and a master of the guild of the Holy Cross and supported the local monastery of the order of St. Clare. His house, "Het Paradijs," in the middle of the city's central business district was the focal point of an extensive circle of friends. Like Hans Dernschwam, Occo took an interest in books and rare manuscripts, and his library made him highly esteemed within the circles of the Dutch humanists. And like Matthäus Schwarz, he was a patron of the visual arts. In 1515, he commissioned a domestic altar from Jacob Cornelisz, on which the donor and his wife, Gerbrich Claes, are represented. Occo's splendid portrait, executed by Dirck Jacobsz in 1531 and exhibited in the Rijksmuseum today, is considered as an early pinnacle of Renaissance painting in Amsterdam. Finally, the reputation that Occo acquired for himself and his family in Amsterdam society is underscored by the fact that his son Sybrant was later elected as the city's mayor.

DIFFICULT RELATIONS: SILVESTER RAID AND MATTHÄUS ÖRTEL

In 1564, Augsburg's chief criminal investigators interrogated a woman named Anna Megerler, who was suspected of practicing magic. During the interrogations, the woman claimed that she had repeatedly visited Anton Fugger, who had died in 1560, in his house at his request and held astrological sessions with him in front of a crystal glass bowl. Thereupon, the investigators, who obviously felt uneasy about the matter, released her. The historian Lyndal Roper, who has uncovered this remarkable case, leaves it open whether the aging merchant-banker really met with a woman who apparently came from the lower classes for secret astrological sessions. For Roper, the case provides a starting point for reflections on the relationship between economic rationality and magic in the sixteenth century. According to Roper, a medium like the crystal glass bowl could actually exert considerable fascination for a merchant such as Anton Fugger, because it might enable him to control the behavior of employees in distant places: "With the help of this wonderful peace of satellite spy equipment, Fugger could see without being seen—a powerful fantasy about the visual domination of a group of employees on whose loyalty and subservience he was completely dependent." Apart from the possibility of monitoring the behavior of factors who might be acting on their own or neglecting their duties, the crystal glass bowl, according to Roper's interpretation, could also give Anton Fugger the power to imprison the spirits of his "enemies" and make them subservient to him.[62] As the cases of Silvester Raid and Matthäus Örtel show, Fugger indeed had such enemies. Their careers and their relationship with Anton Fugger exemplify the problems that could arise between the managers of large mercantile companies and their employees. They also demonstrate that the commercial employee's professional profile was still in flux in the sixteenth century, despite the trend toward professionalization.

Silvester Raid first appears in Augsburg as a notary and recorder of the hospital in the 1530s. For a few years, he lived in the same house as Clemens Jäger, the city council's servant and chronicler whom Hans Jakob Fugger later commissioned to write the family's Book of Honors. In late 1538, Anton Fugger gave Raid instructions for negotiating with King Christian III of Denmark on an issue that had already occupied Pompejus Occo for many years: the passage of ships transporting Hungarian copper from the Baltic ports to the Netherlands through the Danish Sound. It is not clear why Fugger selected Raid for the task and provided him with extensive powers of attorney. There is no information on earlier sojourns in Scandinavia; the committed Protestant Raid was at odds with his employers in religious matters; and Raid generally appeared "odd as an adventurous figure amidst a conservative workforce," as Pölnitz has written.[63]

In any case, Raid initially acted with remarkable success. He managed to get Duke Albrecht of Prussia involved as a mediator, and with Albrecht's help, he concluded a treaty with the Danish king in May 1539 that secured the passage of Fugger ships through the sound. Upon his return to Augsburg, Raid assumed the role of a diplomatic agent for the Prussian duke, whom he regularly supplied with political news flowing into the Fugger headquarters. Moreover, scores of new musical compositions also found their way from Augsburg to Königsberg through Raid's mediation. In late 1540, Silvester Raid undertook a second journey to the north on commission for Anton Fugger to obtain the Danish king's agreement to the postponement of a loan payment that originally had been promised for Christmas of 1540. Once again, he successfully brought the duke of Prussia in as a mediator; his careful cultivation of relations had thus paid off. In the summer of 1541, Fugger sent Raid, who was now accompanied by a team of mining experts, on a third voyage to Scandinavia, this time to explore the condition of mines in Norway. Apparently on his own initiative, Raid subsequently went on to Sweden, where he was suspected of espionage, however, and was barred from entering the mines. Nor did Raid's attempt to mediate in negotiations between Sweden and Prussia meet with the success he had hoped for. With all of these activities, it is difficult to decide where Raid acted on Anton Fugger's orders and where he pursued his own goals and interests. Pölnitz claimed that he "often served the Fuggers skillfully, but hardly ever honestly." At the end of 1541, Raid quit Fugger's service and worked in Augsburg as a lawyer during the following years. In 1543, the city council admonished him for uttering invectives and "inappropriate expressions" in court. Five years later, Raid gave up his citizenship in Augsburg and moved to Donauwörth, where he accepted the position of city secretary.[64]

Raid's subsequent relations with his former place of residence Augsburg and his former employer, Anton Fugger, were marked by severe strife. In 1549, he was imprisoned because of a business transaction using prohibited coins and sentenced to a fine of 100 florins by the Augsburg city council. In court, Raid insisted on his innocence and apparently viewed himself as the victim of a conspiracy. In 1552, the imperial councilor Dr. Heinrich Hase and Anton Fugger appeared in Donauwörth and persuaded the city council to dismiss Raid. Hase had been in charge of the reform of the southern German imperial city governments decreed by Emperor Charles V in 1548—that is, the abolition of the guilds and the establishment of patrician councils (which were derisively called *Hasenräte* thereafter—a pun on Hase's name that literally means "rabbit councils"). The action taken by Hase and Fugger against Raid indicates that he had agitated for restitution of the guild constitution and had advocated resistance to the emperor even before the revolt of the princes in 1552. Raid subsequently entered the service of Margrave Albrecht Alcibiades of Brandenburg-Kulmbach, whose commissioner for military supplies he became. He was able to use this position during the revolt of the princes to become a leader of the Protestant opposition in Donauwörth. Moreover, he engaged in a series of diplomatic initiatives on behalf of his new master. Among other things, he conducted negotiations with the bishop of Arras and the duke of Alba that led to the margrave's employment in the emperor's service at the beginning of 1553. In the same year, however, a military alliance headed by Elector Moritz of Saxony drove Albrecht Alcibiades out of his territory because of his attacks on the Franconian prince-bishoprics of Würzburg and Bamberg, and the margrave went into exile in France. Now it was Raid's task to prepare for the margrave's return by negotiating alliances and arranging for loans, and during the following years he was continuously traveling on secret missions in France, Switzerland, and southern Germany. Eventually, however, his participation in the knight Wilhelm von Grumbach's armed robbery of a messenger en route from Augsburg to Venice sealed his fate. Raid had substantial claims against the bankrupt Weyer company of Augsburg, and as the merchant Hans Langnauer had grabbed the bankrupts' estate, Raid claimed that he only wanted to take back what was his by robbing Langnauer's firm, the Haug-Langnauer-Linck company. In May 1558, an imperial commissioner had Raid arrested in Donauwörth. He was taken to Wiener Neustadt, interrogated under torture, and executed in November 1558.[65]

By this time, however, Anton Fugger most likely focused his attention on the transactions of his Antwerp factor Matthäus Örtel, who had brought his firm into great difficulties. Örtel initially represented the Welser company in Rome before joining Anton Fugger's firm.[66] In the mid-1540s, he is mentioned as the Fuggers' factor in Naples, and in the fall of 1548, he moved on to the Antwerp office.[67] There Örtel became involved in ever larger loan transactions with the Spanish crown and the government of the Netherlands from 1552 onward. He did not heed the warnings of the Augsburg headquarters and the Spanish factor Christoph Hörmann to beware of putting too much trust in the Spanish court—probably because of his anticipation of high returns and the fact that high-ranking members of the government in Brussels personally guaranteed repayment. When the Spanish crown's suspension of payments triggered a severe crisis on the Antwerp financial market, Anton Fugger bitterly reproached his factor in August 1557, holding him responsible for what had happened. Örtel was "not to defend himself with the good words that the court had given him"; he had "had warnings enough." The anger and frustration that the great merchant felt toward his servant culminated in the exclamation: "Let the devil thank you for your services." Moreover, an audit of the Antwerp office account for 1557–58 found that Örtel had recorded interest payments that had not yet been collected. Fugger also held Örtel partly responsible for the confiscation of American silver shipments that had been destined for the Fuggers in Antwerp: "If we had been able to fish in time we would not have lost anything. But as things now stand, others have made the catch."[68]

Although Anton Fugger fired him and sued him in court, Matthäus Örtel apparently remained on good terms with the nephews Hans Jakob, Christoph, and Georg Fugger. Moreover, he became a wealthy man in the service of the Fuggers, owning his own house in Antwerp. Three years before this death in 1564, his estate was estimated at 100,000 florins. Shortly before he died, he was still trying to forge business ties with the new Dutch regent, Margaret of Parma.[69] Örtel's case hints at a trend that can be observed more frequently under Anton Fugger's successors: the benefit of the mercantile company and the private gain of its employees were no longer identical. This problem grew in significance as the partners withdrew from the active management of the firm. Whereas Anton Fugger had still considered traveling to the Netherlands himself in 1557 and eventually sent his son Hans to Antwerp, such business trips by family members had practically ceased by 1600. Effective control of the factors on the spot became very difficult under these circumstances—not even a gaze into the crystal glass bowl was bound to be of much help in this respect.

THE EMPLOYEES IN THE COMPANY'S FINAL PHASE

The gradual withdrawal of the Fugger family's male members from the active management of the firm and their increasing concentration on other fields of interest and activity—military careers, service at princely courts, office holding, patronage of the arts, and learned studies—resulted in a paradoxical situation in the first half of the seventeenth century. On the one hand, the highest-ranking employees in the firm's headquarters and the remaining offices gained greater influence over the management than ever before, for it was they who guaranteed the continuity of the company and grasped complex economic issues. On the other hand, the Fuggers' complaints about the negligence and "unfaithfulness" of their commercial servants multiplied after 1600. The causes of the negative turn that business affairs took were attributed to highhanded and irresponsible employees who allegedly looked after only their own advantage.[70] The cases of the main bookkeeper Anton Bidermann, the Spanish factor Andreas Hyrus, and the Tyrolean administrator Ulrich Truefer illustrate the employees' broad scope of action in the final phase of the Fugger company, as well as the risks that this involved.

Anton Bidermann, who had already been active in the firm's headquarters at the time of Marx Fugger and served as main bookkeeper from 1610, at the latest, until his death in 1628, was the "soul of the business," to use Hildebrandt's phrase. Like many of his colleagues, he was integrated into the kinship network of Fugger employees through his marriage to Melchior Griesstetter's daughter. During the period in which he was active for the company, his taxable property increased twenty-fold, from between 1,450 and 2,900 florins in 1575 to between 29,000 and 58,000 florins in 1618. With this assessment, he ranked among the one hundred largest taxpayers in Augsburg on the eve of the Thirty Years' War.[71] But when severe strife among the descendants of the brothers Marx, Hans, and Jakob Fugger about their respective shares in the firm's profits broke out in the 1620s, the venerable chief bookkeeper, like the other high-ranking employees of the headquarters, was accused of "great partiality" and repeatedly called before the imperial commission that had been set up to mediate the conflict in 1628. The eighty-six-year-old Bidermann partly proved his critics correct when he freely confessed that his sympathies lay with Hans Fugger's heirs while he thought "not much of Jakob Fugger's [descendants]."[72]

Andreas Hyrus came from a patrician family in the imperial city of Ravensburg; therefore, he was of higher rank than most commercial employees in his time. However, it was fairly typical that kinship ties smoothed his entry into the Fugger firm in 1606, for the Spanish Fugger factor Sigmund Hinderofen was his cousin. In 1615, Hyrus replaced Hinderofen as head of the Madrid office, and in 1621–22, he and Julio Cesar Scazuola were occupied with a general visitation that had the task of compiling a detailed survey of the state of the Fuggers' affairs in Spain. Although an employee reported to Augsburg in 1622 that the visitation had been "damaging and useless" and that the visitors had proved to be incompetent, Hyrus was appointed as chief factor of the Spanish trade, with an annual salary of 1,000 ducats, in 1624. The close ties with the Spanish royal court that this position involved helped Hyrus obtain a knighthood in the Order of Santiago, among other things.[73] The pressing demands of creditors, the crown's complaints, and reports about incompetence and wastefulness in the Spanish trade, however, caused the management to dismiss the chief factor in 1630. The lawyer Dr. Johann Jakob Holzapfel was commissioned to manage the affairs and carry out a new visitation. Holzapfel passed a devastating judgment on Hyrus's business abilities and the state of the company office's accounts, claiming that the Fuggers' leading representative in Spain "diligently rode to court every day" and "played the courtier, but not the factor" there. He also accused Hyrus of disloyalty and of squandering funds.[74]

In the meantime, the chief factor who faced these serious charges had been elected mayor of his home town in his absence and returned to Ravensburg in 1630. Repeated summons to come to Augsburg and render an account of his conduct to the management initially went unheeded. When he did come to Augsburg in 1631, he was immediately arrested. His arrest, however, triggered the intervention of the city of Ravensburg with the emperor. The Fuggers also turned to the emperor, pointing out that Hyrus had severely damaged their "family credit" and "reputation" while his own fortune had increased from 6,000 florins to 90,000 florins within only five years. Considering that the investigations that followed found him guilty of forging balance sheets and transacting business on his own account, and that the Fuggers had been prosecuting him in court for years, it is no small irony that they sent none other than Hyrus to the Iberian Peninsula for a visitation tour of the Spanish trade in 1639. One reason for this was an ultimatum by the Spanish monarch, Philip IV, who threatened to have the Fuggers declared bankrupts unless they either appeared in Spain in person or sent Hyrus as their representative. Another reason was that Hyrus was considered a trusted friend of the Spanish trade's major creditor, the Genoese Bartolomeo Spinola. Shortly after Hyrus completed his visitation, the Fuggers gave up their business in Spain. In the meantime, Hyrus had become a very wealthy man in the service of the Fuggers. By 1631, he was able to lend the city of Ravensburg 25,000 florins, and by 1645, he had advanced the city another 5,000 florins.[75]

Ulrich Truefer was at the head of the Tyrolean trade from 1620 until his death in 1655. According to Ludwig Scheuermann, he was the one Fugger employee who "kept the whole business afloat all by himself" during this period. Truefer commanded comprehensive knowledge of technical, administrative, and economic matters, and his regular reports on the state of Tyrolean mining testify to his conscientiousness. He sought to compensate for the decline of production in the old mining districts of Schwaz and Rattenberg by opening new mines, and his attempts were at least temporarily successful in Palleiten and Sterzing. In addition, he put the moribund mines at Röhrerbühel and the smelting works at Lützelfelden back to work for a few years in 1634. In the years after 1630, however, Truefer was confronted time and again with demands from Fugger family members for cash withdrawals from the trading company, which continued to weaken the already shrinking capital stock. In 1645, he managed to convince Friedrich and Marquard Fugger to undertake a rehabilitation plan that envisioned the repayment of the debts to the Jenbach company and a redistribution of shares, but the plan foundered when new conflicts broke out within the family. In the final years of his life, Truefer had great difficulties meeting current expenses and other liabilities. As he wrote on February 27, 1651, he could "not be as prompt [as usual] because the already enormous pile of debt as well as the continuously deficient credit and the universal lack of money." In the end, all of the efforts of the Tyrolean factor had merely a delaying effect: Two years after Truefer's death, the Tyrolean trade was abandoned, as well.[76]

6

PATRONAGE

AND

SELF-DISPLAY

When the French humanist Michel de Montaigne visited Augsburg in 1580, he noted in his diary: "The Fuggers, of whom there are several lines, all of them very rich, take up the most important social positions within the city. We were permitted to see two rooms in their palace: one of them large, high, and with marble floors, the other one low and filled with old and modern medallions, with a small cabinet in the back. These are the most magnificent rooms I have ever seen." He was also impressed by the family's summer houses and gardens: "With their extravagant splendor they contribute towards the further embellishment of the city, which is grateful to them for it."[1] Montaigne's was no isolated case: Visits to the Fugger houses and gardens were part of the standard program of high-ranking travelers who came to the imperial city in the sixteenth century. Apart from their wealth and economic strength, the Fuggers aroused their contemporaries' interest mainly by their patronage and lifestyle.[2] Although the family also had numerous castles in the countryside (either remodeled or newly built and lavishly decorated), it mainly used the imperial city as a stage on which to display itself.[3]

Aside from the Fuggers' economic activities, researchers have paid most attention to their patronage of the arts. Norbert Lieb devoted several volumes to this topic, and Paul Lehmann wrote a two-volume history of the Fugger libraries. Historical exhibitions have repeatedly brought the Fuggers' role as collectors, patrons, and promoters of the arts to the attention of an interested public. In 1950, an exhibition entitled "Fugger and Welser" in Augsburg, which still bore the marks of wartime destruction at the time, invited visitors to revel in the imperial city's glorious past. Three decades later, the city's cultural heyday from the Renaissance to the early Baroque was exhibited under the title "World in Transition," and in 1993, the five-hundredth anniversary of Anton Fugger's birth was acknowledged with the exhibition "The Fuggers and Music."[4]

The results of these investigations into the history of art, music, and libraries cannot be displayed exhaustively here. Instead, the following account focuses on six central areas: the Fugger houses as centers of urban representation; the burial chapel at St. Anna as a major work of the early Renaissance in southern Germany and focal point of the family's memory; the social settlement of the Fuggerei as an architectural monument to Jakob Fugger's charitable activities; the patronage of painters and musicians, as exemplified by Christoph Amberger and Melchior Neusidler; the family's collections of books; and the Fuggers' *Book of Honors* as a medium of family identity and tradition. Throughout, the visual arts, architecture, music, and extensive collections of books should not be viewed in isolation from the family's economic activities. In accordance with recent scholarship, the manifold interconnections, interdependencies, and processes of "osmosis" between economy and art require particular attention.[5]

THE FUGGER HOUSES IN AUGSBURG

At the beginning of the sixteenth century, members of the Fugger family already owned substantial houses in Augsburg—at the Judenberg (the old Jewish quarter), on the Rindermarkt (cattle market), and in the Kleesattlergasse. By midcentury, these estates had been extended and redecorated according to their occupants' tastes and needs for self-representation.[6] After his wedding to Sibylla Artzt in 1498, Jakob Fugger moved into his mother-in-law's house fronting the Weinmarkt (wine market) and purchased it, along with a neighboring house, in 1511. By 1515, he had had the estates remodeled and joined together into one representative city palace, turning the Weinmarkt, which was centrally located on the old imperial road (the present-day Maximilianstraße) into the firm's headquarters and the center of most family members' lives. In 1523, Jakob Fugger also bought the adjacent house of Georg Kunigsperger and his wife, Regina Artzt. His nephews added to this estate, which eventually made up almost an entire city block, and Anton Fugger continued to remodel the houses on the Weinmarkt. The palace-like complex finally included three interior courts, among which the Damenhof (Ladies' Court) with its arcades shows the conspicuous influence of the Italian Renaissance. The frescoes embellishing the Ladies' Court were devoted to the heroic deeds of Maximilian I, thereby emphasizing the Fugger family's loyalty to the emperor. The façade fronting the Weinmarkt, which is almost seventy-five yards wide, was covered with allegorical and historical paintings probably executed by Hans Burgkmair the Elder. The lavish interior decoration with marble, wooden coffered ceilings, and tapestries soon aroused the admiration of visitors such as Antonio de Beatis, who described the Fug-

FIGURE 10

*The citizens of Augsburg paying homage to King Gustavus Adolphus of Sweden
in front of the Fugger houses on the wine market. Copper engraving, 1655.
(Staats- und Stadtbibliothek Augsburg)*

ger houses in 1517. Another novelty was the covering of the roofs, for which
Jakob Fugger obtained a special import license for copper from Hungary. On
a piece of ground acquired in 1531, Anton Fugger erected magnificent visitors' and festival quarters, which were specially designed for the emperor and
other members of the House of Habsburg, by 1536. Charles V resided in this
"imperial *palatium*" during his sojourns in the city in 1547–48 and 1551, and
it is here that the Venetian painter Titian executed the famous portraits of
the emperor during the imperial Diet of 1547–48. Among the other guests
entertained in these quarters were King Philip II of Spain, Mary of Hungary,
and Emperor Ferdinand I.[7]

In 1568–73, Hans Fugger commissioned a magnificent remodeling of the
rear part of the Fugger palace on the Weinmarkt, which he had inherited
from his father, Anton, employing the late Renaissance style. As his model,
he obviously borrowed the decoration which Giorgio Vasari had designed
for the Palazzo Vecchio in Florence. For the redecoration of the festival hall,

house chapel, living quarters, garden loggias, collection galleries, and library, he recruited Friedrich Sustris, a native Dutchman living in Florence; the painters Alessandro Scalzi, known as Paduano, and Antonio Ponzano; and the sculptor and stucco artist Carlo di Cesari Pallago. Duke Wilhelm V of Bavaria subsequently commissioned this team of talented artists for the remodeling of his own residence, and Sustris in particular exerted a strong influence on Munich court art in the late sixteenth century. Marble floors, leather wall coverings painted with gold, rich stucco decorations, fantastic wall paintings in the style called "grotesque," and ceilings painted with mythological and allegorical themes impressed visitors. The entire cost for the remodeling of these rooms has been estimated at 10,000 florins. In a letter written in 1573, Hans Fugger referred to Sustris and his colleagues as "costly people" who had severely strained his purse. The highlight among the works of art displayed in the galleries was the so-called Amazon sarcophagi, brought to Augsburg via Venice on Hans Fugger's orders in 1568 and located in Vienna today. Fugger was less interested in the pieces' authenticity, however, than in their representative effect: Damaged antique sculptures were "repaired," and Venetian artists supplied imitations of Roman emperors' busts. Any evaluation of Hans Fugger's standing as collector and patron of the arts, however, has to consider that he usually left the purchase of art works to employees and agents. A typical Renaissance "chamber of arts and curiosities," his collection comprised all sorts of exotic rarities and finely crafted precious objects in addition to paintings, sculptures, books, coins, and medallions. Hans Fugger's "Italian garden" in Augsburg was stocked with Mediterranean plants and tended by a gardener from Italy.[8]

In 1575, the brothers Philipp Eduard and Octavian Secundus Fugger purchased from the patrician Hans Paul Herwart an estate on the Weinmarkt in the vicinity of their relatives Marx and Hans Fugger. Octavian Secundus, who became proprietor of the house when the inheritance was partitioned in the following year, had it remodeled according to his wishes; by 1584, he had spent almost 5,500 florins on it. The inventory compiled after the owner's death in 1600 listed forty rooms lavishly decorated with paintings and precious and exotic objects. The highlight was the house chapel into which Octavian Secundus Fugger had invested about 4,300 florins in 1586–87. The altar was adorned by a Dutch altar painting, an ivory crucifix, large silver candelabras, and silver busts of the apostles Peter and Paul. Paintings by Venetian masters lined the entrance hall. According to Lieb, the chapel space as a whole was "densely filled with sacral preciousness—a patrician counterpart to the princely chapels" of the Bavarian dukes.[9]

Octavian Secundus Fugger's house passed into the hands of another line of the family when Ott Heinrich Fugger acquired it in 1622. The estate inventory drawn up after Ott Heinrich's death in 1644 recorded about 320 paintings, as well as hundreds of drawings and graphic prints, along with numerous exquisite pieces of furniture and finely crafted objects. Ott Heinrich Fugger owned works by Old Masters such as Albrecht Altdorfer, Giovanni Bellini, Albrecht Dürer, and Titian, as well by contemporary artists such as Hans von Aachen, Georg Petel, and Johann Rottenhammer. At least some of the rooms were devoted to specific visual programs. Moreover, Ott Heinrich purchased two versions of the Assumption of St. Mary from the workshop of Peter Paul Rubens in the 1620s, one of which was destined for the church of the Holy Cross in Augsburg and the other for the domestic chapel in the house on the Weinmarkt. Despite the fact that many works of art were obviously of high quality, Ott Heinrich Fugger was not an art collector in the strict sense of the term. Instead, his main thematic interest in portraits of family members, princes, and officers, as well as in religious and mythological subjects, city views, and landscapes, primarily reflects his noble way of life, rootedness in family tradition, religious orientation, and liking for art that depicted warfare.[10]

Apart from the architectural design and decoration of their houses in Augsburg, feasts and festivals provided the Fuggers with numerous opportunities to display their wealth and status within the city to great effect. Weddings and funerals of family members, which were attended by high noblemen; the visits of rulers to the Fugger houses; and tournaments, shooting competitions, sleigh rides, and carnivals were staged as lavish spectacles.[11] The family's *Book of Honors* notes on Anton Fugger's wedding with Anna Rehlinger in 1527 that "no man in Augsburg [had] ever imagined or seen . . . such a costly, honorable wedding."[12] The wedding celebration of Octavian Secundus and Maria Jakobäa Fugger, which lasted four whole days in 1579, was attended by numerous "counts, barons, and other noble lords as well as the honorable patrician and merchant families belonging to the two exclusive drinking halls of the city of Augsburg."[13] Regarding the extravagant expenditures on ostentatious display, Anton Fugger and Barbara Montfort's wedding in 1591 marked a climax of urban festive culture and the family's self-presentation. The entry of the wedding guests with 345 horsemen and twenty festival carriages was a colorful spectacle, and the festivities, which lasted several days, included tournaments, costume balls, fireworks, and opulent festive dinners. The departure of the wedding company for the tournament likewise attracted the attention of contemporary chroniclers because of the fantastic costumes and décor. On the whole, the chroniclers' accounts reflect the odd mixture of fascination and critical distance with which contemporaries regarded these ostentatious displays of splendor. The wedding spectacle's costs were estimated at more than 48,000 florins.[14]

THE BURIAL CHAPEL AT ST. ANNA

In the medieval and early modern periods, burial monuments of princes, noblemen, and wealthy merchants were central media of representation. They communicated the self-image of the deceased to posterity; demonstrated prestige, power, wealth, and piety; and symbolized the family's origins and continuity. From the early sixteenth century onward, the Fuggers' economic rise manifested itself in lavishly decorated burial sites and intense efforts to preserve the liturgical memory of deceased family members. After the early death of her son Marx, Regina Fugger set up a Holy Mass foundation in the provost's church of St. Peter at Augsburg's central square, the Perlach, in 1511; according to Baron Götz von Pölnitz, she "showered" the church "with exquisite presents."[15] The outstanding artistic monument of the Fuggers' sepulchral representation, however, is undoubtedly the burial chapel of the brothers Ulrich, Georg, and Jakob Fugger in the Carmelite church of "our Lady's brothers," the present-day church of St. Anna in Augsburg.

Plans to build this burial chapel apparently date back to the year 1505. The groundwork for their realization was laid in a contract that the brothers Ulrich and Jakob Fugger concluded with Augsburg's Carmelite convent in 1509. The contract is characterized by a marked asymmetry, for the brothers basically reserved all rights regarding the decoration and use of the burial chapel to themselves, while the convent essentially committed itself to maintain it according to the founders' will.[16] Because the history of the building and decoration of the Fugger chapel is poorly documented in the sources, research has focused on art-history methods of attribution and reconstruction. The construction work on the extension of the church itself probably took place from 1509 to 1512, and by 1517, essential parts of the decoration had been completed: the altar, which takes up almost the entire end wall of the chapel and is adorned with a freestanding sculptured Corpus Christi group and passion reliefs; the epitaphs of Georg and Ulrich Fugger, who died in 1506 and 1510, respectively; the choir stalls; and the organ. According to Bruno Bushart, the basic concept for the chapel, which was consecrated in 1518, was probably designed by Albrecht Dürer. What is certain is that Dürer made the designs for Ulrich and Georg Fugger's epitaphs depicting the resurrection of Christ and Samson's fight with the Philistines; documents also prove that the Nuremberg coppersmith Peter Vischer forged the wrought-iron work, and Jan von Dobrau built the organ. Art historians have attributed the sculptural work to the Augsburg master Adolf Daucher and

his workshop, while the Corpus Christi group on the altar probably was the work of Daucher's son Hans. The paintings on the organ's wings were most likely carried out by Jörg Breu the Elder, and designs for the choir stalls may have been provided by Hans Burgkmair the Elder. In a foundation charter drawn up in 1521, Jakob Fugger finally provided for the liturgical acts commemorating the deceased family members and ordered that the foundation's capital was to remain under the exclusive control of the founder and his descendants.[17]

Considering its size, its prominent location in the church's west choir, the exquisite nature of the materials used, the artistic quality of the decoration, and, last but not least, the estimated cost of 15,000 florins, the Fugger chapel by far exceeded the dimensions of burial monuments of wealthy bourgeois families in southern German imperial cities up to this time. Although the decoration bears the signature of various artists and combines elements of the southern German late gothic and Italian early Renaissance styles, art historians have rightly characterized it as a remarkably coherent artistic synthesis.[18]

The chapel's size and splendor drew the admiration of contemporary visitors, and modern researchers have compared it to papal and princely burial chapels. Were the Fuggers therefore primarily interested in showing off their noble pretensions, as Otto Gerhard Oexle thinks?[19] Undoubtedly, the chapel reflects the founders' exalted self-consciousness, but we can assume that concern for the salvation of their souls was at least as important to them. Like the circle of partners who constituted the Fugger trading company, the burial chapel in St. Anna was exclusively for the male members of the Fuggers' "name and lineage." Benjamin Scheller has interpreted the altar decoration as the "visualization of a concept of individual salvation." The "combination between veneration of the Eucharist and memory of the dead" in the Fugger chapel's architecture, decoration, and liturgy was to ensure the permanent commemoration of the male members of the mercantile dynasty, as well as the salvation of their souls.[20]

THE FUGGEREI

Even more than the burial chapel in the Church of St. Anna, another foundation is indelibly linked in historical memory with the name of Jakob Fugger the Rich. This is the housing project for poor people in a suburb of Augsburg, the Jakober Vorstadt (parish of St. James), a project that was first referred to as the Fuggerei in 1531. Although later generations of the family set up other substantial foundations,[21] none became nearly as well-known as the Fuggerei, where poor, Catholic citizens of Augsburg can live for a yearly rent of one Rhenish florin (.88 Euro-cents) to the present day. The Fuggerei constitutes one of Augsburg's main tourist attractions. Scheller has characterized it as the "ideal type of an autocratic act of creation," for Jakob Fugger could realize his visions there largely independent of other interests.[22]

The firm's general balance of 1511, which Jakob Fugger drew up after the death of his brothers Georg and Ulrich, contains a first hint of his intention to establish a settlement for the poor, inasmuch as it reserved 15,000 florins for charitable foundations. Even earlier, the company Ulrich Fugger and Brothers had kept an account for "St. Ulrich," the profits of which were set aside for charity, but it was only after the death of his brothers that Jakob Fugger's plans for a foundation for the poor became specific. In February 1514, he purchased from Hieronymus Welser's widow, Anna Strauss, a piece of real estate with four houses and a garden Am Kappenzipfel (a street in the city of Augsburg), in a thinly inhabited part of the suburb. Two years later, he acquired three more houses and concluded a contract with the city of Augsburg concerning the taxation of the future settlement for the poor. Under the direction of the Augsburg mason Thomas Krebs, the settlement was built within no more than a few years: Twenty-two houses had been finished by 1517, forty-five houses were standing three years later, and fifty-two houses inhabited by 102 taxable citizens had eventually been completed by 1522. The exterior appearance of the Fuggerei, which was slightly altered by later extensions and new buildings, is characterized by the "lines of houses of uniform type" along straight alleys. This construction principle saved costs and made optimal use of the building site. Deviations from the settlement's geometrical floor plan were primarily the result of the particular shape of the building site. Another cost-saving measure was the use of standardized building parts such as doors and windows. Access to the walled settlement was provided by three gates, which were locked at night. In his foundation charter of 1521, Jakob Fugger explicitly formulated the settlement's purpose and provided for its future financial support and administration. According to the document, the houses were to be rented out to poor day laborers and artisans who were citizens of Augsburg and were not dependent on alms for a yearly rent of one Rhenish florin. As this sum was equivalent to the monthly income of a day laborer at the time, it was not originally a merely symbolic payment. Moreover, the settlement's inhabitants were obliged to pray daily for the members of the Fugger family. Four executors, two of them from the male lineage of the Fuggers "von der Lilie," were to administer the foundation's capital. An administrator, who received the settlement's gatehouse as living quarters, oversaw activities on location.[23]

There has been considerable discussion of the possible architectural and intellectual models for the Fuggerei. Otto Nübel's opinion that the late medieval beguine courts in the Netherlands, above all, have to be considered as models for the Augsburg housing project has been viewed skeptically by more recent researchers. According to Marion Tietz-Strödel, the Fuggerei reflects architectural tendencies in social housing projects that can be found in several European countries—England, the Netherlands, northern Germany, Italy—while no particular settlement can be identified as the direct model.[24] Most recently, Benjamin Scheller has interpreted the Fuggerei as a variant of the houses for the poor that emerged from the fourteenth century on that were based on a new concept of poor relief. In contrast to the medieval hospital, a settlement project like the Fuggerei assigned separate living spaces to its individual inhabitants, which ensured a degree of privacy. This kind of housing foundation was especially designed for the so-called *Hausarmen*— that is, pious resident inhabitants who were willing to work but still needed relief. Confronted with a growing number of beggars and alms recipients,

The Fuggerei.
(Städtische Kunstsammlungen Augsburg)

late medieval urban governments began to distinguish between "honorable" and "fraudulent" poor. Only the first category, the resident and honorable poor, continued to be considered worthy of relief. By founding a settlement for poor, God-fearing citizens of Augsburg, Jakob Fugger conformed to this new conception of poor relief. With more than one hundred apartments (two apartments per house), however, the dimensions of the Fuggerei far exceeded those of other contemporary urban housing projects for the poor. Although elderly people were accepted from the beginning, the settlement also housed numerous young resident poor. Many of the households, which measured 45 square meters (490 square feet), were occupied by families with children, and most male household heads earned their living as craftsmen or day laborers. The Fuggerei did not become an exclusive settlement for the elderly until the twentieth century.[25]

Compared with earlier settlements for the poor, another peculiar aspect of the Fuggerei is the lack of public spaces and centers of communication. The settlement did not have a central courtyard or square, and even the chapel of St. Mark was only built in 1581. In Scheller's view, this highlights the disciplinary character of the social settlement, for the inhabitants of the Fuggerei were entirely confined to the private spaces of their living quarters. There were no sociable or festive events within the settlement to keep the inhabitants from a God-fearing and hardworking life or to give them any occasion for "leisure." Those who came back from the tavern too late at night would find the gates closed.[26]

Whereas modern observers are inclined to regard the Fugger chapel at St. Anna primarily as a great work of art and the Fuggerei as an important social settlement, for Jakob Fugger, the burial chapel, the settlement for the poor, and the foundation of a preachership in the church of St. Moritz in Augsburg, which will be considered in the next chapter, constituted an integrated whole. This is evident from the foundation charter of 1521, in which Jakob Fugger provided for the organization and administration of all three foundations, as well as from his last will of 1525. Beyond the particular purposes of each foundation—the creation of a family burial site, the relief of poverty, and the improvement of preaching—they all stand as testimony to the founder's deep concern for the salvation of his soul and his belief that this salvation could be promoted by good and pious works. But they also testify to the great merchant's interest in legitimating his wealth and permanently securing his own reputation and that of his family before his contemporaries and posterity. Liturgical acts of commemoration in the burial chapel and the daily prayers of the Fuggerei's inhabitants were meant to preserve the founder's memory, and those who saw the inscriptions and the lily coat of arms in the chapel or above the gates of the social settlement were reminded of who had created these works.[27]

THE PATRONAGE OF ART AND MUSIC: CHRISTOPH AMBERGER AND MELCHIOR NEUSIDLER

My descriptions of the Fugger houses have already indicated that members of the family surrounded themselves with works of art. The Fuggers' art patronage operated on two levels. On one level, they—like many other rich merchant families—used their commercial relations to purchase artworks abroad. During the late Middle Ages, an art market emerged in the Italian cities in which the demand of bourgeois customers largely determined the supply. With the growing wealth of urban elites in the southern German cities, a market for paintings, sculpture, antiques, and finely crafted objects developed there, as well, from the late fifteenth century onward. Because of its trans-Alpine commercial relations, Augsburg in particular became a "gateway, collection point, and distribution center for Italian art."[28]

Anton Fugger's brother Raymund, who is referred to as *rerum antiquarum amantissimus* (the most devoted lover of ancient objects) in his epitaph, is considered the first genuine art collector within the family. According to the draft version of the Fuggers' *Book of Honors,* he was "not only a particular enthusiast, but a credit to all true historians, an eager collector of antique objects and medallions—verily, a diligent inquirer into all the above-mentioned areas of knowledge [*gutwissender sachen*], and a patron [*begaber*] of all good arts, as his diligence may well be felt and seen in the art gallery that he left behind, which stands as wonderful testimony to everyone with eyes to see." Raymund Fugger owned paintings by Italian masters and Lucas Cranach the Elder, but artworks from Greek and Roman antiquity were his particular passion. Using the Fugger firm's commercial relations with Italy and southeastern Europe, he acquired antique bronzes, stone sculpture, and coins and probably owned the most extensive and sophisticated central European collection of antiquities of his time. When his estate was distributed among his heirs, the value of the "antiques, paintings, and other curiosities" was estimated at 8,000 florins.[29] As has been mentioned, Raymund's nephew Hans, his grandson Octavian Secundus, and his great-grandson Ott Heinrich also owned numerous works of art, but they were less concerned with the building of collections than with display, the accumulation of prestige, and the preservation of family property and family tradition.[30]

Members of the urban elite not only made purchases on the free art market, however, but deliberately patronized individual artists. In this respect, the portrait in particular became increasingly popular during the sixteenth century, for more than other genres of painting it satisfied its patrons' desire for self-presentation and ostentatious display. More than almost any other contemporary southern German family, the Fuggers made use of this medium of self-display and visual distinction. Georg Fugger was depicted as a young man by the Venetian painter Giovanni Bellini in 1474, and Jakob Fugger and his nephews Raymund and Anton were drawn by Hans Holbein the Elder around 1510. Hans Burgkmair portrayed Jakob Fugger in a colored woodcut in 1511, and Albrecht Dürer made a portrait drawing of the rich merchant in 1518, which then became the model for the famous portrait of Jakob Fugger in a fur coat and with a Venetian cap executed in Dürer's workshop. In 1524–25, Hans Maler of Schwaz painted portraits of Jakob Fugger's nephews Anton and Ulrich. Anton's brother Raymund Fugger was portrayed by the Italian Vincenzo Catena in 1525 and by Martin Schaffner a few years later. In addition, a series of portrait medallions has been preserved.[31] The patronage of very different artists from whom family members ordered portraits may also be due to the fact that no specialized portrait painter was resident in Augsburg until 1530. This market niche was finally filled when Christoph

Amberger, probably a native of Kaufbeuren, became a resident of the city. With his numerous portraits of well-to-do citizens, Amberger became the "visual chronicler of Augsburg's heyday."[32]

Christoph Amberger is first recorded in the imperial city in May 1530, when he obtained a painter's privilege. Shortly before he had married the daughter of the Augsburg painter Leonhard Beck and thus acquired the rights of citizenship. Whereas older researchers have assumed that Amberger had already been trained by Beck or some other Augsburg painter, Annette Kranz's exhaustive study demonstrates that he was decisively influenced by the specialized portrait painter Hans Maler of Schwaz in Tyrol in the late 1520s. During his stay with Maler, who worked for the Innsbruck court as well as for wealthy Tyrolean mining entrepreneurs, Amberger may also have become aware of the growing demand for portraits. His hand is first identifiable on an image of Wolfgang Roner, a Fugger employee in Schwaz, which Hans Maler began in 1529 and Amberger completed. In the following year, Amberger portrayed Anton Fugger's trusted friend Georg Hörmann, the head of the Schwaz trading post. Hörmann, who like Roner (and, most likely, Amberger) hailed from Kaufbeuren, may have arranged the promising painter's move to Augsburg, where the imperial Diet of 1530 provided him with an excellent opportunity to establish himself. Amberger seized this opportunity with a portrait of Emperor Charles V and was subsequently well supplied with orders. Merging the "old German" tradition of Augsburg painters such as Hans Holbein the Elder and Hans Burgkmair the Elder with Italian influences, his paintings obviously suited the taste of the urban elite.[33]

The Fuggers initially were reluctant to order portraits from Amberger, but from the mid-1530s they used his abilities for other works. In February 1536, they paid him "for making a golden rose," and in 1539, Amberger executed a map of the New World destined for King Ferdinand (the future emperor), a drawing of a piece of jewelry, and four windows with coats of arms for the parish church of Mickhausen, the center of a landed Fugger estate.[34] In 1541, the brothers Hans Jakob and Christoph Fugger ordered two large portraits from Amberger, which are considered as highlights of his career and mark a stylistic caesura in his oeuvre. A characteristic feature of this "sustained expansion" of Amberger's "professional horizon" is his adoption of a "courtly" style that suited the predilection of his clients for ostentatious self-display. Amberger's artistic development went hand in hand with his increasing reception of Italian influences and manifests itself in larger formats and sizes, with standing or sitting three-quarter figures, freer gestures, an expanded range of colors, the use of additional attributes such as gold chains and weapons, and a perspective background design showing architectural and

FIGURE 13
Hans Jakob Fugger. Portrait by Christoph Amberger.
(Los Angeles County Museum of Art [LACMA]; gift of John Passi [M.87.280];
© 2011; Digital Image Museum Associates/LACMA/Art Resource NY/Scala/Florence)

FIGURE 14
Christoph Fugger. Portrait by Christoph Amberger.
(Bayerische Staatsgemaeldesammlungen—Alte Pinakothek, München)

landscape elements. This stylistic change was probably the result not of a journey to Italy—for which there are no records—but of Amberger's study of Italian works of art, which were brought to Augsburg in great numbers at the time, and his encounter with the Austrian court painter Jakob Seiseneg-ger, who had become familiar with the "courtly" pictorial style in Italy and successfully adapted it. Seisenegger's full-size portrait of Georg Fugger was executed at the same time as Amberger's images of his brothers Hans Jakob and Christoph.

A particular occasion for which these three portraits were painted cannot be identified. After their elevation to the ranks of the hereditary nobility of the empire in 1530, their reception into the Hungarian nobility in 1535, and their rise to the Augsburg patriciate in 1538, the brothers may have felt that it was time to visually display their gain in status and prestige. It is also possible that they wished to create a demonstrative response to the subjection to their uncle's authority that the company contract of 1538 had imposed on them. And maybe the portraits were also "a contribution to the patrons' efforts to retain their position within the imperial city's structures of power" at a time that the family played only a marginal role in Augsburg politics. In any case, with their elegant black dress, gold chains, shining weapons, and proud postures, Hans Jakob and Christoph Fugger demonstrate their acute consciousness of their rank and identity. The fact that these Fugger portraits were obviously modeled on official images of Emperor Charles V can also be interpreted as an expression of a courtly and aristocratic sense of identity, as well as a demonstration of their close allegiance to the House of Habsburg. The Fuggers' main bookkeeper Matthäus Schwarz may have been stimulated by these impressive portraits to have himself and his wife, Barbara, painted by Amberger, as well.[35] After Amberger's death in 1562, the imperial city lacked a portrait painter of comparable quality and popularity, and members of the Fugger family who had themselves portrayed in the final third of the sixteenth century therefore turned once again to foreign masters such as Hans von Aachen and Nicolaus Juvenel.[36]

The Fuggers' musical interests not only manifested themselves in their own musical activities—handwritten lute books have been preserved for Georg Fugger and his son Octavian Secundus—but also in the foundation of church organs and organists' positions, the acquisition of instruments, the patronage of musicians and composers, and the financing of musical prints. During his stay in Antwerp in 1556–57, Hans Jakob Fugger, to whom Sigmund Salminger dedicated a collection of motets as early as 1545, helped to recruit Orlando di Lasso for the court in Munich. After his own move to Munich, Fugger also served as "musical impresario" of the duke's court. Several of Orlando di Lasso's compositions were printed with dedications to members of the Fugger family. The Flemish composers Philippe de Monte and Karel Luython, who worked as musicians at the court of Emperor Rudolf II in Prague, as well as the Italians Gregorio Turini and Orazio Vecchi, dedicated compositions to Hans Fugger. In 1566, Raymund Fugger the Younger owned no fewer than 145 musical instruments, including works by renowned instrument builders. Hans Leo Hassler, a native of Nuremberg, was active in Augsburg as chamber organist for Octavian Secundus Fugger from 1586 onward. Hassler received an annual salary of 200 Thaler and invested deposit capital in the Fugger company. The Regensburg organist Gregor Aichinger began to play the Fugger organ in the basilica church of St. Ulrich and Afra in 1584. Aichinger's patron Jakob Fugger, who had spent 2,500 florins on the organ, established contact with the Venetian master Giovanni Gabrieli, with whom the organist took lessons. Aichinger for his part instructed Jakob Fugger's sons and dedicated a whole series of compositions to family members. In their capacity as administrators of the Fugger foundations, Philipp Eduard and Marx Fugger employed the organ builder Marx Günzer and the painter Hans Freyberger in 1612 to modernize and expand the organ in Augsburg's Dominican church.[37] The Fuggers' relations with the lute player and composer Melchior Neusidler (1531–90/91) are a particularly good example of the family's patronage of music, which intensified during the second half of the sixteenth century.

Neusidler's curriculum vitae shows some parallels with Amberger's. Like the painter, the musician moved to Augsburg as a young man, and like Amberger, Neusidler soon occupied a leading position in his profession there by blending older traditions with "modern" Italian influences. Finally, like Amberger, Neusidler enjoyed the special patronage of members of the patrician and mercantile elite. His relations with Hans Fugger, whom Neusidler invited to his wedding to a chamber lady of the widowed Palatine Electress Dorothea in Neumarkt in 1573, were particularly close. Fugger did not attend the musician's wedding in person but ordered the company's factor in Nuremberg, Carl Heel, to make the journey to Neumarkt and present Neusidler with a valuable drinking cup. In 1574, Neusidler sold a painting to Hans Fugger for his musical chamber. The lute book that Neusidler had printed in Strasbourg in the same year included a piece entitled "Lady Fugger's Dance (Der Fuggerin Dantz)." In December 1580, Hans Fugger extended a loan of 100 florins to the musician, and in March 1585, Neusidler played at Ursula Fugger's wedding to Baron Kaspar von Meckau. From 1583 until his death, the aging musician, who was afflicted with gout, was financially supported by Ursula's brother Octavian Secundus Fugger. The patronage of Augsburg's leading family not only contributed to Neusidler's income; it also may have given him access to the courts of Munich and Innsbruck. The Tyrolean Archduke Ferdinand, however, who had invited Neusidler to Innsbruck as a court musician in 1580, dismissed him from service after only a few months, because the Protestant Neusidler had not observed the strict rules for Lent.[38]

Along with the House of Habsburg and the Bavarian and Palatine branches of the Wittelsbach dynasty, members of the Fugger family were among the largest book collectors in central Europe in the sixteenth century. Holdings from the Fuggers' collections are now among the treasured possessions of the Bavarian State Library in Munich, the Austrian National Library in Vienna, and the Vatican Library in Rome. In the terminology of the French sociologist Pierre Bourdieu, the collecting of books and manuscripts can be conceived as the transformation of economic into social and cultural capital. The Fugger libraries were investments in education and learning; they represented the progressive turn of the family, which had become wealthy in commerce, toward learned and literary interests; and they helped to prepare coming generations for careers at princely courts, as well as in municipal and territorial administrations.[39]

No significant book collections are documented for the generation of the brothers Ulrich, Georg, and Jakob Fugger at the beginning of the family's economic rise. Ulrich Fugger's donation of a number of books to Augsburg's Dominican convent in 1509 and the translation of a treatise on eastern European peoples that the theologian Johannes Eck dedicated to Jakob Fugger in 1518 are relatively isolated instances of their support of education and learning.[40] In the generation that followed, the references to bibliophile activities and the patronage of learning become more numerous. Raymund Fugger was apparently the first family member to assemble an important library, one that formed the basis for the much more voluminous collections of his sons. Moreover, he supported the printing of a large work on inscriptions compiled by the humanists Petrus Apianus and Bartholomäus Amantius in 1534. Around 1530, Anton Fugger unsuccessfully tried to lure the great humanist Erasmus of Rotterdam to Augsburg. Although neither gifts nor flattery could entice Erasmus to move from Freiburg in the Breisgau to Augsburg, the great merchant's efforts at least found an echo in the dedicatory epistle to the translation of Xenophon that Erasmus published in Basel in 1533.[41] Works by the humanists Johannes Cochlaeus and Georg von Logau were likewise printed with dedicatory epistles to Anton Fugger. In the 1550s, Fugger financed the publication of Byzantine manuscripts edited by the humanist Hieronymus Wolf and printed by Johannes Oporinus of Basel. Some of the manuscripts had been purchased by the senior Fugger employee Hans Dernschwam in Constantinople.[42]

The "heyday of the Fugger book collections" (in the words of Paul Lehmann), however, came with Anton Fugger's nephews Hans Jakob, Ulrich, and Georg. After 1535, Hans Jakob Fugger systematically expanded the collection he had inherited from his father, Raymund. Dedications by Thomas Naogeorgius in 1538, Hieronymus Ziegler in 1542, Sixtus Betuleius (Sixt Birck) in 1544, Conrad Gesner in 1546 and 1556, Wolfgang Musculus in 1549, and other scholars testify to his role as a patron of classical scholars, theologians, and natural scientists. Hans Jakob Fugger also financed the university education of Lorenz Gryll, who later became a professor of medicine in Ingolstadt, and the Augsburg jurist Hieronymus Fröschel. His collecting activities took on a new dimension after the humanist Hieronymus Wolf was hired as the family's librarian in 1551. Wolf filled this post until he became rector of the Augsburg grammar school (*Gymnasium*) of St. Anna in 1557. His tenure coincided with the purchase of the library of the Nuremberg physicians Hermann and Hartmann Schedel, which was famous at the time for its numerous manuscripts and early prints, in 1552. Wolf also placed regular book orders from Italy, especially Venice, which was then the most important market for Greek and Hebrew manuscripts and prints in Europe. There the German-born merchant David Ott; Nicolaus Stoppius, who hailed from Flanders; and Jacopo Strada from Mantua made purchases for Hans Jakob Fugger and other family members. Apart from acquiring printed works and manuscripts, Hieronymus Wolf and Hans Jakob Fugger commissioned numerous copies of Greek and Hebrew manuscripts, which were executed by Greeks and Jews who had fled to Venice because of the Ottoman expansion in the eastern Mediterranean. Greek and Jewish copyists also worked for the Fuggers in Augsburg. During the early 1560s, the librarian of the Vatican, Onophrio Panvinio, likewise helped Hans Jakob Fugger with the acquisition of books. After his move to Munich, Fugger gave numerous works of art and antiquities from his collection to his employer and patron Duke Albrecht V of Bavaria. In 1571, the entire library, which comprised about 12,000 volumes, became the property of the Bavarian dukes, who had commissioned a new library building shortly before. This collection formed the basis of the present Bavarian State Library.[43]

As a bibliophile and patron, Ulrich Fugger was completely equal to his brother Hans Jakob. Sickly since his childhood and a lifelong bachelor, Ulrich was considered an eccentric who could not be usefully employed in the trading company. He was also relatively isolated within his own family after his conversion to Protestantism. One of his friends, the physician Achilles Pirmin Gasser, characterized him as a *homo generosus et singularis melancholicus*. Like his brother Hans Jakob, Ulrich assembled a large collection of Greek and Hebrew manuscripts and printed works, which is exceptionally well documented through several contemporary library catalogues. By 1555, he owned 250 Greek codices. In contrast to Hans Jakob, however, he also purchased numerous Reformation treatises and works on theological controversies and was interested in medieval German literature and popular texts—satires, defamatory writings, pamphlets, and horoscopes. A unique aspect of Ulrich Fugger's activities is his patronage of the Parisian printer Henri Etienne (or Henricus Stephanus), who is referred to as *Typographus illustris viri Huldrichi Fugger* from 1558 onward and received a yearly rent from his patron along with gifts and loans. With Fugger's support, Etienne published at least twenty-one Latin and Greek editions between 1558 and 1568. The Scottish scholar Henricus Scrimger and the Protestant theologian and historian Mathias Flacius Illyricus also acquired numerous manuscripts and printed works for him. When Ulrich Fugger fled Augsburg in 1567 because of his high private debts and moved to the court of the Palatine Elector Friedrich III, he also arranged for the transfer of his library to Heidelberg. Despite his financial difficulties, he was still able to expand the library there by adding the collection of his friend Achilles Pirmin Gasser, who had died in 1577. When the treasures of the court library were transported to Rome after the occupation of Heidelberg by troops of the Catholic League during the Thirty Years' War in 1622–23, Ulrich Fugger's collection of books and manuscripts also became part of the Bibliotheca Vaticana.[44]

The library assembled by Georg Fugger does not match the wealth of Greek and Hebrew texts in the holdings of his brothers Ulrich and Hans Jakob but put the main emphasis on mathematical, astronomical, astrological, and other scientific works. With the collection of Johann Schöner, he was able to acquire an important scholar's library from Nuremberg; the Bohemian astronomer and astrologer Cyprianus Leovitius also sent him numerous works. A clause in Georg Fugger's will of 1563 demonstrates the importance of this library to its owner. Georg provided that his library remain undivided in the care of his eldest son but might be used by the younger brothers. From this eldest son it was to be passed on within the male lineage. Georg Fugger's firstborn, Philipp Eduard, not only adhered faithfully to his father's will but further enlarged the library with his own purchases. Philipp Eduard Fugger's Catholicism is reflected in numerous works by Jesuits and other Counter-Reformation authors, but he also collected in various other genres and fields of knowledge. Philipp Eduard's library, which comprised more than 15,000 volumes, survived the Thirty Years' War and was sold in 1655 to the court library in Vienna for the bargain price of 15,000 florins.[45]

While the libraries of Anton Fugger's sons pale in comparison with those of their cousins, they still have to be included among the great southern German book collections of their time. Anton Fugger's eldest son Marx systematically began to purchase books during his studies at the University of

Leuven in the Netherlands, and he continued his acquisitions and epigraphic studies during a journey to Spain in 1552. His library eventually held more than one thousand volumes, with an emphasis on ancient philosophical and historiographical works, as well as humanist literary, philosophical, and historical writings. In addition, he assembled a numismatic collection and supported humanists such as Guilelmus Xylander and the Augsburg city physician Adolph Occo. With a book on the breeding of horses published in 1578, he also made his mark as an author, and he translated several works on theology and church history. His translation of Cesare Baronio's voluminous ecclesiastical history was printed in 1594–95. According to Georg Lutz, this work communicates a view of history that stresses the continuity of the old church primarily and served the "defense, preservation, and strengthening of tradition" in the interest of Catholic confessionalization.[46]

There is no doubt that the important libraries assembled by family members in the two generations after Anton Fugger indicate a shift away from economic activities and toward learned and literary interests; therefore, they can be interpreted as expressions of a shift in mentalities. It was precisely during the heyday of the Fugger company between 1545 and 1560 that family members invested large sums in book purchases—Ulrich Fugger alone spent 126,000 florins on books from 1546 to 1553[47]—and thus reinvested commercial profits in a form of cultural capital. In this respect, they benefited from the fact that the market situation for Greek and Hebrew manuscripts and printed works was particularly favorable at precisely this time because of the presence of numerous Greek and Jewish refugees in Venice. On closer inspection, it is also evident, however, that the book collections of individual family members not only had different emphases but also served different purposes. His scholarly and literary inclinations notwithstanding, Marx Fugger primarily remained the head of the trading company and held high public office in the city. Hans Jakob Fugger's collections and his reputation as a bibliophile and art expert were important factors in his career at the ducal court in Munich. Ulrich Fugger, who was unfit for the professions of merchant and politician because of his bodily constitution and mental disposition, wholeheartedly and passionately dedicated himself to his learned and bibliophile activities.

THE FUGGERS' *BOOK OF HONORS*

"In honor of the whole Fugger name," Clemens Jäger, an employee of the Augsburg city council, wrote a work on the history of the family during the years 1542 to 1548. At a time when the contract between Anton Fugger and his nephews, which provided for the division of family property, signaled the gradual separation of the various family lineages, the work, which was lavishly decorated with colored miniatures, impressively reaffirmed the idea of family unity. Jäger's history underlined the Fuggers' self-image as a family that had risen from the ranks of the urban bourgeoisie to the landed nobility. Historiography of the kind that Clemens Jäger practiced for the Fuggers— and for other rich Augsburg families in a number of similar works—was not only to document dates and facts but also to help ensure that "the Fuggers' honor remain[ed] in good memory for many years and future times."[48]

A characteristic feature of the Fuggers' *Book of Honors*, which was primarily addressed to the circles of close and more distant relatives, is the correspondence of text and images, which puts it in a kind of intermediary position between ancestral gallery and family history. The text primarily consists of genealogical notes that are supplemented by biographical information on the respective individuals. The relatively copious texts that have been preserved in a draft version, however, were significantly abbreviated in the final version. Therefore, the emphasis shifted to the family's visual representation through a series of half-figure portraits and heraldic coats of arms. Coats of arms and labels documented the family's rise from the weavers' craft via the mercantile profession to the ranks of imperial counts. Although the entire family—including the impoverished Fuggers "vom Reh" branch—was included, Hans Jakob Fugger as the book's "founder" (*Fundator*) attached great importance to his own memory and that of his father, Raymund, as a collector and patron of the arts, which were duly emphasized.[49]

In his detailed analysis of the Fuggers' *Book of Honors*, Gregor Rohmann has shown that both images and texts carried multiple levels of meaning. The attributes, gestures, and facial expressions of the depicted individuals, for example, are renderings of gender-specific assignments of roles. The active postures and sweeping gestures of the male family members contrast with the passive, controlled bearing of the women, which expresses an "ideal female disposition." The figures' fine dress and golden jewelry reflect the Fuggers' social rise.[50] The texts do not deny the family's origins in the weavers' craft but carefully stylize its ascent "as a successive, continuous process," thus making it compatible with prevailing social norms, according to which upward social mobility was acceptable only as a long, gradual process encompassing several generations. This intention also corresponds with the strong emphasis on the Fuggers' commitment to the city's common good and their services to the emperor. From this perspective, it was not his desire for wealth and profit that formed the basis of Jakob Fugger's business success and social advancement but, rather, his piety, humility, modesty, and moderation. The "defensive need for legitimacy" that Rohmann attributes to

FIGURE 15
Raymund Fugger and Katharina Thurzo.
Page from the Fugger family's Book of Honors.
(Bayerische Staatsbibliothek München [Clm 9460, Fol. 74r])

the Fuggers is also reflected in the treatment of the darker spots within the family's history in the *Book of Honors.* Illegitimate children, family scandals, and the nonconformist behavior of individual members are systematically excluded, and the work is completely silent on the importance of women to the family's rise in the fifteenth century.[51]

Although the *Book of Honors* is an outstanding example of the construction of family tradition, it is not the only one of its kind in the house of Fugger. The indefatigable Clemens Jäger also wrote a "Fugger Chronicle" that has not yet been analyzed in detail or critically edited. Almost half a century after their uncle Hans Jakob, Philipp Eduard and Octavian Secundus Fugger commissioned the copper engraver Dominicus Custos to execute a series of family portraits in 1592. This gallery of family engravings was later updated by Wolfgang and Lukas Kilian and published by the Augsburg printer Andreas Aperger under the title *Fuggerorum et Fuggerarum ... imagines* in 1618. The 120-page ancestral gallery once again demonstrated the family's rise and the high degree of self-confidence that was the result of the Fuggers' material success and their acceptance into the imperial nobility.[52]

7

THE FUGGERS IN SIXTEENTH-CENTURY URBAN SOCIETY

SPECIAL CASE OR ELITE NETWORK?

When Jakob Fugger died in 1525, the Benedictine monk Clemens Sender of Augsburg wrote that his name was "known in all realms and countries, and in the heathen world as well. . . . Emperors, kings, princes, and lords have sent their embassies to him, the pope greeted and received him as his beloved son, the cardinals rose before him: he has been the ornament of all Germany, but especially of the city of Augsburg."[1] But what was the role of this wealthy and prominent family in the political and social life of its native city? In many of the great Italian city republics, the richest and most powerful families brought the governments under their control in the course of the fifteenth century and sixteenth century. The Medici in Florence are only the most prominent example of this process. Did the Fuggers play a comparable role in the imperial city of Augsburg?

According to Olaf Mörke's and Katarina Sieh-Burens's analyses of the Fuggers' role within the city's social hierarchy and the political careers of family members, the answer to this question is decidedly negative. The brothers Ulrich, Georg, and Jakob Fugger were members of the respected merchants' guild, and by virtue of their marriages to women from the Lauginger, Imhof, and Artzt families, they also had access to the Gentlemen's Drinking Hall (*Herrentrinkstube*), the exclusive meeting place of the patricians and related families. In contrast to the Welser, Herwart, and Langenmantel families, however, they were not part of the patriciate, the highest prestige group within the imperial city, which had been largely closed since 1368. Only when the patriciate, which had shrunk to merely seven families, was expanded in 1538 were the Fuggers accepted into its ranks, along with thirty-eight other families. Other than the old patrician families, moreover, the Fuggers did not play a prominent role in the city council and its most important offices during the period of their economic rise. Whereas members of the Welser family accumulated a total of 131 years; the Langenmantels, a total of 317 years; and the Rehlingers, a total of 355 years of office holding between 1520 and 1548, the five Fuggers who held seats on the city council during this period held office for a combined total of only thirty-five years. Even more remarkable, Jakob Fugger and his nephew Anton, the heads of the family trading company, only sat on the Grand Council, which had little political influence. They were represented neither in the forty-two–member Small Council nor in the Committee of Thirteen, the real center of urban power. As "adjunct" to the Small Council during the brief period from 1523 to 1525, Jakob Fugger was not a member of the body with full rights. In these years, only Anton Fugger's nephew Hans Jakob sat on the Small Council from 1542 to 1546. It was only after Emperor Charles V had imposed a new patrician constitution on the imperial city in 1548 that members of the Fugger family acceded to the highest urban offices. According to Mörke, the Fuggers had "no place" under the old guild regime, "Perhaps because they were barred from it, but more likely because they did not seek it to begin with." At the same time, however, their contemporaries and fellow citizens closely watched the Fuggers' activities within the city. In the imperial city chronicles, they are mentioned much more frequently than other families of the Augsburg elite. Time and again, the chroniclers picked out their ostentatious displays of wealth and their close relationships with the emperor, princes, and the Roman curia. For Mörke, the Fuggers' political restraint and their contemporaries' assessments of them are indicators of their detachment from the "traditional urban value system." Within the imperial city's social fabric, the family thus constituted a "special structure (*Sonderstruktur*)."[2]

Sieh-Burens has added two important modifications to Mörke's portrait. On the one hand, her examination of the highest public officials demonstrates that the imperial city's political elite was made up of several family groups, or "networks," that competed and cooperated with one another. Each of these networks coalesced around a particularly influential family. The extensive "Welser network" primarily recruited its members from the ranks of the rich patricians and great merchants while remaining open to social climbers and including Catholics, as well as Protestants. The smaller "Fugger network," by contrast, was characterized by strict adherence to the Catholic faith and the "formation of a small, elitist cluster of persons" with strong ties to the landed nobility. The Protestant "Herbrot network" was made up of "flexible, venturesome social climbers from the guilds," whereas the "Seitz network" consisted of "well-respected members of the middling artisans'

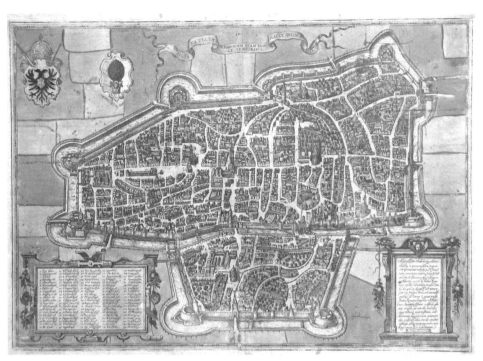

FIGURE 16

Plan of the city of Augsburg, from Braun and Hogenberg,
Civitates orbis terrarium, *Cologne, 1572.*
(Staats- und Stadtbibliothek Augsburg)

ranks."[3] In addition, Sieh-Burens points out how the positions of these four networks within the city's political elite shifted in the course of the sixteenth century. While the bi-confessional Welser network continued to play an important role throughout the century, the Herbrot network attained significance only during the Reformation years, and the Catholic Fugger network became significant only after the abolition of the guild regime in 1548.[4]

In this context, the most important aspects with which an account of the Fuggers' role in urban society has to deal are their responses to issues of church reform and the Reformation; their position as a rich Catholic family in a city with a Catholic minority and a Protestant majority after 1548; their role in important political events such as the War of the Schmalkaldic League of 1546–47 and the conflict about the introduction of the new papal calendar and the right to appoint preachers in the 1580s; and, finally, the ways in which they were perceived by contemporaries.

From the end of the fifteenth century onward, the Fuggers' economic rise, their close relationships with the emperor and the papal curia, their wealth, and their patronage drew increasing attention in their native city. The chronicles of urban citizens and clerics mentioned earlier are important sources for the perception of the Fuggers within the imperial city. In the early sixteenth century, the monk Clemens Sender and the merchant Wilhelm Rem were particularly astute observers of contemporary events. Regarding the Fuggers, however, neither of these two chroniclers can be considered a non-partisan reporter: Sender, who viewed the Fuggers as benefactors of the church and faithful servants to the emperor, was full of praise and admiration, whereas Rem, who was married to one of Ulrich Fugger's daughters, had few kind things to say about his relatives by marriage. It is precisely in their partisanship and one-sidedness, though, that the two chronicles reveal different facets of the assessment of the Fuggers by other inhabitants of Augsburg.[5]

For Sender, the Fuggers' foundations and festivals, as well as their cordial relationships with church and emperor, were a pillar of the city's welfare. When Cardinal Bernardino Carvajal, the papal legate, passed through Augsburg in 1507 and celebrated Holy Mass in the cathedral, Jakob Fugger subsequently invited him and his entourage to a festive dinner followed by a dance. On this occasion, Carvajal dispensed "mercy and indulgence" to all those present.[6] In his obituary for Jakob Fugger, quoted briefly at the beginning of the chapter, Sender praised the character traits of the deceased—hospitality, charity toward the poor, reasonableness, fairness, virtue, and honor— as well as his achievements as a merchant, banker, founder, and patron and mentioned the honors that the emperor and princes had conferred on him. Sender also had only good things to say about Jakob Fugger's role in Augsburg society: Despite his wealth, he had lived "entirely without ostentation" and spent a large portion of his fortune on charitable foundations. Finally, Sender emphasized the compatibility of the Fuggers' business activities with the common good: "Their great trade in commercial goods, harming nobody but promoting the common good and support of the poor, has encompassed the entire globe to the praise of all."[7]

Rem could not agree with this kind of praise. When he wrote about the Fuggers, he nearly always did so with critical detachment. Among the remarkable events of 1497, Rem recorded the wedding of Georg Thurzo and Ulrich Fugger's daughter Anna. At the wedding, the bride was led to church "in a gown and bare-headed with tied-up braids, according to noble custom." Something like this had never happened in Augsburg before, as brides there had always worn a coat over their gown and a large brown veil. After the Fuggers and Thurzos created a precedent, however, "Sundry other burghers and merchants also took it up, and thus it became customary for the first time." With their great wealth and lavish displays, therefore, the Fuggers initiated a change in social norms and introduced "noble customs" into urban society.[8] Rem's subsequent entries on the Fuggers return to this theme. The wedding of Ulrich Fugger the Younger and Veronika Gassner appeared "strange" to the chronicler, considering both the high cost and the fact that the two families had earlier "been averse to one another" and "spoke ill of each other." Lukas Gassner had given his daughter the unheard-of sum of 12,000 florins as a dowry, while Fugger spent 13,000 florins on his marriage portion. Moreover, the bridegroom had given the bride clothing and jewelry worth 3,000 florins as a gift and spent the same amount on gifts to "other relatives and servants": "silk clothing, and velvet, and sateen, and other sorts of clothes." Including the costs of the celebration, Ulrich Fugger allegedly spent 7,000 florins. For Rem, this "overweening pride" clearly exceeded the limits that weddings within the bourgeois elite had observed so far.[9]

In his view, the same criticism applied to the Fuggers' foundations. When the Fugger chapel at St. Anna was completed in 1517, Rem noted that it had "cost a lot of money," and some people estimated the costs at 30,000 florins. A "good workman" doubted this estimate, however, and put the cost at no more than 8,000 florins; the workman himself would have been able to build it for 6,000 florins. The Fuggers' expenses on self-display and self-commemoration therefore were a subject of lively public debate. The same year also saw the completion of the new convent church of St. Katharina. The nun Felicitas Fugger, a daughter of Ulrich Fugger, had contributed 1,000 florins to meet the building expenses but demanded that her coat of arms be affixed to the vault of the new choir in return. This reportedly gave the other nuns cause to regret that they had not paid for the church in full, "For many years from now people might think that the same Fugger woman had had the whole church built at her expense." For Rem, both incidents illustrated a basic principle of the Fuggers' self-advertisement: Even though the expenditures were high, the public effect was even greater.[10]

Emperor Maximilian's visit to Augsburg in 1518, the celebrations of the election of Charles V in 1519, and Archduke Ferdinand's visit in 1521 served as additional examples with which Rem could illustrate the changing norms in the imperial city, with special emphasis on the Fugger family. At a dance in Augsburg's dance house, the emperor asked the young burgher women to remove the large veils that covered almost the entire face. "Thus," Rem reports, "the Fugger and Adler people began to wear little veils like the noble women." Along with the women of Philipp Adler's household, therefore, it was the female members of the Fugger family who once again appeared to lead the way in introducing new noble customs. When the news of Charles V's election reached Augsburg, Jakob Villinger, Jakob Fugger, and Ambrosius Höchstetter allegedly wanted to celebrate the event by shooting fireworks in front of their houses on the Weinmarkt. Until this point, however, it had "not been the custom that burghers should make bonfires in the city; the city had never made bonfires before." The council intervened against this attempted self-display by wealthy citizens and organized the fireworks on its own. When Archduke Ferdinand came to Augsburg on a visit in May 1521, Jakob Fugger once again seized the occasion to vaunt himself, inviting Ferdinand, Duke Wilhelm of Bavaria, and Cardinal Matthäus Lang to his house and treating them to twenty different dishes, including no fewer than eight courses of fish.[11]

Both Sender and Rem closely adhered to the fundamental norms and values of late medieval and early modern society: civic unity as the basis of social life; the common good as the goal of political and economic behavior; and honor as the yardstick of the city's and its inhabitants' reputation.[12] Whereas Sender viewed the Fuggers as great promoters of the honor and common good of the city, the empire, and other European monarchies, Rem considered their behavior incompatible with these very norms. Where Sender saw virtue, honor, and Christian charity, Rem perceived only vanity, wastefulness, self-interest, and the decay of good old urban traditions.

The Fuggers were not only an object of their contemporaries' admiration and criticism, however. They also took an active part in the debates that agitated the urban public in the years preceding the Reformation. This applies particularly to Jakob Fugger's role in the disputes between the clerics of the collegiate chapter and the parish congregation within the Augsburg church of St. Moritz and his intervention in the debate about the canonical prohibition of interest. In the parish of St. Moritz, a lengthy dispute was simmering between the clerics of the collegiate chapter, who lived off their benefices, and the lay administrators of the parish (*Zechpfleger*), who demanded improvements in preaching and pastoral care on behalf of the congregation. The conflict reached a climax in 1511 when the congregation hired its own sexton without the chapter's consent and refused to pay its dues to the chapter for several months. In this dispute, which was typical for many imperial cities before the Reformation, Jakob Fugger was one of the representatives of the congregation who participated in negotiations with the chapter. The great merchant took the side of the reform-oriented members of the congregation. A contract that allowed both sides to hire their own sextons initially settled the dispute, but the issue of pastoral care contained the seeds of

Ecclefia Collegiata S.Mauritij, cum foro. S. Moritzen Kirchen und Blaz.

Simon Grimm delineavit.

FIGURE 17

Church of St. Moritz in Augsburg, view from the west. Copper engraving by Simon Grimm, 1687.

(Staats- und Stadtbibliothek Augsburg)

further conflict. Dissatisfied with how the pastor, who had been appointed by the chapter, exercised his office, the parish congregation eventually obtained the right to call and pay its own preacher. It conferred this office on the learned theologian Dr. Johannes Speiser.[13]

As the settlement was limited to four years and the chapter barred Speiser from preaching after its expiration, the conflict flared up again in 1515. Jakob Fugger now decided to donate 1,000 florins toward the establishment of a preachership (preacher's position) and approach the papal curia, with whom he cultivated excellent relations through his Roman office, to obtain a papal bull that would give him and his heirs the *ius patronatus,* or the right to appoint the preacher. The preachership was to be tied to a canon's benefice from which the incumbent would receive a large part of his income. On the surface, Jakob Fugger's 1,000 florins served to supplement his income; in fact, however, they were mainly intended as a kind of emergency insurance to provide for the continuous spiritual welfare of the parish in case an incumbent became unable to carry out his duties. Although it was not Jakob Fugger but the parish community that originally raised the sum, Fugger's involvement was still decisive for the establishment of the preachership, for only he could overcome the chapter's resistance, thanks to his cordial relations with the emperor and the curia. In January 1517, Pope Leo X issued the desired bull. The collegiate chapter still tried to prevent the calling of a preacher, however, and both sides cultivated influential allies. While the chapter brought the bishop of Augsburg and the dukes of Bavaria into the affair, Jakob Fugger activated his connections to the emperor. As Johannes Speiser had meanwhile been accepted into the chapter and refused to take up the preacher's position once again, Fugger temporarily favored his trusted adviser Johannes Eck, who later became famous as an opponent of Martin Luther, as candidate for the preachership. After Jakob Fugger had successfully prevented Speiser's appointment as suffragan bishop of Constance, Speiser finally gave up his resistance and in September 1518 took up the preacher's position, which was now also tied to the office of parish pastor. Thus, the great merchant had "pushed through his quest for authority over the chapter by all possible means" His success in this lengthy conflict had cost him nearly 2,000 florins.[14]

Apart from this involvement in an affair that touched on the relationship between the city and the church, Jakob Fugger tried to influence public opinion in a matter that was of considerable relevance to the large Augsburg merchant companies: the debate about the canonical prohibition of taking interest. Although it had long been common practice to lend money at interest in public and private credit transactions, it was still prohibited in canon law, and church reformers demanded that the prohibition be applied more strictly. Therefore, it was important for Jakob Fugger and other large merchants to obtain the church's official approval of an interest rate of 5 percent. It is highly likely that Fugger's influence stood behind a pro-interest memorandum by the jurist Sebastian Ilsung, a man who came from a patrician family of Augsburg and was in the service of Bavaria, in 1513. Fugger also commissioned a memorandum on the question of interest from the theologian Johannes Eck of Ingolstadt, who had indicated that he basically accepted the termination of the prohibition on interest in a lecture on economic ethics and who had participated in a disputation in Augsburg's Carmelite convent in 1514. In a *consilium* written in September 1514, Eck argued that loan contracts at 5 percent interest were justified. He insisted, "One should always assume good intentions among participants in business and not the damnable intent of usury, unless the latter could be positively proven." Eck intended to defend his arguments in a public disputation at the University of Ingolstadt, but the plan foundered when the bishop of

Eichstätt, Gabriel von Eyb, refused his permission. Eck then sent his tract on interest to several universities, which mostly remained reluctant, and finally defended his theses in a disputation with Johannes Faber, the prior of Augsburg's Dominican convent, an event that took place in Bologna in July 1515. Jakob Fugger financed the journey of Eck and his companions to Bologna, and a debate about the same issue at the University of Tübingen was initiated by Dr. Gregor Lamparter, chancellor of the Duchy of Württemberg and husband of Mechthild Belz, an illegitimate daughter of Jakob Fugger. While the jurists Sebastian Ilsung and Conrad Peutinger, who had close ties to the Augsburg elite, were the preeminent supporters of Eck's position, his theses were unequivocally rejected by the Nuremberg humanists Christoph Scheurl, Willibald Pirckheimer, and Johannes Cochlaeus; the Freiburg jurist Ulrich Zasius; and the Augsburg cathedral canon Bernhard Adelmann of Adelmannsfelden. It is primarily due to the critiques and lampoons by his opponents that Eck's reputation as a corrupt mouthpiece for the great merchant companies has found its way even into modern scholarly accounts. Although the debate on interest did not alter the church's official position, the practice of taking interest continued to be tacitly tolerated. For the merchant companies, therefore, nothing changed.[15]

THE FUGGERS AND THE EVANGELICAL MOVEMENT
IN THE ERA OF THE PROTESTANT REFORMATION

After the theses against indulgences of the Augustinian friar Martin Luther of Wittenberg were published in October 1517, his teachings spread throughout the Holy Roman Empire via the correspondence networks of humanists and church reformers, but primarily via the medium of printing. Augsburg's printers contributed substantially to the popularization of Luther's ideas, and his appearance in Augsburg in 1518, where he submitted himself to an interrogation by Cardinal Legate Cajetan in the Fugger palace after the termination of the imperial Diet, added to his popularity within the city. By the early 1520s, the evangelical movement had gained a foothold in Augsburg. Evangelical sermons took place in several of the city's churches, and the first priest married in 1523. The evangelical preachers' following grew especially rapidly among urban craftsmen.[16] Luther himself did not hesitate to criticize the large trading companies in his reform pamphlets and writings on economic ethics, and in the tract *To the Christian Nobility of the German Nation*, published in 1520, he urged authorities to put "a bridle into the mouth of the Fuggers and similar companies." For Luther, the large firms' conduct of business was incompatible with the principles of justice and the common good, and in his view, their high profits could not have been earned honestly.

The humanist Ulrich von Hutten, a supporter of Luther, sharply attacked the Fuggers' business practices and their connections with the Roman curia in several of his writings.[17]

Meanwhile, Jakob Fugger had taken his stand early against the new teaching. In a piece of scholarly detective work, Götz-Rüdiger Tewes has reconstructed the connections between Fugger's company, the Roman curia, and early opponents of Luther at the University of Cologne and in ducal Saxony. The central nodes within this "imposing, closely knit network" of the reformer's opponents, which was "capable of integrating powerful forces and continued to operate into the Reformation period," were Johannes Eck and the theologian Michael Schwab of Cologne, a native of Augsburg whose family had long cultivated close ties to the Fuggers. Schwab used the correspondence network of the Fugger trading posts to expedite his letters, which coordinated the activities of Luther's opponents in Cologne, Augsburg, Leipzig, and Rome.[18]

The chroniclers Clemens Sender and Wilhelm Rem demonstrate that people in Augsburg were well aware of Fugger's position. Sender wrote that Fugger had "been a good, true, faithful Christian and totally opposed to Lutheranism." Rem linked Fugger's position on the reformer to his business interests. In his view, Luther had pointed out how "the pope had begun to turn his powers into cash, selling them to the Fuggers of Augsburg, so that they now grant, exchange, and sell bishoprics and fiefs, and carry on a trade in ecclesiastical properties." Fugger did not like this at all, and when the city council issued a decree against the pro-Reformation writings, it was said that "Fugger brought it about." It was in fact Jakob Fugger and the city recorder, Dr. Conrad Peutinger, who communicated the council's decision to suppress the printing of controversial religious writings to Augsburg's printers in 1520. During a civic uprising in 1524, which had been prompted by the impending expulsion of the reform-minded Franciscan preacher Johannes Schilling, Jakob Fugger temporarily left the city and retreated to his manorial estate of Biberbach for his own safety.[19] Moreover, Fugger obtained an imperial letter of protection that explicitly exempted him and his family from the application of the imperial Edict of Worms against Luther and his adherents, and he gave financial support to the Swabian League when it suppressed the Peasants' War. In a letter to Duke Georg of Saxony, Fugger accused Martin Luther of being "the initiator and primary cause of this uprising, rebellion, and bloodshed in the German nation."[20] Confronted with the progress of the Reformation in Augsburg and the dissolution of the Carmelite convent of St. Anna, Jakob Fugger's second will, which he dictated on his deathbed in

1525, also foresaw the possibility that St. Anna might be permanently lost to the old church. Although he provided for his burial in the family chapel that he had built at such great expense, he left to his heirs the option of celebrating the liturgical memory of the deceased in another church. Indeed, the Holy Masses and anniversaries for which Jakob Fugger had made provisions were never celebrated in St. Anna. Moreover, the visual program and decoration of the Fugger chapel were apparently not finished according to the original plan.[21]

While more and more members of the patrician and mercantile elite joined the evangelical movement, Jakob Fugger's nephews remained faithful to the old church. According to contemporary accounts, Raymund Fugger publicly provoked the evangelical inhabitants of the city with derogatory remarks—"He shit on the gospels"—as early as 1523 without being punished by the council. In general, a large part of the Fugger network rejected the Reformation.[22] This religious antagonism underlay a series of conflicts between the Fuggers and other members of Augsburg's elite that occurred during the following years. The remarriage of Jakob Fugger's widow, Sibylla, only seven weeks after her husband's death created a sensation in Augsburg. Although her second husband, Konrad Rehlinger, was a highly respected long-distance merchant and patrician city councilor, the rapid remarriage fed rumors that Rehlinger had "secretly courted the Fugger woman." Clemens Sender even claimed that the couple had been "found in each other's company" after Jakob Fugger's death. In fact, Rehlinger had been a trusted friend and close business partner of the deceased who also officiated as administrator of the Fuggerei foundation. As Jakob Fugger had left a generous legacy to his wife and allowed her to reside in one of his houses in his will but had made these provisions only for the term of her widowhood, the remarriage triggered a dispute over Sibylla Fugger's dowry and inheritance. According to Sender, Rehlinger—whom he characterized as "a little old man" with eight children—had prompted the widow to move into his house silently, with all her dowry and inherited property, and marry him "after Lutheran fashion." Another chronicle of Augsburg reports, however, that Jakob Fugger's nephews had ordered the widow and her second husband to be driven out of her deceased husband's house "violently and with armed force," and that Sibylla Fugger had lost part of her property in the incident. The dispute was finally settled in July 1526 with a contract in which Jakob Fugger's nephews promised 20,000 florins to the widow and an "adequate gift" to her new husband, while Rehlinger relinquished any claims to the Fugger houses. Ill feeling lingered between the two parties for a long time, however, as one can see from Sibylla's will, which does not say a word about her first husband, Jakob Fugger, and from the Fugger *Book of Honors,* which remains silent on Sibylla's marriage to Rehlinger.[23]

The rift between the Fuggers and the evangelical part of Augsburg's citizenry deepened in the late 1520s when Anton Fugger, in his capacity as lord of the manor of the Swabian territory of Weißenhorn, assented to the execution of the Augsburg patrician Eitelhans Langenmantel. Langenmantel had been banished from the city after he had joined the Anabaptist movement, which was feared by both adherents of the old church and most evangelicals, and he had later been seized in a village near Augsburg along with a manservant and a maidservant and taken to Weißenhorn. The Fugger-friendly monk Clemens Sender reported that Langenmantel had earlier renounced Anabaptism and that leaders of Augsburg's city council had sent a messenger to Weißenhorn, allegedly to find out "in what faith Langenmantel wanted to die," but more likely to prevent the execution.[24]

A dispute between Matthäus Ehem, a leading representative of the evangelical party in Augsburg who was lord of the manor in the Swabian village of Langenneufnach, and the neighboring territorial lord Raymund Fugger in 1529 caused quite a stir and convinced many members of the elite that the Fuggers were exceeding the limits of their authority. Ehem had ordered the seizure of a Langenneufnach peasant who had attacked another villager with an ax. As the peasant was farming a piece of land that belonged to Raymund Fugger, however, Fugger entered Langenneufnach with his entourage, liberated the peasant, and arrested the village bailiff and took him to his own territory of Mickhausen as a prisoner. In the eyes of critical observers, Fugger mainly hoped to demonstrate "his great power" and intimidate the lords of neighboring territories to underscore his own claims to authority over the village. Augsburg's city council responded by ordering Raymund Fugger's arrest and only released him upon the intercession of the emperor and the duke of Bavaria. Seventeen years later, Matthäus Ehem sold Langenneufnach to the Fuggers.[25]

As the Protestant Reformation progressed in the imperial city, the Fuggers' foundation of a preachership in the church of St. Moritz became an object of contention between the patrons, who adhered to the old church, and the evangelical majority of the parish congregation. Johannes Speiser, whose appointment as preacher Jakob Fugger and the congregation had pushed through against the prolonged opposition of the collegiate chapter, was now one of the first clerics in Augsburg to spread evangelical doctrines in the early 1520s. In 1522, the bishop of Augsburg demanded that Speiser be handed over to him, but the city council refused to do so and took the two evangelical preachers Speiser and Johann Frosch under its explicit protection the following year. Speiser's abrupt turnabout in 1524, when he reaffirmed his allegiance to the old church, may be ascribed at least partly to the pressure that his patron Jakob Fugger exerted on him. Because the parish congregation now turned against him with this sudden change of mind, Speiser shortly afterward defied Jakob Fugger's will and gave up his preaching position. In 1525, he left Augsburg and moved to Leipheim. Jakob Fugger then pushed through Ottmar Nachtigall, a clergyman with a humanist education, as Speiser's successor. The fact that Nachtigall served as Jakob Fugger's confessor and testamentary witness indicates that close bonds of trust tied him to his patron. Although some of his religious beliefs were close to evangelical doctrine, in political matters he was considered a representative of the old church. In the long run, however, Nachtigall proved unable to straddle the divide between the adherents of the old church and the evangelical party. After he voiced sharp criticism of evangelical positions in a sermon in September 1528, the Augsburg council put him under house arrest and barred him from preaching. This finally obliged Anton, Raymund, and Hieronymus Fugger to consent to his dismissal, a move that he had already requested. Subsequently, the rift between the Catholic minority and the evangelical majority was temporarily patched up by appointing two preachers to the position.[26]

The latent conflict between the patrons and the congregation erupted openly on Ascension Day of 1533, and once again it was a member of the Ehem family who emerged as the Fuggers' primary opponent. Marx Ehem, the lay administrator of St. Moritz parish and a devout Zwinglian, had begun to restrict the celebration of Catholic mass and other religious rites and to remove images and sculpture from the church. Among other things, he had ordered a figure of Christ, a statue that traditionally had been ceremoniously hoisted up into the church vault with a winch to celebrate and commemorate the ascension of Christ, to be locked away. Anton Fugger, however, had secretly commissioned a new Christ figure, and on the appointed day, Anton and Raymund Fugger went to the church along with relatives, servants, and fellow believers to carry out the rite of ascension in accordance with traditional custom. According to the chronicler Jörg Breu, this demonstration of old-church piety was "obnoxious to the whole council and the city community." When Marx Ehem appeared in church with adherents of the evangelical party, mutual threats and recriminations ensued. After the Fuggers and their entourage had left the church, Ehem ordered the Christ figure to be hurled down, and it smashed on the church floor. The matter did not end with this dramatic confrontation of the two religious parties. Anton Fugger was summoned before the council and sentenced to eight days in one of the city towers for disobeying the city government. Although this punishment was later reduced—Fugger eventually had to spend one night in the tower and discharged the remaining sentence in cash—it marked a rift in the relations between the Fuggers and the city. Anton Fugger, who apparently considered the punishment a severe insult to his honor, removed to his territory of Weißenhorn, where he mainly resided until 1536. By going into exile, he intended to "do great harm" to the community that had taken a stand against him, as Breu put it. In Weißenhorn he "wanted to wait until another God came"—that is, until Catholicism was restored in the city.[27]

Anton Fugger's departure from Augsburg was not merely a personal act of revenge, though, for it also coincided with a decisive moment in the imperial city's ecclesiastical policy. Until the late 1520s, the Augsburg city council had pursued a "middle course" in matters of church doctrine, a moderate policy conceived by the influential city recorder Dr. Conrad Peutinger. In the interest of the city's internal peace, this policy was characterized by a general openness toward the innovations associated with the Protestant Reformation, as well as tolerance for the minority who adhered to the old faith. Because of the religious split within Augsburg's elite, the city's close ties to the emperor, and its proximity to influential Catholic princes—the duke of Bavaria and the bishop of Augsburg—this course of compromise initially appeared more than reasonable. From 1529–30 on, however, such a middle course increasingly threatened to lead Augsburg into political isolation. By accepting the final decisions of the imperial Diet of Speyer in 1529 and by refusing to sign the Augsburg Confession, the city became estranged from the Protestant camp, even though it offended the Catholic party by tolerating Protestant innovations and refusing to accept the final decrees of the imperial Diet of 1530. Faced with this situation, the evangelical preachers, whose ranks were reinforced from Protestant Strasbourg, agitated in the early 1530s for an unequivocal decision in favor of the new doctrine. Prompted by a petition of the preachers in January 1533, the Augsburg council set up a committee to deliberate the city's future religious policy. Based on several legal memorandums, the Grand Council, which had been summoned for a special session on this occasion, decided to introduce the Reformation in July 1534. Preaching was hitherto reserved for preachers called by the city council, and Catholic services were to be confined to eight selected churches. Two years later, Augsburg joined the Schmalkaldic League, and in January 1537, the Reformation was completed: All Catholic clerics were now dismissed; mass was prohibited; the remaining monasteries were dissolved; and church property that was not directly controlled by the bishop was taken over by the council. Clergy who refused to become citizens had to leave the city. By passing a church ordinance as well as a moral and police ordinance, regulating religious festivals and holidays, and establishing a marriage court and a censorship office, the city council demonstrated unequivocally that the church within the city was now subject to its authority. Augsburg had officially become a Protestant city.[28]

For the religious practices of Catholic families such as the Fuggers, the religious changes of the years from 1534 to 1537 signified a sharp break. The Carmelite church of St. Anna, where the family's burial chapel was located, remained closed between 1534 and 1548. Although Raymund and Hieronymus Fugger were buried there in 1535 and 1538, respectively, upon their own wish, the burials had to take place silently, and the actual mourning services were held in Weißenhorn, thirty miles west of Augsburg.[29] Moreover, the Fugger network was largely ousted from political office. Still, the bridges between the city and its richest family were not completely destroyed even during these years. Augsburg concluded a new tax agreement with Anton, Raymund, and Hieronymus Fugger in 1535.[30] When Raymund Fugger died on his manorial estate of Mickhausen in the same year, even a dedicated Protestant like the painter Jörg Breu acknowledged him as a generous and virtuous man who had always treated craftsmen well and paid them punctually—something that did not seem to be the norm with Protestant merchants and patricians—and a benefactor who took great responsibility for the care of the poor and the sick.[31] In addition, the Fuggers retained close business contacts with leading evangelical politicians, such as the patricians Hans Welser and Georg Herwart and the guild burgomaster Jakob Herbrot, even during the heyday of the Reformation.[32] And even in the Reformation period, Jakob Fugger's most important charitable foundation, the Fuggerei, completely agreed with urban notions of promoting the common good and providing poor relief only to the "truly needy"—that is, the honest resident poor who were willing to work. Therefore, the Fuggerei not only continued to operate according to its founder's will but could even be expanded with the construction of a so-called wood house for treating syphilis patients. In 1548, Anton Fugger provided this "wood house" with foundation capital of 20,000 florins.[33]

Moreover, when the Augsburg patriciate, which had shrunk to seven families, was enlarged with the acceptance of thirty-eight families in 1538, the Fuggers and their trusted adviser Konrad Mair were among the beneficiaries of the measure. The inclusion of leading Catholic families in such a matter of prestige made particular sense with respect to economic policy, for in this way "the politically dominant Protestant elites prevented the possible emigration of important taxpayers and economic players within the Fugger network."[34] The family was once again represented in the Small Council by the theologically open-minded and personally tolerant Hans Jakob Fugger from 1542 on, and between 1543 and 1546, Fugger even belonged to the Committee of Thirteen, the inner circle of leadership, holding the office of receiver. In 1545, the Augsburg city council granted the Fuggers a water pipe from the city well to their houses "in view of . . . [their] manifold services and good deeds to the city community." Although the Fuggers and the families that were close to them in terms of kinship and religious belief continued to be underrepresented among the political elite, the imperial city's leading politicians were apparently careful to retain them.[35] This strategy would pay off during the War of the Schmalkaldic League between the emperor and his Protestant opponents.

THE WAR OF THE SCHMALKALDIC LEAGUE AND THE CONSTITUTIONAL REFORM OF 1548: A TURNING POINT?

When the efforts to reach a compromise between the emperor and the Protestant estates in matters of religious policy failed in the early 1540s, Charles V sought to break the Protestant princes' and cities' resistance by military means. After the Peace of Crépy with France in 1544 gave Charles the necessary military and political freedom of action, the war against the Schmalkaldic League broke out in July 1546. In that conflict, the league's leaders, Elector Johann Friedrich of Saxony and Landgrave Philipp of Hesse, wasted their initial strategic advantage in southern Germany through disunity and indecision, and the emperor, allied with the pope, Duke Wilhelm of Bavaria, and even some Protestant princes, was able to defeat them in the decisive battle at Mühlberg on the Elbe River in 1547. The imperial city of Augsburg, which had entered the war on the side of the Schmalkaldic League, was forced to submit to the emperor as early as January 1547. This submission also signaled the failure of the city's attempts to export the Reformation to the surrounding countryside through the occupation of monasteries and the dispatch of Protestant preachers in hopes of making territorial and political gains.[36]

In spite of the council's orders that all citizens had to participate in the city's defense, several members of the leading families loyal to the emperor left the city when the conflict began. Along with Bartholomäus Welser, his sons-in-law Hieronymus Sailer and Hans Paul Herwart, and Hans Baumgartner, Anton Fugger and his nephew Hans Jakob decided to await the conflict's outcome from a safe distance. Anton Fugger, after trying unsuccessfully to keep the city neutral during a stay in Regensburg as late as June 1546, went with his family to Schwaz in Tyrol, to which the firm's business documents were also transferred. Hans Jakob initially stayed in Regensburg but later moved to Passau. His brothers Georg and Christoph also left Augsburg. For their absence, the Fuggers paid 40,000 florins to the city treasury; in addition, they delivered grain and Tyrolean silver to the city in the summer of 1546. Although the Augsburg city council knew that the Fuggers were supporting the emperor with significant loans during this time, it refrained from confiscating their property, even though Hans Baumgartner's estates were seized. The council also declined repeated demands from the camp of the Schmalkaldic League for a forced loan from the Fuggers. Moreover, leading city politicians such as Jakob Herbrot continued to correspond regularly with Anton Fugger, and the captain of the league's troops, Sebastian Schertlin of Burtenbach, spared the family's estates during his military operations in eastern Swabia. This consideration would pay off when the emperor's side regained the upper hand in southern Germany at the end of 1546. Anton Fugger now urged Jakob Herbrot to negotiate a settlement with the emperor, and when the council finally assented in mid-January 1547, Fugger agreed to lead Augsburg's delegation to the emperor. When the six members of the delegation humbled themselves before the ruler on January 29, 1547, the event also marked "a demonstration of the great merchant's identification with the imperial city," as Sieh-Burens has pointed out. By showering important imperial advisers such as the Duke of Alba and Nicolas Perrenot de Granvelle with gifts, Anton Fugger tried to prevent the city's punishment, and when the emperor demanded a fine of 150,000 florins from Augsburg, the firm helped out with a loan of 80,000 florins. In addition, Anton Fugger paved the way for a negotiated settlement between the imperial city and the bishop of Augsburg, Cardinal Otto Truchsess of Waldburg, by granting a loan to the latter. His actions on behalf of the imperial city may well have been triggered by the same motives that led his Protestant opponents to remain in contact with him: Both sides had an overriding interest in mending broken commercial ties and restoring Augsburg's economic life to normalcy as quickly as possible.[37]

In the wake of his victory over the Protestant estates, Charles V enforced decisive religious and constitutional changes at the "armored Diet" that was held in Augsburg in 1547–48, and these changes were of great significance for the future history of the imperial city and its wealthiest family. To begin with, under pressure from the emperor, the city had to conclude a treaty with the bishop of Augsburg that restored him to his former rights and formed the basis for the return of Catholic clergy to the city and the restitution of the dissolved monasteries and collegiate chapters. In addition, the emperor decreed the introduction of the *Interim* in the Protestant imperial cities and territories, a state of suspense of sorts between old and new doctrines in matters of religious policy. According to the emperor's conception, the *Interim* was to remain the basis of religious practice and congregational services until the Council of Trent, which had begun in 1545, issued its final rulings. These measures had grave consequences for Augsburg's religious development, as Catholicism could now be openly practiced again for the first time since 1537, and Augsburg's Protestant church, which had been strongly inclined toward the teachings of the theologians Martin Bucer of Strasbourg and Huldrych Zwingli of Zurich before, subsequently assumed an increasingly Lutheran character. An important factor shaping this development was the expulsion in 1551 of those preachers who would not accept the *Interim*. The religious dualism of a Catholic minority and a Lutheran majority that now began to take shape received legal sanction with the Religious Peace of Augsburg in 1555. Finally, the emperor ordered the abolition of the guilds and the introduction of patrician council regimes in Augsburg and twenty-six other imperial cities in southern Germany at the beginning of August 1548. On the one hand, these measures, which had also been recommended by the Augsburg patricians Hans Baumgartner and Hans Jakob Fugger, clearly amounted to a punishment of the guilds, which had been essential supporters of the Reformation movement, for their "disobedience" to the emperor and the empire. On the other hand, they also confirmed the consolidation of the city council's supreme authority, which had been under way in the imperial cities for quite some time. After the guilds were disbanded and their representatives ousted from the city governments, the councils, which were now dominated by patricians, ruled the cities as quasi-aristocratic bodies. The imperial city of Nuremberg, which had long been governed by patricians, served as the model for these regime changes.[38]

For the Fuggers, these changes meant that they could fully resume their role as supporters of the old church and patrons of St. Moritz parish. In 1555, they were finally able to fill the preaching position there permanently according to the will of its founder, Jakob Fugger, a matter that had been contentious for so long. But the former Carmelite church of St. Anna remained Protestant after 1548, and in 1555, Jakob Fugger's heirs transferred the liturgical commemoration of their great ancestor to Augsburg's Dominican convent.[39] Furthermore, the transformation of the guild constitution into a patrician city regime meant that the Fuggers, who had become members of this highest social group, could now rise for the first time to the highest urban offices. The emperor appointed Anton Fugger to one of the five seats on the Privy Council, which subsequently formed the top layer of the city's regime along with the two mayors (*Stadtpfleger*). While Anton Fugger gave up this post as early as 1551 and withdrew from urban politics, his nephew Hans Jakob and his brother-in-law Heinrich Rehlinger, who held the office of mayor from 1549 on, became the two most important city politicians of the 1550s. Hans Jakob Fugger was elected burgomaster in 1548, and while this office had lost much of the political importance it had had under the guild constitution, Fugger was able to use it as a springboard for his political career. As early as 1551, he took over his uncle's seat on the Privy Council. "The Fuggers," Sieh-Burens has said, "became the decisive factor supporting the new political system because of their economic power and influence, which extended far beyond the boundaries of the city."[40]

THE FUGGERS IN THE BI-CONFESSIONAL IMPERIAL CITY

After the turbulent period of the Reformation, the War of the Schmalkaldic League, and the abolition of the guild constitution, Augsburg's leadership faced the task of preserving the peace among the religious and social groups within the city while balancing relations with the emperor and Augsburg's powerful Catholic neighbors. In view of his irenic, tolerant position on religious issues, which manifested itself in friendships with Protestant scholars and his cordial relations with the Habsburg and Wittelsbach courts, Hans Jakob Fugger appeared to be the ideal man for these tasks. From his university days, he was personally acquainted with the imperial councilors Georg Sigmund Seld and Johann Ulrich Zasius, as well as Bavaria's Chancellor Wiguleus Hundt, and both the emperor and King Ferdinand demonstrated their esteem for Hans Jakob Fugger by making him their honorary councilor in 1549 and 1551, respectively. The Fuggers' confessional open-mindedness during this period, which manifested itself in several marriage alliances with Protestant noble families, and their simultaneous cultivation of cordial relations with the houses of Habsburg und Wittelsbach, paid off especially during the rebellion of Protestant imperial princes against Emperor Charles V in 1552. Although a guild regime led by the Protestant long-distance merchants Jakob Herbrot and Georg Österreicher temporarily reassumed power in the city, Hans Jakob Fugger characteristically kept his seat on the council and cleverly maneuvered between urban and imperial interests. After the end of the princes' rebellion, he successfully lobbied for the restoration of the patrician regime and a compromise between the confessional camps. But in 1556, Fugger and his brother-in-law Heinrich Rehlinger also prompted Augsburg to join the League of Landsberg, an alliance of imperial estates loyal to the emperor led by Bavaria, thus setting the course for a pro-Habsburg foreign policy.[41]

After 1560, however, the Fuggers' religious position began to change, and this also affected their role within the bi-confessional city. Whereas Hans Jakob Fugger and his brother Ulrich, a committed Protestant, left Augsburg because of their private debts,[42] their brothers and cousins who remained in the city turned toward decidedly Counter-Reformation positions under the influence of the Jesuit Order and became leading representatives and supporters of the Catholic confessionalization within the imperial city. The sermons that the Jesuit Father Petrus Canisius delivered in Augsburg's cathedral from the summer of 1559 on not only revived piety among the city's Catholics, who only numbered about 7,000 at the time, but also resulted in numerous conversions. Among the most prominent converts were the Protestant spouses of members of the Fugger family. In 1560, Marx Fugger's wife. Sibylla von Eberstein, and Georg Fugger's wife, Ursula von Liechtenstein, converted to Catholicism, and they were followed by Hans Fugger's wife, Elisabeth Nothafft von Weissenstein, as well as by Katharina Fugger and her husband, Count Jakob of Montfort, in 1561. The Catholic faith now became the norm for the Fuggers and the people around them. In the final third of the sixteenth century, the marriage contracts of family members regularly stipulated that weddings were to be performed according to Catholic rites. In addition, Fugger wills explicitly provided for Catholic burials, and the brothers Hans and Marx Fugger paid increasing attention to the "correct" faith of their servants and their children's educators. During Philipp Eduard Fugger's stay in Antwerp in 1569, for example, the employee Hans Bechler informed him "that my lord Hans [Fugger] does not want to permit any Lutheran in his house any longer." Georg, Marx, and Hans Fugger also lent vigorous support to Augsburg's Jesuits and even had their libraries "purged" of pro-Reformation writings. Georg Fugger's sons Octavian Secundus and Philipp Eduard attended the Collegium Germanicum in Rome, and Octavian Secundus for a while seriously considered joining the Society of Jesus. Their mother, Ursula, presented the Jesuits with gifts and financial support. Several exorcisms that the Jesuits practiced on maidservants of the Fugger family in 1568–69 caused a sensation among Augsburg's inhabitants. Ursula Fugger even went on a pilgrimage to Rome in the company of her brother-in-law Hans because she believed that one of her maidservants, who was allegedly "possessed," could only be helped there. An exorcism that Petrus Canisius performed on Sibylla Fugger's noble chambermaid in Altötting in 1570 substantially contributed to the boom of the Altötting pilgrimage in the late sixteenth century.[43]

The most important project that emerged in the context of the confessional policy of Augsburg's Jesuits and their supporters was the founding of a Jesuit college in the imperial city. Members of the Fugger family actively promoted this project from the 1560s on. Around 1576, relations between the order and the family were strained because the Jesuits, of all people, revived the old issue of the canonical prohibition of taking interest and proclaimed the practice of charging 5 percent interest on loans to be sinful. For some time they even denied absolution for this reason to those family members who were active in the family firm. Viewed against this background, the Fuggers' decision to facilitate the founding of the college of St. Salvator with particularly generous gifts and legacies may be interpreted as a conciliatory gesture toward the order—and, perhaps, an expression of their bad conscience. A sum of 30,000 florins came from the estate of Christoph Fugger, and the brothers Octavian Secundus and Philipp Eduard Fugger donated eight houses on the city's outskirts worth 12,000 florins to the Jesuits. The college, which started instruction in 1582, was built on this site. The Fuggers' wives donated money and valuable objects to decorate the church of St. Salvator. In 1586, the college received another 16,000 florins from the Fugger family, and twelve years later, Hans Fugger's son Christoph donated 40,000 florins for its maintenance. Subsequently, the Fuggers also supported the establishment of a branch of the Capuchin Order in Augsburg and put considerable land at the order's disposal for the building of the church and monastery of St. Sebastian in 1602. The founding of St. Salvator with the approval of the leading city councilors and the fact that the Jesuits were offering courses free of charge provided Augsburg's Protestants with an incentive to embark on a new initiative in the field of higher education. In 1581, the evangelical college at St. Anna was founded with financial contributions from numerous patrician and merchant families. The establishment of two competing institutions of higher education, in turn, was an indication of the hardening of confessional lines that became apparent in the years around 1580.[44]

During this phase of confessional polarization, in which the Fuggers also demonstrated their adherence to the Catholic faith by taking part in religious processions,[45] Marx Fugger and Anton Christoph Rehlinger, another committed Catholic, held the city's top position of mayor (*Stadtpfleger*). Marx Fugger had only agreed to accept this high office in 1576 after an urgent appeal to his duties as a citizen of Augsburg, however, and in 1581, he unsuccessfully asked to be relieved of his duties. Three years later he was discharged after the emperor had intervened on his behalf.[46] By then the confessional polarization within the imperial city had already escalated into open rebellion on account of the introduction of the Gregorian calendar.

This conflict began when the leaders of Augsburg's city council decided

FIGURE 18

Jesuit college of St. Salvator in Augsburg. Copper engraving by Simon Grimm, 1687.
(Staats- und Stadtbibliothek Augsburg)

in January 1583 to adopt the new calendar, which Pope Gregory XIII had introduced the year before. The council justified this decision by pointing out the danger of economic losses the city might suffer if Augsburg's religious holidays diverged from those of the neighboring Catholic territories. These territories—the duchy of Bavaria and the prince-bishopric of Augsburg—had already introduced the new calendar. While the population of Augsburg was overwhelmingly Protestant, the Catholics held a slight majority on the city council. Apart from Mayor Marx Fugger, Octavian Secundus Fugger, a son of Marx's cousin Georg, held a seat on the Small Council from 1580, and later, from 1594 to 1600, Octavian Secundus, whom the Protestant chronicler Jörg Siedeler described as "a main pillar of the Roman church," filled the office of mayor himself.[47] Although several Protestant council members had consented to the introduction of the new calendar, a group of Protestant councilors and church administrators considered the reform a violation of the principle of liberty of conscience and a breach of the Religious Peace of Augsburg. They appealed to the imperial chamber court. When the council enforced the reform, the Protestant majority of the citizenry intentionally ignored the new dates for Sundays and religious holidays. In consequence, numerous artisans were punished for working on these days. Anonymous defamatory writings accused the council of trying to turn Augsburg into a city controlled by Catholic priests, using the insulting term *Pfaffenstadt* (city of clerics), by deploying the "made-up" papal calendar. If the new calendar were not repealed, the community would take the matter into its own hands. The Protestant preachers assumed the leadership of the opposition. The superintendent of Augsburg's Protestant church, Dr. Georg Müller, was particularly strident in his criticism, denouncing the councilors as hypocrites and tyrants. Mayor Marx Fugger in turn regarded the Protestant preachers as troublemakers who should best be banished. As early as 1580, he had written to his colleague Anton Christoph Rehlinger: "If they are allowed to get away with everything they will become more and more impudent until an uprising will finally ensue. . . . [I]t is better to have such inflammatory preachers out of the city than within it."[48]

In late 1583 and early 1584, additional measures taken by the council aggravated the situation. It hired soldiers for its own safety and claimed the authority to fill two vacant preaching positions itself. Up to this point this had traditionally been the preserve of the body of Protestant preachers, the Ministerium, but its recommendation had been rejected by the council. After a ruling of the imperial chamber court had confirmed the legality of the introduction of the new calendar, the council took vigorous action and dismissed the leaders of the Protestant opposition. The preachers reacted by continuing to foment disobedience. Their position was supported by a legal opinion of the University of Tübingen, which argued for the Protestants' claim to legal equality. At the beginning of June 1584, the preachers summoned their congregations from the pulpits to celebrate the upcoming festival of Ascension according to the old calendar. The council reacted by prohibiting the closing of shops on that day and expelled the superintendent, Dr. Müller, from the city. This attempt to get rid of the leading Protestant preacher triggered an open rebellion. The carriage taking Müller and his family out of the city was stopped by an angry crowd, and the preacher was released. Several thousand people then assembled in St. James's parish (the Jakober Vorstadt), the suburb mostly inhabited by poor craftsmen and day laborers. Although the council had ordered the inner city gates to be closed, the crowd forced its way into the upper city, stormed the armory, and armed itself. Some shots were fired in front of the city hall, where the soldiers hired by the council had taken up positions, but the preachers managed to calm the angry crowd, thus possibly preventing major bloodshed.

While the city council subsequently attempted to settle the calendar conflict through negotiations with the citizenry, the argument about the right to call the preachers continued. An imperial commission set up in July 1584 and including people from the Fuggers' circle of relatives (Count Wilhelm of Oettingen and Ottheinrich von Schwarzenberg) questioned more than one hundred citizens of Augsburg, whose answers revealed a great degree of dissatisfaction with the council regime. Hans Fugger, who was one of the first to be questioned, voiced his opinion that the conflict was not primarily about religion: "He thinks the cause [was] the malice and poverty of sundry who would have liked to see everything turned upside down." The statements of most people interrogated show that resistance to the "papal" calendar had become intertwined with social and political issues. Augsburg was marked by a deep rift between fabulously wealthy patricians and merchants on one side and poor craftsmen on the other. The poorer inhabitants complained about rising food prices and the deteriorating economic conditions (particularly in the textile sector, which was of crucial importance for Augsburg). Essential points of criticism were the numerical relationship of Catholics and Protestants within the council, the kinship networks among the councilors, the unfair electoral code, the authorities' interventions in the affairs of the Protestant church, the activities of the Jesuits, and the preferential treatment of rich patrician families, particularly the Fuggers, in matters of taxation. The Protestant merchant David Weiß, himself a member of the upper class, reported that the "common man" was complaining that the Fuggers all together paid only 2,000 gold florins in property taxes, even though each family member could easily pay that sum alone. Meanwhile, Mayor Marx Fugger conspicuously stayed in the background. It is more than likely, however, that he pulled the strings behind the scenes to win over allies and secure the dominance of the patriciate.[49]

The letters of Hans Fugger, the mayor's brother, offer revealing insights into the perception of this conflict by a member of the imperial city's Catholic elite. Although Protestant patricians such as Hans Honold and Hans Sigmund Stammler were among his personal friends, Fugger consistently took the perspective of the Augsburg city council in his correspondence. The activities of the calendar's Protestant opponents left him with the impression that "they are trying to cover up all sorts of villainy under the cloak of religion." He regarded the Protestant preachers and particularly the superintendent, Dr. Müller, as instigators of the trouble. They had stirred up the common people so much that they had "run about in the city like madmen" in arms. Writing to his nephew Jörg von Montfort, Hans Fugger even expressed his hopes that the emperor would bring Müller to Vienna and have him executed there, just as Ferdinand I had once done with Silvester Raid, for "otherwise we will have evil deeds and no more peace and quiet once and for all." His words not only reveal Hans Fugger's uncompromising stance toward "rebels" who were threatening the council's legitimate authority; they also demonstrate that the memory of the former Fugger employee and political schemer Silvester Raid was still very much alive a quarter-century after Raid's death. Fugger's unyielding position was obviously rooted in his deep concern for the future of Catholicism and for patrician authority in the city. When "once we lose the Catholic religion in this place now," he wrote to Dr. Johann Tonner in Prague in August 1584, then it was "well to be feared that no Emperor Charles [V] would restore it again so soon, and that the city would eventually perish on account of it, and grass would grow on the wine market before long." Hans Fugger thus regarded the future of his own family as closely bound up with the fate of the patrician regime. The conflict over the right to call the Protestant preachers kept these fears alive during the following year; Fugger referred to the preachers as "vermin" who wanted to turn "this glorious city into a dive (*ein spelunca*)." If the preachers actually prevailed, he would rather live on the (dangerous) Hungarian border than in Augsburg. During the conflict, Fugger tried to activate his contacts with Munich, Speyer, Vienna, and Prague to mobilize support for Augsburg's city council while also acting as a mediator toward a neighboring Lutheran prince, Philipp Ludwig of Pfalz-Neuburg.[50]

After the imperial commission's negotiations failed to bring about a settlement between the religious factions within the council, the Catholic majority of councilors resorted to force in August 1585. An opposition group of eighteen Protestants, which included members of prominent elite families, was interrogated, and ten of them were expelled from the city. Other opponents of the new calendar voluntarily went into exile. In 1586, all Protestant pastors were expelled and replaced with new incumbents. The successors appointed by the council were boycotted by the Protestant citizenry, however, and attendance at religious services as well as charitable donations in the Protestant congregations declined dramatically. Protestant citizens met in private Bible groups that the council tried in turn to dissolve. It was not before 1591 that a compromise on the issue of calling the preachers could be reached with the help of other imperial cities. The Protestant church administrators, whose number was fixed at six, were given the right to nominate candidates for vacant preaching positions, while the actual calls to the preachers were issued by the council. On the whole, the calendar conflict deepened the confessional divide within the imperial city and shaped religious mentalities. The demands of the Protestant opposition, however, had also sketched a possible solution to religious conflicts in a city like Augsburg: equality in the filling of council offices, as well as internal autonomy and "liberty of conscience" for each of the two confessional camps. This solution—religious parity—was later inscribed into the constitutions of Augsburg and several other bi-confessional cities in the Peace of Westphalia in 1648.[51]

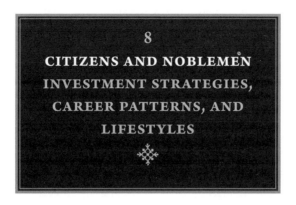

8

CITIZENS AND NOBLEMEN
INVESTMENT STRATEGIES, CAREER PATTERNS, AND LIFESTYLES

✤

FROM URBAN BOURGEOISIE TO LANDED NOBILITY?

In the history of the late medieval and early modern bourgeoisie, the frequency with which newly rich patrician and merchant families invested part of their wealth in rural property is well known. This process has been observed for the upper strata of the large southern German imperial cities, as well as for urban elites in Italy, England, France, and the Netherlands.[1] Sometimes the acquisition of landed property went hand in hand with the conferring of noble titles, marriage alliances with the landed nobility, and a withdrawal from urban life. These phenomena often have been described as a "feudalization" of the bourgeoisie. It was not economic and social success in urban society but the ascent into the ranks of the nobility that supposedly formed the model for the bourgeoisie.[2]

At first glance, the history of the Fuggers looks like the ideal example of this process of "feudalization." The weavers who had immigrated to Augsburg in the fourteenth century first became respected merchants and then international entrepreneurs and bankers. In the course of the sixteenth century, they invested ever larger sums in rural estates, and by the early seventeenth century, they owned more than one hundred villages in eastern Swabia alone. They were elevated to the rank of hereditary imperial counts in 1530 and were granted additional privileges, such as the right to exercise manorial jurisdiction and a partial exemption from Augsburg's municipal jurisdiction. From this time on, the Fuggers formed marriage alliances with landed noble families almost exclusively. By the mid-seventeenth century, they eventually had given up merchant banking entirely, the activity that had once formed the very basis of their economic and social ascent, and now derived their income from land rents or served as high clergymen, officers, and princely bureaucrats.[3]

As the preceding chapters have shown, however, this schematic view of a linear rise from the bourgeoisie to the nobility is much too simple. Although the Fuggers invested considerable sums in landed property as early as 1507 and benefited from the conferment of imperial titles and privileges from 1511 on, they retained their trading company for almost a century and a half. Although they married into the landed nobility and turned their rural manors into splendid and ostentatious castles, the Fugger houses in Augsburg remained the centers of life for most family members until the Thirty Years' War. Moreover, family members assumed high city offices and actively participated in urban life. The Fuggers' patronage and collecting activities, their learning and educational trips, and their self-display and cultural consumption increased their prestige among fellow citizens, foreign scholars, landed noblemen, and central Europe's princely courts alike and formed the basis of their elevated status in urban society, as well as the acceptance of their noble rank. Throughout the sixteenth century and early seventeenth century, the Fuggers were *both* merchants and landed noblemen, thus taking up a social position that defies overly simple classifications of rank. When family members referred to themselves as "citizens of Augsburg and estates of the Roman Empire" in 1592, they succinctly described their special status.[4] Moreover, a comparison with other leading urban families shows that the combination of bourgeois and aristocratic values, behavioral patterns, and lifestyles was not confined to the Fuggers; it can also be observed in families such as the Vöhlins, Langenmantels, Imhofs, Rehlingers, and Stettens. What distinguishes the Fuggers' rural estates most clearly from those of other Augsburg families was their size and stability. Whereas other families frequently resold their estates, landed property in the Fuggers' case became "an inalienable element of family wealth."[5]

Therefore the changing lifestyle and self-image of urban families in the sixteenth and seventeenth centuries should not be viewed as "feudalization." Rather, it indicates a pluralism of social norms and career options. Although commerce was the basis of these families' wealth, prestige, and status, there were several ways to preserve and increase prestige and wealth: continuing involvement in trade and banking, the assumption of public office in the city, a lifestyle befitting the receivers of feudal rents, as well as ecclesiastical, military, courtly, and administrative careers in early modern territorial states.[6] Members of the Fugger family pursued all of these career paths in the sixteenth century and early seventeenth century. Men like Marx and Octavian Secundus Fugger simultaneously were heads of a merchant company, high-ranking city officials, and landed noblemen. Ott Heinrich Fugger held all of these functions in addition to those of military entrepreneur and official of

the duke of Bavaria.[7] This chapter illustrates this pluralism of family strategies, career paths, and lifestyles by describing the growth of the Fuggers'
landed territories and the motives behind the acquisition of these estates, on
the one hand, and by outlining the careers of family members in the church
and in early modern princely states, on the other.

THE FUGGERS AS RURAL PROPRIETORS IN SWABIA

Although the Fuggers also held landed property outside Swabia (e.g., the
territory of Bibersburg in present-day Slovakia, acquired in 1535, as well as
estates in the southern part of Alsace, Thurgau, and Lower Austria[8]), eastern Swabia—that is, the area between the rivers Danube, Iller, and Lech
and Lake Constance—was the center of their property acquisitions. The
French historian Robert Mandrou has counted no fewer than 633 large and
small purchases of manorial estates, farms, smallholdings, and other kinds
of landed property on which the Fuggers spent a total of 2.6 million florins
between the early sixteenth century and the outbreak of the Thirty Years'
War. In 1618, the Fuggers were owners and manorial lords of more than one
hundred villages. According to Mandrou's calculations, this complex of
landed properties comprised between 94 and 98 square miles.[9]

Jakob Fugger the Rich laid the foundations of the family's later territorial
complex when he acquired the county of Kirchberg, along with the territories of Wullenstetten, Weißenhorn, and Pfaffenhofen, as a lien at the imperial Diet of Constance in 1507, paying 50,000 florins for it to King Maximilian,
who was heavily indebted to him and urgently needed money for a projected
journey to Rome for his imperial coronation. Two years later, Jakob Fugger
purchased the manorial estate (*Hofmark*) of Schmiechen from Maximilian
for 8,000 florins. By 1512, he had spent 3,000 florins more on the construction
of a new castle there. Finally, in 1514, he acquired the territory of Biberbach,
which had passed from the marshals of Pappenheim into Maximilian's possession, paying 20,000 florins, along with a loan of 12,000 florins. By the end
of his life, Jakob Fugger was manorial lord of more than fifty villages.[10]

Nevertheless, we should be cautious before we interpret these early activi-
ties as a systematic reinvestment of commercial capital in landed property.
The investments in the Tyrolean and Hungarian trades were much larger, and
Jakob Fugger spent comparable sums on other types of property. A few years
before the acquisition of Kirchberg, the Fuggers purchased jewels out of the
Burgundian treasure of Charles the Bold from the city of Basel for 40,000
florins, and in 1508, they bought a diamond from the estate of an insolvent
Venetian merchant for 20,000 florins.[11] Initially, the sole motivation for the
elevation of Jakob Fugger and his nephews to the ranks of imperial barons in

1511 and counts in 1514, which was confirmed to his heirs in 1526, was a matter of feudal law. As the Swabian landed nobility did not accept the granting of fiefs by a mere Augsburg merchant, Jakob Fugger's elevation to noble rank ensured his full right of disposal over his landed estates. Within the imperial city of Augsburg, however, citizens were prohibited from using noble titles, and there is no indication that Jakob Fugger ever employed them there.[12]

We find the main indication that Jakob Fugger's land acquisitions and the conferment of noble status on him not only served to secure the family property but were also linked to the long-term goal of social advancement in the marriage alliances with the Swabian nobility, which were first formed in the early sixteenth century. The marriage of Ulrich Fugger's daughter Ursula to the knight Philipp von Stain in 1503 was accompanied by a remarkably large dowry payment to the bridegroom, and the wedding, at which numerous noblemen were present, was celebrated with great splendor. The marriage of Sibylla Fugger to the knight Hans Marx von Bubenhofen in 1512 was a particularly festive occasion. When the bridegroom came to Augsburg, the imperial city's councilors and citizens met them "upon their entry with two of the city's soldier companies to honor the city." Most marriages of family members in the second and third decades of the sixteenth century, however, still allied the Fuggers with other leading families of Augsburg, such as the Stettens, Gassners, Baumgartners, and Rehlingers.[13]

Jakob Fugger's nephews Anton and Raymund systematically expanded the family's landed estates. Initially, Raymund was the more active of the brothers in this respect: In 1527, he purchased the village of Gablingen near Augsburg from the knight Sebastian von Knöringen for 13,200 florins, and in the following year, he bought the eastern Swabian manorial estate of Mickhausen from King Ferdinand I, where he built a new castle "merely for the pleasure which he took in building, and to provide the poor with a means of relief and nourishment," as the Fuggers' *Book of Honors* claims. After the bankruptcy of the Höchstetter company in 1529, Ambrosius Höchstetter's territory of Burgwalden was temporarily pawned to the Fuggers. Four years later, Oberndorf, which was close to Biberbach, and Dürrlauingen were taken over by the Fuggers. Between 1536 and 1539, Anton Fugger purchased the territories of Glött und Babenhausen, Dorndorf, and the imperial estate (*Reichspflege*) of Donauwörth. For the most important among these acquisitions, Babenhausen along with the Swabian territory of Brandenburg, he paid a total of 68,000 florins to the heirs of Veit von Rechberg. The acquisition of Pless and Rettenbach, as well as the village of Roth, which was located in the territory of the imperial city of Biberach, followed in the mid-1540s. A further series of land purchases began after 1550 when Anton Fugger planned to liquidate the trading company and systematically reinvested his capital in real estate. Between 1550 and 1557, the territories of Kirchheim on the Mindel, Boos, and Kettershausen, as well as the villages and hamlets of Untersulmentingen, Druisheim, Ehingen, and Ortlfingen, were added. In January 1551, the purchase from the imperial councilor Hans Walter von Hirnheim of Kirchheim, along with the villages of Eppishausen, Duttenstein, Niederalfingen, and Stettenfels, alone cost him 250,000 florins. In the same year, Anton Fugger purchased from Ludwig Stebenhaber the territory of Boos, north of the imperial city of Memmingen, for 29,000 florins. In addition, substantial sums were invested in the expansion of existing landholdings and in the purchase of numerous smaller properties. On the estate of Oberndorf near the town of Rain on the river Lech, for example, which had been acquired for 21,000 florins in 1533, a four-winged castle was built between 1535 and 1546 that cost a further 75,000 florins. Another new castle was constructed in the territory of Glött from 1550 onward. The separation of Anton Fugger's interests from those of his brother Raymund's heirs, which was apparent in the brothers' individual real-estate purchases, was formalized in a division of property in 1548. On this occasion, Anton's and Raymund's lineages received real estate and feudal rights worth 379,000 florins each. Anton Fugger and Raymund Fugger's sons pledged to preserve these landholdings and pass them on to the family's male descendants. In the event of property sales, the male family members had an option to purchase. This agreement also marked the final stage in the establishment of a family trust, which had its origins in the company contracts of 1502.[14]

The acquisitions of substantial landed estates coincided with the conferment of the rank of hereditary counts on Anton, Raymund, and Hieronymus Fugger in 1530 and the addition of the title and heraldic coat of arms from the extinct counts of Kirchberg to those of the Fuggers "von der Lilie." Among other things, the noble privilege of 1530 included exemptions from civic duties and offices as well from the court tribunal (*Hofgericht*) in Rottweil and other foreign law courts. Of particular significance, moreover, was the minting privilege granted to the Fuggers in 1534.[15] Like his uncle Jakob, however, Anton Fugger refrained from actually using the title count (*Graf*) that had been conferred on him; it was only after 1620 that the family officially employed it.[16] However, from the 1530s on, Anton pursued a marriage policy that systematically targeted alliances with southern German and Austrian noble families—that is, families from the ranks of the imperial knights, barons, and counts. Between 1538 and 1549, seven of Raymund Fugger's children married members of the landed nobility, and between 1553 and 1570, eight of Anton Fugger's children married into the families of barons or counts. The daughters' weddings in particular were promoted at considerable financial expense: Raymund Fugger's daughter Regina, who became the wife of Johann Jakob von Mörsberg in 1538, brought a dowry of 30,000 florins to the marriage. Count Joachim of Ortenburg received the same sum on the occasion of his wedding with Ursula Fugger in 1549, while the bridegroom's marriage portion came to no more than 13,000 florins. The size of these dowries was unusual for the time and the rank of the couples involved, but we also need to take into account that the women were excluded from the family trading company, which meant that the dowries were also a kind of compensation. The fact that these marriages were celebrated with great extravagance and sought to increase the Fuggers' prestige is underscored by an entry in the family *Book of Honors* on the occasion of the wedding of Raymund Fugger's daughter Barbara and Ferdinand von Vels. During the Augsburg Diet of 1547–48, the couple celebrated its wedding "very expensively and splendidly . . . Count Haug of Montfort and Count Carl of Zollern led the bride; princes and high rulers greatly rejoiced." Raymund and Anton Fugger's descendants consistently followed this marriage policy in the late sixteenth century and early seventeenth century. Until 1600, marriage alliances were concluded, among others, with the counts of Ortenburg in 1549 and 1585; the counts of Helfenstein in 1578, 1583, and 1590; the counts of Montfort in 1553 and 1587; and the counts Oettingen-Wallerstein and Hohenzollern, both in 1589. The title *wohlgeboren* (well-born, or noble), repeatedly mentioned in documents from the final third of the sixteenth century onward, confirms the Fuggers' acceptance by their noble peers.[17]

At the time of Anton Fugger's death in 1560, the family's real-estate holdings had a distinct spatial structure. They extended over "a trapezoidal area between Ulm, Donauwörth, Augsburg, and Babenhausen." Their geographical centers were the region south of the Danube between the town of Günzburg and the imperial city of Ulm, with the river valleys of the Iller, Kammel, and Mindel, as well as the region between Augsburg and Donauwörth.[18] In the 1560s, Anton Fugger's sons Marx, Hans, and Jakob took over the manorial estate of Mickhausen, which Raymund Fugger had acquired in 1528, from Raymund's bankrupt son Ulrich; beyond that, they were initially reluctant to invest in rural properties. This changed in 1573 when they purchased the territory of Mering east of Augsburg from the duke of Bavaria and the eastern Swabian villages of Ellgau, Lauterbrunn, and Waltershofen from the Pappenheim family. All together they spent 132,000 florins on these purchases. The division of estates on which Marx, Hans, and Jakob Fugger agreed in 1575 marks another important caesura. On this occasion, Marx received the complex of estates and territories extending to the north of Augsburg and west of

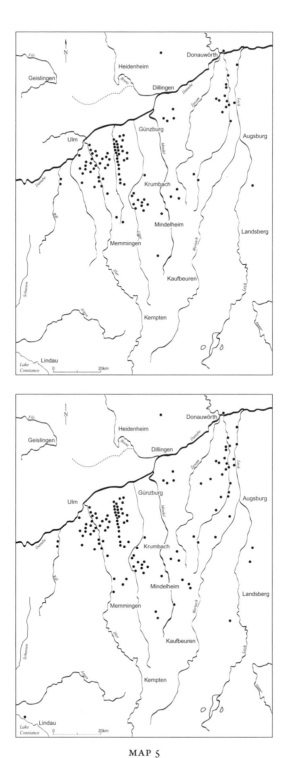

MAP 5

Fugger territories in Swabia, 1560 and 1618; dots indicate the family's real-estate holdings.
(Adapted from Mandrou, Die Fugger als Grundbesitzer in Schwaben, 1560–1618*)*

the river Lech: Gablingen, Biberbach, Druisheim, the imperial estate (*Reichs-pflege*) of Donauwörth, Oberndorf, Lauterbrunn, Ehingen, Ellgau, Dutten-stein, and Niederalfingen. This area also included criminal jurisdiction over Biberbach and the right to collect tolls at a station between Gablingen and Biberbach. Hans Fugger obtained the territories of Kirchheim, Dürrlauin-gen, Glött, Schmiechen, Mickhausen, and Mering, while at the division of 1575, Jakob became manorial lord and proprietor of Babenhausen, Ketters-hausen, Pless, Boos, Waltenhausen, and Rettenbach. Each of these three property complexes was valued at roughly 415,000 florins.[19]

This division was a kind of starting signal for a further series of property acquisitions. The period between 1575 and the death of the three brothers in 1597–98 was one of the most active in the history of Fugger real-estate pur-chases. Marx bought Nordendorf with the fortress of Donnersberg, which was adjacent to his territory of Biberbach, for 30,000 florins in 1580; the vil-lages of Hirblingen and Täfertingen northwest of Augsburg in the follow-ing year; Meitingen in 1585; and Welden in 1597. Hans became the owner of the estates of Hardt and Reinhartshausen east of his territory of Kirchheim in 1587 and Pestenacker south of his estate of Schmiechen in 1598. His son Christoph invested 116,000 florins in the territories of Mattsies and Rammin-gen after the death of his father, and Christoph's brother Marx obtained the Bavarian manorial estate (*Hofmark*) of Türkenfeld in 1598. Hans and Chris-toph Fugger, however, were unable to realize their ambitions for the impor-tant territory of Mindelheim. Compared with those of his brothers, Jakob Fugger's purchases had the widest geographical extent. They included the territories of Gottenau and Heimertingen in the Memmingen region in 1584 and 1589; Wasserburg on Lake Constance in 1592; Leeder near Landsberg on the Lech in 1595; and Wellenburg just outside the city gates of Augsburg, also in 1595. Jakob Fugger spent huge sums on these purchases: 131,000 florins on Heimertingen, acquired from the Ettlinstett family; 62,000 florins on Was-serburg, bought from the counts of Montfort; and 70,000 florins on Wellen-burg. Apart from these large territories and manorial estates, this phase was conspicuous for Fugger purchases of numerous smaller pieces of real estate, many of them from farmers and smallholders. During the last two decades before the outbreak of the Thirty Years' War, the Fuggers concentrated their purchases on smaller properties.[20]

In 1589, Georg Fugger's sons likewise agreed on a division of their real-estate holdings. Philipp Eduard became the proprietor of the territories of Weißenhorn and Pfaffenhofen and the county of Marstetten; his younger brother Octavian Secundus received the county of Kirchberg and the terri-tory of Wellenstetten; and Raymund became the owner of the territory of

Brandenburg (Swabia), as well as the estate of Obenhausen. The total value of these territories was estimated at 304,000 florins. Their brother Anton (1552–1616) presents a special case, for after his separation from the trading company Georg Fugger's Heirs, he made an ambitious attempt to form a new complex of estates in the immediate vicinity of Augsburg. After purchasing Hainhofen in 1580 and Aystetten, he tried to obtain the villages of Neusäß, Schlipsheim, Biburg, and Ottmarshausen but became heavily indebted in the attempt and was unable to hold on to his properties. Because his debts amounted to almost 224,000 florins, Augsburg's city council had his assets sealed and inventoried in 1594. This measure and Anton Fugger's verbal attacks on the council triggered a lengthy controversy that eventually occupied the imperial chamber court and an imperial commission. In contrast with Anton's ambition to form a new territorial complex within just a few years, the acquisitions policy of other family members aimed more at the long-term consolidation and preservation of their holdings.[21]

But what were the motives behind these extensive property holdings that the Fuggers acquired in the course of a century? Researchers have provided very different answers to this question. Baron Götz von Pölnitz expressed the view that Anton Fugger, by pursuing a "persistent and costly real estate acquisition policy, aimed at nothing less than the establishment of a loose federation of territories between the Iller, Lech, and Danube rivers and Lake Constance." Hermann Kellenbenz agreed that Anton Fugger, "in view of his expanding property holdings, dreamed of following the example of the house of Medici and turn his territories into a principality." Robert Mandrou, however, rejected this notion of a coherent territorial policy. First, no sources prove that such an overall concept existed, and second, the pattern of the actual acquisitions indicates the opposite, for the Fuggers bought numerous territories, estates, farms, and smallholdings that never formed a coherent geographic area. Like Mandrou, Peter Blickle regards the Fuggers' acquisition policy as rather haphazard: "The indiscriminate purchase of territories . . . on the Fuggers' side apparently was primarily a form of capital investment." Pankraz Fried, however, has emphasized an element of "territorial planning" in the structure of the Fuggers' real-estate purchases denied by Mandrou and Blickle: "The acquisition of territorial bases between the rivers Lech and Iller, the Alps and the Danube was anything but accidental; it was not merely characterized by the accumulation of ground rents and feudal dues." To a certain extent, the assessment of the Fuggers' acquisition policy depends on the importance one attaches to plans that in the end could *not* be realized. The Fuggers' policy of territory building certainly would have taken on a new dimension if Anton Fugger had been able to obtain the margravate of Burgau from his debtor Ferdinand I and the duchy of Pfalz-Neuburg during the Schmalkaldic War, and if Anton's son Hans had succeeded in taking over the territory of Mindelheim. But this did not happen.[22]

Undoubtedly, the revenues in cash and kind from feudal dues that the peasants and smallholders had to pay from their holdings were an important motive for acquiring rural properties. These dues provided a secure rent income to their receivers, as well as the opportunity to produce and market agrarian surpluses. Although the Fuggers generally adhered to traditional legal systems and agrarian practices, the administration of their estates was marked by great circumspection and care. According to Mandrou, it followed "the iron laws of the house of Fugger: meticulous recording of all business transactions, calculation of all individual accounts, and annual accounting of the income obtained."[23] In economic terms, this careful estate administration was extremely profitable. According to Mandrou's calculations, the Fuggers' estates yielded average annual returns of 5–6 percent on capital invested in the late sixteenth century, making them a significant source of income. An important factor in this calculation were the loans the Fuggers made to their feudal subjects. When the brothers Marx, Hans, and Jakob Fugger divided their real estate in 1575, they had claims against farmers and smallholders amounting to nearly 45,000 florins, with 21,000 florins bearing interest. When Hans Fugger had his landed properties assessed once more in 1596, Swabian villagers owed him almost 33,000 florins, including interest-bearing loans of 24,000 florins. "Long-term planning, persistent watchfulness, and meticulous administration" were, in Mandrou's terms, "the three decisive elements of successful managements for the Fuggers, in commerce as in the management of real estate."[24]

Another motivation is indicated by the remark in the Fuggers' *Book of Honors* that Raymund's and Anton's purchases served the family's "honor and benefit." The expansion of real-estate holdings and the remodeling of their centers into splendid castles increased the family's prestige and transformed economic capital into social capital.[25] Like no other Fugger castle-building project of the sixteenth century, the new castle of Kirchheim, for which Hans Fugger had commissioned the Augsburg city architect Jakob Eschay from 1578 to 1585, demonstrated this desire for prestige and self-display. Hans Fugger spared neither trouble nor expense on the construction and splendid decoration of the four-winged renaissance castle. By 1585, the costs amounted to more than 150,000 florins. In return for these enormous expenses, Hans Fugger obtained work of the highest quality: He commissioned the Flemish Hubert Gerhard and the Italian Carlo Pallago for the sculptural work and the Augsburg master carpenter Wendel Dietrich for the

FIGURE 19
View of Kirchheim castle. Painting, anonymous artist, seventeenth century.
(Fürstl. Fugger Glött'sche Domänenverwaltung)

wooden doors and the ceilings of the halls and rooms reserved for public
display. The finely structured and lavishly ornamented ceiling of the grand
festival hall, which was decorated with inlay work and measured 375 square
meters, is considered a masterpiece of southern German craftsmanship of
the late sixteenth century.[26]

But this does not mean that the real-estate acquisitions were motivated
exclusively by the striving for social prestige or the desire to invest capital at
low risk and securely against crises. Georg Lutz has suggested that there may
have also been an ethical and moral aspect to the increasing property acquisitions of the final quarter of the sixteenth century, for the Fuggers were repeatedly confronted with the accusation that their business strategy violated the
canonical prohibition on taking interest. This accusation, which had already
occupied scholars at the beginning of the sixteenth century, was revived in
the late 1570s by Augsburg's Jesuits, of all people, whose establishment in the
imperial city the Fuggers had actively promoted. While the taking of interest
in commercial and financial transactions thus remained ethically controversial, the church raised no objects against feudal rents on landed property.[27]
Most recently, Dietmar Schiersner has argued that the margravate of Burgau in eastern Swabia, where many of the Fuggers' real-estate acquisitions

FIGURE 20
Grand Festival Hall of Kirchheim castle.
(Fürstl. Fugger Glött'sche Domänenverwaltung)

were concentrated, also formed a virtually ideal investment area due to its
proximity to the imperial cities of Augsburg and Ulm and its flexible political
and constitutional structure. The character of the region as a *territorium non
clausum*—an area where territorial sovereignty was not concentrated in the
hands of a single prince or lord but dispersed among a variety of families and
institutions—made the acquisition of territorial rights and feudal privileges
relatively easy.[28]

The functions and significance of the Fuggers' landed estates and the
strategies employed to extend their authority in the countryside can be illustrated by the case of Mickhausen, situated in the upper Schmutter Valley
southwest of Augsburg. This noble estate had once belonged to the barons
of Freiberg before becoming part of the Habsburg margravate of Burgau;
in 1528, it was sold by Archduke Ferdinand of Austria to Raymund Fugger
for 4,000 florins. At the time, the estate comprised the village of Mickhausen, two hamlets, and scattered property in two neighboring villages and two
more distant places. Raymund Fugger systematically expanded and devel-

oped the estate; in 1531, for example, he bought the neighboring village of Münster, for which he paid 3,000 florins to the Augsburg collegiate chapter of St. Moritz. In the following year, Raymund Fugger issued a jurisdictional ordinance for Mickhausen and installed a bailiff. Moreover, he succeeded in uniting the two villages of Mickhausen and Münster into a single parish in which he had the right of presentation—that is, to install the pastor—and for which he planned a large parish church. After Raymund's death, his brother Anton, who took over the estate, actually had the church built, and it was completed by 1538. Together with the castle, the parish church of Mickhausen subsequently formed the center of the estate. Anton Fugger also continued to expand these holdings, buying the upper part of the village of Langenneufnach from the Augsburg citizen Matthäus Ehem for 18,500 florins in 1546. At the division of landed property in 1548, the estate, which was now valued at roughly 54,000 florins, fell to Raymund Fugger's son Ulrich. Fifteen years later, the heavily indebted Ulrich sold it to Anton's sons for 100,000 florins. When the property was divided in 1575, Mickhausen came into Hans Fugger's hands, from whom it passed to his son Christoph and his grandson Ott Heinrich.

On the eve of the Thirty Years' War, the estate consisted of landholdings in twenty-three villages and important territorial rights, including civil and petty criminal jurisdiction and the privilege to hunt large game. Mickhausen's subjects had to provide substantial dues in kind to the manorial household—dues that included grain, poultry, venison, hay, straw, building timber, and firewood. In 1617, the estate's value was assessed at 191,000 florins, with an average annual income of 5,700 florins, plus 2,200 florins from grain sales. Ott Heinrich Fugger, who was the proprietor of Mickhausen at the time, resided there several times a year, but generally these sojourns were confined to a few days. Continuity of government and administration was provided by the senior official, Hans Stotz, who regularly corresponded with his master or his representatives, and with the main bookkeeper in Augsburg. During the Thirty Years' War, however, the well-functioning and profitable administration crashed to a halt: From 1628 on, the quartering of troops put a heavy burden on Mickhausen, and after an outbreak of the plague in 1630, virtually no more rents were collected. Ten years later, Ott Heinrich Fugger complained that the village of Mickhausen was nearly depopulated. After his death, the estate's value was assessed at only 111,000 florins, and the yearly returns had fallen below 1,400 florins.[29]

The Fuggers' income from their rural estates was not confined to rents in cash and kind, however. In addition, several family members pursued a strategic economic policy and promoted fustian weaving in their territories.

The beginnings of export-oriented fustian production in the Fugger territories date back to Jakob Fugger's time: He delivered cotton to the weavers
in the county of Kirchberg and supported the establishment of a fustian
fair (*Barchentschau*) in the small town of Weißenhorn in 1517. The fair was
intended to serve the purpose of quality control, on the one hand, and to
keep the weavers of Weißenhorn and its environs away from the textile fair
in the imperial city of Ulm, on the other.[30] Jakob Fugger's nephew Anton
promoted fustian production in Weißenhorn especially during the 1530s,
when he resided on his estates for extended periods because of the religious
and political turmoil in Augsburg. During this period, scales and two flax
bleacheries were established, and the company's cotton purchases in Venice
increased markedly. By 1535, the Fuggers' investments in fustian production
amounted to roughly 30,000 florins, and from November 1538 to late December 1539, the Augsburg head office spent 63,741 florins on the fustian trade.
Weißenhorn fustian was mostly exported to the Netherlands, England, and
Spain. The accounts of the Fuggers' Antwerp factory for 1539–40 recorded
a total of 11,125 pieces of fustian among the inventory. The Castilian fairs
served as distribution centers for the Iberian Peninsula, and Weißenhorn
cloth was sold to the New World via the office in Seville. In 1552, 295 weavers
in Weißenhorn and its environs produced fustian for the Fuggers' commerce
in a putting-out system. The rise of Weißenhorn's textile production aroused
the opposition of the imperial city of Ulm, however, because the city viewed
fustian weaving in the Fugger territory as undesirable competition for its
own craftsmen. While Augsburg, which was worried about the yarn supply
to its own weavers, supported Ulm's position, the Fuggers sought the protection of the Habsburg rulers. In 1538, King Ferdinand I renewed the privilege
for the Weißenhorn fustian fair. The military events of the Schmalkaldic War
and the princes' rebellion of 1552 severely handicapped cloth production,
however, and in view of the permanent squabbles with Ulm, Anton Fugger
finally agreed in 1555 that all fustian produced in Weißenhorn and its environs was to be sold to Ulm merchants. Moreover, he left the entire stock of
cotton in Weißenhorn to the city of Ulm for 11,000 florins.[31]

In later years, the Fuggers remained alert to the economic potential of
rural textile production. In 1583, Anton Fugger's son Jakob considered establishing a fair in the market town of Babenhausen, and Jakob's sons pursued
these plans. According to an Ulm source of 1604, a new fustian fair had been
set up there, and from 1613, this institution is recorded in the official accounts
of the Fugger territory of Babenhausen. During the following years, the Babenhausen fair was very active. In 1620 and 1621, more than 18,000 pieces of
fustian and almost 15,000 pieces of linen were inspected there. Apparently,

the initiative for promoting Babenhausen's textile production came from Maximilian Fugger, who obtained the territory at a division of inheritance in 1620. In the following year, Fugger, his steward (*Hofmeister*) Hans Sigmund Jäcklin of Hohenrealt, the Babenhausen official Hans Verckh, and Julio Cesar Scazuola formed their own company for trade with Spain. The company aimed to organize fustian production in a putting-out system by supplying raw materials to Babenhausen's weavers and selling their products on the Iberian Peninsula. Maximilian Fugger, who was responsible for quality control for the cloth produced, invested 80,000 florins in the enterprise. After a promising start, a Spanish ban on the import of foreign textiles put an abrupt end to the trade. On the advice of his partners, Maximilian Fugger then invested the profits made in the textile trade in the farming of a royal tax, the *cruzada,* which proved to be a bad decision. Because of the import ban and the Thirty Years' War, cloth production declined dramatically, and after 1640, the fair temporarily came to a complete standstill. While fustian production failed to revive after the Peace of Westphalia, the textile fair continued as an institution for the quality control of linen into the eighteenth century.[32]

The example of textile production underscores once again that the acquisition of landed estates cannot simply be viewed as an expression of a conservative economic mentality. At least until the Thirty Years' War, rural property certainly was a comparatively low-risk form of capital investment and served to increase the social prestige of a family that also aimed to rise into the ranks of the nobility by marrying into noble families and obtaining noble privileges. But the marketing of agrarian surpluses, the provision of credit, and trade in textiles produced in the countryside also opened up economic perspectives that went beyond the mere collection of ground rents. When we consider their role as rural proprietors, therefore, the Fuggers defy easy categorization, for they simultaneously were manorial and territorial lords, rentiers, and entrepreneurs.

CLERGYMEN, PRINCELY SERVANTS, AND MILITARY OFFICERS: CAREER PATHS IN THE LATE SIXTEENTH AND EARLY SEVENTEENTH CENTURIES

Even in the late Middle Ages it was common for sons and daughters of urban patricians and long-distance merchants to enter the clergy. Monasteries and ecclesiastical benefices were important institutions to provide for descendants who were expected neither to marry nor to enter the trading company. With Jakob Fugger's brother Marx, who died in 1478, and his nephew of the same name we have already encountered two family members who accumulated clerical benefices at a young age but whose early death ended their social ascent.[33] Over the course of the sixteenth century, as the family's wealth and social prestige grew, opportunities to install family members as cathedral canons or provosts multiplied, as well. In the second half of the century, moreover, as a result of confessional polarization, ecclesiastical careers assumed a new character as the efforts of Catholics as well as Protestants to strengthen their own position and discipline their respective adherents intensified. The Fuggers' support of the Jesuits has already been mentioned in another context, but the number of family members who entered the ranks of the clergy also grew significantly in the second half of the sixteenth century.

The expansion of the early modern territorial state and the consolidation of bureaucratic institutions also resulted in a growing demand for qualified administrative personnel, and the sons of urban patricians, who increasingly benefited from university educations in the course of the sixteenth century and whose families functioned as princely creditors, formed an important group within the emerging territorial bureaucracy. Because of the Fuggers' decades-long financial relations with the houses of Habsburg and Wittelsbach, their marriage alliances with Bavarian and Austrian noble families, and their religious beliefs, service at the courts of Munich, Innsbruck, and Vienna or employment in the Bavarian and Austrian territorial administrations were obvious career options for members of the family. In the second half of the sixteenth century, a number of family members can be found at the courts and in the bureaucracies of the Habsburgs and Wittelsbachs; between the 1540s and the 1620s, fourteen Fuggers served as salaried officials at the court of the dukes of Bavaria alone, four of them as court councilors (*Hofräte*).[34]

The best-known representative of the family to enter the service of a territorial prince was certainly Hans Jakob Fugger, Anton's nephew and the hapless manager of the family firm from 1560 to 1563. After Hans Jakob Fugger had fled to Munich because of his private debts, his longtime friendly relations with Duke Albrecht V and Duke Wilhelm V and the esteem that he enjoyed as an adviser on political and artistic matters opened up a career for him in the duchy's administration. After handling Duke Albrecht's Italian correspondence for several years, serving as the court's musical director, and accompanying one of the duke's sons on a journey to Florence in 1565, he was appointed to the court council (*Hofrat*) in 1570, with an annual salary of 1,000 florins. Two years later, he became president of the newly formed court chamber (*Hofkammer*), the duchy's central financial institution. Maximilian Lanzinner has taken the fact that a bankrupt like Hans Jakob Fugger could advance to such an influential position as an indicator that the Bavarian dukes valued personal trust, wide-ranging connections, language skills, competence in artistic matters, and common political convictions more highly than expertise in financial matters. Moreover, the instruction for the Hofkammer that Hans Jakob Fugger drafted in 1572 proved its author to be a well-versed expert in administrative matters with the ability to make a substantial contribution to the consolidation of central state power in sixteenth-century Bavaria. The Bavarian dukes supported their trusted adviser, who intermittently had great difficulties in meeting his payment obligations, by granting loans to him (a remarkable inversion of the usual relationship between princes and merchants in the early modern period) and acting as sponsors of several of his children. Duke Albrecht V helped Hans Jakob Fugger with a loan of 65,000 florins in 1562 and five years later gave him a house on Munich's cattle market as a present. In the will he made in 1573, the duke ordered that Hans Jakob Fugger's debts to the Munich court chamber, which then stood at 80,000 florins, should not be called in after his death. After Hans Jakob's demise in 1575, high-ranking courtiers and government bureaucrats acted as preceptors and guardians for his children and handled his unsettled debt claims and court cases. As manorial lord of Taufkirchen, Altenerding, and Helfenbrunn, moreover, Hans Jakob Fugger was among the duchy's large rural proprietors.[35]

Most of the thirteen sons born to Hans Jakob Fugger after his marriages to Ursula von Harrach in 1540 and to Sidonia von Colaus in 1560 pursued clerical, courtly, or military careers. Four sons from his first marriage entered the clergy: Sigmund Friedrich, born in 1542, became bishop of Regensburg; his younger brother Alexander Secundus, cathedral provost in Freising and provost of St. Viktor near Mainz; and Viktor Augustus became cathedral provost in Regensburg, cathedral canon in Passau, and president of the ecclesiastical council of Emperor Maximilian II in Vienna. Their brother Maximilian, born in 1550, was a knight of the Teutonic Order and rose to the position of commander at Sterzing before he resigned and married. In the Bavarian territorial administration, Severin Fugger (1551–1601) served as administrator (*Pfleger*) in Friedberg; his half-brother Joachim (b. 1563) became chamberlain of Duke Wilhelm V and *Vizedom* (judge and military commander) in Burghausen; and Konstantin Fugger became *Vizedom* in Landshut. Joachim Fugger served as member of the court council in 1593 and rose to the council presidency two years later; in addition, he was chief steward (*Obersthofmeister*) of Albrecht, the brother of Duke Maximilian I. As cupbearer, Hans Jakob Fugger's son Alexius was also a member of the duke's court. Close relationships with the elites of the Habsburg courts and administration, moreover, were established through the marriages of their sister Aemilia to Alexander von Sprinzenstein, the imperial court councilor and governor of Lower Austria, and of their sister Constantia to Archduke Ferdinand's chief constable, Baron Bernhard von Herberstein. Finally, two sons from Hans Jakob Fugger's first marriage became military officers. Carl Fugger (b. 1543) initially served at the court of King Philip II as a cupbearer and later commanded a Spanish regiment in the Netherlands as colonel. Carl's younger brother Ferdinand likewise became a colonel in the service of Spain.[36]

Regarding the lineage of Georg Fugger's heirs, Octavian Secundus Fugger's son Ferdinand (1587–1644) became cathedral canon in Bressanone, and his cousin Carl (1587–1642), one of Philipp Eduard's sons, became cathedral canon in Constance and dean of the cathedral chapter in Salzburg. Among Marx Fugger's sons, Anton (1563–1616) obtained the offices of chief constable and court councilor of the duke of Bavaria and served as administrator in Rain on the Lech river from 1611 onward. His cousin Georg Fugger (1577–1643), a son of Jakob Fugger and Anna Ilsung, was governor of the Habsburg province of Swabia from 1597 on and chamberlain at the Innsbruck court. Hans Fugger's son Marx (1564–1614) became chamberlain to Archduke Ernst, Bavarian councilor, and administrator of Landsberg, as well as president of the imperial chamber court. Hans Ernst Fugger (1590–1639) filled the same honorable post and later moved on to the presidency of the imperial Aulic Council in Vienna. Hans Ernst's brother Ott Heinrich was a chamberlain at the court of Ferdinand II (1578–1637), archduke of Inner Austria and later emperor, in Graz from 1611 onward and in 1626 became majordomo of Duke Maximilian I of Bavaria. Two years later, he advanced to the position of head chamberlain of the Munich court. Moreover, he served as administrator of Landsberg from 1627 onward. No fewer than five of Ott Heinrich Fugger's sons, in turn, entered Bavarian and Habsburg service.[37]

As an officer and military entrepreneur, Ott Heinrich pursued "a logical course of action for a young nobleman in an age of intensifying warfare," according to his biographer. In 1617, he recruited his own regiment for Spain's war against Savoy, a regiment that fought the Bohemian rebels after the outbreak of the Thirty Years' War and was stationed in the Netherlands in 1624. After an interruption of several years, Ott Heinrich became active again in the southern German theater of war in 1631 and temporarily rose to the rank of chief commander of the troops of the Catholic League. After Augsburg had been taken by imperial troops, Ott Heinrich Fugger in 1635 became governor of the city where his predecessors had risen to prominence. He assumed the imperial governorship not as a member of the established urban elite but as the representative of a military occupation regime that intended "to reduce the renegade imperial city once again to obedience and enforce law and order." With his reprisals against the Protestant citizenry, arrests, spying, and interference with urban justice, he made numerous enemies, however, and the Augsburg city council managed to persuade the emperor by 1639 to confine his authority to the command of the city guard. At a time that other sources of income were drying up, as the trading company was incurring losses and his manorial estates, devastated by the Thirty Years' War, were not yielding returns, Ott Heinrich Fugger's salary as an officer was an essential source of income. Moreover, Ott Heinrich could hope to receive property grants as a war profiteer; he repeatedly applied for such grants, but his expectations ultimately failed to materialize. Military honors and the prospect of imperial privileges, as well as other displays of favor, however, were probably as important as material gain. The fact that King Philip IV of Spain accepted Ott Heinrich Fugger into the knightly Order of the Golden Fleece in 1627 was very likely the result of his military service and the recommendation of the head of the Catholic League, Maximilian I of Bavaria.[38]

Like other family members, Hans Fugger strategically employed his good relations with the courts of the Wittelsbach and Habsburg dynasties and the Roman curia to promote the careers of his sons, as well as those of his nephews from the Montfort family.[39] His son Jakob (1567–1626) deserves to be singled out, for he rose into the ranks of the ecclesiastical princes of the empire. After attending the universities of Dillingen in 1575 and Ingolstadt in 1577, Jakob Fugger lived in Italy for several years and was appointed one of the pope's secret chamberlains in Rome. Thanks to his connections with the curia, he received canon's benefices in Regensburg and Constance. After his sojourn in Rome ended in 1590 and he had taken a brief turn at the University of Alcalá in Spain, he was ordained a priest in 1592 and became cathedral provost in Constance in the following year. In 1604, he was elected prince-bishop of Constance and thus became head of an important ecclesiastical territory. During his twenty-year tenure, Jakob Fugger energetically pursued reforms in the spirit of the Council of Trent: Like his relatives in Augsburg, he promoted the Jesuits, who established a college in Constance from 1607 to 1610, but also the Capuchins. In addition, he supported the efforts of the abbot of Weingarten, Georg Wegelin, to reform the Benedictine monasteries, commissioned church visitations, and put his bishopric's relations with the Catholic Swiss cantons on a new foundation with the establishment of an episcopal commissariat in the town of Lucerne. The statutes passed at a diocesan synod in 1609 regulated the distribution of the sacraments, the celebration of Holy Mass, the duties and behavior of the clergy, the administration and discipline of convents, and ecclesiastical jurisdiction in accordance with the Council of Trent. In the ongoing conflicts with Protestant-

Within the engraving:

IACOBVS FVGGER FILIVS. IV. IOANNIS,
EPISCOPVS CONSTANTIENSIS.

L. Kilian excl.   103.

Mathias Kager. inuentor.   Lucas Kilian. sculpsit.

FIGURE 21
Prince-bishop Jakob Fugger of Constance (1567–1626)
from Fuggerorum and Fuggerarum . . . imagines, 1618.
(Bayerische Staatsbibliothek München)

ism, Jakob Fugger pursued an aggressive course in his own diocese, as well as in the political alliances he formed: The prince-bishopric of Constance was one of the founding members of the Catholic League.[40]

This survey of the careers and fields of activity of family members in the late sixteenth century and early seventeenth century demonstrates that an economic and social-history perspective that perceives the Fuggers merely as merchants, bankers, and feudal lords is inadequate. In an era that, according to modern historians, was mainly characterized by processes of confessionalization and state formation,[41] we find representatives of the Fugger family at the head of ecclesiastical territories, central government bodies, and imperial courts. These offices brought high reputation with them, as well as significant income and political influence. While the family's commercial and financial affairs confronted mounting difficulties, the extensive manorial and territorial possessions formed a solid economic foundation for the family's future, while activities in the church, government bureaucracies, and the military opened up promising new fields of employment and advancement for the Fuggers, as well as for other leading urban families such as the Herwarts, Welsers, and Rehlingers.[42]

CONCLUSION

Compared with older histories of the Fugger family, this book has attempted to provide some new perspectives. The rise of the enterprise under the leadership of Jakob and Anton Fugger was not only the work of individual personalities, but part of a general upsurge of the European economy in which an increasing demand for precious metals, as well as the emerging modern states' need for credit, opened up new business opportunities. To realize these opportunities, the firm depended on a large number of agents and experts. The history of the Fugger firms after 1560 was not so much a story of decline as a case of structural adjustment to changing economic and political conditions. The Fugger company itself was not a unique phenomenon but a prominent version of the southern German family trading firm of the long sixteenth century. The Fuggers' patronage of the arts and their foundations were closely tied to the family's economic capability and wide-ranging business connections, while its contributions to the family's increasing status and prestige were substantial. The family's large-scale real-estate acquisitions were not a mere withdrawal to the countryside but an investment strategy that promised both economic profit and social recognition. Finally, the entry of family members into court service, princely administrations, and ecclesiastical and military careers appeared as a logical course of action when viewed against the background of the early modern processes of state formation and confessionalization. The history of the Fuggers from the late fourteenth century to the mid-seventeenth century, which has been the subject of this book, presents not a linear case of a rise from the urban bourgeoisie into the imperial nobility but, rather, a multilayered, tension-filled period in which family members simultaneously moved within different economic, political, social, and cultural spheres. The fact that family members mainly derived their living from their manorial estates and territories after the Thirty Years' War and pursued careers at princely courts, in the church, and in the military reflects changing political and economic circumstances as well as long-term changes in family ideals and social norms.

If finally we return to the question posed in the introduction concerning the norms and motivations that guided the Fuggers' actions during the period under consideration, we encounter the twin terms "honor" (*Ehre*) and "benefit" (*Nutzen*) in the sources time and again. In his dispositions for the future of the Hungarian trade and the family's real estate in 1512, Jakob Fugger referred to the "honor, benefit, and advancement" of the Fuggers' "name and lineage."[1] In letters he wrote a few weeks before his death on the occasion of the crisis of the Hungarian trade, Fugger emphasized that the conflict was not merely about a lucrative field of business, but also about rescuing his honor.[2] In a privilege that he granted to the Fugger firm on October 26, 1525, Emperor Charles V stressed that the firm had substantially promoted the "honor, welfare, benefit, and advancement" of the House of Habsburg with the provision of credit and other "useful and beneficial demonstrations of obedience and loyalty".[3] In 1531, Anton Fugger remarked on the family's real-estate purchases: "For we are not doing it for profit's sake, but for honor's sake."[4] In the company contract that they concluded in the following year, Raymund, Anton, and Hieronymus Fugger emphasized the obligation, inherited from their uncle, to preserve the family's "name and lineage still further in a good and honorable state."[5] When Anton Fugger learned about plans to resell the Swabian territories of Kirchberg and Weißenhorn to the imperial city of Ulm in 1538, he reminded King Ferdinand what his family had done for the "highest honor, benefit, welfare, and rise of the house of Austria."[6] In the same year, Georg Hörmann, Anton Fugger's factor at Schwaz and trusted adviser, admonished Hans Jakob Fugger "that you consider well those matters which are conducive to your own honor and benefit as well as that of your house and the Fuggers' name".[7] The family's *Book of Honors,* which Hans Jakob Fugger commissioned, explicitly served the purpose that "the Fugger' honor remain in good memory for many years and future times." In portraying Jakob Fugger, the *Book of Honors* emphasized his commitment to the city's common good, as well as the "honor and benefit" of the imperial family. Through his close relations with Emperor Maximilian, "the whole name and commerce of the Fuggers" acquired "a high reputation and wealth . . . , so that they subsequently showed remarkable help and financial assistance to many kings, princes, and lords, to their great honor and benefit."[8]

What is striking in these quotations is that they completely agree with the fundamental norms of early modern society. The family's benefit was understood not as a striving for profit for its own sake, but as a legitimate effort to accumulate prestige and wealth. Moreover, they emphasized the compatibility of the Fuggers' wealth and esteem with the common good of the city of Augsburg and the interests of the emperor and the Empire. These legitimating terms undoubtedly were defensive, for critics repeatedly questioned the Fuggers' honor and the compatibility of their business transactions with the common good. "What kind of nobility is this," the humanist Ulrich von Hutten asked, for example, "which . . . is acquired by dishonorable financial wealth and replaces the lack of virtue with material goods? When money acquires honor, then every yardstick for measuring the true value of things is gone."[9] Other critics did not hesitate to characterize the Fuggers as "Jews," thereby evoking a semantic affiliation with an oppressed religious minority that was always confronted with charges of usury and fraud.[10] And the duke of Württemberg's councilors cast doubt on the family's social honor as late as 1553 when they described Anton Fugger as "the fustian weaver of Augsburg."[11]

Despite widespread criticism of their business practices and public self-display, however, the Fuggers' efforts to increase their status and family honor were remarkably successful. By the end of the sixteenth century, they were securely anchored among the ranks of the southern German imperial nobility and had largely achieved recognition as members of the ruling estates of the Holy Roman Empire. To a considerable extent, this success can be ascribed to the fact that the Fuggers' rise—once again in accord with the norms of feudal estate society—was a gradual process that spanned several generations.[12] The moment in time when the family moved from the bourgeoisie to the nobility cannot be fixed precisely; it cannot be identified with a specific imperial privilege or a project such as the building of the burial chapel of St. Anna. Rather, it was the sum of imperial privileges and favors, splendid festivals and weddings with members of the nobility, foundations for the common good, and loans to kings and princes that ultimately resulted in the social recognition that the family desired and paved the way into the imperial nobility. In the meantime, the Fuggers remained citizens of Augsburg, occupied high office there, ran one of the most important southern German trading companies, and took an active part in the city's interior political and religious conflicts of the sixteenth century. Thus, the family presents an extremely revealing example of the normative power of the values of feudal estate society at the beginning of the modern era, as well as the dynamics that were inherent in this social order.

NOTES

INTRODUCTION

1. Karg, "Betreff."
2. Jansen, *Anfänge,* 7.
3. Strieder, *Jakob Fugger der Reiche,* vii–viii, 2–3, 29, 41.
4. Ibid., 15–17; cf. Böhm, *Reichsstadt Augsburg,* 106; Maschke, "Berufsbewusstsein," 308; Pölnitz, *Jakob Fugger,* 1:465, 476–77; Roeck, *Geschichte Augsburgs,* 100; Wurm, *Johannes Eck,* 42.
5. Ogger, *Kauf dir einen Kaiser.*
6. Pölnitz, *Jakob Fugger,* 1:231, 266.
7. Ibid., 1:81, 131, 477.
8. Pölnitz, "Fugger und Medici." See esp. the final paragraph on p. 23.
9. Pölnitz, *Die Fugger,* 310.
10. See esp. Kellenbenz, *Die Fugger in Spanien.*
11. Hildebrandt, *Die "Georg Fuggerischen Erben";* Mandrou, *Fugger;* Sieh-Burens, *Oligarchie.*
12. Bourdieu, *Distinction* and "Ökonomisches Kapital."
13. Dauser, *Informationskultur;* Haberer, *Ott Heinrich Fugger;* Rohmann, *Ehrenbuch;* Scheller, *Memoria;* Wölfle, *Kunstpatronage.*
14. Cf. Dinges, "Ehre," and particularly for the case of the Fuggers, Rohmann, *Ehrenbuch.*

1. THE FUGGER FAMILY IN LATE MEDIEVAL AUGSBURG

1. Jansen, *Anfänge,* 8–10; Kalesse, *Bürger in Augsburg,* 88; Pölnitz, *Jakob Fugger,* 1:7, 2:1; Rohmann, *Ehrenbuch,* 1:208–9; Stromer, *Gründung,* 32–33. An image of the first tax book entry can be found in Roeck, *Geschichte Augsburgs,* 85.
2. Jansen, *Anfänge,* 20–21.
3. Kießling, *Die Stadt und ihr Land,* 722–23, and "Stadt und Land im Textilgewerbe," 117.
4. Jansen, *Anfänge,* 14–16, 89–90, 95–96; Lieb, *Die Fugger und die Kunst,* 1:5–7; Pölnitz, *Jakob Fugger,* 1:8, 2:2; Rohmann, *Ehrenbuch,* 1:208; Schad, *Frauen,* 9–10.
5. Peter Geffcken, "Steuer(n)," in *Augsburger Stadtlexikon,* 854–57.
6. Rohmann, *Ehrenbuch,* 1:78, 208.
7. Geffcken, "Soziale Schichtung," app., 6–7 (table 1). Since Geffcken uses the property assessment as a category that allows comparisons over time, his data are clearly preferable to those in Strieder, *Zur Genesis des modernen Kapitalismus,* 163–72. See also Jansen, *Anfänge,* 16–20; Pölnitz, *Jakob Fugger,* 2:2.
8. Pölnitz, *Jakob Fugger,* 1:7–8; Strieder, *Zur Genesis des modernen Kapitalismus,* 165–67.
9. Geffcken, "Soziale Schichtung," app., 14 (table 2), 21 (table 3), 29 (table 4), 36 (table 5).
10. Aloys Schulte, as quoted in Strieder, *Zur Genesis des modernen Kapitalismus,* 167.
11. Schad, *Frauen,* 11–15; Wunder, *Er ist die Sonn',* 125–26.

12. See Geffcken, "Soziale Schichtung," app., 82 (table 11), 91 (table 12); Jansen, *Anfänge*, 23–24, 30, 172–73;

13. Geffcken, "Soziale Schichtung," app., 102–3 (table 13); Peter Geffcken et al., "Fugger," in *Augsburger Stadtlexikon*, 420; Jansen, *Anfänge*, 23, 31, 33; Lieb, *Die Fugger und die Kunst*, 1:8–10; Pölnitz, *Jakob Fugger*, 1:9; Rohmann, *Ehrenbuch*, 1:265–66; Strieder, *Zur Genesis des modernen Kapitalismus*, 170.

14. In 1462, she paid taxes on 4,908 florins; in 1466, on 4,462 florins: Geffcken, "Soziale Schichtung," 111 (table 14), 121 (table 15). See Jansen, *Anfänge*, 25, 33; Strieder, *Zur Genesis des modernen Kapitalismus*, 164. On the Stammler family, see Peter Geffcken, "Stammler," in *Augsburger Stadtlexikon*, 843–44.

15. Peter Geffcken, "Grander," in *Augsburger Stadtlexikon*, 452. Geffcken partly corrects the information given in Strieder, *Zur Genesis des modernen Kapitalismus*, 181–83. See also Rohmann, *Ehrenbuch*, 1:96, 267.

16. Rohmann, *Ehrenbuch*, 1:268.

17. Jansen, *Anfänge*, 36–37, 44, 104–7, 176–77; Schulte, *Geschichte*, 2:55 (nos. 62, 66), 89 (no. 169).

18. Jansen, *Anfänge*, 37, 44–45, 109, 182–83; Pölnitz, *Jakob Fugger*, 2:14, 27.

19. Jansen, *Anfänge*, 38, 105. For the Fuggers' relationship to Gastel Haug, see Peter Geffcken, "Haug," in *Augsburger Stadtlexikon*, 478; Rohmann, *Ehrenbuch*, 1:269.

20. Jansen, *Anfänge*, 184–85; Pölnitz, *Jakob Fugger*, 2:15; Simonsfeld, *Fondaco*, 1:315 (no. 583).

21. Jansen, *Anfänge*, 36–37.

22. Ibid., 38–41, 102, 121, 189–90; Pölnitz, *Jakob Fugger*, 2:70–71; Trauchburg-Kuhnle, "Kooperation und Konkurrenz," 214–15.

23. Jansen, *Anfänge*, 41–42, 110–13, 188–89; Simonsfeld, *Fondaco*, 1:323 (no. 594), 328–29 (nos. 603–4, 606), 2:61.

24. Rohmann, *Ehrenbuch*, 1:268–69.

25. Häberlein, *Brüder, Freunde und Betrüger*, 261–74, 280–81, 324–27, 331–36.

26. Rohmann, *Ehrenbuch*, 1:271.

27. Pölnitz, *Jakob Fugger*, 2:70.

28. See Häberlein, *Brüder, Freunde und Betrüger*.

29. *Die Chroniken der deutschen Städte*, 5:99–101; Jahn, "Augsburger Sozialstruktur," 188; Jansen, *Anfänge*, 26–27, 173; Pölnitz, *Jakob Fugger*, 1:9–10.

30. Rohmann, *Ehrenbuch*, 1:213.

31. Jansen, *Anfänge*, 31–32; Rohmann, *Ehrenbuch*, 1:89.

32. Geffcken, "Soziale Schichtung," app., 149 (table 18), 157 (table 19), 166–67 (table 20). See also Jansen, *Anfänge*, 63.

33. Rohmann, *Ehrenbuch*, 1:92, 269.

34. Jansen, *Anfänge*, 47, 64–65, 90–95, 175–76; Lieb, *Die Fugger und die Kunst*, 1:27, 32–33; Pölnitz, *Jakob Fugger*, 1:13–14; Strieder, *Jakob Fugger der Reiche*, 57–58.

35. Rohmann, *Ehrenbuch*, 1:88–89; Schad, *Frauen*, 12–13; Strieder, *Jakob Fugger der Reiche*, 55–56, 64–65.

36. Jansen, *Anfänge*, 48, 104–7; Pölnitz, *Anfänge*, 199; Rohmann, *Ehrenbuch*, 1:168.

37. Jansen, *Anfänge*, 48–50, 60, 181, 184, 186–87, and *Jakob Fugger*, 6–8; Strieder, *Jakob Fug-*

ger der Reiche, 59. For relations with Italy, see Schulte, *Geschichte*, 2:56 (no. 74); Simonsfeld, *Fondaco*, 1:309 (no. 568), 315 (no. 582), 2:15, 61.

38. Jansen, *Anfänge*, 65–66.

39. Ibid., 48–50; Pölnitz, *Jakob Fugger*, 2:62; Schulte, *Die Fugger in Rom*, 11–12.

40. Jansen, *Anfänge*, 50–51, 174; Kießling, *Bürgerliche Gesellschaft*, 324–25; Rohmann, *Ehrenbuch*, 1:82.

41. Jansen, *Anfänge*, 52–53, 102–3; Pölnitz, *Jakob Fugger*, 2:62–63.

42. The respected guild of the *Salzfertiger* initially consisted of only the urban salt traders, but from the late fifteenth century on, it also accepted numerous people from other crafts and commercial branches: see Peter Geffcken, "Salzfertiger," in *Augsburger Stadtlexikon*, 773.

43. Peter Geffcken, "Lauginger II," in *Augsburger Stadtlexikon*, 602; Geffcken, "Imhof II," in ibid., 527; Geffcken, "Fugger," in ibid., 420; Jansen, *Anfänge*, 28–30, 47, 61, 65–66; Nebinger, "Standesverhältnisse," 262; Rohmann, *Ehrenbuch*, 1:213–18; Schad, *Frauen*, 17–20.

44. Georg Kreuzer, "Mülich, Hektor," in *Augsburger Stadtlexikon*, 666–67 (with bibliographical references).

45. Jahn, "Augsburger Sozialstruktur," 188; Kießling, *Die Stadt und ihr Land*, 715–17.

46. Kießling, "Augsburgs Wirtschaft," 175, and *Die Stadt und ihr Land*, 721, 723–25; Stromer, *Gründung*, 31.

47. Jahn, "Augsburger Sozialstruktur," 188–89; Kießling, "Augsburgs Wirtschaft," 174, 176; Kießling, "Bürgerlicher Besitz auf dem Land," 121–22; Kießling, *Die Stadt und ihr Land*, 725; Rogge, *Für den Gemeinen Nutzen*, 30–41.

48. Kalesse, *Bürger in Augsburg*, 226–29.

49. Kießling, "Augsburgs Wirtschaft," 175–76; Kießling, "Bürgerlicher Besitz auf dem Land," 117–19; Kießling, *Die Stadt und ihr Land*, 725; Stromer, *Gründung*, 31–32.

50. Kießling, "Augsburgs Wirtschaft," 176–77; Kießling, "Bürgerlicher Besitz auf dem Land," 123–24; Kießling, *Die Stadt und ihr Land*, 726–29; Rogge, *Für den Gemeinen Nutzen*, 107–18.

51. Kießling, "Augsburgs Wirtschaft," 177; Jahn, "Augsburger Sozialstruktur," 188.

52. Steinmeyer, *Nördlinger Pfingstmesse*, 84–89.

53. Pölnitz, "Die Anfänge der Weißenhorner Barchentweberei," 197.

54. Kießling, "Augsburgs Wirtschaft," 176, and *Die Stadt und ihr Land*, 731–32.

55. Ehrenberg, *Zeitalter*, 1:187–88; Hildebrandt, "Augsburger und Nürnberger Kupferhandel," 206–7; Kießling, "Augsburgs Wirtschaft," 177; Strieder, *Jakob Fugger der Reiche*, 42–43.

56. Jahn, "Augsburger Sozialstruktur," 190; Kießling, "Augsburgs Wirtschaft," 178; Rogge, *Für den Gemeinen Nutzen*, 33, 101–3.

57. Kießling, "Augsburg zwischen Mittelalter und Neuzeit," 241–42; Rogge, *Für den Gemeinen Nutzen*, 12–16, 299–301 (quote on 13).

58. Jahn, "Augsburger Sozialstruktur," 191; Rogge, *Für den Gemeinen Nutzen*, 16–27. On the character of elections in the imperial city, see Rogge, "Ir freye Wale zu haben."

59. Geffcken, "Soziale Schichtung," 192.

60. Jansen, *Anfänge*, 23; Pölnitz, *Jakob Fugger*, 1:9.

61. Geffcken, "Soziale Schichtung," 188, 191, 193, 196; Jansen, *Anfänge*, 34–35; Pölnitz, *Jakob Fugger*, 2:69; Rohmann, *Ehrenbuch*, 1:95.

62. See the table in Geffcken, "Soziale Schichtung," 205–6.

63. Rogge, *Für den Gemeinen Nutzen*, 184–91.

64. Jahn, "Augsburger Sozialstruktur," 191; Kießling, "Augsburg zwischen Mittelalter und Neuzeit," 244.

65. Jansen, *Anfänge*, 43–44.

66. Rohmann, *Ehrenbuch*, 1:175.

67. Jansen, *Anfänge*, 66–67, 178–82, 185–86, 190–91; Lieb, *Die Fugger und die Kunst*, 1: 47–50.

68. Jansen, *Anfänge*, 47.

69. Pölnitz, *Jakob Fugger*, 1:11–12; Strieder, *Jakob Fugger der Reiche*, 56.

70. Jansen, *Anfänge*, 47–48, and *Jakob Fugger*, 3–6; Rohmann, *Ehrenbuch*, 1:213–18.

71. Rohmann, *Ehrenbuch*, 1:174.

72. Pölnitz, *Jakob Fugger*, 1:12.

73. Geffcken, "Jakob Fuggers frühe Jahre," 5–7. See also Ehrenberg, *Zeitalter*, 1:87–88; Simonsfeld, *Fondaco*, 2:61.

2. JAKOB FUGGER THE RICH

1. For the texts, see Jansen, *Jakob Fugger*, 263–70. See also ibid., 30–32; Strieder, "Geschäfts- und Familienpolitik," 194–96, and *Jakob Fugger der Reiche*, 66–67, 72–73.

2. The quotes are from Pölnitz, *Jakob Fugger*, 1:58.

3. See Häberlein, *Brüder, Freunde und Betrüger*, 341–43, 377–79; Lutz, *Struktur*.

4. According to Jansen, *Jakob Fugger*, 14–15, Tyrolean sources mention Jakob Fugger's company even before 1490.

5. Pölnitz, *Jakob Fugger*, 1:347, 2:369.

6. Jansen, *Jakob Fugger*, 32–35. For the texts, see ibid., 268–86; cf. Pölnitz, *Jakob Fugger*, 1:137–38, 2:122–23; Strieder, "Geschäfts- und Familienpolitik," 196–99, and *Jakob Fugger der Reiche*, 73–77.

7. Jansen, *Jakob Fugger*, 1:36–38. For the texts, see ibid., 286–306 (quote on 291). See Pölnitz, *Jakob Fugger*, 1:285–88, 2:244–46, 270; Strieder, "Geschäfts- und Familienpolitik," 200–1, and *Jakob Fugger der Reiche*, 78–83.

8. Jansen, *Jakob Fugger*, 272, 298. In this case, the term "secular" (*weltlich*) refers to male family members who did not become clergymen.

9. Jansen, *Anfänge*, 54–55; Kellenbenz, "Jakob Fugger," 39; Pölnitz, *Jakob Fugger*, 1:30–31, 2:9–10; Unger, *Die Fugger in Hall*, 32–33. For Cavalli, see Noflatscher, *Räte und Herrscher*, 43–44.

10. Ehrenberg, *Zeitalter*, 1:89–90; Jansen, *Anfänge*, 55–56, and *Jakob Fugger*, 10–19; Kellenbenz, "Jakob Fugger," 39–40; Palme, "Fugger in Tirol," 300–1; Pölnitz, *Jakob Fugger*, 1:34–37; Schick, *Un grand homme d'affaires*, 21–26; Strieder, *Jakob Fugger der Reiche*, 105–7; Unger, *Die Fugger in Hall*, 33–35.

11. Jansen, *Anfänge*, 124–26, and *Jakob Fugger*, 19–21; Kellenbenz, "Jakob Fugger," 40–41; Pölnitz, *Jakob Fugger*, 1:39–42, 2:12–13, 16–17; Schick, *Un grand homme d'affaires*, 33–37; Unger, *Die Fugger in Hall*, 35–36.

12. Ehrenberg, *Zeitalter*, 1:90–91; Jansen, *Anfänge*, 57, 131–34, and *Jakob Fugger*, 24–25, 27, 79–81, 195–97; Pölnitz, *Jakob Fugger*, 1:45–49, 63, 2:17–18, 29–33, 58; Schick, *Un grand homme d'affaires*, 37–41; Unger, *Die Fugger in Hall*, 36–38.

13. Jansen, *Jakob Fugger*, 23–24; Pickl, "Kupfererzeugung," 136; Pölnitz, *Jakob Fugger*, 1:44, 60–61, 2:16.

14. Jansen, *Anfänge*, 58–59, and *Jakob Fugger*, 26–27; Kellenbenz, "Gold Mining Activities," 197; Ludwig and Gruber, *Gold- und Silberbergbau*, 100, 135–41; Pölnitz, *Jakob Fugger*, 1:29–30, 2:20–21, 73, 111–12, 147.

15. Böhm, *Reichsstadt Augsburg*, 289–90; Hollegger, *Maximilian I.*, 185; Jansen, *Jakob Fugger*, 197–225; Pölnitz, *Jakob Fugger*, 1:91–96, 134–44, 149–52 and passim, 2:60, 71–72, 78–90, 187–88 and passim.

16. Ehrenberg, *Zeitalter*, 1:91–93; Jansen, *Jakob Fugger*, 79–131; Kellenbenz, "Jakob Fugger," 45–46, 51–52; Pölnitz, *Jakob Fugger*, 2:124–26, 159, 164, 179, 183, 194–95, 223; Schick, *Un grand homme d'affaires*, 62–74, 83–85.

17. Westermann, *Die Listen der Brandsilberproduktion*, 60–94, and "Zur Silber- und Kupferproduktion," 206.

18. See Kellenbenz, "Schwäbische Kaufherren," 209; Westermann, "Zur Silber- und Kupferproduktion," 193–94.

19. Kellenbenz, "Kapitalverflechtung," 24–27; Kellenbenz, "Schwäbische Kaufherren," 209–10; Kellenbenz, "Wirtschaftsleben der Blütezeit," 265.

20. Hollegger, *Maximilian I.*, 147–48; Noflatscher, *Räte und Herrscher*, 60, 68, 74, 84, 144, 148–49, 184, 209, 224, 250, 252, 278, 291, 374, 402.

21. Böhm, *Reichsstadt Augsburg*, 286; Ehrenberg, *Zeitalter*, 1:91; Jansen, *Jakob Fugger*, 80–84, 88, 195–203; Rolf Kießling, "Gossembrot," in *Augsburger Stadtlexikon*, 449–50; Pölnitz, *Jakob Fugger*, 1:66, 68, 83–85, 2:17–19, 29–30, 33, 39, 58–60, 68, 72, 87–88.

22. Pölnitz, *Jakob Fugger*, 2:19, 28, 31, 87, 160. For Hans von Stetten, see also Noflatscher, *Räte und Herrscher*, 144, 148, 197, 224, 250, 252, 257, 281, 408.

23. Pölnitz, *Jakob Fugger*, 2:24–25, 57.

24. See Fuhrmann, "'Öffentliches' Kreditwesen," 14; Kießling, *Bürgerliche Gesellschaft*, 187; Wurm, *Johannes Eck*, 47, 52.

25. Jansen, *Jakob Fugger*, 133–37; Kalus, *Die Fugger in der Slowakei*, 43–46, 51–54; Kellenbenz, "Jakob Fugger," 43–44; Pölnitz, *Jakob Fugger*, 1:52–54, 77, 2:22–23, 33–34, 53; Schick, *Un grand homme d'affaires*, 47–55.

26. Jansen, *Jakob Fugger*, 137–38, 152–53; Kalus, *Die Fugger in der Slowakei*, 54–58, 65–66, 72–73; Pölnitz, *Jakob Fugger*, 1:69–77 (figures on 71, 77), 2:35–38, 46–50, 53–56, 76–77, 99–101; Strieder, *Jakob Fugger der Reiche*, 114–15; Vlachović, "Kupfererzeugung," 150.

27. Kalus, *Die Fugger in der Slowakei*, 37–39, 59; Pölnitz, *Jakob Fugger*, 1:73–74, 2:39–40.

28. Jansen, *Jakob Fugger*, 68–72; 138–44, 150–51, 191–93; Kalus, *Die Fugger in der Slowakei*, 58–59, 65–66; Kellenbenz, "Gold Mining Activities," 186; Pölnitz, *Jakob Fugger*, 1:129–30, 186, 2:40–44, 53–55, 74–77, 104–19, 319–20; Strieder, *Jakob Fugger der Reiche*, 115–17.

29. Schick, *Un grand homme d'affaires*, 117, 160. See also Jansen, *Jakob Fugger*, 158–59; Kalus, *Die Fugger in der Slowakei*, 58; Vlachović, "Kupfererzeugung," 150. The accounts of the Hungarian trade during this period are summarized in Pölnitz, *Jakob Fugger*, 2:224–31, 252–54, 282–99, 352–68, 430–35, 447–50, 455–62, 580–88.

30. Hildebrandt, "Augsburger und Nürnberger Kupferhandel," 193; Kalus, *Die Fugger in der Slowakei*, 62–64.

31. Hildebrandt, "Augsburger und Nürnberger Kupferhandel," 208; Jansen, *Jakob Fugger*, 155–56; Kalus, *Die Fugger in der Slowakei*, 64; Strieder, *Jakob Fugger der Reiche*, 117–18.

32. Jansen, *Jakob Fugger*, 52–53; Kellenbenz, "Jakob Fugger," 45; Pickl, "Kupfererzeugung,"

137; Pölnitz, *Jakob Fugger,* 1:96–108, 126–28, 133–34; 2:78, 81, 83–84, 98–99; Schick, *Un grand homme d'affaires,* 61–62; Strieder, *Jakob Fugger der Reiche,* 118–19.

33. Lutz, *Conrad Peutinger,* 39–41.

34. Jansen, *Jakob Fugger,* 59–60; 144–47; Pölnitz, *Jakob Fugger,* 1:289–97; 2:278–81.

35. Kalus, *Die Fugger in der Slowakei,* 66–99; see also Jansen, *Jakob Fugger,* 160–78; Pölnitz, *Jakob Fugger,* 1:540–542, 602–5; Schick, *Un grand homme d'affaires,* 103–7.

36. Kellenbenz, "Jakob Fugger," 46–47; Pölnitz, *Jakob Fugger,* 1:87–90; 2:34, 62–67, 74–75, 80; Schick, *Un grand homme d'affaires,* 119–25; Schulte, *Die Fugger in Rom,* 1:6–18; Tewes, "Luthergegner," 288–89.

37. On Schwab, see Tewes, "Luthergegner," 282–95.

38. Pölnitz, *Jakob Fugger,* 1:121–23; 2:90–96, 129–30; Schulte, *Die Fugger in Rom,* 1:22–32, 109–11, 279–89.

39. Pölnitz, *Jakob Fugger,* 1:263–64.

40. Kellenbenz, "Jakob Fugger," 47; Lutz, *Conrad Peutinger,* 102; Pölnitz, *Jakob Fugger,* 1: 275–77; 2:130–31, 153–54; Schulte, *Die Fugger in Rom,* 1:27–29.

41. Kellenbenz, "Jakob Fugger," 47–48, 56; Pölnitz, *Jakob Fugger,* 1:146, 163–66, 171, 184–85, 211, 222; 2:130–31, 146, 152–53, 155–57, 169–70, 196–97, 204, 254–56, 268–69; Schick, *Un grand homme d'affaires,* 134–35; Schulte, *Die Fugger in Rom,* 1:33–54, 207–8; Strieder, *Jakob Fugger der Reiche,* 144–51.

42. Pölnitz, *Jakob Fugger,* 1:298–99; Schick, *Un grand homme d'affaires,* 125–33; Schulte, *Die Fugger in Rom,* 1:55–92, 155–65; Tewes, "Luthergegner," 330 and passim.

43. Ehrenberg, *Zeitalter,* 1:98–99; Kellenbenz, "Jakob Fugger," 54–55; Pölnitz, *Jakob Fugger,* 1:306–11, 320; 2:321–27; Schulte, *Die Fugger in Rom,* 1:93–145.

44. Burkhardt, *Reformationsjahrhundert,* 33–34; Reinhard, *Probleme deutscher Geschichte,* 268–69.

45. Kellenbenz, "Jakob Fugger," 56; Pölnitz, *Jakob Fugger,* 1:502–503; 2:412, 475–76, 498–99, 542–43, 545–47, 569, 573–74; Schulte, *Die Fugger in Rom,* 1:188–92, 207–10, 226–28, 235.

46. See Knittler, "Europas Wirtschafts- und Handelsräume."

47. Braunstein, "Le marché du cuivre," 92–93; Jansen, *Jakob Fugger,* 1:13; Pölnitz, *Jakob Fugger,* 2:15, 79–80, 134; Simonsfeld, *Fondaco,* 1:315 (no. 582); 2:15, 61; Strieder, *Jakob Fugger der Reiche,* 99–100.

48. Böhm, *Reichsstadt Augsburg,* 52, 64–65; Jansen, *Jakob Fugger,* 60–61, 208; Lutz, *Conrad Peutinger,* 77–96; Pickl, "Kupfererzeugung," 137–38; Pölnitz, *Jakob Fugger,* 1:162–63, 205–15, 302; 2:199–200; Schick, *Un grand homme d'affaires,* 86–88; Simonsfeld, *Fondaco,* 1:360 (no. 653), 364 (no. 658); 2:177; Weitnauer, *Venezianischer Handel,* 48–51.

49. Ehrenberg, *Zeitalter,* 1:98; Lieb, *Die Fugger und die Kunst,* 2:81; Pölnitz, *Jakob Fugger,* 2: 210–11; Schulte, *Die Fugger in Rom,* 1:193; Simonsfeld, *Fondaco,* 2:61–62.

50. Weitnauer, *Venezianischer Handel,* 40–41.

51. Ibid., 65–106.

52. Kellenbenz, "Neues zum oberdeutschen Ostindienhandel," 82–85; Mathew, *Indo-Portuguese Trade,* 154. On German interest in the Portuguese discovery, see also Johnson, *The German Discovery of the World.*

53. Johnson, *The German Discovery of the World,* 96; Lutz, *Conrad Peutinger,* 154–57; Mathew, *Indo-Portuguese Trade,* 155–57; Pölnitz, *Jakob Fugger,* 1:147–49; 2:133–35.

54. See Kellenbenz, *Die Fugger in Spanien*, 1:49, and "Neues zum oberdeutschen Ostindienhandel," 86–87.

55. Johnson, *German Discovery of the World*, 96–97; Kellenbenz, "Neues zum oberdeutschen Ostindienhandel," 88; Pölnitz, *Jakob Fugger*, 2:179; Schaper, *Hirschvogel*, 219–20, 230–31.

56. Kellenbenz, *Die Fugger in Spanien*, 1:52–53; Pölnitz, *Jakob Fugger*, 2:233–34.

57. Kellenbenz, *Die Fugger in Spanien*, 1:54–61, and "Jakob Fugger," 63; Mathew, *Indo-Portuguese Trade*, 162–67.

58. Limberger, "Economies of Agglomeration"; Van der Wee and Materné, "Antwerp". For the German merchants in Antwerp, see Harreld, *High Germans*; Trauchburg-Kuhnle, "Auf den Spuren."

59. Jansen, *Jakob Fugger*, 68, 200; Kellenbenz, "Jakob Fugger," 41; Pölnitz, *Jakob Fugger*, 2: 14, 30.

60. Harreld, *High Germans*, 131; Jansen, *Jakob Fugger*, 156–58; Kalus, *Die Fugger in der Slowakei*, 65; Pölnitz, *Jakob Fugger*, 1:161–62, 211; 2:108, 195, 233, 275, 283–84; Vlachović, "Kupfererzeugung," 154.

61. Doehaerd, *Etudes anversoises*, 3:199 (nos. 3586, 3587); Kellenbenz, *Die Fugger in Spanien*, 1:437; Lieb, *Die Fugger und die Kunst*, 1:69 (Dürer quote); Pölnitz, *Jakob Fugger*, 2:149–50; Strieder, *Jakob Fugger der Reiche*, 98–99; Trauchburg-Kuhnle, "Auf den Spuren," 268, and "Kooperation und Konkurrenz," 216.

62. Doehaerd, *Etudes anversoises*, 2:256–59 (no. 1780); 3:192–93 (no. 3531); Häberlein, "Handelsgesellschaften," 305–6; Jansen, *Jakob Fugger*, 147; Lutz, *Conrad Peutinger*, 62–64.

63. Doehaerd, *Etudes anversoises*, 3:207 (no. 3642), 233 (no. 3813), 239 (no. 3861), 241 (no. 3874). See also Harreld, *High Germans*, 140; Kellenbenz, *Die Fugger in Spanien*, 1:437–38.

64. Pölnitz, *Jakob Fugger*, 2:502–3; Strieder, *Aus Antwerpener Notariatsarchiven*, 3–11, 13.

65. Ehrenberg, *Zeitalter*, 1:96–97; Jansen, *Jakob Fugger*, 44–45, 213–25; Kellenbenz, *Die Fugger in Spanien*, 1:63, 438; Pölnitz, *Jakob Fugger*, 1:297, 343–44, 365, 378, 2:308–9, 361–62, 376–77; Tracy, *Emperor Charles V*, 92; Weitnauer, *Venezianischer Handel*, 71–72.

66. Geffcken, "Welser," 145–57; Kießling, "Wirtschaftlicher Strukturwandel in der Region."

67. Häberlein, "Handelsgesellschaften," 313–14, and "Welser-Vöhlin-Gesellschaft," 20–22.

68. Häberlein, "Handelsgesellschaften," 315–22, and "Welser-Vöhlin-Gesellschaft," 23–29.

69. See Häberlein, "Fugger und Welser," 225–28.

70. Noflatscher, *Räte und Herrscher*, 79, 148–49; Pölnitz, *Jakob Fugger*, 1:253, 300, 2:218, 223, 241, 278, 307–8, 385, 393; Katarina Sieh-Burens, "Adler," in *Augsburger Stadtlexikon*, 223–24.

71. Burschel and Häberlein, "Familie, Geld und Eigennutz," 57–59; Ehrenberg, *Zeitalter*, 1: 212–18; Kern, "Studien," 164–73; Westermann, "Brass-works."

72. Böhm, *Reichsstadt Augsburg*, 103–7; Ehrenberg, *Zeitalter*, 1:95; Jansen, *Jakob Fugger*, 54, 56, 104–5, 108–9, 112, 115–16, 121–22; Palme, "Fugger in Tirol," 301; Pickl, "Kupfererzeugung," 138; Pölnitz, *Jakob Fugger*, 1:257, 272–73, 300, 335–36, 2:163, 246–47, 270, 278, 316, 345, 349–50, 428; Schick, *Un grand homme d'affaires*, 150–55; Strieder, *Jakob Fugger der Reiche*, 120–21, 124–25; Unger, *Die Fugger in Hall*, 54–55, 66–67, 72; Westermann, "Brass-works," 165.

73. Häberlein, *Brüder, Freunde und Betrüger*, 282–87.

74. Böhm, *Reichsstadt Augsburg*, 319; Pölnitz, *Jakob Fugger*, 2:97–98, 111; Strieder, *Jakob Fugger der Reiche*, 68.

75. Jansen, *Jakob Fugger*, 65–66; Pölnitz, *Jakob Fugger*, 2:116, 224, 252, 282.

76. See Davis, *The Gift*; Groebner, *Gefährliche Geschenke*. I explore the Fuggers' practices of gift giving in more detail in Häberlein, "Geschenke und Geschäfte."

77. Böhm, *Reichsstadt Augsburg*, 95, 200; Jansen, *Jakob Fugger*, 225–30 (quote on 229); Kalus, *Die Fugger in der Slowakei*, 77; Kellenbenz, "Jakob Fugger," 52–53; Pölnitz, *Jakob Fugger*, 1:105–6, 127, 255–56, 329–31, 2:82, 117, 127, 346; Strieder, *Jakob Fugger der Reiche*, 134–35.

78. Böhm, *Reichsstadt Augsburg*, 199; Jansen, *Jakob Fugger*, 40–41, 43, 51, 105, 126; Kellenbenz, "Jakob Fugger," 49; Lieb, *Die Fugger und die Kunst*, 1:78–80; Pölnitz, *Jakob Fugger*, 1: 59–60, 64, 84, 140–41, 292, 301, 2:78, 126, 149, 159, 192, 231, 236–37, 406, 453 and passim; Weitnauer, *Venezianischer Handel*, 53.

79. Pölnitz, *Jakob Fugger*, 2:248, 384.

80. Jansen, *Jakob Fugger*, 41–42, 206, 209; Kellenbenz, "Jakob Fugger," 49, 52; Pölnitz, *Jakob Fugger*, 1:43, 85, 182, 205–6, 252, 265, 2:38, 189, 240, 277.

81. See Pieper, "Informationszentren," and the essays in Calabi and Christensen, *Cities and Cultural Exchange*.

82. Jansen, *Jakob Fugger*, 47–51; Pölnitz, *Jakob Fugger*, 1:46, 144, 2:128–29; Schulte, *Die Fugger in Rom*, 1:193; Weitnauer, *Venezianischer Handel*, 117–20.

83. Pölnitz, *Jakob Fugger*, 1:543, 2:438, 452, 455, 476, and "Jakob Fuggers Zeitungen."

84. Kalus, *Die Fugger in der Slowakei*, 82; Kellenbenz, "Jakob Fugger," 55–56; Pölnitz, *Jakob Fugger*, 1:102–3, 112, 221, 251, 331, 2:80, 203; Schulte, *Die Fugger in Rom*, 1:32, 51, 194.

85. Noflatscher, *Räte und Herrscher*, 38–41 (quote on 40), 60, 69–70, 154, 220, 335, 404. See also Schick, *Un grand homme d'affaires*, 44–46.

86. Kellenbenz, "Jakob Fugger," 42–43; Noflatscher, *Räte und Herrscher*, 74; Pölnitz, *Jakob Fugger*, 1:59, 61, 79–80, 2:17–19, 28, 57, 72.

87. Kellenbenz, "Jakob Fugger," 46, 49–50; Pölnitz, *Jakob Fugger*, 1:218–23, 2:178, 200–2, 205, 220; Schick, *Un grand homme d'affaires*, 89–96.

88. Noflatscher, *Räte und Herrscher*, 50–52, 60, 62, 78–79, 182, 200, 245, 273–74, 279–80, 351, 371, 404.

89. Böhm, *Reichsstadt Augsburg*, 54, 65–66, 170–71; Jansen, *Jakob Fugger*, 100–7, 206, 209; Noflatscher, *Räte und Herrscher*, 256, 316; Pölnitz, *Jakob Fugger*, 1:134–38, 172, 189, 199, 210, 253, 273, 292–93, 300, 2:86–87, 126, 306–7 and passim.

90. Pölnitz, *Jakob Fugger*, 2:220–21.

91. Ibid., 1:223–29, 238–40. See also Kellenbenz, "Jakob Fugger," 50–51; Pölnitz, "Streit um den Nachlass."

92. Ehrenberg, *Zeitalter*, 1:94; Hollegger, *Maximilian I.*, 212–14; Pölnitz, *Jakob Fugger*, 1: 267–71; Schulte, *Die Fugger in Rom*, 1:53–54.

93. Jansen, *Jakob Fugger*, 132–33; Kalus, *Die Fugger in der Slowakei*, 40–46; Pölnitz, *Jakob Fugger*, 1:51–53, 255, 2:19–22, 26, 102–7; Strieder, *Jakob Fugger der Reiche*, 108–12.

94. Jansen, *Jakob Fugger*, 149–50; Kalus, *Die Fugger in der Slowakei*, 60–62; Kellenbenz, "Gold Mining Activities," 188, and "Jakob Fugger," 52–53; Pölnitz, *Jakob Fugger*, 1:77–78, 101, 120, 2:56, 78–79, 90, 96–97.

95. Kalus, *Die Fugger in der Slowakei*, 42, 77, 82; Pölnitz, *Jakob Fugger*, 1:122, 322, 2:94, 256; Schulte, *Die Fugger in Rom*, 1:19–20, 25, 47.

96. Kalus, *Die Fugger in der Slowakei*, 42; Lieb, *Die Fugger und die Kunst*, 2:23; Pölnitz, *Jakob Fugger*, 1:55, 2:23.

97. Rohmann, *Ehrenbuch*, 1:37, 174.

98. Kalus, *Die Fugger in der Slowakei*, 89; Pölnitz, *Jakob Fugger*, 2:477–78.

99. Kellenbenz, "Jakob Fugger," 57; Pölnitz, *Jakob Fugger*, 1:386, 410, 2:391.

100. Ehrenberg, *Zeitalter*, 1:100; Kellenbenz, *Die Fugger in Spanien*, 1:62–63; Pölnitz, *Jakob Fugger*, 1:362, 364, 2:362.

101. Detailed coverage of the events of 1518–19 from Jakob Fugger's perspective can be found in Jansen, *Jakob Fugger*, 232–48; Pölnitz, *Jakob Fugger*, 1:365–441, 2:416–23, and *Die Fugger*, 117–35; Schick, *Un grand homme d'affaires*, 161–79. See also Ehrenberg, *Zeitalter*, 1: 100–10; Kellenbenz, *Die Fugger in Spanien*, 1:64–65, and "Jakob Fugger," 58–60; Kohler, *Karl V.*, 72–74; Strieder, *Jakob Fugger der Reiche*, 136–40; Tracy, *Emperor Charles V*, 99, and, most recently, Häberlein, "Jakob Fugger und die Kaiserwahl Karls V."

102. Lutz, *Conrad Peutinger*, 150; Pölnitz, *Jakob Fugger*, 1:437–39, 2:429.

103. Jansen, *Jakob Fugger*, 127–28; Kellenbenz, "Jakob Fugger," 61; Pölnitz, *Jakob Fugger*, 1: 458–59, 496–501. See also Kohler, *Ferdinand I.*, 72–76.

104. Jansen, *Jakob Fugger*, 128–29; Kellenbenz, "Jakob Fugger," 61–62; Palme, "Fugger in Tirol," 298; Pickl, "Kupfererzeugung," 138–39; Pölnitz, *Jakob Fugger*, 1:522–23, 532, 2:516–19, 533–34, 554–56, 590–91; Strieder, *Jakob Fugger der Reiche*, 104–5.

105. Kellenbenz, "Jakob Fugger," 63, 66–67; Lutz, *Conrad Peutinger*, 248; Pölnitz, *Jakob Fugger*, 1:479–81, 515–16, 523–26, 540, 545–46, 550, 553, 2:466, 472, 526, 528–29, 537, 551–53, 565–66, 569–70, 580–81, 586.

106. Ehrenberg, *Zeitalter*, 1:111–15; Kellenbenz, *Die Fugger in Spanien*, 1:65–67; Kellenbenz, "Jakob Fugger," 62; Pölnitz, *Jakob Fugger*, 1:518–19, 549–50, 553.

107. Haebler, *Geschichte*, 45–55; Kellenbenz, *Die Fugger in Spanien*, 1:153–55, 169; Pölnitz, *Jakob Fugger*, 1:519–20, 2:507–8, 569.

108. Jansen, *Jakob Fugger*, 54–56, 259–62; Kellenbenz, "Jakob Fugger der Reiche," 64–66; Pölnitz, *Jakob Fugger*, 1:504–17, 527–30, 532–39, 544–47, 555–65; Schick, *Un grand homme d'affaires*, 187–207; Strieder, *Jakob Fugger der Reiche*, 121–24. See also Lutz, *Conrad Peutinger*, 184–86, 214–22, 269–70, and more generally, with some revisions of the older literature, Mertens, *Im Kampf gegen die Monopole*.

109. Jansen, *Jakob Fugger*, 38–39; Kellenbenz, "Jakob Fugger," 71; Lieb, *Die Fugger und die Kunst*, 2:24; Pölnitz, *Jakob Fugger*, 1:471–76, 642; Simnacher, *Fuggertestamente*, 77–78, 104–17; Strieder, "Geschäfts- und Familienpolitik," 202–3, and *Jakob Fugger der Reiche*, 83–84. The wills are edited in Preysing, *Fuggertestamente*, 51–97 (quotes on 88, 91).

110. *Die Chroniken der deutschen Städte*, 23:167; Pölnitz, *Jakob Fugger*, 1:649–57.

3. ANTON FUGGER, THE HOUSE OF HABSBURG, AND THE EUROPEAN WORLD ECONOMY, 1525–1560

1. Burkhardt, "Jubiläumsvortrag Anton Fugger," 138–43. See also Burkhardt, *Reformationsjahrhundert*, 149–52.

2. See chapter 7 in this volume.

3. Pölnitz, *Anton Fugger*, 1:27–63, 3:2:304–9. *Anton Fugger* was published in five parts within three volumes; the co-author of volume 3, part 2, is Hermann Kellenbenz. Kellenbenz, "Anton Fugger," 48–56; Lieb, *Die Fugger und die Kunst*, 2:67–68; Simnacher, *Fuggertestamente*, 102–4.

4. For this and the following paragraph, see Kalus, *Die Fugger in der Slowakei*, 100–54; Pölnitz, *Jakob Fugger*, 1:602–25; Schick, *Un grand homme d'affaires*, 207–23.

5. Pölnitz, *Jakob Fugger*, 1:613–40.

6. Kellenbenz, "Anton Fugger," 59–60; Pölnitz, *Anton Fugger*, 1:66–73.

7. Pölnitz, *Jakob Fugger*, 1:74–80, 590–98 (quote on 595). See also Blickle, *Revolution*, 18–19, 188–89; Kohler, *Ferdinand I.*, 84–86.

8. Fischer, "Bergbeschau."

9. Kellenbenz, "Anton Fugger," 64; Pölnitz, *Anton Fugger*, 1:96–97, 3:2:310; Scheller, *Memoria*, 182; Schulte, *Die Fugger in Rom*, 1:236–44; Strieder, *Inventur*, 10.

10. Burschel and Häberlein, "Familie, Geld und Eigennutz," 58–61; Ehrenberg, *Zeitalter*, 1:215–18; Kellenbenz, "Anton Fugger," 65, 68–69; Pölnitz, *Anton Fugger*, 1:102–4, 113–14, 118, 128–35, 143–46, 156–63, 234; Trauchburg-Kuhnle, "Kooperation und Konkurrenz," 221–22; Westermann, "Brass-works," 170–71. On the Höchstetter bankruptcy, cf. Safley, "Staatsmacht und geschäftliches Scheitern."

11. Ehrenberg, *Zeitalter*, 1:118–19, 122–25; Jansen, *Jakob Fugger*, 73–76; Strieder, *Inventur* and *Jakob Fugger der Reiche*, 87–89.

12. For the text, see Lutz, *Struktur*, 2:84'–103' (quotes on 84'–85', 91'); see also Kellenbenz, "Anton Fugger," 57–59; Pölnitz, *Anton Fugger*, 1:252–57.

13. Ehrenberg, *Zeitalter*, 1:132–35; Kellenbenz, "Anton Fugger," 85; Pölnitz, *Anton Fugger*, 2: 1:33–35, 331–33, 3:2:373.

14. For the text, see Lutz, *Struktur*, 2:104'–15' (quotes on 107'–8', 112'). See also Ehrenberg, *Zeitalter*, 1:139; Kellenbenz, "Hans Jakob Fugger," 52–53; Pölnitz, *Anton Fugger*, 2:1:51, 54, 69–70.

15. Tracy, *Emperor Charles V*, 100–1. For slightly different figures, see Carande, *Carlos V*, 3: 28–33. Cf. also Kellenbenz, *Die Fugger in Spanien*, 1:397–409; Kohler, *Karl V.*, 145–47.

16. Carande, *Carlos V*, 3:124–41, 226–39, 324–51; Ehrenberg, *Zeitalter*, 1:139–44; Kellenbenz, "Anton Fugger," 91–92 and passim, and *Die Fugger in Spanien*, 1:67–116, 479–80; Kirch, *Die Fugger und der Schmalkaldische Krieg*, 7–19, 67–72, 86–91, 100–10. On the cooperation between the Fugger and Welser companies, see Großhaupt, "Die Welser als Bankiers"; Häberlein, "Fugger und Welser," 228–33. On the Villach *asiento*, cf. Ehrenberg, *Zeitalter*, 1:152–55; Kellenbenz, "Anton Fugger," 99–100; Kohler, *Karl V.*, 148; Pölnitz, *Anton Fugger*, 3:1:292–96.

17. Kellenbenz, *Die Fugger in Spanien*, 1:28–35, 123–49, 337–38, 342, 445–46.

18. Ibid., 1:245–317, 378–82, 485–86; Kellenbenz, *Die Fuggersche Maestrazgopacht*.

19. Kellenbenz, *Die Fugger in Spanien*, 1:317; Lieb, *Die Fugger und die Kunst*, 2:278–82.

20. Kellenbenz, "Anton Fugger," 73–75, 84, and *Die Fugger in Spanien*, 1:157–62, 170; Pölnitz, *Anton Fugger*, 1:222–33. For the Welsers in America, see esp. Denzer, *Konquista*; Otte, "Die Welser in Santo Domingo"; Simmer, *Gold und Sklaven*.

21. Kellenbenz, *Die Fugger in Spanien*, 1:323–60, 374–78, 442. Numerous documents on the commercial and banking transactions of the Fuggers in Seville are contained in Kellenbenz and Walter, *Oberdeutsche Kaufleute*.

22. Kellenbenz, *Die Fugger in Spanien*, 1:439, 444; Pölnitz, *Anton Fugger*, 2:2:561–63; Strieder, *Aus Antwerpener Notariatsarchiven*, 451–54, and "Deutscher Metallwarenexport."

23. Kellenbenz, *Die Fugger in Spanien*, 1:391–93; Johnson, *The German Discovery of the World*, 159–62; Scheller, *Memoria*, 225–30.

24. Ehrenberg, *Zeitalter,* 1:129–30; Kellenbenz, "Anton Fugger," 72, and *Die Fugger in Spanien,* 1:72; Pölnitz, *Anton Fugger,* 1:110, 207–9, 532–33n132, 3:2:340; Strieder, *Inventur,* 18–21.

25. Ehrenberg, *Zeitalter,* 1:130, 134, 137; Müller, *Quellen,* 188–89 (no. 450), 192–93 (no. 462); Kellenbenz, "Anton Fugger," 81, 89; Pölnitz, *Anton Fugger,* 2:1:208–10, 223, 251.

26. Ehrenberg, *Zeitalter,* 1:147; Kellenbenz, "Anton Fugger," 107; Pölnitz, *Anton Fugger,* 2:2:341, 3:1:550, 3:2:343.

27. Hipper, "Beziehungen," 8–9; Kellenbenz, "Anton Fugger," 59, and "Kapitalverflechtung," 23–24; Pölnitz, *Anton Fugger,* 1:64–65, 425n10; Strieder, *Inventur,* 24–25, 42–46, 69; Unger, *Die Fugger in Hall,* 80.

28. Westermann, *Die Listen der Brandsilberproduktion,* 100–9. On the firms involved, see Häberlein, *Brüder, Freunde und Betrüger,* 123–32, 172–77; Kellenbenz, "Kapitalverflechtung," 32–39; Müller, *Quellen,* passim.

29. See Westermann, "Zur Silber- und Kupferproduktion," 196, 206.

30. See Pölnitz, *Anton Fugger,* 1:168, 249, 309, 336, 2:1:57–58, 76, 136–37, 204, 399–400n95, 518n156.

31. Häberlein, *Brüder, Freunde und Betrüger,* 125–26; Müller, *Quellen,* 188–89 (no. 450), 191 (no. 457), 195 (no. 469); Pölnitz, *Anton Fugger,* 2:1:226–27, 281, 284, 538–39nn319–320, 2:2:65, 75–76, 3:1:14, 358; Scheuermann, *Die Fugger als Montanindustrielle,* 28–32, 412–18.

32. Palme, "Fugger in Tirol," 303–4; Pickl, "Kupfererzeugung," 139–40; Pölnitz, *Anton Fugger,* 1:389n5, 424–25 n9, 431–32n36, 451–52n135, 480–84n41, 575–77n116, 2:1:118, 313n95, 362–70n111, 447–48n148, 3:2:319–20, 335–36, 379–80; Strieder, *Inventur,* 53–56, 68–70. On the Hall trading post, see Unger, *Die Fugger in Hall,* esp. 76–28, 231–37.

33. Pölnitz, *Anton Fugger,* 3:2:320–24. On the separation of the Tyrolean business from the family firm, see Scheuermann, *Die Fugger als Montanindustrielle,* 5–47, esp. 10–12, 17–19. On the development of the company's capital and profits, cf. Scheuermann, *Die Fugger als Montanindustrielle,* 50–51, 55–56, and with slightly different figures, Pölnitz, *Anton Fugger,* 3:1:435, 553–54.

34. Kellenbenz, "Anton Fugger," 113–14; Pölnitz, *Anton Fugger,* 3:1:97, 108, 131, 142, 187–88, 215, 226–27, 238, 241, 381, 3:2:26, 34–35, 45–46, 51–52, 54–56, 72–73, 90–91, 102–3, 138–41, 197–98, 221–22, 247–50; Scheuermann, *Die Fugger als Montanindustrielle,* 68–73, 77–78, 108–17.

35. Kellenbenz, "Konto Neapel," 365–67; Pölnitz, *Anton Fugger,* 1:65, 108, 384n142, 388–89n4, 445n118.

36. Ehrenberg, *Zeitalter,* 1:138; Kellenbenz, *Die Fugger in Spanien,* 1:460–61, 477, and "Konto Neapel," 367–72; Kirch, *Die Fugger und der Schmalkaldische Krieg,* 91–96, 161–62; Pölnitz, *Anton Fugger,* 1:209, 230, 237, 534n138, 536n142, 567–69n86, 611n132, 619n148, 2:1:26, 50, 58, 62, 71, 137, 145–48, 151–54, 293–94n3, 306n39, 313–14n97, 337n16, 353n77, 414n140, 522n79, 2:2:70, 75, 123, 221, 279, 294, 345, 3:1:54–56, 154–55, 199, 425, 3:2:390.

37. Kalus, *Die Fugger in der Slowakei,* 163–66, 185–88; Pölnitz, *Anton Fugger,* 3:2:312–18; Strieder, *Inventur,* 46–52.

38. Kalus, *Die Fugger in der Slowakei,* 166–69, 179–84, 194; Kellenbenz, "Anton Fugger," 62–63, 65–66, 69–71, 75–77, 83–84; Pölnitz, *Anton Fugger,* 1:84–85, 88, 92, 106–7, 169–73, 176–99, 202–5, 214–25, 233–38, 243–44, 335–41, 422n156, 427–28n13, 444n105, 464–65n186.

39. Hildebrandt, "Augsburger und Nürnberger Kupferhandel," 193, 197; Pölnitz, *Anton Fugger,* 3:2:314; Strieder, *Inventur,* 46.

40. Kalus, *Die Fugger in der Slowakei*, 184–85, 196–212; Pölnitz, *Anton Fugger*, 1:606–7n113, 2:1:98–99, 166–73, 181–83, 192–202, 321–23n146, 540–42n333.

41. Kalus, *Die Fugger in der Slowakei*, 213–26; Pölnitz, *Anton Fugger*, 2:2:103–4, 126–29, 237–40, 263–64, 298–301, 311–14, 419–23, 433–34, 440–51, 457–61, 480–88, 494–97, 501–4, 509–12, 565–67, 3:2:315; Seibold, *Die Manlich*, 74–79. See also Hildebrandt, "Augsburger und Nürnberger Kupferhandel," 197; Pickl, "Kupfererzeugung," 141.

42. Pölnitz, *Anton Fugger*, 3:2:315–18; Strieder, *Inventur*, 44–45.

43. Kellenbenz, "Gold Mining Activities"; Pölnitz, *Anton Fugger*, 3:1:22–23, 36–37, 43, 78–79 and passim, 3:2:325–28.

44. Kellenbenz, "Anton Fugger," 67; Pölnitz, *Anton Fugger*, 1:119–20, 135–43, 146–51, 178–79, 187–90, 3:2:328–29; Strieder, "Ein Bericht des Fuggerschen Faktors Hans Dernschwam."

45. See chapter 2 in this volume.

46. Ehrenberg, *Zeitalter*, 1:134, 140, 147; 2:53–54; Kellenbenz, *Die Fugger in Spanien*, 1: 440–443; Pölnitz, *Anton Fugger*, 1:619n148, 2:1:470n254, 2:2:340, 3:2:340, 345.

47. Ehrenberg, *Zeitalter*, 1:148, 150–51, 166, 2:53, 57–59; Kellenbenz, "Anton Fugger," 90–91, 95, 97; Pölnitz, *Anton Fugger*, 2:2:74, 97–101, 109–10, 113–17, 150–51, 173, 201, 214, 219–20, 250, 340, 561, 3:1:47–48, 85, 138–39, 150–51, 181, 193–94, 203, 253–54, 263–64, 282, 286, 301, 315, 323, 329–30, 366–67, 396, 409–10, 419, 520–21, 3:2:26, 64, 225–26, 338, 342.

48. Pölnitz, *Anton Fugger*, 2:1:112, 115, 166–67, 188, 3:2:343.

49. Ehrenberg, *Zeitalter*, 1:156, 159; Kellenbenz, "Anton Fugger," 97, 101–3, 108–9; Lieb, *Die Fugger und die Kunst*, 2:137; Pölnitz, *Anton Fugger*, 2:2:515–16, 3:1:70–71, 161, 199, 303, 309–10, 342, 373, 400, 425, 465, 540–41, 3:2:3, 46, 263, 338, 343–44; Wölfle, *Kunstpatronage*, 289–90.

50. Ehrenberg, *Zeitalter*, 1:145–49; Kellenbenz, "Anton Fugger," 95; Pölnitz, *Anton Fugger*, 2:2:329–45, 3:2:373.

51. Ehrenberg, *Zeitalter*, 1:157–58; Kellenbenz, "Anton Fugger," 105–7; Pölnitz, *Anton Fugger*, 3:1:481–83.

52. Ehrenberg, *Zeitalter*, 1:148; 2:53–54; Kellenbenz, *Die Fugger in Spanien*, 1:481; Kirch, *Die Fugger und der Schmalkaldische Krieg*, 31, 105–6; Pölnitz, *Anton Fugger*, 2:2:340–41.

53. Blendinger and Blendinger, *Zwei Augsburger Unterkaufbücher*. See also Kellenbenz, *Die Fugger in Spanien*, 1:101.

54. Ehrenberg, *Zeitalter*, 1:157.

55. Ibid., 1:155–62; Kellenbenz, "Anton Fugger," 98–99, 101, 108, 110–11, and *Die Fugger in Spanien*, 1:101–16, 444; Pölnitz, *Anton Fugger*, 3:2:9–12, 25–26, 36, 40, 50, 60–63, 74–75, 94–95, 98–100, 123–34; Strieder, *Aus Antwerpener Notariatsarchiven*, 432–44.

56. Ehrenberg, *Zeitalter*, 1:162–66, 2:153–59; Kellenbenz, "Anton Fugger," 111–12, 114, and *Die Fugger in Spanien*, 1:116–22, 446–48; Maasen, *Hans Jakob Fugger*, 33; Pölnitz, *Anton Fugger*, 3:2:118–34, 158–62.

57. Pölnitz, *Anton Fugger*, 3:2:251–54.

58. Ehrenberg, *Zeitalter*, 1:166; Kellenbenz, "Anton Fugger," 113–16; Pölnitz, *Anton Fugger*, 3:2, 88, 101, 164–66, 190–97, 209–21, 239–47, 259–60, 252, 282–83; Scheuermann, *Die Fugger als Montanindustrielle*, 106–7.

59. Preysing, *Fuggertestamente*, 114–65 (quotes on 125, 152–53). Cf. Ehrenberg, *Zeitalter*, 1: 144, 167; Kellenbenz, "Anton Fugger," 97, 116, and "Hans Jakob Fugger," 76; Maasen, *Hans Jakob Fugger*, 31–32; Pölnitz, *Anton Fugger*, 3:1:123–25, 3:2:292; Simnacher, *Fuggertestamente*, 79–83.

60. Rabe, *Deutsche Geschichte*, 65.

61. Cf. Landsteiner, "Kein Zeitalter der Fugger," 97–101.

62. Cf. Palme, "Fugger in Tirol," 298–99, 306–7; Pölnitz, *Anton Fugger*, 3:2:141, 262–63 and passim.

63. See Hildebrandt, "Augsburger und Nürnberger Kupferhandel," 209–16; Kellenbenz, "Kapitalverflechtung," and "Wirtschaftsleben der Blütezeit," 265, 275–76.

64. See Häberlein, "Wirtschaftsgeschichte," 149; Kellenbenz, "Wirtschaftsleben der Blütezeit," 265.

65. Blendinger and Blendinger, *Zwei Augsburger Unterkaufbücher;* Häberlein, "Wirtschaftsgeschichte," 150.

66. Häberlein, *Brüder, Freunde und Betrüger,* 79–97, 120–47. See also Kellenbenz, "Wirtschaftsleben der Blütezeit," 275, 287.

67. Kellenbenz, "Wirtschaftsleben der Blütezeit," 271–74. Cf. the example of the Böcklin firm in Häberlein, "Familiäre Beziehungen."

68. Häberlein, "Jakob Herbrot"; Kellenbenz, "Wirtschaftsleben der Blütezeit," 276–77, 280–81.

69. Kellenbenz, "Wirtschaft im Zeitalter der Reformation"; Peters, *Der Handel Nürnbergs.*

70. For a good summary of these processes, see Landsteiner, "Kein Zeitalter der Fugger," 101–18.

71. Häberlein, *Brüder, Freunde und Betrüger,* 341–43, 377–79; Kellenbenz, "Wirtschaftsleben der Blütezeit," 282–83.

72. See Hildebrandt, "Effects of Empire"; Kellenbenz, "Wirtschaftsleben der Blütezeit."

73. Landsteiner, "Kein Zeitalter der Fugger," 97–106.

4. DECLINE OR REORIENTATION?

1. Ehrenberg, *Zeitalter,* 1:170–86; Pölnitz, "Generationenproblem."

2. Hildebrandt, *Die "Georg Fuggerischen Erben,"* 53.

3. Karnehm, "Korrespondenznetz," 303–4, and *Die Korrespondenz Hans Fuggers,* 1:4*–8*; Lieb, *Die Fugger und die Kunst,* 2:309–10; Lutz, "Marx Fugger," 432–35, 442–43; Pölnitz, *Anton Fugger,* 3:1:248–49, 314, 412, 3:2:293–94; Simnacher, *Fuggertestamente,* 123–25; Wölfle, *Kunstpatronage,* 14–15, 22–23.

4. Hildebrandt, *Die "Georg Fuggerischen Erben,"* 22–23; Kellenbenz, "Hans Jakob Fugger," 49–57; Lehmann, *Fuggerbibliotheken,* 1:42–44; Maasen, *Hans Jakob Fugger,* 4–26; Rohmann, *Ehrenbuch,* 1:18–19.

5. Edelmayer and Strohmeyer, *Die Korrespondenz der Kaiser,* 111–12, 149–50 (quote), 186–87, 197, 234 (quote), 248, 322, 335, 346, 405, 445; Ehrenberg, *Zeitalter,* 1:166. See also Haebler, *Geschichte,* 129–36.

6. Ehrenberg, *Zeitalter,* 1:173–76; Hildebrandt, *Die "Georg Fuggerischen Erben,"* 53–54; Pölnitz, *Die Fugger,* 307, and "Die Fuggersche Generalrechnung."

7. Hildebrandt, "Effects of Empire," 62–74; Häberlein, *Brüder, Freunde und Betrüger,* 37–40 and passim.

8. *Die Chroniken der deutschen Städte,* 33:161, 164–65, 174, 183, 210, 379; Ehrenberg, *Zeitalter,* 1:176; Kellenbenz, "Hans Jakob Fugger," 76–79; Lutz, "Marx Fugger," 451; Maasen, *Hans Jakob Fugger,* 33–36; Rohmann, *Ehrenbuch,* 1:20.

9. Kellenbenz, "Hans Jakob Fugger," 79–81; Maasen, *Hans Jakob Fugger,* 38–42.

10. Karnehm, *Die Korrespondenz Hans Fuggers,* 1:nos. 128, 544. See also Lietzmann, "Briefwechsel," 440.

11. Bastl, *Tagebuch,* 325–26; Ehrenberg, *Zeitalter,* 1:183; Hildebrandt, *Die "Georg Fuggerischen Erben,"* 23–24, 57–76; Lutz, "Marx Fugger," 451–52; Sieh-Burens, *Oligarchie,* 103.

12. Hans Fugger's participation in the management of the firm is clearly evident from his letters: Dauser, *Informationskultur,* 84–87; Karnehm, "Korrespondenznetz," 305, and *Die Korrespondenz Hans Fuggers,* 1:nos. 337–38, 1065a and passim. See also Ehrenberg, *Zeitalter,* 1: 176–77; Lill, *Hans Fugger,* 7–8.

13. Karnehm, *Die Korrespondenz Hans Fuggers,* 1:no. 356.

14. Ehrenberg, *Zeitalter,* 2:30, 32; Hassler, *Ausgang,* 31–32; Hildebrandt, "Wirtschaftsentwicklung und Konzentration," 43; Reinhard, *Augsburger Eliten,* 159–63 (no. 246).

15. Karnehm, *Die Korrespondenz Hans Fuggers,* 1:nos. 3, 314.

16. Ibid., 1:nos. 411, 494, 1116, and nos. 681, 901, 1033.

17. Ibid., 1:60*–61* and no. 971, 2:1, nos. 1001, 1011. Cf. Dauser, *Informationskultur,* 163–66; Ehrenberg, *Zeitalter,* 1:181–82; Harreld, *High Germans,* 181; Zorn, *Augsburg,* 236.

18. Lutz, "Marx Fugger," 453–56 (quotes on 454–55). See also Ehrenberg, *Zeitalter,* 1:182–83; Hildebrandt, *Die "Georg Fuggerischen Erben,"* 57.

19. For recent contributions, see Behringer, "Fugger und Taxis"; Pieper, *Die Vermittlung einer neuen Welt;* Schilling, "Zwischen Mündlichkeit und Druck."

20. Karnehm, "Korrespondenznetz," 305–9, and, more extensively, Dauser, *Informationskultur,* 140–312.

21. Karnehm, *Die Korrespondenz Hans Fuggers,* 1:26*–30*. On relations with Venice, see Backmann, "Kunstagenten oder Kaufleute?" 176, 182–84; Wölfle, *Kunstpatronage,* 274–79 and passim.

22. Hildebrandt, *Die "Georg Fuggerischen Erben,"* 56.

23. Haebler, *Geschichte,* 132, 136, 138–44; Johnson, *The German Discovery of the World,* 112; Kellenbenz, "Los Fugger en España."

24. Haebler, *Geschichte,* 144–56.

25. Ibid., 151, 168.

26. Ibid., 158–64, 166, 169. Ehrenberg, *Zeitalter,* 1:178–81; 2:205–21; Hildebrandt, *Die "Georg Fuggerischen Erben,"* 56; Strieder, *Aus Antwerpener Notariatsarchiven,* 445–51; Zorn, *Augsburg,* 235–36.

27. Karnehm, *Die Korrespondenz Hans Fuggers,* 2:1:nos. 940, 1468.

28. Haebler, *Geschichte,* 170–71, 176–77, 190–91, 193–94.

29. Hildebrandt, *Quellen und Regesten,* 1:66–67 (no. 26).

30. Karnehm, *Die Korrespondenz Hans Fuggers,* 1:nos. 356, 821.

31. Hildebrandt, *Quellen und Regesten,* 1:90 (no. 44), 92–94 (nos. 45–47), 101–4 (nos. 56–60), 105–9 (nos. 62–66), 114–15 (nos. 71–73), 121–25 (nos. 77–79), 126 (no. 82), 127 (nos. 84–85); Rauscher, *Zwischen Ständen und Gläubigern,* 170, 232–33. See also Karnehm, *Die Korrespondenz Hans Fuggers,* 1:nos. 591, 976.

32. Edelmayer, *Söldner und Pensionäre,* 166, 168; Hildebrandt, "Der Kaiser und seine Bankiers," 240, and *Quellen und Regesten,* 1:143 (no. 104). See also Bastl, *Tagebuch,* 233, 235.

33. Karnehm, *Die Korrespondenz Hans Fuggers,* 2:2:no. 2309; Lill, *Hans Fugger,* 35–36.

34. Sigelen, "Die Fugger und Reichspfennigmeister Zacharias Geizkofler," 83, 99–102.

Dauser, *Informationskultur,* 203, mentions a loan of 340,000 florins granted in 1594; this was probably the same loan with interest included.

35. Dauser, *Informationskultur,* 235–37; Hildebrandt, *Die "Georg Fuggerischen Erben,"* 104–5, 108; Karnehm, *Die Korrespondenz Hans Fuggers,* 1:48*–49*; Lietzmann, "Briefwechsel," 438–39, 445, 448–59; Wölfle, *Kunstpatronage,* 244–45.

36. Numerous entries in Karnehm, *Die Korrespondenz Hans Fuggers,* passim. For the "moors," who may have been slaves, see Dauser, *Informationskultur,* 87–90, 357–62; Karnehm, *Die Korrespondenz Hans Fuggers,* 1:nos. 752, 762, 1088, 1107;

37. Harreld, *High Germans,* 177.

38. Backmann, "Kunstagenten oder Kaufleute?" 184–86.

39. Karnehm, "Die Korrespondenz Hans Fuggers," 28–29, and *Die Korrespondenz Hans Fuggers,* 1:44*–46*.

40. Edelmayer, *Söldner und Pensionäre,* 239; Karnehm, *Die Korrespondenz Hans Fuggers,* 1: nos. 89, 108–9, 111, 123, 127, 131, 134, 145, 159, 220.

41. Karnehm, *Die Korrespondenz Hans Fuggers,* 1:nos. 188, 208, 210.

42. Ibid., 1:nos. 648, 656, 663, 673, 677, 682, 692, 704, 770.

43. Ibid., 1:nos. 1051, 1052, 1081–82, 1092, 1109, 1220, 1221, 1240.

44. Ibid., 2:1:nos. 8–9, 969–71, 1008, 1065, 1396. Cf. Dauser, *Informationskultur,* 65, 87.

45. Kellenbenz, "Kapitalverflechtung," 39–41; Scheuermann, *Die Fugger als Montanindustrielle,* 132–67; Seibold, *Die Manlich,* 118–22; Spranger, "Der Metall- und Versorgungshandel," 181–82.

46. Scheuermann, *Die Fugger als Montanindustrielle,* 168–323, esp. 180–82, 204–7, 223–25, 260–95, 302–3, 317–22. See also Kellenbenz, "Kapitalverflechtung," 41; Pickl, "Kupfererzeugung," 143–45; Seibold, *Die Manlich,* 122–24; Spranger, *Der Metall- und Versorgungshandel* and "Der Metall- und Versorgungshandel," 186–98. For data on silver production at Falkenstein, see Westermann, *Die Listen der Brandsilberproduktion,* 113–15.

47. Preysing, *Fuggertestamente,* 245–46; Simnacher, *Fuggertestamente,* 83–84.

48. Haberer, *Ott Heinrich Fugger,* 112–13; Haebler, *Geschichte,* 180–90; Karg, "Hans Fugger wird 'Regierer.'"

49. The essential work on which the following paragraphs rely is Hildebrandt, *Die "Georg Fuggerischen Erben."*

50. Bastl, *Tagebuch,* 300–13 and passim; Hildebrandt, *Die "Georg Fuggerischen Erben,"* 24–30, 42–44 (quote on 43).

51. Hildebrandt, *Die "Georg Fuggerischen Erben,"* 71–74, 76, 81–85.

52. Ibid., 39, 86–121; Sigelen, "Die Fugger und Reichspfennigmeister Zacharias Geizkofler," 98.

53. Hildebrandt, *Die "Georg Fuggerischen Erben,"* 131–39.

54. Hildebrandt, "Wirtschaftsentwicklung und Konzentration," 33–37; Warnemünde, "Augsburger Handel," 148–50.

55. Hildebrandt, "Wirtschaftsentwicklung und Konzentration," 37–46; Johnson, *The German Discovery of the World,* 191–95; Reinhard, *Augsburger Eliten,* 713–15 (no. 1088); Warnemünde, "Augsburger Handel," 150–51.

56. Hildebrandt, *Die "Georg Fuggerischen Erben,"* 144–45; Mathew, *Indo-Portuguese Trade,* 172–73.

57. Hildebrandt, *Die "Georg Fuggerischen Erben,"* 145–72; Mathew, *Indo-Portuguese Trade,* 173–83, 186–88.

58. Cf. Haberer, *Ott Heinrich Fugger,* 102–3, 105, 114–15, 124–27.

59. Ibid., 114.

60. Ehrenberg, *Zeitalter,* 1:184–85; Haberer, "Handelsdiener und Handelsherren," 137, 140–45, 152, and *Ott Heinrich Fugger,* 106–7, 128–30, 133–38; Haebler, *Geschichte,* 197–222.

61. Backmann, "Kunstagenten oder Kaufleute?" 186.

62. Haberer, *Ott Heinrich Fugger,* 110–11, 130–31; Pickl, "Kupfererzeugung," 144–46; Scheuermann, *Die Fugger als Montanindustrielle,* 326–65.

63. Haberer, *Ott Heinrich Fugger,* 116–23 (quote on 119).

64. Haberer, *Ott Heinrich Fugger,* 117 (quote), 136, 141–46; Scheuermann, *Die Fugger als Montanindustrielle,* 345–55.

65. Haberer, *Ott Heinrich Fugger,* 101.

5. SERVANTS AND MASTERS

1. Sieh-Burens, *Oligarchie,* 68 (quote).

2. Denzel, "Professionalisierung," 417; Hildebrandt, "Diener und Herren," 152.

3. Hildebrandt, "Diener und Herren," 154–56. On the administration of the Fuggers' rural landholdings, see Mandrou, *Fugger,* 94–99.

4. Jansen, *Jakob Fugger,* 148–49; Pölnitz, *Jakob Fugger,* 2:48, 50–52, 458–62; Schick, *Un grand homme d'affaires,* 242–43. For testamentary bequests, cf. Pölnitz, *Anton Fugger,* 3:2: 298–99; Preysing, *Fuggertestamente,* 75, 163–65; Simnacher, *Fuggertestamente,* 108, 127, 153. On employees' deposit investments, see Strieder, *Inventur,* 65–67. The exceptional nature of provision for old age is emphasized in Hildebrandt, "Diener und Herren," 168.

5. Pölnitz, *Jakob Fugger,* 2:55, 117–18, 237–38.

6. Dauser, "Fern-Gespräche," 38–42; Hildebrandt, "Diener und Herren," 166.

7. Pölnitz, *Jakob Fugger,* 2:44, 238, 460.

8. Kellenbenz, *Die Fugger in Spanien,* 1:172–73, and "Sebastian Kurz"; Kirch, *Die Fugger und der Schmalkaldische Krieg,* 152–53 and passim; Lieb, *Die Fugger und die Kunst,* 2:84–85.

9. See Hildebrandt, *Die "Georg Fuggerischen Erben,"* 45–50.

10. Karnehm, *Die Korrespondenz Hans Fuggers,* 1:nos. 668, 851, 911, 945, 950, 992, 1203; Kellenbenz, *Die Fugger in Spanien,* 1:449; numerous references in Pölnitz, *Anton Fugger,* vols. 1–3: 2 (cf. index); Pölnitz, *Jakob Fugger,* 1:164; 2:144–45. See also Fuchs, "Une famille de négociants banquiers."

11. Häberlein, *Brüder, Freunde und Betrüger,* 81, 84–85; Strieder, *Inventur,* 105.

12. Karnehm, *Die Korrespondenz Hans Fuggers,* 1:26* and passim (cf. index). See also chapter 4 in this volume.

13. Pölnitz, *Anton Fugger,* 1:53, and *Jakob Fugger,* 1:278; Schulte, *Die Fugger in Rom,* 1: 197–206.

14. Kellenbenz, *Die Fugger in Spanien,* 1:445; Koutná-Karg, "Die Ehre der Fugger," 95–96; Lieb, *Die Fugger und die Kunst,* 2:90–124; Pölnitz, *Anton Fugger,* 1:628–29n148, 2:2:335–37.

15. Kellenbenz, *Die Fugger in Spanien,* 1:174–77. Cf. Kranz, *Christoph Amberger,* 312.

16. Jansen, *Jakob Fugger,* 67; Pölnitz, *Anton Fugger,* 1:343 and passim (see index), and *Jakob Fugger,* 2:36, 48, 50, 76, 111; Rohmann, *Ehrenbuch,* 1:96–100, 271, 278, 280, 285.

17. Pölnitz, *Jakob Fugger*, 2:36, 76, 190, 461; Rohmann, *Ehrenbuch*, 1:279.

18. Jansen, *Jakob Fugger*, 50, 67–68; Pölnitz, *Jakob Fugger*, 2:14, 20, 30–31, 195, 218, 248, 311; Rohmann, *Ehrenbuch*, 1:217; Unger, *Die Fugger in Hall*, 43–44.

19. Jansen, *Jakob Fugger*, 68; Pölnitz, *Jakob Fugger*, 2:18; Reinhard, *Augsburger Eliten*, 690–91 (no. 1054); Rohmann, *Ehrenbuch*, 1:95, 217.

20. Kellenbenz, *Die Fugger in Spanien*, 1:168–69; Reinhard, *Augsburger Eliten*, 673–74 (no. 1030).

21. Jansen, *Jakob Fugger*, 67; Pölnitz, *Jakob Fugger*, 1:128, 150, 237, 69, 136–37; Schick, *Un grand homme d'affaires*, 242; Unger, *Die Fugger in Hall*, 44–45.

22. Pölnitz, *Jakob Fugger*, 2:43, 51, 460; Sommerlad, "Die Faktorei."

23. Hildebrandt, "Diener und Herren," 161–63.

24. With the reform of the city constitution decreed by Emperor Charles V in 1548, the office had lost its original function as highest city office but retained important functions related to the policing of the city and the maintenance of public order.

25. Denzel, "Professionalisierung," 422; Hildebrandt, "Wirtschaftsentwicklung und soziale Mobilität," 44–46; Pölnitz, *Jakob Fugger*, 2:516; Reinhard, *Augsburger Eliten*, 494–95 (no. 752); Sieh-Burens, *Oligarchie*, 54, 92, 104–5, 154–56, 171, 188, 348; Unger, *Die Fugger in Hall*, 227 and passim.

26. Hildebrandt, "Wirtschaftsentwicklung und soziale Mobilität," 46–51; Pölnitz, *Anton Fugger*, 3:1:80–85 and passim.

27. Kellenbenz, *Die Fugger in Spanien*, 1:174, 226–27.

28. Denzel, "Professionalisierung," 429, 431; Hildebrandt, *Die "Georg Fuggerischen Erben,"* 86–87, 90, 93, and "Wirtschaftsentwicklung und soziale Mobilität"; Reinhard, *Augsburger Eliten*, 30 (no. 42); Sieh-Burens, *Oligarchie*, 54, 92–93, 104–5, 188, 347.

29. See Hildebrandt, "Diener und Herren," 166–67.

30. Haebler, *Geschichte*, 132–33; Kellenbenz, *Die Fugger in Spanien*, 1:174, 232–33.

31. Haebler, *Geschichte*, 177–78; Karnehm, *Die Korrespondenz Hans Fuggers*, 2:2:no. 2357; Kellenbenz, *Die Fugger in Spanien*, 1:270; Pölnitz, *Anton Fugger*, 3:2:387.

32. Hildebrandt, *Die "Georg Fuggerischen Erben,"* 90–92. Cf. Haebler, *Geschichte*, 149.

33. Reinhard, *Augsburger Eliten*, 436 (no. 647). Cf. Hildebrandt, *Die "Georg Fuggerischen Erben,"* 89.

34. Denzel, "Professionalisierung," 429; Hipper, "Beziehungen," 2–19; Kranz, *Christoph Amberger*, 244–45; Lieb, *Die Fugger und die Kunst*, 2:81–84; Pölnitz, *Anton Fugger*, 3:2:379–80; Safley, "Fuggerfaktoren," 120; Sieh-Burens, *Oligarchie*, 98–100. Numerous references to his activities on behalf of the Fuggers can be found in Pölnitz, *Anton Fugger*, vols. 1–3:1 (see index).

35. Pölnitz, *Anton Fugger*, 1:499n158, 2:1:465.

36. Denzel, "Professionalisierung," 431; Haebler, *Geschichte*, 134–35, 147; Hipper, "Beziehungen," 19–29; Kellenbenz, *Die Fugger in Spanien*, 1:173–74, 232–43.

37. Kellenbenz, "Konto Neapel," 371, 375; Pölnitz, *Anton Fugger*, 2:1:137, 145, 151–52, 187 and passim; Reinhard, *Augsburger Eliten*, 320 (no. 459).

38. Hipper, "Beziehungen," 29–30; Mandrou, *Fugger*, 96, 98; Scheuermann, *Die Fugger als Montanindustrielle*, 475.

39. Pölnitz, *Anton Fugger*, 3:1:434.

40. Preysing, *Fuggertestamente*, 180–81, 254, 256–57; Reinhard, *Augsburger Eliten*, 987–

88 (nos. 1506, 1508). See also the examples in Hildebrandt, "Diener und Herren," 173, and Sigelen, "Die Fugger und Reichspfennigmeister Zacharias Geizkofler," 85–92.

41. Preysing, *Fuggertestamente*, 180–81; Reinhard, *Augsburger Eliten*, 790 (no. 1233).

42. Reinhard, *Augsburger Eliten*, 826 (no. 1287), 894 (no. 1385).

43. Karnehm, *Die Korrespondenz Hans Fuggers*, 1:no. 95; Reinhard, *Augsburger Eliten*, 502 (no. 766).

44. Sieh-Burens, *Oligarchie*, 101, 104.

45. Cf. Hildebrandt, "Diener und Herren," 164; Sieh-Burens, *Oligarchie*, 189. For the exceptional cases of members the Zech and Geizkofler families, who made their careers in the Fuggers' service while remaining Protestants, see Sigelen, "Die Fugger und Reichspfennigmeister Zacharias Geizkofler," 90.

46. For his biography, cf. Bechtel, *Matthäus Schwarz*; Fink, *Trachtenbücher*, esp. 11–19; Kranz, *Christoph Amberger*, 318–19; Lieb, *Die Fugger und die Kunst*, 2:86–87; Pölnitz, *Jakob Fugger*, 1: 356–59.

47. Fink, *Trachtenbücher*, 17–18, 43–44, 206–24; Hildebrandt, *Die "Georg Fuggerischen Erben,"* 67; Reinhard, *Augsburger Eliten*, 760–62 (nos. 1176–77, 1180).

48. Weitnauer, *Venezianischer Handel*.

49. See Denzel, "Handelspraktik" and "Professionalisierung," 435–39; Westermann, "Gewichtsverhältnisse."

50. August Fink's groundbreaking study reproduces the entire costume book in black and white. Some of the images are also reproduced in Grüber, *"Kurzweil viel."* The images in Braunstein, *Un banquier mis à nu*, are in color, but they are based on a copy of the original manuscript, which was produced in the early eighteenth century and is preserved in the Bibliothèque Nationale de France in Paris.

51. See Grüber, *"Kurzweil viel,"* 112–13, 132–33.

52. Cf. Arnold, *"Da het ich die gestalt"*; Groebner, "Die Kleider des Körpers"; Mentges, "Fashion."

53. Groebner, "Die Kleider des Körpers."

54. Grüber, *"Kurzweil viel,"* 139–44; Habich, "Gebetbuch"; Lieb, *Die Fugger und die Kunst*, 2:88; Fink, *Trachtenbücher*, 25–30.

55. Fink, *Trachtenbücher*, 31–34; Grüber, *"Kurzweil viel,"* 78–79; Habich, "Der Augsburger Geschlechtertanz."

56. Fink, *Trachtenbücher*, 10 and passim; Kranz, *Christoph Amberger*, 317–25 and passim; Lieb, *Die Fugger und die Kunst*, 2:88–89.

57. The basic text on Dernschwam is the introduction to Babinger, *Hans Dernschwam's Tagebuch*, xiii–xxx. Examples of his reports on the state of affairs in Hungary can be found in Pölnitz, *Anton Fugger*, 1:135–43, 146–51, 195–201, 214–19, 221–25, 234–36, 2:1:127–28, 131– 35, 3:1:392–96; Strieder, "Ein Bericht des Fuggerschen Faktors Hans Dernschwam." See also Birnbaum, "The Fuggers"; Jeggle, "Die fremde Welt"; Kalus, *Die Fugger in der Slowakei*, 179, 182–83, 216–17, 283–84; Lieb, *Die Fugger und die Kunst*, 2:79–80.

58. Babinger, *Hans Dernschwam's Tagebuch*, xvii–xvix; Birnbaum, "The Fuggers," 124, 127, 143; Jeggle, "Die fremde Welt," 416.

59. Jeggle, "Die fremde Welt," 418–426 (quotes on 424, 426).

60. Birnbaum, "The Fuggers," 131–43.

61. This and the next two paragraphs are mainly based on Nübel, *Pompejus Occo.* Cf. also Pölnitz, *Anton Fugger,* 2:1:372–79n115; Pölnitz, *Fugger und Hanse,* 29, 33, 40, 44–45, 57, 138–41, 146; Pölnitz, *Jakob Fugger,* 2:383–84. On his family, see Nübel, "Das Geschlecht Occo."

62. Roper, *Oedipus and the Devil* (quote on 133).

63. Häberlein, *Brüder, Freunde und Betrüger,* 207–8; Pölnitz, *Anton Fugger,* 2:1:53, 87–88.

64. Häberlein, *Brüder, Freunde und Betrüger,* 208–9, 211; Pölnitz, *Anton Fugger,* 2:1:100–2, 112, 124, 128, 144, 149, 157, 168, 177–78, 185–86, 216–17, 226 (quote).

65. This paragraph summarizes Häberlein, *Brüder, Freunde und Betrüger,* 209–15, 257–59.

66. Pölnitz, *Anton Fugger,* 1:97, 433n44; Schulte, *Die Fugger in Rom,* 1:238.

67. Kellenbenz, *Die Fugger in Spanien,* 1:173; Pölnitz, *Anton Fugger,* 2:1:61, 106, 112, 178, 206, 249, 294, 355–56, 2:2:14, 178.

68. Pölnitz, *Anton Fugger,* 3:1:45, 104, 140, 170, 210, 263, 337–38, 369, 409, 412, 426–27, 521–22, 534–35, 3:2:60–63, 74–75, 94–95, 98, 123–34, 158–59 (quotes on 129, 159). Cf. Kellenbenz, *Die Fugger in Spanien,* 1:99–122, 446–47.

69. Kellenbenz, *Die Fugger in Spanien,* 1:447–48; Pölnitz, *Anton Fugger,* 3:2:134, 183–84.

70. Haberer, "Handelsdiener und Handelsherren," 139.

71. Hildebrandt, "Diener und Herren," 154–55.

72. Haberer, *Ott Heinrich Fugger,* 121–23.

73. Haberer, "Handelsdiener und Handelsherren," 144–47. See also Denzel, "Professionalisierung," 424–25.

74. Dauser, "Fern-Gespräche," 42–43; Haberer, "Handelsdiener und Handelsherren," 147–49.

75. Haberer, "Handelsdiener und Handelsherren," 149–54.

76. Scheuermann, *Die Fugger als Montanindustrielle,* 324–64 (quotes on 324, 363). See also Dauser, "Fern-Gespräche," 44–49; Haberer, *Ott Heinrich Fugger,* 132–33.

6. PATRONAGE AND SELF-DISPLAY

1. Montaigne, *Tagebuch,* 79–80. Cf. Karg, "Anton Fugger," 128; Lieb, *Die Fugger und die Kunst,* 2:204–5; Trauchburg, *Häuser und Gärten,* 34–35, 132–33.

2. Wölfle, *Kunstpatronage,* 37–39; Wüst, "Das Bild der Fugger," 76–81.

3. Rohmann, *Ehrenbuch,* 1:16.

4. See Eikelmann, *Die Fugger und die Musik* and the exhibition catalogues *Fugger und Welser; Welt im Umbruch.*

5. Cf. Burkhardt, "Handelsgeist und Kunstinteresse," 31–33, as well as the contributions in Bergdolt and Brüning, *Kunst und ihre Auftraggeber.*

6. Lieb, *Die Fugger und die Kunst,* 1:88; 2:16–18, 34–39, 202–3.

7. Lieb, *Die Fugger und die Kunst,* 1:92–100, 2:71–73, 155–56, 158–96, 204–5; Pölnitz, *Jakob Fugger,* 1:261–62; 2:158, 250–51. Cf. Diemer, "Sammlungskabinette," 21; Kranz, *Christoph Amberger,* 79–80; Roeck, *Geschichte Augsburgs,* 101; Trauchburg, *Häuser und Gärten,* 32–35.

8. Bushart, "Kunst und Stadtbild," 372; Diemer, "Hans Fugger und die Kunst" and "Sammlungskabinette"; Kellenbenz, "Augsburger Sammlungen," 83–84; Kuhoff, "Augsburger Handelshäuser," 265–66; Lill, *Hans Fugger,* 41–80 (quote on 66), 128–74; Trauchburg, *Häuser und Gärten,* 36–37; Wölfle, *Kunstpatronage,* 104–34, 247, 315. Numerous references to the deco-

ration of the Fugger houses and to collections can be found in Karnehm, *Die Korrespondenz Hans Fuggers,* vol. 1 passim. See also the introduction in Karnehm, *Die Korrespondenz Hans Fuggers,* 78*–101*.

9. Lieb, *Octavian Secundus Fugger,* 7–18 (quote on 18). Cf. Garas, "Die Fugger und die venezianische Kunst," 128; Trauchburg, *Häuser und Gärten,* 40–42.

10. Haberer, *Ott Heinrich Fugger,* 379–93, 411–29.

11. *Die Chroniken der deutschen Städte,* 32:332–33, 33:44 (quote), 59–62, 116–18, 197, 237–38, 241, 407; Kellenbenz, "Anton Fugger," 63, 101–2; Koutná, "Feste und Feiern der Fugger," 100–11; Koutná-Karg, "Die Ehre der Fugger," 90–94; Lutz, "Marx Fugger," 444–50; Mauer, *"Gemain Geschrey,"* 101–8; Rohmann, *Ehrenbuch,* 1:78.

12. Rohmann, *Ehrenbuch,* 1:184.

13. Hildebrandt, *Die "Georg Fuggerischen Erben,"* 35.

14. Koutná, "Feste und Feiern der Fugger," 101–4, 108; Mauer, *"Gemain Geschrey,"* 102–4.

15. Pölnitz, *Jakob Fugger,* 1:277, 2:264.

16. Scheller, *Memoria,* 47–53.

17. See esp. Bushart, *Fuggerkapelle* (on Dürer's role, see esp. 99–111); Kellenbenz and Preysing, "Stiftungsbrief," 100, 105–7; Lieb, *Die Fugger und die Kunst,* 1:135–249; Scheller, *Memoria,* 53–90.

18. Bushart, *Fuggerkapelle,* 319–28. Cf. also Bellot, "Auf welsche art."

19. Oexle, "Adel, Memoria und kulturelles Gedächtnis," 345–56. For a critical view on this thesis, see Rohmann, *Ehrenbuch,* 1:16–17; Scheller, *Memoria,* 80–82.

20. Scheller, *Memoria,* 65–90 (quotes on 70, 77).

21. For the hospital and school foundations of Hieronymus and Anton Fugger, see Karg, "Anton Fugger," 130; Koutná-Karg, "Die Ehre der Fugger," 102; Lieb, *Die Fugger und die Kunst,* 2:286–90; Simnacher, *Fuggertestamente,* 97–100. On the Fuggers' role in the establishment of the Jesuit college in Augsburg, see chapter 7 in this volume.

22. On the history of the foundation and building of the *Fuggerei,* see esp. Pölnitz, *Jakob Fugger,* 1:348–56; 2:380–84; Scheller, *Memoria,* 127–58 (quote on 127); Tietz-Strödel, *Die Fuggerei,* 20–106.

23. Kellenbenz and Preysing, "Stiftungsbrief," 99–101, 104–5, 107–8; Scheller, *Memoria,* 128–32; Tietz-Strödel, *Die Fuggerei,* 27–33, 43–96 (quote on 71).

24. Nübel, *Mittelalterliche Beginen- und Sozialsiedlungen;* Tietz-Strödel, *Die Fuggerei,* 107–217.

25. Scheller, *Memoria,* 132–45.

26. Ibid., 145–51. See also Tietz-Strödel, *Die Fuggerei,* 36–38, 71, 77, 230–31.

27. Bushart, *Fuggerkapelle,* 34–35; Kießling, *Bürgerliche Gesellschaft,* 237; Pölnitz, *Jakob Fugger,* 1:466–71; Roeck, *Kunstpatronage,* 44; Scheller, *Memoria,* 13–16, 55–57, 129–30, 152–58; Simnacher, *Fuggertestamente,* 96–97; Tietz-Strödel, *Die Fuggerei,* 27–35 and passim. The foundation charter of 1521 is printed in Kellenbenz and Preysing, "Stiftungsbrief," 103–16.

28. Kranz, *Christoph Amberger,* 78 (quote). See more generally the essays in Bergdolt and Brüning, *Kunst und ihre Auftraggeber;* North, "Kunst und bürgerliche Repräsentation"; Roeck, *Kunstpatronage.*

29. Kellenbenz, "Augsburger Sammlungen," 77–78; Kuhoff, "Augsburger Handelshäuser,"

261–65; Lieb, *Die Fugger und die Kunst,* 2:42–51, 61–63; North, "Kunst und bürgerliche Repräsentation," 38, 41; Rohmann, *Ehrenbuch,* 1:183.

30. Cf. Kellenbenz, "Augsburger Sammlungen," 81–82; Lieb, *Octavian Secundus Fugger,* 150–60; North, "Kunst und bürgerliche Repräsentation," 44–45.

31. Bushart, *Fuggerkapelle,* 24; Eikelmann, *Die Fugger und die Musik,* 114–21, 128–39; Garas, "Die Fugger und die venezianische Kunst," 123–24; Koutná-Karg, "Die Ehre der Fugger," 101; Kranz, *Christoph Amberger,* 15, 84–86, 117, 138–39; Lieb, *Die Fugger und die Kunst,* 1:268–77, 2: 4–5, 53–59, 291–300; *Welt im Umbruch,* 2:165, 181, 187.

32. Kranz, *Christoph Amberger,* 11 (quote), 48–49 (origins), 117, 124–27.

33. Ibid., 27, 44–46, 54–62, 166, 233–38, 243–47.

34. Ibid., 37, 39, 456–457; Lieb, *Die Fugger und die Kunst,* 2:33, 43, 122, 134, 150, 302, 341–42; Pölnitz, *Anton Fugger,* 2:1:26.

35. Kranz, *Christoph Amberger,* 13, 53 (quote), 88, 93–94, 120, 130–35, 140–41, 151–52, 156–60, 168, 175–76 (quote on 176), 307–14, 317–27. Cf. also *Welt im Umbruch,* 2:106–7, 129.

36. Bushart, "Kunst und Stadtbild," 372; Eikelmann, *Die Fugger und die Musik,* 122–25; Karnehm, *Die Korrespondenz Hans Fuggers,* 1:98*–101*; Lill, *Hans Fugger,* 32, 132–35; *Welt im Umbruch,* 1:317–18, 2:96–97, 120–22.

37. Eikelmann, *Die Fugger und die Musik,* 41–48, 61–68, 142–71; Kellenbenz, "Hans Jakob Fugger," 85, 89–90; Küster, "Beziehungen," 83–89. Cf. also Huber, *Musikpflege.*

38. Eikelmann, *Die Fugger und die Musik,* 47, 146–47, 158–59; Krautwurst, "Melchior Neusidler."

39. Bourdieu, "Ökonomisches Kapital." Cf. Haberer, *Ott Heinrich Fugger,* 11, 410–11.

40. Lehmann, *Fuggerbibliotheken,* 1:1–9.

41. Ibid., 10–19; Lieb, *Die Fugger und die Kunst,* 2:142–43, 309 and passim. See also Burkhardt, "Handelsgeist und Kunstinteresse," 28; Kellenbenz, "Anton Fugger," 70–71, 76, and "Augsburger Sammlungen," 76–78; Kuhoff, "Augsburger Handelshäuser," 264–67; Pölnitz, *Anton Fugger,* 1:153, 157, 163, 177, 241, 572n104.

42. Bellot, "Humanismus," 347–48; Karg, "Anton Fugger," 135; Kellenbenz, "Augsburger Sammlungen," 78; Lehmann, *Fuggerbibliotheken,* 1:20–40; Pölnitz, *Anton Fugger,* 3:1:166–67, 217, 3:2:13–14, 84–86, 109–10, 145–46, 171–72, 201–2, 208, 234.

43. Backmann, "Kunstagenten oder Kaufleute?" 178, 182; Hartig, *Gründung;* Kellenbenz, "Augsburger Sammlungen," 78–79, and "Hans Jakob Fugger," 86–93; Kuhoff, "Augsburger Handelshäuser," 266, 268; Lehmann, *Fuggerbibliotheken,* 1:41–73; Maasen, *Hans Jakob Fugger,* 74–80; Meadow, "Merchants and Marvels"; Mondrain, "Copistes et collectionneurs"; Weber "Vermächtnis." On the copyists in Augsburg, cf. Lehmann, *Fuggerbibliotheken,* 1:65, 114.

44. Kellenbenz, "Augsburger Sammlungen," 79–80; Kuhoff, "Augsburger Handelshäuser," 269; Lehmann, *Fuggerbibliotheken,* 1:73–195.

45. Lehmann, *Fuggerbibliotheken,* 1:195–224. Cf. Bastl, *Tagebuch,* 359–67; Hildebrandt, *Die "Georg Fuggerischen Erben,"* 23, 30–31; Kellenbenz, "Augsburger Sammlungen," 80–81; Preysing, *Fuggertestamente,* 175; Simnacher, *Fuggertestamente,* 139.

46. Kellenbenz, "Augsburger Sammlungen," 82–83; Kuhoff, "Augsburger Handelshäuser," 271; Lehmann, *Fuggerbibliotheken,* 1:238–49; Lutz, "Marx Fugger," 425–42, 461–75, 495–508 (quote on 473); Wölfle, *Kunstpatronage,* 17–18.

47. Lehmann, *Fuggerbibliotheken*, 1:166.

48. Rohmann, *Ehrenbuch*, vol. 1 (quotes on 40–41, 205). See also Bayerische Staatsbibliothek, *Die Fugger im Bild*, 31–89; Koutná-Karg, "Die Ehre der Fugger," 96–98.

49. Rohmann, *Ehrenbuch*, 1:31–43.

50. Ibid., 1:47–51, 54–63.

51. Ibid., 1:71–89 (quotes on 77, 81).

52. Bayerische Staatsbibliothek, *Die Fugger im Bild*, 115–98; Burkhardt, "Handelsgeist und Kunstinteresse," 25–26; Koutná-Karg, "Die Ehre der Fugger," 100; Rohmann, *Ehrenbuch*, 1: 41–42; *Welt im Umbruch*, 1:370–71; Wölfle, *Kunstpatronage*, 222–23.

7. THE FUGGERS IN SIXTEENTH-CENTURY URBAN SOCIETY

1. *Die Chroniken der deutschen Städte*, 23:166–67.

2. Mörke, "Fugger" (quotes on 146, 152). Cf. also Rohmann, *Ehrenbuch*, 1:13–14, 19; Scheller, *Memoria*, 38–42; Wüst, "Das Bild der Fugger," 70–71.

3. Sieh-Burens, *Oligarchie*, 74–132 (quotes on 127, 129).

4. Ibid., 133–213.

5. Cf. Mörke, "Fugger," 146–52; Wüst, "Das Bild der Fugger," 71–76.

6. *Die Chroniken der deutschen Städte*, 23:115–16.

7. Ibid., 23:165–70. Cf. Rohmann, *Ehrenbuch*, 1:15.

8. *Die Chroniken der deutschen Städte*, 25:272.

9. Ibid., 25:48, 66.

10. Ibid., 25:82–83. Cf. Bushart, *Fuggerkapelle*, 25; Scheller, *Memoria*, 63–64.

11. *Die Chroniken der deutschen Städte*, 25:83–84, 109–10, 157. See also Noflatscher, *Räte und Herrscher*, 241; Rohmann, *Ehrenbuch*, 1:57–58.

12. Rohmann, *Ehrenbuch*, 1:15, 71–73; Rublack, "Grundwerte"; Schulze, "Gemeinnutz."

13. Kießling, *Bürgerliche Gesellschaft*, 111–13; Pölnitz, *Jakob Fugger*, 1:279–81; Scheller, *Memoria*, 104–6.

14. The most important study is Scheller, *Memoria*, 101–25 (quote on 113). Cf. also Kellenbenz and Preysing, "Stiftungsbrief," 101, 108–9; Kießling, *Bürgerliche Gesellschaft*, 302–5, 356–57; Pölnitz, *Jakob Fugger*, 1:368–74, 380–84; Tewes, "Luthergegner," 334–35.

15. For an extensive account that partly corrects older works, see Wurm, *Johannes Eck*, 66–220. Cf. also Johnson, *German Discovery of the World*, 127–32; Kießling, *Bürgerliche Gesellschaft*, 192–93; Lutz, *Conrad Peutinger*, 106–9; Oberman, *Werden und Wertung*, 161–200 (quote on 175; on the Fugger-Lamparter relationship, see 181–83); Pölnitz, *Jakob Fugger*, 1: 312–19.

16. For a good overview of the Reformation in Augsburg, see Kießling, "Augsburg in der Reformationszeit," esp. 22–24. Cf. Scheller, *Memoria*, 175–76, 179. On the role of printing, see esp. Künast, *"Getruckt zu Augspurg,"* 200–5, 225–26, 231–34, 295–98.

17. Pölnitz, *Jakob Fugger*, 1:484–95. Cf. Burkhardt, "Luther und die Augsburger Handelsgesellschaften," 50; Tewes, "Luthergegner," 339–40.

18. Cf. Scheller, *Memoria*, 179–80; Tewes, "Luthergegner" (quote on 364).

19. *Die Chroniken der deutschen Städte*, 23:169, 25:137, 172, 206; Gößner, *Weltliche Kirchenhoheit*, 35–36; Künast, *"Getruckt zu Augspurg,"* 201; Lutz, *Conrad Peutinger*, 235; Pölnitz, *Jakob Fugger*, 1:570–72; Scheller, *Memoria*, 180; Tewes, "Luthergegner," 337–38. On the Schilling

uprising, see Kießling, "Augsburg in der Reformationszeit," 24–25; Rogge, *Für den Gemeinen Nutzen,* 249–84.

20. Lutz, *Conrad Peutinger,* 248; Pölnitz, *Jakob Fugger,* 1:576–77, 599.

21. Pölnitz, *Jakob Fugger,* 1:642–43; Preysing, *Fuggertestamente,* 75, 78; Scheller, *Memoria,* 185–98; Simnacher, *Fuggertestamente,* 105–6.

22. *Die Chroniken der deutschen Städte,* 25:204; Schad, *Frauen,* 173; Sieh-Burens, *Oligarchie,* 135–39.

23. Burschel and Häberlein, "Familie, Geld und Eigennutz," 52; *Die Chroniken der deutschen Städte,* 23:169; Pölnitz, *Jakob Fugger,* 2:271–73; Rohmann, *Ehrenbuch,* 1:82; Schad, *Frauen,* 172–75; Simnacher, *Fuggertestamente,* 111–14.

24. *Die Chroniken der deutschen Städte,* 23:189, 201–2; Kellenbenz, "Anton Fugger," 67–68; Pölnitz, *Anton Fugger,* 1:125–27.

25. Bauer, *Schwabmünchen,* 258–59, 272, 366; *Die Chroniken der deutschen Städte,* 23:237–44; Häberlein, *Brüder, Freunde und Betrüger,* 185; Hoffmann, "Delinquenz und Strafverfolgung," 378–79; Lutz, *Conrad Peutinger,* 302–4; Pölnitz, *Anton Fugger,* 1:164–66.

26. Pölnitz, *Anton Fugger,* 1:114–16; Scheller, *Memoria,* 205–17.

27. *Die Chroniken der deutschen Städte,* 23:340–42, 29:53–54, 59–60; Hoffmann, "Delinquenz und Strafverfolgung," 374–75; Kellenbenz, "Anton Fugger," 78–79; Mörke, "Fugger," 148–49; Pölnitz, *Anton Fugger,* 1:265–74, 277, 283–86; Scheller, *Memoria,* 181, 217–24.

28. Gößner, *Weltliche Kirchenhoheit,* 46–61, 92–212; Kießling, "Augsburg in der Reformationszeit," 28–32; Scheller, *Memoria,* 186.

29. Bushart, *Fuggerkapelle,* 41; Scheller, *Memoria,* 186–87; Simnacher, *Fuggertestamente,* 117.

30. Kellenbenz, "Anton Fugger," 84; Sieh-Burens, *Oligarchie,* 209.

31. *Die Chroniken der deutschen Städte,* 29:60. Cf. Wüst, "Das Bild der Fugger," 73.

32. Häberlein, "Fugger und Welser," 232–33, and "Jakob Herbrot," 73–74; Sieh-Burens, *Oligarchie,* 155, 168.

33. Scheller, *Memoria,* 225–34, 271–75.

34. Sieh-Burens, *Oligarchie,* 143–45, 148–55 (quote on 154–55). See also Kellenbenz, "Anton Fugger," 85; Mörke and Sieh, "Führungsgruppen," 303, 307; Nebinger, "Standesverhältnisse," 263, 269.

35. Kellenbenz, "Hans Jakob Fugger," 55–57; Maasen, *Hans Jakob Fugger,* 12–13; Rohmann, *Ehrenbuch,* 1:19; Sieh-Burens, *Oligarchie,* 156, 168.

36. Kießling, "Augsburg in der Reformationszeit," 33–37; Sieh-Burens, *Oligarchie,* 155–69.

37. *Die Chroniken der deutschen Städte,* 33:323–25; Ehrenberg, *Zeitalter,* 1:142, 144; Kellenbenz, "Anton Fugger," 91–94, and "Hans Jakob Fugger," 58–62; Kirch, *Die Fugger und der Schmalkaldische Krieg,* 36–61, 113–38, 142–50, 157, 165–71; Maasen, *Hans Jakob Fugger,* 14–16; Pölnitz, *Anton Fugger,* 2:1:198–462, and *Die Fugger,* 205–21; Sieh-Burens, *Oligarchie,* 168–69.

38. Kellenbenz, "Hans Jakob Fugger," 63–67; Kießling, "Augsburg in der Reformationszeit," 37–39; Sieh-Burens, *Oligarchie,* 169–87; Warmbrunn, *Zwei Konfessionen,* 106–14.

39. Scheller, *Memoria,* 257–69.

40. Sieh-Burens, *Oligarchie,* 170–73 (quote on 171). Cf. Kellenbenz, "Hans Jakob Fugger," 65, 71; Kießling, "Augsburg in der Reformationszeit," 38; Kranz, *Christoph Amberger,* 308; Maasen, *Hans Jakob Fugger,* 17–18; Mörke, "Fugger," 145–46; Mörke and Sieh, "Führungsgruppen," 303.

41. Kellenbenz, "Hans Jakob Fugger," 67–74; Maasen, *Hans Jakob Fugger,* 19–26, 53–56;

Pölnitz, *Anton Fugger*, 3:1:216–18, 271–72, 321, 3:2:68–71, 83–84, 110–11, 148–50, 176–77, 204, 237; Rohmann, *Ehrenbuch*, 1:19–20; Sieh-Burens, *Oligarchie*, 171, 178–79, 183–86, 210; Warmbrunn, *Zwei Konfessionen*, 146–47, 150.

42. See chapter 4 in this volume.

43. Bastl, *Tagebuch*, 231 (quote), 303, 330–31; Hildebrandt, *Die "Georg Fuggerischen Erben,"* 37–40; Lutz, "Marx Fugger," 475–80; Schad, *Frauen*, 25–39, 49–70; Sieh-Burens, *Oligarchie*, 188–89, 208; Simnacher, *Fuggertestamente*, 123–24, 140–41, 144, 146, 149, 152; Soergel, *Wondrous in his Saints*, 114–19; Wallenta, *Konfessionalisierung*, 191–98; Warmbrunn, *Zwei Konfessionen*, 240–41, 244–45.

44. Bastl, *Tagebuch*, 331–33; Haberer, *Ott Heinrich Fugger*, 51–53; Hildebrandt, *Die "Georg Fuggerischen Erben,"* 37–38; Lieb, *Octavian Secundus Fugger*, 30–31; Lutz, "Marx Fugger," 480–92; Schad, *Frauen*, 35–36, 62–63; Sieh-Burens, *Oligarchie*, 195–206; Wallenta, *Konfessionalisierung*, 194–96, 199–203; Warmbrunn, *Zwei Konfessionen*, 248–49, 285; Wölfle, *Kunstpatronage*, 228–30, 242.

45. Mauer, "Gemain Geschrey," 118.

46. Lutz, "Marx Fugger," 456–61; Sieh-Burens, *Oligarchie*, 91, 187–88, 347.

47. See Bastl, *Tagebuch*, 323; Hildebrandt, *Die "Georg Fuggerischen Erben,"* 34; Mauer, "Gemain Geschrey," 157–58.

48. Sieh-Burens, *Oligarchie*, 197 (quote). On the development of the calendar dispute, see Roeck, *Eine Stadt in Krieg und Frieden*, 1:125–88 (with a detailed structural analysis); Sieh-Burens, *Oligarchie*, 203–7; Steuer, *Außenverflechtung*, 147–85; Wallenta, *Konfessionalisierung*, 102–16; Warmbrunn, *Zwei Konfessionen*, 360–75.

49. Roeck, *Eine Stadt in Krieg und Frieden*, 1:133–37 (Hans Fugger quote on 134). Cf. Lutz, "Marx Fugger," 498–504; Sieh-Burens, *Oligarchie*, 205; Wallenta, *Konfessionalisierung*, 115.

50. Karnehm, *Die Korrespondenz Hans Fuggers*, 2:2:nos. 2308 (quote), 2435, 2448, 2459, 2508–9, 2511, 2515, 2518–19 (quote), 2521, 2523–24, 2532, 2538, 2544, 2561, 2582 (quote), 2611 (quote), 2612–13, 2615, 2617, 2862 (quote), 2876. For a detailed analysis of Hans Fugger's position on the calendar dispute, see Dauser, *Informationskultur*, 251–83. On Silvester Raid, see chapter 5 in this volume.

51. Lutz, "Marx Fugger," 502–3, 505–8; Roeck, *Eine Stadt in Krieg und Frieden*, 1:169–88; Wallenta, *Konfessionalisierung*, 117–22.

8. CITIZENS AND NOBLEMEN

1. On the Swabian region, see esp. Kießling, "Bürgerlicher Besitz auf dem Land," "Patrizier und Kaufleute," and *Die Stadt und ihr Land*. From a European perspective, the phenomenon is examined in Burke, *Venice and Amsterdam*; Soly, "Bourgeoisie."

2. Cf. Brady, "Patricians, Nobles, Merchants," 239–44; Endres, "Adel und Patriziat," 230–31; Press, "Führungsgruppen," 57–58.

3. For a concise survey of these developments, see Karg, "Dem Fuggerischen namen erkauft"; Nebinger, "Standesverhältnisse."

4. See Hildebrandt, *Die "Georg Fuggerischen Erben,"* 189; Koutná-Karg, "Die Ehre der Fugger," 89 (quote); Lutz, "Marx Fugger," 446–50; Mandrou, *Fugger*, 25; Mörke, "Fugger," 153–54.

5. Kießling, "Patrizier und Kaufleute," 220–30; Mandrou, *Fugger*, 73–78 (quote on 77).

6. Cf. Häberlein, "Sozialer Wandel."

7. See Haberer, *Ott Heinrich Fugger*; Hildebrandt, *Die "Georg Fuggerischen Erben"*; Lutz, "Marx Fugger."

8. On the territory of Bibersburg, see Kalus, *Die Fugger in der Slowakei*, 230–68. For the landholdings in Alsace and Thurgau, see Deininger, "Gütererwerbungen," 2:86–110; Lieb, *Die Fugger und die Kunst*, 2:262–65; Maasen, *Hans Jakob Fugger*, 34–35. On the Fuggers' properties in Lower Austria, cf. Haberer, *Ott Heinrich Fugger*, 162–66.

9. Mandrou, *Fugger*, 36–37, 68–70.

10. Deininger, "Gütererwerbungen," 3–6; Düvel, *Gütererwerbungen*, 14–89; Jansen, *Jakob Fugger*, 301–2; Karg, "Dem Fuggerischen namen erkauft," 239; Kellenbenz, "Jakob Fugger," 48; Mandrou, *Fugger*, 48–50; Pölnitz, *Jakob Fugger*, 1:177–82, 196–97, 200–1, 234–35, 240, 303–4, 2:165–67, 179–82, 184–86, 216–17, 221–22, 274, 312–15; Strieder, *Jakob Fugger der Reiche*, 89.

11. Kellenbenz, "Jakob Fugger," 48–49; Lieb, *Die Fugger und die Kunst*, 1:81–86; Pölnitz, *Jakob Fugger*, 1:155–58, 229; Schick, *Un grand homme d'affaires*, 74–76.

12. Düvel, *Gütererwerbungen*, 97–131, 200–10; Hadry, "Jakob Fugger"; Karg, "Dem Fuggerischen namen erkauft," 245; Mandrou, *Fugger*, 24; Nebinger, "Standesverhältnisse," 265–68; Pölnitz, *Jakob Fugger*, 1:260–61; 2:249, 540; Rohmann, *Ehrenbuch*, 1:15; Strieder, *Jakob Fugger der Reiche*, 92.

13. Nebinger, "Standesverhältnisse," 263–64; Pölnitz, *Jakob Fugger*, 1:142, 347, 2:369–70; Rohmann, *Ehrenbuch*, 1:66, 78, 221–29; Sieh-Burens, *Oligarchie*, 94.

14. The basic works in this context are Deininger, "Gütererwerbungen"; Lieb, *Die Fugger und die Kunst*, 2:27–33, 207–60. See also Blickle, *Memmingen*, 336, 341, 357; Fried, *Fugger*, 13–14; Jahn, *Augsburg Land*, 436–37, 465; Karg, "Anton Fugger," 123–28, and "Dem Fuggerischen namen erkauft," 239–41; Kießling, *Die Stadt und ihr Land*, 444, 487–88, 670–71, 739–40; Mandrou, *Fugger*, 35, 37, 50, 54, 67; Merten, "Landschlösser," 66–71; Pölnitz, *Anton Fugger*, vols. 1–3:2 passim; Rohmann, *Ehrenbuch*, 1:37–38; Simnacher, *Fuggertestamente*, 68–74.

15. Deininger, "Gütererwerbungen," 2:268–78; Karg, "Dem Fuggerischen namen erkauft," 245; Kellenbenz, "Anton Fugger," 61, 73, 78, 83; Lieb, *Die Fugger und die Kunst*, 2:25–26, 68–69; Pölnitz, *Anton Fugger*, 1:76, 209–10, 262–63, 333; Scheller, *Memoria*, 183–84.

16. Cf. Haberer, *Ott Heinrich Fugger*, 347–54; Karg, "Anton Fugger," 123; Nebinger, "Standesverhältnisse," 266, 268–69; Rohmann, *Ehrenbuch*, 1:16.

17. Bastl, *Tagebuch*, 340–53; Koutná-Karg, "Die Ehre der Fugger," 88–89; Lieb, *Die Fugger und die Kunst*, 2:52–53, 73–75; Nebinger, "Standesverhältnisse," 270–74; Nebinger and Rieber, *Genealogie*, no. 5; Rohmann, *Ehrenbuch*, 1:12–13, 16, 66–67, 78, 230–43; Schad, *Frauen*, 74–81; Sieh-Burens, *Oligarchie*, 93–98; Völkel, "Der alte und der neue Adel."

18. Mandrou, *Fugger*, 52, 54.

19. Fehn, *Wertingen*, 32–34; Karg, "Dem Fuggerischen namen erkauft," 240–41, 245; Mandrou, *Fugger*, 47, 54–55, 67–72; Simnacher, *Fuggertestamente*, 132–35.

20. Blickle, *Memmingen*, 347, 357, 362; Fried, *Fugger*, 14–15; Jahn, *Augsburg Land*, 449, 453–54, 463; Karg, "Dem Fuggerischen namen erkauft," 241; Kießling, *Die Stadt und ihr Land*, 383; Mandrou, *Fugger*, 54–58.

21. Hildebrandt, *Die "Georg Fuggerischen Erben,"* 72–73, 83; Hoffmann, "Delinquenz und Strafverfolgung," 377–78; Karg, "Dem Fuggerischen namen erkauft," 244.

22. Blickle, *Memmingen*, 333–34; Fried, *Fugger*, 20–21; Kellenbenz, "Anton Fugger," 47; Mandrou, *Fugger*, 25, 35; Pölnitz, *Anton Fugger*, 2:1:20, 75, and *Die Fugger*, 225–26, 306 (quote).

23. Mandrou, *Fugger*, 87–94, 99–113 (quote on 112).

24. Ibid., 134–88, 192 (quote).

25. Rohmann, *Ehrenbuch*, 1:37, 183.

26. Karnehm, *Die Korrespondenz Hans Fuggers*, 1:101*–110*; Lill, *Hans Fugger*, 86–127; Merten, "Landschlösser," 75–80. On the decoration of Kirchheim castle, see also Lutz, "Gegenreformation," and the recent Wölfle, *Kunstpatronage*, 135–204, which focuses especially on the sculptural program.

27. Lutz, "Marx Fugger," 488–89.

28. Schiersner, "In der Region zu Hause," 28–32.

29. Bauer, *Schwabmünchen*, 254–83; Haberer, *Ott Heinrich Fugger*, 158–60, 170–73, 177–78, 183–84, 211–13, 219–20; Jahn, *Augsburg Land*, 467–69; Lieb, *Die Fugger und die Kunst*, 2:29–33, 51, 218.

30. Kellenbenz, "Fustian Industry," 264; Pölnitz, "Die Anfänge der Weißenhorner Barchentweberei," 206–19.

31. Kellenbenz, "Fustian Industry," 264–69, and *Die Fugger in Spanien*, 1:375; Pölnitz, *Anton Fugger*, 2:1:4–7, 89–90, 99, 193, 303–5nn27–28, 330n189, 420–21nn169–170, 2:2:21, 51, 71, 119, 130, 141, 149–51, 246–47, 265–66, 276–77, 302–5, 344, 360, 3:1:420–25, 482–83, 531, 3:2:32–33, 331–33.

32. Sczesny, *Kontinuität*, 108–12, 137–40.

33. Pölnitz, *Jakob Fugger*, 1:275; 2:262–63. See chapters 1–2 in this volume.

34. See esp. Lanzinner, *Fürst, Räte und Landstände*; Steuer, *Außenverflechtung*, 87–146. On the number of Fuggers in Bavarian service, see Steuer, *Außenverflechtung*, 120, 123.

35. Kellenbenz, "Hans Jakob Fugger," 81–85; Lanzinner, *Fürst, Räte und Landstände*, 71–73, 208, 343–44; Maasen, *Hans Jakob Fugger*, 45–58; Steuer, *Außenverflechtung*, 121, 124–25, 194–95.

36. Armer, "Zwischen Religion und Politik," 204–6; Kellenbenz, "Hans Jakob Fugger," 95; Lanzinner, *Fürst, Räte und Landstände*, 205, 208, 344; Nebinger and Rieber, *Genealogie*, no. 9a; Rohmann, *Ehrenbuch*, 1:244–52; Steuer, *Außenverflechtung*, 127–33, 189–99. On Carl Fugger, cf. Edelmayer, *Söldner und Pensionäre*, 176; Haberer, "Fugger als Offiziere," 233–35; Karnehm, *Die Korrespondenz Hans Fuggers*, 1:nos. 1025, 1054–55, 1059, 1072, 1088, 1177, 1204–5.

37. Egermann-Krebs, "Fugger"; Haberer, *Ott Heinrich Fugger*, 223–36; Nebinger and Rieber, *Genealogie*, no. 13a, 14; Steuer, *Außenverflechtung*, 93, 99, 102, 116–18, 189–99.

38. Haberer, *Ott Heinrich Fugger*, 239–346 (quotes on 243, 322).

39. Dauser, *Informationskultur*, 334–57.

40. The basic study still is the biography of Holl, *Fürstbischof Jakob Fugger*—unfortunately, confessionally a very one-sided work. For a recent account, see Armer, "Zwischen Religion und Politik."

41. Cf. Burkhardt, *Reformationsjahrhundert*, esp. parts 2–3; Reinhard, *Geschichte der Staatsgewalt*; Schilling, "Konfessionalisierung."

42. Häberlein, "Die Augsburger Welser und ihr Umfeld" and "Sozialer Wandel"; Lanzinner, "Johann Georg Herwarth."

CONCLUSION

1. Jansen, *Jakob Fugger*, 272, 298.

2. Pölnitz, *Jakob Fugger*, 1:632, 645–46.

3. Ibid., 1:625–27.

4. Ibid., 1:573n107. Cf. Stollberg-Rilinger, "Gut vor Ehre," 44.

5. Lutz, *Struktur,* 2:84'–85'.

6. Pölnitz, *Anton Fugger,* 2:1:72.

7. Kellenbenz, "Hans Jakob Fugger," 54.

8. Rohmann, *Ehrenbuch,* 1:40–41, 71–73, 76, 174–75, 205. Cf. Koutná-Karg, "Die Ehre der Fugger," 96–97.

9. Quoted in Stollberg-Rilinger, "Gut vor Ehre," 35.

10. Staudinger, "Juden am Reichshofrat," chap. 7.1.1.

11. Rohmann, *Ehrenbuch,* 1:16.

12. See ibid., 1:118.

BIBLIOGRAPHY

Armer, Stephanie. "Zwischen Religion und Politik: Fürstbischof Jakob Fugger von Konstanz (1604–1626). Ein Reichsfürst am Vorabend des Dreißigjährigen Krieges." In *Die Fugger und das Reich: Eine neue Forschungsperspektive zum fünfhundertjährigen Jubiläum der ersten Fuggerherrschaft Kirchberg-Weißenhorn,* ed. Johannes Burkhardt, 197–227. Augsburg, 2008.

Arnold, Klaus. "*Da het ich die gestalt:* Bildliche Selbstzeugnisse in Mittelalter und Renaissance." In *Das dargestellte Ich: Studien zu Selbstzeugnissen des späteren Mittelalters und der frühen Neuzeit,* ed. Klaus Arnold et al., 201–21. Bochum, 1999.

Augsburger Stadtlexikon, 2d ed., ed. Günther Grünsteudel et al. Augsburg, 1998.

Babinger, Franz, ed. *Hans Dernschwam's Tagebuch einer Reise nach Konstantinopel und Kleinasien (1553/55),* repr. ed. Berlin, 1986 (1923).

Backmann, Sibylle. "Kunstagenten oder Kaufleute? Die Firma Ott im Kunsthandel zwischen Oberdeutschland und Venedig (1550–1650)." In *Kunst und ihre Auftraggeber im 16. Jahrhundert: Venedig und Augsburg im Vergleich,* ed. Klaus Bergdolt and Jochen Brüning, 175–97. Berlin, 1997.

Bastl, Beatrix. *Das Tagebuch des Philipp Eduard Fugger (1560–1569) als Quelle zur Fuggergeschichte.* Tübingen, 1987.

Bauer, Hans. *Schwabmünchen* (Historischer Atlas von Bayern, Teil Schwaben, 15). Munich, 1994.

Bayerische Staatsbibliothek, ed. *Die Fugger im Bild: Selbstdarstellung einer Familiendynastie der Renaissance* (exhibition catalogue). Luzern, 2010.

Bechtel, Heinrich. *Matthäus Schwarz: Lebensbild nach der "Kostümbiographie" und dem "dreyerley buchhalten".* Frankfurt on the Main, 1953.

Behringer, Wolfgang. "Fugger und Taxis. Der Anteil Augsburger Kaufleute an der Entstehung des europäischen Kommunikationssystems." In *Augsburger Handelshäuser im Wandel des historischen Urteils,* ed. Johannes Burkhardt, 241–48. Berlin, 1996.

Bellot, Christoph. "'Auf welsche art, der zeit gar new erfunden:' Zur Augsburger Fuggerkapelle." In *Humanismus und Renaissance in Augsburg: Kulturgeschichte einer Stadt zwischen Spätmittelalter und Dreißigjährigem Krieg,* ed. Gernot Michael Müller, 445–490. Berlin, 2010.

Bellot, Josef. "Humanismus—Bildungswesen—Buchdruck und Verlagsgeschichte." In *Geschichte der Stadt Augsburg von der Römerzeit bis zur Gegenwart,* 2d ed., ed. Gunther Gottlieb et al., 343–57. Stuttgart, 1985.

Bergdolt, Klaus, and Jochen Brüning, eds. *Kunst und ihre Auftraggeber im 16. Jahrhundert: Venedig und Augsburg im Vergleich.* Berlin, 1997.

Birnbaum, Marianna D. "The Fuggers, Hans Dernschwam, and the Ottoman Empire." *Südost-Forschungen* 50 (1991): 119–44.

Blendinger, Friedrich, and Elfriede Blendinger, eds. *Zwei Augsburger Unterkaufbücher aus*

den Jahren 1551 bis 1558: Älteste Aufzeichnungen zur Vor- und Frühgeschichte der Augsburger
Börse. Stuttgart, 1994.

Blickle, Peter. Memmingen (Historischer Atlas von Bayern, Teil Schwaben, 4). Munich, 1967.

———. Die Revolution von 1525, 3d ed. Munich, 1993.

Böhm, Christoph. Die Reichsstadt Augsburg und Kaiser Maximilian I. Untersuchungen
zum Beziehungsgeflecht zwischen Reichsstadt und Herrscher an der Wende zur Neuzeit.
Sigmaringen, 1998.

Bourdieu, Pierre. Distinction: A Social Critique of Judgement and Taste. Cambridge, Mass., 1987.

———. "Ökonomisches Kapital, kulturelles Kapital, soziales Kapital." In Soziale
Ungleichheiten, ed. Reinhard Kreckel, 183–98. Göttingen, 1983.

Brady, Thomas A. "Patricians, Nobles, Merchants: Internal Tensions and Solidarities in
South German Urban Ruling Classes at the Close of the Middle Ages." In Social Groups
and Religious Ideas in the Sixteenth Century, ed. Miriam Usher Chrisman and Otto
Gründler, 38–45, 159–64. Kalamazoo, Mich., 1978.

Braunstein, Philippe. "Le marché du cuivre à Venise à la fin du Moyen-Age." In
Schwerpunkte der Kupferproduktion und des Kupferhandels in Europa, 1500–1650, ed.
Hermann Kellenbenz, 78–94. Cologne, 1977.

———, ed. Un banquier mis à nu. Autobiographie de Matthäus Schwarz, bourgeois
d'Augsbourg. Paris, 1992.

Burke, Peter, Venice and Amsterdam: A Study of Seventeenth-Century Elites. London, 1974.

Burkhardt, Johannes, ed. Anton Fugger (1493–1560): Vorträge und Dokumentation zum
fünfhundertjährigen Jubiläum. Weißenhorn, 1994.

———, ed. Augsburger Handelshäuser im Wandel des historischen Urteils. Berlin, 1996.

———, ed. Die Fugger und das Reich: Eine neue Forschungsperspektive zum
fünfhundertjährigen Jubiläum der ersten Fuggerherrschaft Kirchberg-Weißenhorn. Augsburg,
2008.

———. "Handelsgeist und Kunstinteresse in der Fuggergeschichte." In Anton Fugger
(1493–1560): Vorträge und Dokumentation zum fünfhundertjährigen Jubiläum, ed. Johannes
Burkhardt, 19–33. Weißenhorn, 1994.

———. "Jubiläumsvortrag Anton Fugger." In Anton Fugger (1493–1560): Vorträge und
Dokumentation zum fünfhundertjährigen Jubiläum, ed. Johannes Burkhardt, 137–50.
Weißenhorn, 1994.

———. "Luther und die Augsburger Handelsgesellschaften." In Reformation und
Reichsstadt: Luther in Augsburg, ed. Helmut Gier and Reinhard Schwarz, 50–64.
Augsburg, 1996.

———. Das Reformationsjahrhundert: Deutsche Geschichte zwischen Medienrevolution und
Institutionenbildung, 1517–1617, Stuttgart, 2002.

Burkhardt, Johannes, and Franz Karg, eds. Die Welt des Hans Fugger (1531–1598). Augsburg,
2007.

Burschel, Peter, and Mark Häberlein. "Familie, Geld und Eigennutz: Patrizier und
Großkaufleute im Augsburg des 16. Jahrhunderts." In "Kurzweil viel ohn' Maß und Ziel:"
Alltag und Festtag auf den Augsburger Monatsbildern der Renaissance, ed. Deutsches
Historisches Museum Berlin, 48–65. Munich, 1994.

Bushart, Bruno. Die Fuggerkapelle bei St. Anna in Augsburg. Munich, 1994.

———. "Kunst und Stadtbild." In *Geschichte der Stadt Augsburg von der Römerzeit bis zur Gegenwart*, 2d ed., ed. Gunther Gottlieb et al., 363–85. Stuttgart, 1985.

Calabi, Donna, and Sören T. Christensen, eds. *Cities and Cultural Exchange in Europe, 1400–1700*. Cambridge, 2007.

Carande, Ramón. *Carlos V y sus banqueros*, 3 vols. Madrid, 1942–57.

Die Chroniken der deutschen Städte vom 14. bis zum 16. Jahrhundert, vols. 5, 23, 25, 29, 32, 33, repr. ed. Göttingen, 1966.

Dauser, Regina. "Fern-Gespräche zwischen Herren und Dienern: Kommunikation in der Fugger-Firma zu Zeiten Hans Fuggers und Ott Heinrich Fuggers." In *Die Welt des Hans Fugger (1531–1598)*, ed. Johannes Burkhardt and Franz Karg, 35–50. Augsburg, 2007.

———. *Informationskultur und Beziehungswissen — Das Korrespondenznetz Hans Fuggers (1531–1598)*. Tübingen, 2008.

Davis, Natalie Zemon. *The Gift in Sixteenth-Century France* (The Curti Lectures). Madison, Wisc., 2000.

Deininger, Heinz. "Die Gütererwerbungen unter Anton Fugger (1526–1560), seine Privilegien und Standeserhöhung, sowie Fideikommissursprung." Ph.D. diss., University of Munich, 1924.

Denzel, Markus A. "Eine Handelspraktik aus dem Hause Fugger (erste Hälfte des 16. Jahrhunderts): Ein Werkstattbericht." In *Kaufmannsbücher und Handelspraktiken vom Spätmittelalter bis zum beginnenden 20. Jahrhundert*, ed. Markus A. Denzel et al., 125–52. Stuttgart, 2002.

———. "Professionalisierung und sozialer Aufstieg bei oberdeutschen Kaufleuten und Faktoren im 16. Jahrhundert." In *Sozialer Aufstieg: Funktionseliten im Spätmittelalter und in der frühen Neuzeit. Büdinger Gespräche 2000–2001*, ed. Günther Schulz, 413–42. Munich, 2002.

Denzer, Jörg. *Die Konquista der Augsburger Welser-Gesellschaft in Südamerika 1528–1556: Historische Rekonstruktion, Historiografie und lokale Erinnerungskultur in Kolumbien und Venezuela*. Munich, 2005.

Diemer, Dorothea. "Hans Fugger und die Kunst." In *Die Welt des Hans Fugger (1531–1598)*, ed. Johannes Burkhardt and Franz Karg, 165–76. Augsburg, 2007.

———. "Hans Fuggers Sammlungskabinette." In *"Lautenschlagen lernen und ieben": Die Fugger und die Musik. Anton Fugger zum 500. Geburtstag*, ed. Renate Eikelmann, 13–40. Augsburg, 1993.

Dinges, Martin. "Die Ehre als Thema der Stadtgeschichte: Eine Semantik im Übergang vom Ancien Régime zur Moderne." *Zeitschrift für Historische Forschung* 16 (1989): 409–40.

Doehaerd, Renée. *Etudes anversoises: Documents sur le commerce international à Anvers, 1488–1514*, 3 vols. Paris, 1962–63.

Düvel, Thea. *Die Gütererwerbungen Jakob Fuggers des Reichen (1494–1525) und seine Standeserhöhung: Ein Beitrag zur Wirtschafts- und Rechtsgeschichte*. Munich, 1913.

Edelmayer, Friedrich. *Söldner und Pensionäre. Das Netzwerk Philipps II. im Heiligen Römischen Reich*. Vienna, 2002.

Edelmayer, Friedrich, and Arno Strohmeyer, eds. *Die Korrespondenz der Kaiser mit ihren Gesandten in Spanien, Band 1: Der Briefwechsel zwischen Ferdinand I., Maximilian II. und Adam von Dietrichstein 1563–1565*. Vienna, 1997.

Egermann-Krebs, Diana. "Die Fugger und die Reichslandvogtei in Schwaben—ein Weg in kaiserliche Dienste." In *Die Fugger und das Reich: Eine neue Forschungsperspektive zum fünfhundertjährigen Jubiläum der ersten Fuggerherrschaft Kirchberg-Weißenhorn,* ed. Johannes Burkhardt, 53–61. Augsburg, 2008.

Ehrenberg, Richard. *Das Zeitalter der Fugger: Geldkapital und Creditverkehr im 16. Jahrhundert,* 2 vols. Jena, 1896.

Eikelmann, Renate, ed. *"Lautenschlagen lernen und ieben": Die Fugger und die Musik. Anton Fugger zum 500. Geburtstag.* Augsburg, 1993.

Endres, Rudolf. "Adel und Patriziat in Oberdeutschland." In *Ständische Gesellschaft und soziale Mobilität,* ed. Winfried Schulze, 221–38. Munich, 1988.

Fehn, Klaus. *Wertingen* (Historischer Atlas von Bayern, Teil Schwaben, 3). Munich, 1967.

Fink, August. *Die Schwarzschen Trachtenbücher.* Berlin, 1963.

Fischer, Peter. "Bergbeschau am Falkenstein, 1526: Zum Stellenwert oberdeutscher Handelshäuser, insbesondere der Fugger, bei der Versorgung des Tiroler Montansektors in der frühen Neuzeit." *Scripta Mercaturae* 33, no. 2 (1999): 92–114.

Fried, Pankraz. *Die Fugger in der Herrschaftsgeschichte Schwabens.* Munich, 1976.

Fuchs, François-Joseph. "Une famille de négociants banquiers du XVIe siècle: Les Prechter de Strasbourg." *Revue d'Alsace* 95 (1956): 146–94.

Fugger und Welser: Oberdeutsche Wirtschaft, Politik und Kultur im Spiegel zweier Geschlechter, exhibition catalogue. Augsburg, 1950.

Fuhrmann, Bernd. "'Öffentliches' Kreditwesen in deutschen Städten des 15. und 16. Jahrhunderts." *Scripta Mercaturae* 37, no. 1 (2003): 1–17.

Garas, Klára. "Die Fugger und die venezianische Kunst." In *Venedig und Oberdeutschland in der Renaissance: Beziehungen zwischen Kunst und Wirtschaft,* ed. Bernd Roeck et al., 123–29. Sigmaringen, 1993.

Geffcken, Peter. "Jakob Fuggers frühe Jahre." In *Jakob Fugger (1459–1525): Sein Leben in Bildern,* ed. Martin Kluger, 4–7. Augsburg, 2009.

———. "Soziale Schichtung 1396 bis 1521: Beitrag zu einer Strukturanalyse Augsburgs im Spätmittelalter." Ph.D. diss., University of Munich, 1995.

———. "Die Welser und ihr Handel 1246–1496." In *Die Welser: Neue Forschungen zur Geschichte und Kultur des oberdeutschen Handelshauses,* ed. Mark Häberlein and Johannes Burkhardt, 27–167. Berlin, 2002.

Gößner, Andreas. *Weltliche Kirchenhoheit und reichsstädtische Reformation: Die Augsburger Ratspolitik des ,milten und mitleren weges', 1520–1534.* Berlin, 1999.

Gottlieb, Gunther et al., eds. *Geschichte der Stadt Augsburg von der Römerzeit bis zur Gegenwart,* 2d ed. Stuttgart, 1985.

Groebner, Valentin. *Gefährliche Geschenke: Ritual, Politik und die Sprache der Korruption in der Eidgenossenschaft im späten Mittelalter und am Beginn der Neuzeit.* Constance, 2000. (English translation: *Liquid Assets, Dangerous Gifts: Presents and Politics at the End of the Middle Ages.* Philadelphia, 2002.)

———. "Die Kleider des Körpers des Kaufmanns: Zum 'Trachtenbuch' eines Augsburger Bürgers im 16. Jahrhundert." *Zeitschrift für Historische Forschung* 25 (1998): 323–58.

Großhaupt, Walter. "Die Welser als Bankiers der spanischen Krone." *Scripta Mercaturae* 21 (1987): 158–88.

Grüber, Pia Maria, ed. *"Kurzweil viel ohn' Maß und Ziel": Augsburger Patrizier und ihre Feste zwischen Mittelalter und Neuzeit,* exhibition catalogue. Munich, 1994.

Haberer, Stephanie. "Fugger als Offiziere—im Dienst von Kaiser und Reich?" In *Die Fugger und das Reich: Eine neue Forschungsperspektive zum fünfhundertjährigen Jubiläum der ersten Fuggerherrschaft Kirchberg-Weißenhorn,* ed. Johannes Burkhardt, 229–42. Augsburg, 2008.

———. "Handelsdiener und Handelsherren—Andreas Hyrus und die Fugger." *Zeitschrift des Historischen Vereins für Schwaben* 88 (1995): 137–55.

———. *Ott Heinrich Fugger (1592–1644): Biographische Analyse typologischer Handlungsfelder in der Epoche des Dreißigjährigen Krieges.* Augsburg, 2004.

Habich, Georg. "Der Augsburger Geschlechtertanz von 1522." *Jahrbuch der Königlich Preußischen Kunstsammlungen,* 1911, 213–35.

———. "Das Gebetbuch des Matthäus Schwarz." *Sitzungsberichte der Bayerischen Akademie der Wissenschaften, philosophisch-philologische und historische Klasse,* 1910, 8.

Hadry, Sarah. "Jakob Fugger (1459–1525)—ein falscher Graf? Kirchberg-Weißenhorn als Ausgangsbasis für den Aufstieg einer Augsburger Familie in den Reichsadel." In *Die Fugger und das Reich: Eine neue Forschungsperspektive zum fünfhundertjährigen Jubiläum der ersten Fuggerherrschaft Kirchberg-Weißenhorn,* ed. Johannes Burkhardt, 33–51. Augsburg, 2008.

Häberlein, Mark. "Die Augsburger Welser und ihr Umfeld zwischen karolinischer Regimentsreform und Dreißigjährigem Krieg: Ökonomisches, kulturelles und soziales Kapital." In *Die Welser: Neue Forschungen zur Geschichte und Kultur des oberdeutschen Handelshauses,* ed. Mark Häberlein and Johannes Burkhardt, 382–406. Berlin, 2002.

———. *Brüder, Freunde und Betrüger: Soziale Beziehungen, Normen und Konflikte in der Augsburger Kaufmannschaft um die Mitte des 16. Jahrhunderts.* Berlin, 1998.

———. "Familiäre Beziehungen und geschäftliche Interessen: Die Augsburger Kaufmannsfamilie Böcklin zwischen Reformation und Dreißigjährigem Krieg." *Zeitschrift des Historischen Vereins für Schwaben* 87 (1994): 39–58.

———. "Fugger und Welser: Kooperation und Konkurrenz, 1498–1614." In *Die Welser: Neue Forschungen zur Geschichte und Kultur des oberdeutschen Handelshauses,* ed. Mark Häberlein and Johannes Burkhardt, 223–39. Berlin, 2002.

———. "Geschenke und Geschäfte: Die Fugger und die Praxis des Schenkens im 16. Jahrhundert." In *Faszinierende Frühneuzeit: Festschrift für Johannes Burkhardt zum 65. Geburtstag,* ed. Wolfgang E.J. Weber and Regina Dauser, 135–49. Berlin, 2008.

———. "Handelsgesellschaften, Sozialbeziehungen und Kommunikationsnetze in Oberdeutschland zwischen dem ausgehenden 15. und der Mitte des 16. Jahrhunderts." In *Kommunikation und Region,* ed. Carl A. Hoffmann and Rolf Kießling, 305–26. Constance, 2001.

———. "Jakob Fugger und die Kaiserwahl Karls V. 1519." In *Die Fugger und das Reich: Eine neue Forschungsperspektive zum fünfhundertjährigen Jubiläum der ersten Fuggerherrschaft Kirchberg-Weißenhorn,* ed. Johannes Burkhardt, 65–81. Augsburg, 2008.

———. "Jakob Herbrot (1490/95–1564), Großkaufmann und Stadtpolitiker." In *Lebensbilder aus dem Bayerischen Schwaben,* vol. 15, 69–111. Weißenhorn, 1997.

———. "Sozialer Wandel in den Augsburger Führungsschichten des 16. und frühen 17.

Jahrhunderts." In *Sozialer Aufstieg: Funktionseliten im Spätmittelalter und in der frühen Neuzeit. Büdinger Gespräche 2000–2001,* ed. Günther Schulz, 73–96. Munich, 2002.

———. "Die Welser-Vöhlin-Gesellschaft: Fernhandel, Familienbeziehungen und sozialer Status an der Wende vom Mittelalter zur Neuzeit." In *Geld und Glaube: Leben in evangelischen Reichsstädten. Katalog zur Ausstellung im Antonierhaus, Memmingen, 12. Mai bis 4. Oktober 1998,* ed. Wolfgang Jahn et al., 17–37. Munich, 1998.

———. "Wirtschaftsgeschichte vom Mittelalter bis zur Gegenwart." In *Augsburger Stadtlexikon,* 2d ed., ed. Günther Grünsteudel et al., 146–61. Augsburg, 1998.

Häberlein, Mark, and Johannes Burkhardt, eds. *Die Welser: Neue Forschungen zur Geschichte und Kultur des oberdeutschen Handelshauses.* Berlin, 2002.

Haebler, Konrad. *Die Geschichte der Fugger'schen Handlung in Spanien.* Weimar, 1897.

Harreld, Donald J. *High Germans in the Low Countries: German Merchants and Commerce in Golden Age Antwerp.* Leiden, 2004.

Hartig, Otto. *Die Gründung der Münchener Hofbibliothek durch Albrecht V. und Johann Jakob Fugger.* Munich, 1917.

Hassler, Friedrich. *Der Ausgang der Augsburger Handelsgesellschaft David Haug, Hans Langnauer und Mitverwandte (1574–1606).* Augsburg, 1928.

Hildebrandt, Reinhard. "Augsburger und Nürnberger Kupferhandel, 1500–1619: Produktion, Marktanteile und Finanzierung im Vergleich zweier Städte und ihrer wirtschaftlichen Führungsschicht." In *Schwerpunkte der Kupferproduktion und des Kupferhandels in Europa, 1500–1650,* ed. Hermann Kellenbenz, 190–224. Cologne, 1977.

———. "Diener und Herren: Zur Anatomie großer Unternehmen im Zeitalter der Fugger." In *Augsburger Handelshäuser im Wandel des historischen Urteils,* ed. Johannes Burkhardt, 149–74. Berlin, 1996.

———. "The Effects of Empire: Changes in the European Economy after Charles V." In *Industry and Finance in Early Modern History: Essays Presented to George Hammersley to the Occasion of his 74th Birthday,* ed. Ian Blanchard et al., 58–76. Stuttgart, 1992.

———. *Die "Georg Fuggerischen Erben": Kaufmännische Tätigkeit und sozialer Status, 1555–1620.* Berlin, 1966.

———. "Der Kaiser und seine Bankiers: Ein Beitrag zum kaiserlichen Finanzwesen im 16. Jahrhundert." In *Finanzen und Herrschaft: Materielle Grundlagen fürstlicher Politik in den habsburgischen Ländern und im Heiligen Römischen Reich im 16. Jahrhundert,* ed. Friedrich Edelmayer et al., 234–45. Vienna, 2003.

———, ed. *Quellen und Regesten zu den Augsburger Handelshäusern Paler und Rehlinger 1539–1642: Wirtschaft und Politik im 16./17. Jahrhundert, Band 1: 1539–1623.* Stuttgart, 1996.

———. "Wirtschaftsentwicklung und Konzentration im 16. Jahrhundert: Konrad Rot und die Finanzierungsprobleme seines interkontinentalen Handels." *Scripta Mercaturae* 4, no. 1 (1970): 25–50.

———. "Wirtschaftsentwicklung und soziale Mobilität Memmingens, 1450–1618: Die Handelsdiener Konrad Mair, Hans und Friedrich Bechler." *Memminger Geschichtsblätter* (1969): 41–61.

Hipper, Richard. "Die Beziehungen der Faktoren Georg und Christoph Hörmann zu den Fuggern: Ein Beitrag zur Familiengeschichte der Freiherrn von Hermann auf Wain."

Familiengeschichtliche Beilage der Zeitschrift des Historischen Vereins für Schwaben und
  Neuburg 46 (1926): 1–32 (supp.).

Hoffmann, Carl A. "Delinquenz und Strafverfolgung städtischer Oberschichten im
  Augsburg des 16. Jahrhunderts." In *Die Welser: Neue Forschungen zur Geschichte und
  Kultur des oberdeutschen Handelshauses,* ed. Mark Häberlein and Johannes Burkhardt,
  347–81. Berlin, 2002.

Holl, Konstantin. *Fürstbischof Jakob Fugger von Konstanz (1604–1626) und die katholische
  Reform der Diözese im ersten Viertel des 17. Jahrhunderts.* Freiburg, 1898.

Hollegger, Manfred. *Maximilian I. (1459–1519). Herrscher und Mensch einer Zeitenwende.*
  Stuttgart, 2005.

Huber, Herbert. *Musikpflege am Fuggerhof Babenhausen (1554–1836).* Augsburg, 2003.

Jahn, Joachim. *Augsburg Land* (Historischer Atlas von Bayern, Teil Schwaben, 11). Munich,
  1984.

———. "Die Augsburger Sozialstruktur im 15. Jahrhundert." In *Geschichte der Stadt
  Augsburg von der Römerzeit bis zur Gegenwart,* 2d ed., ed. Gunther Gottlieb et al., 187–93.
  Stuttgart, 1985.

Jansen, Max. *Die Anfänge der Fugger.* Leipzig, 1907.

———. *Jakob Fugger der Reiche: Studien und Quellen.* Leipzig, 1910.

Jeggle, Christof. "Die fremde Welt des Feindes: Hans Dernschwams Bericht einer Reise
  nach Konstantinopel und Kleinasien 1553–1556." In *Das Osmanische Reich und die
  Habsburgermonarchie. Akten des internationalen Kongresses zum 150-jährigen Bestehen des
  Instituts für Österreichische Geschichtsforschung Wien, 22.–25. September 2004,* ed. Marlene
  Kurz et al., 413–26. Munich, 2005.

Johnson, Christine R. *The German Discovery of the World: Renaissance Encounters with the
  Strange and Marvelous.* Charlottesville, Va., 2008.

Kalesse, Claudia. *Bürger in Augsburg: Studien über Bürgerrecht, Neubürger und Bürgen anhand
  des Augsburger Bürgerbuchs I (1288–1497).* Augsburg, 2001.

Kalus, Peter. *Die Fugger in der Slowakei.* Augsburg, 1999.

Karg, Franz. "Anton Fugger: Kaufmann und Bauherr, Mäzen und Stifter." In *Anton Fugger
  (1493–1560): Vorträge und Dokumentation zum fünfhundertjährigen Jubiläum,* ed. Johannes
  Burkhardt, 117–36. Weißenhorn, 1994.

———. "'Betreff: Herstellung einer Geschichte des Hauses Fugger': Die Fugger als
  Forschungsthema im 20. Jahrhundert." In *Augsburger Handelshäuser im Wandel des
  historischen Urteils,* ed. Johannes Burkhardt, 308–21. Berlin, 1996.

———. "'Dem Fuggerischen namen erkauft': Bemerkungen zum Besitz der Fugger." In
  Herrschaft und Politik: Vom Frühen Mittelalter bis zur Gebietsreform (Der Landkreis
  Augsburg, 3), ed. Walter Pötzl, 239–49. Augsburg, 2003.

———. "Hans Fugger wird 'Regierer' der Fuggerschen Firma." In *Die Welt des Hans Fugger
  (1531–1598),* ed. Johannes Burkhardt and Franz Karg, 131–42. Augsburg, 2007.

Karnehm, Christl. "Die Korrespondenz Hans Fuggers: Adressaten und Themen." In
  Die Welt des Hans Fugger (1531–1598), ed. Johannes Burkhardt and Franz Karg, 19–33.
  Augsburg, 2007.

———. "Das Korrespondenznetz Hans Fuggers (1531–1598)." In *Kommunikation und*

Medien in der Frühen Neuzeit, ed. Johannes Burkhardt and Christine Werkstetter, 301–11. Munich, 2005.

——, ed. *Die Korrespondenz Hans Fuggers von 1566 bis 1594: Regesten der Kopierbücher aus dem Fuggerarchiv,* 2 vols. Munich, 2003.

Kellenbenz, Hermann. "Anton Fugger (1493–1560)." In *Lebensbilder aus dem Bayerischen Schwaben,* vol. 2, 46–124. Weißenhorn, 1976.

——. "Augsburger Sammlungen". In *Welt im Umbruch: Augsburg zwischen Renaissance und Barock,* exhibition catalogue, vol. 1, 76–88. Augsburg, 1980.

——. "Los Fugger en España en la época de Felipe II. ¿Fue un buen negocio el arrendamiento de los Maestrazgos después de 1562?" In *Dinero y credito (siglos XVI al XIX),* ed. Alfonso Otazu, 19–36. Madrid, 1978.

——. *Die Fugger in Spanien und Portugal bis 1560: Ein Großunternehmen des 16. Jahrhunderts,* 3 vols. Munich, 1990.

——. *Die Fuggersche Maestrazgopacht (1525–1542).* Tübingen, 1967.

——. "The Fustian Industry of the Ulm Region in the Fifteenth and Early Sixteenth Centuries." In *Cloth and Clothing in Medieval Europe: Essays in Memory of Professor E.M. Carus-Wilson,* ed. N.B. Harte and K.G. Ponting, 259–76. London, 1983.

——. "The Gold Mining Activities of the Fugger and the Cementation Privilege of Kremnitz." In *Industry and Finance in Early Modern History: Essays Presented to George Hammersley to the Occasion of his 74th Birthday,* ed. Ian Blanchard et al., 186–204. Stuttgart, 1992.

——. "Hans Jakob Fugger (1516–1575)." In *Lebensbilder aus dem Bayerischen Schwaben,* vol. 12, 48–105. Weißenhorn, 1981.

——. "Jakob Fugger der Reiche (1459–1525)." In *Lebensbilder aus dem Bayerischen Schwaben,* vol. 10, 35–76. Weißenhorn, 1973.

——. "Kapitalverflechtung im mittleren Alpenraum: Das Beispiel des Bunt- und Edelmetallbergbaus vom fünfzehnten bis zur Mitte des siebzehnten Jahrhunderts." *Zeitschrift für bayerische Landesgeschichte* 51 (1988): 13–50.

——. "Das Konto Neapel in der Augsburger Rechnung der Fugger." In *Mut zur Kritik: Hanns Linhardt zum 80. Geburtstag,* ed. Oswald Hahn and Leo Schuster, 369–87. Bern, 1981.

——. "Neues zum oberdeutschen Ostindienhandel, insbesondere der Herwart in der ersten Hälfte des 16. Jahrhunderts." In *Forschungen zur schwäbischen Geschichte,* ed. Pankraz Fried, 81–96. Sigmaringen, 1991.

——. "Schwäbische Kaufherren im Tiroler Bergbau (1400–1650)." In *Schwaben—Tirol. Band 2: Beiträge,* ed. Wolfram Baer and Pankraz Fried, 208–18. Rosenheim, 1989.

——, ed. *Schwerpunkte der Kupferproduktion und des Kupferhandels in Europa, 1500–1650.* Cologne, 1977.

——. "Wirtschaft im Zeitalter der Reformation." In *Nürnberg—Geschichte einer europäischen Stadt,* ed. Gerhard Pfeiffer, 186–93, repr. ed. Munich, 1982.

——. "Wirtschaftsleben der Blütezeit." In *Geschichte der Stadt Augsburg von der Römerzeit bis zur Gegenwart,* 2d ed., ed. Gunther Gottlieb et al., 258–301. Stuttgart, 1985.

Kellenbenz, Hermann, and Maria Gräfin von Preysing. "Jakob Fuggers Stiftungsbrief von 1521." *Zeitschrift des Historischen Vereins für Schwaben* 68 (1974): 104–16.

Kellenbenz, Hermann, and Rolf Walter, eds. *Oberdeutsche Kaufleute in Sevilla und Cádiz (1525–1560). Eine Edition von Notariatsakten aus den dortigen Archiven.* Stuttgart, 2001.

Kern, Ernst. "Studien zur Geschichte des Augsburger Kaufmannshauses der Höchstetter." *Archiv für Kulturgeschichte* 26 (1936): 162–98.

Kießling, Rolf. "Augsburg in der Reformationszeit." In *". . . wider Laster und Sünde": Augsburgs Weg in die Reformation,* ed. Josef Kirmeier et al., 17–43. Cologne, 1997.

———. "Augsburg zwischen Mittelalter und Neuzeit." In *Geschichte der Stadt Augsburg von der Römerzeit bis zur Gegenwart,* 2d ed., ed. Gunther Gottlieb et al., 241–51. Stuttgart, 1985.

———. "Augsburgs Wirtschaft im 14. und 15. Jahrhundert." In *Geschichte der Stadt Augsburg von der Römerzeit bis zur Gegenwart,* 2d ed., ed. Gunther Gottlieb et al., 171–81. Stuttgart, 1985.

———. "Bürgerlicher Besitz auf dem Land—ein Schlüssel zu den Stadt-Land-Beziehungen im Spätmittelalter, aufgezeigt am Beispiel Augsburgs und anderer ostschwäbischer Städte." In *Augsburger Beiträge zur Landesgeschichte Bayerisch-Schwabens,* ed. Pankraz Fried, vol. 1, 121–40. Sigmaringen, 1979.

———. *Bürgerliche Gesellschaft und Kirche im Spätmittelalter: Ein Beitrag zur Strukturanalyse der oberdeutschen Reichsstadt.* Augsburg, 1971.

———. "Patrizier und Kaufleute als Herrschaftsträger auf dem Land." In *Herrschaft und Politik: Vom Frühen Mittelalter bis zur Gebietsreform* (Der Landkreis Augsburg, 3), ed. Walter Pötzl, 217–38. Augsburg, 2003.

———. *Die Stadt und ihr Land: Umlandpolitik, Bürgerbesitz und Wirtschaftsgefüge in Ostschwaben vom 14. bis ins 16. Jahrhundert.* Cologne, 1989.

———. "Stadt und Land im Textilgewerbe Ostschwabens vom 14. bis zur Mitte des 16. Jahrhunderts." In *Bevölkerung, Wirtschaft und Gesellschaft: Stadt-Land-Beziehungen in Deutschland und Frankreich, 14. bis 19. Jahrhundert,* ed. Neithard Bulst et al., 115–37. Trier, 1983.

———. "Wirtschaftlicher Strukturwandel in der Region—Die Welser-Vöhlin-Gesellschaft im Kontext der Memminger Wirtschafts- und Sozialgeschichte des 15. und frühen 16. Jahrhunderts." In *Die Welser: Neue Forschungen zur Geschichte und Kultur des oberdeutschen Handelshauses,* ed. Mark Häberlein and Johannes Burkhardt, 184–212. Berlin, 2002.

Kirch, Hermann Josef. *Die Fugger und der Schmalkaldische Krieg.* Munich, 1915.

Knittler, Herbert. "Europas Wirtschafts- und Handelsräume am Vorabend der atlantischen Expansion." In *Die Geschichte des europäischen Welthandels und der wirtschaftliche Globalisierungsprozess,* ed. Friedrich Edelmayer et al., 12–32. Vienna, 2001.

Kohler, Alfred. *Ferdinand I. 1503–1564: Fürst, König und Kaiser.* Munich, 2003.

———. *Karl V. 1500–1558: Eine Biographie.* Munich, 1999.

Koutná, Dana. "'Mit ainer sollichen kostlichkeit und allerley kurtzweil . . .' Feste und Feiern der Fugger im 16. Jahrhundert." In *Anton Fugger (1493–1560): Vorträge und Dokumentation zum fünfhundertjährigen Jubiläum,* ed. Johannes Burkhardt, 99–115. Weißenhorn, 1994.

Koutná-Karg, Dana. "Die Ehre der Fugger: Zum Selbstverständnis einer Familie." In *Augsburger Handelshäuser im Wandel des historischen Urteils,* ed. Johannes Burkhardt, 87–106. Berlin, 1996.

Kranz, Annette. *Christoph Amberger — Bildnismaler zu Augsburg. Städtische Eliten im Spiegel ihrer Porträts.* Regensburg 2004.

Krautwurst, Franz. "Melchior Neusidler und die Fugger." *Musik in Bayern* 54 (1997): 5–24.

Kuhoff, Wolfgang. "Augsburger Handelshäuser und die Antike." In *Augsburger Handelshäuser im Wandel des historischen Urteils,* ed. Johannes Burkhardt, 258–76. Berlin, 1996.

Künast, Hans-Jörg. *"Getruckt zu Augspurg": Buchdruck und Buchhandel in Augsburg zwischen 1468 und 1555.* Tübingen, 1997.

Küster, Konrad. "Die Beziehungen der Fugger zu Musikzentren des 16. Jahrhunderts." In *Anton Fugger (1493–1560): Vorträge und Dokumentation zum fünfhundertjährigen Jubiläum,* ed. Johannes Burkhardt, 79–98. Weißenhorn, 1994.

Landsteiner, Erich. "Kein Zeitalter der Fugger: Zentraleuropa 1450–1620." In *Globalgeschichte 1450–1620: Anfänge und Perspektiven,* ed. Friedrich Edelmayer et al., 95–123. Vienna, 2002.

Lanzinner, Maximilian. *Fürst, Räte und Landstände: Die Entstehung der Zentralbehörden in Bayern 1511–1598.* Göttingen, 1980.

———. "Johann Georg Herwarth d.Ä. (1553–1622): Territorialpolitik, späthumanistische Gelehrsamkeit und sozialer Aufstieg." *Archiv für Kulturgeschichte* 75 (1993): 301–34.

Lehmann, Paul. *Eine Geschichte der alten Fuggerbibliotheken,* 2 vols. Tübingen, 1956–60.

Lieb, Norbert. *Die Fugger und die Kunst, Band 1: Im Zeitalter der Spätgotik und der frühen Renaissance.* Munich, 1952.

———. *Die Fugger und die Kunst, Band 2: Im Zeitalter der Hohen Renaissance.* Munich, 1958.

———. *Octavian Secundus Fugger (1549–1600) und die Kunst.* Tübingen, 1980.

Lietzmann, Hilda. "Der Briefwechsel Hans Fuggers mit Wilhelm V. von Bayern." *Zeitschrift für bayerische Landesgeschichte* 66 (2003): 435–59.

Lill, Georg. *Hans Fugger (1531–1598) und die Kunst: Ein Beitrag zur Spätrenaissance in Süddeutschland.* Leipzig, 1908.

Limberger, Michael. "'No Town in the World Provides More Advantages': Economies of Agglomeration and the Golden Age of Antwerp." In *Urban Achievement in Early Modern Europe: Golden Ages in Antwerp, Amsterdam and London,* ed. Patrick O'Brien et al., 39–62. Cambridge, 2001.

Ludwig, Karl-Heinz, and Fritz Gruber. *Gold- und Silberbergbau im Übergang vom Mittelalter zur Neuzeit: Das Salzburger Revier von Gastein und Rauris.* Cologne, 1987.

Lutz, Elmar. *Die rechtliche Struktur süddeutscher Handelsgesellschaften in der Zeit der Fugger,* 2 vols. Tübingen, 1976.

Lutz, Georg. "Gegenreformation und Kunst in Schwaben und in Oberitalien: Der Bilderzyklus des Vincenzo Campi im Fuggerschloss Kirchheim." In *Venedig und Oberdeutschland in der Renaissance: Beziehungen zwischen Kunst und Wirtschaft,* ed. Bernd Roeck et al., 131–54. Sigmaringen, 1993.

———. "Marx Fugger (1529–1597) und die *Annales Ecclesastici* des Baronius: Eine Verdeutschung aus dem Augsburg der Gegenreformation." In *Baronio Storico e la Controriforma. Atti del Convegno internazionale di Studi, Sora 6–10 Ottobre 1979,* 421–546. Sora, 1982.

Lutz, Heinrich. *Conrad Peutinger: Beiträge zu einer politischen Biographie.* Augsburg, 1958.

Maasen, Werner. *Hans Jakob Fugger 1516–1575: Ein Beitrag zur Geschichte des 16. Jahrhunderts*, ed. Paul Ruf. Munich, 1922.

Mandrou, Robert. *Die Fugger als Grundbesitzer in Schwaben 1560–1618: Eine Fallstudie sozioökonomischen Verhaltens am Ende des 16. Jahrhunderts*. Göttingen, 1997.

Maschke, Erich. "Das Berufsbewusstsein des mittelalterlichen Fernkaufmanns." In Erich Maschke, *Städte und Menschen: Beiträge zur Geschichte der Stadt, der Wirtschaft und Gesellschaft 1959–1977*, 380–419. Wiesbaden, 1980.

Mathew, K.S. *Indo-Portuguese Trade and the Fuggers of Germany: Sixteenth Century*. New Delhi, 1997.

Mauer, Benedikt. *"Gemain Geschrey" und "teglich Reden": Georg Kölderer—ein Augsburger Chronist des konfessionellen Zeitalters*. Augsburg, 2001.

Meadow, Mark A. "Merchants and Marvels: Hans Jacob Fugger and the Origins of the Wunderkammer." In *Merchants and Marvels: Commerce, Science, and Art in Early Modern Europe*, ed. Pamela H. Smith and Paula Findlen, 182–200. New York, 2002.

Mentges, Gabriele. "Fashion, Time and the Consumption of a Renaissance Man in Germany: The Costume Book of Matthäus Schwarz of Augsburg, 1498–1564." In *Material Strategies: Dress and Gender in Historical Perspective*, ed. Barbara Burman and Carole Turbin, 12–32. Oxford, 2003.

Merten, Klaus. "Die Landschlösser der Familie Fugger im 16. Jahrhundert." In *Welt im Umbruch: Augsburg zwischen Renaissance und Barock*, exhibition catalogue, vol. 3, 66–82. Augsburg, 1980.

Mertens, Bernd. *Im Kampf gegen die Monopole: Reichstagsverhandlungen und Monopolprozesse im frühen 16. Jahrhundert*. Tübingen, 1996.

Mörke, Olaf. "Die Fugger im 16. Jahrhundert: Städtische Elite oder Sonderstruktur? Ein Diskussionsbeitrag." *Archiv für Reformationsgeschichte* 74 (1983): 141–61.

Mörke, Olaf, and Katarina Sieh. "Gesellschaftliche Führungsgruppen." In *Geschichte der Stadt Augsburg von der Römerzeit bis zur Gegenwart*, 2d ed., ed. Gunther Gottlieb et al., 301–11. Stuttgart, 1985.

Mondrain, Brigitte. "Copistes et collectionneurs de manuscrits grecs au milieu du XVIe siècle: Le cas de Johann Jakob Fugger d'Augsbourg." *Byzantinische Zeitschrift* 84–85 (1991–92): 354–90.

Montaigne, Michel de. *Tagebuch der Reise nach Italien über die Schweiz und Deutschland von 1580 bis 1581*, trans. and ed. Hans Stilett. Frankfurt am Main, 2002.

Müller, Karl-Otto, ed. *Quellen zur Handelsgeschichte der Paumgartner von Augsburg (1480–1570)*. Wiesbaden, 1955.

Nebinger, Gerhart. "Die Standesverhältnisse des Hauses Fugger (von der Lilie) im 15. und 16. Jahrhundert: Ein Beitrag zur sozialgeschichtlichen Wertung von Titulaturen." *Blätter des Bayerischen Landesvereins für Familienkunde* 49, no. 15 (1986): 263–76.

Nebinger, Gerhart, and Albrecht Rieber. *Genealogie des Hauses Fugger von der Lilie*. Tübingen, 1978.

Noflatscher, Heinz. *Räte und Herrscher: Politische Eliten an den Habsburgerhöfen der österreichischen Länder 1480–1530*. Mainz, 1999.

North, Michael. "Kunst und bürgerliche Repräsentation in der Frühen Neuzeit." *Historische Zeitschrift* 267 (1998): 29–56.

Nübel, Otto. "Das Geschlecht Occo." In *Lebensbilder aus dem Bayerischen Schwaben*, vol. 10, 77–113. Weißenhorn, 1973.

———. *Mittelalterliche Beginen- und Sozialsiedlungen in den Niederlanden: Ein Beitrag zur Vorgeschichte der Fuggerei*. Tübingen, 1970.

———. *Pompejus Occo, 1483 bis 1537: Fuggerfaktor in Amsterdam*. Tübingen, 1972.

Oberman, Heiko A. *Werden und Wertung der Reformation: Vom Wegestreit zum Glaubenskampf*. Tübingen, 1977.

Oexle, Otto Gerhard. "Adel, Memoria und kulturelles Gedächtnis: Bemerkungen zur Memorial-Kapelle der Fugger in Augsburg." In *Les princes et l'histoire du XIVe au XVIIIe siècle*, ed. Chantal Grell et al., 339–57. Bonn, 1998.

Ogger, Günter. *Kauf dir einen Kaiser: Die Geschichte der Fugger*. Munich, 1978.

Otte, Enrique. "Die Welser in Santo Domingo." In Enrique Otte, *Von Bankiers und Kaufleuten, Räten, Reedern und Piraten, Hintermännern und Strohmännern: Aufsätze zur atlantischen Expansion Spaniens*, ed. Günter Vollmer and Horst Pietschmann, 117–59. Stuttgart, 2004.

Palme, Rudolf. "Historiographische und rezeptionsgeschichtliche Aspekte der Tätigkeit der Fugger in Tirol." In *Augsburger Handelshäuser im Wandel des historischen Urteils*, ed. Johannes Burkhardt, 297–307. Berlin, 1996.

Peters, Lambert F. *Der Handel Nürnbergs am Anfang des Dreißigjährigen Krieges: Strukturkomponenten, Unternehmen und Unternehmer. Eine quantitative Analyse*. Stuttgart, 1994.

Pickl, Othmar. "Kupfererzeugung und Kupferhandel in den Ostalpen." In *Schwerpunkte der Kupferproduktion und des Kupferhandels in Europa, 1500–1650*, ed. Hermann Kellenbenz, 117–47. Cologne, 1977.

Pieper, Renate. "Informationszentren im Vergleich: Die Stellung Venedigs und Antwerpens im 16. Jahrhundert." In *Kommunikationsrevolutionen: Die neuen Medien des 16. und 19. Jahrhunderts*, ed. Michael North, 45–60. Cologne, 1995.

———. *Die Vermittlung einer neuen Welt. Amerika im Nachrichtennetz des Habsburgischen Imperiums (1493–1598)*. Mainz, 2000.

Pölnitz, Götz Freiherr von. "Die Anfänge der Weißenhorner Barchentweberei unter Jakob Fugger dem Reichen." In *Festschrift für Hans Liermann zum 70. Geburtstag*, 196–220. Erlangen, 1964.

———. *Anton Fugger*, 3 vols. Tübingen, 1958–1986.

———. *Die Fugger*. Tübingen, 1960.

———. *Fugger und Hanse: Ein hundertjähriges Ringen um Nordsee und Ostsee*. Tübingen, 1953.

———. "Fugger und Medici." *Historische Zeitschrift* 166 (1942): 1–23.

———. "Die Fuggersche Generalrechnung von 1563." *Kyklos* 20 (1967): 355–70.

———. "Das Generationenproblem in der Geschichte der oberdeutschen Handelshäuser." In *Unser Geschichtsbild*, ed. Karl Rüdinger, 65–79. Munich, 1955.

———. *Jakob Fugger: Kaiser, Kirche und Kapital in der oberdeutschen Renaissance*, 2 vols. Tübingen, 1949–51.

———. "Jakob Fugger und der Streit um den Nachlass des Kardinals Melchior von Brixen (1496–1515)." *Quellen und Forschungen aus italienischen Archiven und Bibliotheken* 30 (1940): 223–94.

———. "Jakob Fuggers Zeitungen und Briefe an die Fürsten des Hauses Wettin in
  der Frühzeit Karls V., 1519–1525." *Nachrichten von der Akademie der Wissenschaften in
  Göttingen, Philosophisch-Historische Klasse 1941*, no. 2 (1941): 89–160.
Press, Volker. "Führungsgruppen in der deutschen Gesellschaft im Übergang zur Neuzeit
  um 1500." In *Deutsche Führungsschichten in der Neuzeit: Eine Zwischenbilanz. Büdinger
  Vorträge 1978*, ed. Hans Hubert Hofmann and Günther Franz, 29–77. Boppard am Rhein,
  1980.
Preysing, Maria Gräfin von. *Die Fuggertestamente des 16. Jahrhunderts. Band 2: Edition*.
  Weißenhorn, 1992.
Rabe, Horst. *Deutsche Geschichte 1500–1600: Das Jahrhundert der Glaubensspaltung*. Munich,
  1991.
Rauscher, Peter. *Zwischen Ständen und Gläubigern: Die kaiserlichen Finanzen unter Ferdinand
  I. und Maximilian II. (1556–1576)*. Munich, 2004.
Reinhard, Wolfgang, ed. *Augsburger Eliten des 16. Jahrhunderts: Prosopographie
  wirtschaftlicher und politischer Führungsgruppen 1500–1620*, comp. Mark Häberlein et al.
  Berlin, 1996.
———. *Geschichte der Staatsgewalt: Eine vergleichende Verfassungsgeschichte Europas von den
  Anfängen bis zur Gegenwart*. Munich, 1999.
———. *Probleme deutscher Geschichte 1495–1806. Reichsreform und Reformation 1495–1555*
  (Gebhardt Handbuch der deutschen Geschichte, 10th ed., vol. 9). Stuttgart, 2001.
Roeck, Bernd. *Eine Stadt in Krieg und Frieden: Studien zur Geschichte der Reichsstadt
  Augsburg zwischen Kalenderstreit und Parität*, 2 vols. Göttingen, 1989.
———. *Geschichte Augsburgs*. Munich, 2005.
———. *Kunstpatronage in der Frühen Neuzeit: Studien zu Kunstmarkt, Künstlern und ihren
  Auftraggebern in Italien und im Heiligen Römischen Reich (15.–17. Jahrhundert)*. Göttingen,
  1998.
Rogge, Jörg. *Für den Gemeinen Nutzen: Politisches Handeln und Politikverständnis von Rat und
  Bürgerschaft in Augsburg im Spätmittelalter*. Tübingen, 1996.
———. "'Ir freye Wale zu haben': Möglichkeiten, Probleme und Grenzen der politischen
  Partizipation in Augsburg zur Zeit der Zunftverfassung (1368–1548)." In *Stadtregiment
  und Bürgerfreiheit: Handlungsspielräume in deutschen und italienischen Städten des Späten
  Mittelalters und der Frühen Neuzeit*, ed. Klaus Schreiner and Ulrich Meier, 244–77.
  Göttingen, 1994.
Rohmann, Gregor. *Das Ehrenbuch der Fugger*, 2 vols. Augsburg, 2004.
Roper, Lyndal. *Oedipus and the Devil: Witchcraft, Religion and Sexuality in Early Modern
  Europe*. London, 1994.
Rublack, Hans-Christoph. "Grundwerte im späten Mittelalter und in der Frühen Neuzeit."
  In *Literatur in der Stadt: Bedingungen und Beispiele städtischer Literatur des 15. bis 17.
  Jahrhunderts*, ed. Horst Brunner, 9–36. Göppingen, 1982.
Safley, Thomas Max. "Die Fuggerfaktoren Hörmann von und zu Gutenberg: Werte und
  Normen einer kaufmännischen Familie im Übergang zum Landadel." In *Augsburger
  Handelshäuser im Wandel des historischen Urteils*, ed. Johannes Burkhardt, 118–29. Berlin,
  1996.
———. "Staatsmacht und geschäftliches Scheitern: Der Bankrott der Handelsgesellschaft

Ambrosius und Hans, Gebrüder Höchstetter, und Mitverwandte im Jahr 1529."
Österreichische Zeitschrift für Geschichtswissenschaften 19, no. 3 (2008): 36–55.

Schad, Martha. *Die Frauen des Hauses Fugger von der Lilie (15.–17. Jahrhundert): Augsburg—Ortenburg—Trient.* Tübingen, 1989.

Schaper, Christa. *Die Hirschvogel von Nürnberg und ihr Handelshaus.* Nuremberg, 1973.

Scheller, Benjamin. *Memoria an der Zeitenwende: Die Stiftungen Jakob Fuggers des Reichen vor und während der Reformation (ca. 1505–1555).* Berlin, 2004.

Scheuermann, Ludwig. *Die Fugger als Montanindustrielle in Tirol und Kärnten: Ein Beitrag zur Wirtschaftsgeschichte des 16. und 17. Jahrhunderts.* Munich, 1929.

Schick, Léon. *Un grand homme d'affaires au début du XVIe siècle: Jacob Fugger.* Paris, 1957.

Schiersner, Dietmar. "In der Region zu Hause—im Reich verankert. 'Fuggerland' im Überblick." In *Die Fugger und das Reich: Eine neue Forschungsperspektive zum fünfhundertjährigen Jubiläum der ersten Fuggerherrschaft Kirchberg-Weißenhorn,* ed. Johannes Burkhardt, 15–32. Augsburg, 2008.

Schilling, Heinz. "Die Konfessionalisierung im Reich: Religiöser und gesellschaftlicher Wandel in Deutschland zwischen 1555 und 1620." *Historische Zeitschrift* 246 (1988): 1–45.

Schilling, Michael. "Zwischen Mündlichkeit und Druck: Die Fuggerzeitungen." In *Editionsdesiderate der Frühen Neuzeit. Beiträge zur Tagung der Kommission für die Edition von Texten der Frühen Neuzeit,* ed. Hans-Gert Roloff, vol. 2, 717–28. Amsterdam, 1997.

Schulte, Aloys. *Die Fugger in Rom, 1495–1523,* 2 vols. Leipzig, 1904.

———. *Geschichte des mittelalterlichen Handels und Verkehrs zwischen Westdeutschland und Italien mit Ausschluss von Venedig,* 2 vols. Leipzig, 1900.

Schulze, Winfried. "Vom Gemeinnutz zum Eigennutz: Über den Normenwandel in der ständischen Gesellschaft der Frühen Neuzeit." *Historische Zeitschrift* 243 (1986): 591–626.

Sczesny, Anke. *Zwischen Kontinuität und Wandel. Ländliches Gewerbe und ländliche Gesellschaft im Ostschwaben des 17. und 18. Jahrhunderts.* Tübingen, 2002.

Seibold, Gerhard. *Die Manlich: Geschichte einer Augsburger Kaufmannsfamilie.* Sigmaringen, 1995.

Sieh-Burens, Katarina. *Oligarchie, Konfession und Politik im 16. Jahrhundert: Zur sozialen Verflechtung der Augsburger Bürgermeister und Stadtpfleger, 1518–1618.* Munich, 1986.

Sigelen, Alexander. ". . . 'durch die mittel der herren Fugger und meiner befreundten': Die Fugger und Reichspfennigmeister Zacharias Geizkofler." In *Die Fugger und das Reich: Eine neue Forschungsperspektive zum fünfhundertjährigen Jubiläum der ersten Fuggerherrschaft Kirchberg-Weißenhorn,* ed. Johannes Burkhardt, 83–110. Augsburg, 2008.

Simmer, Götz. *Gold und Sklaven: Die Provinz Venezuela während der Welser-Verwaltung (1528–1556).* Berlin, 2000.

Simnacher, Georg. *Die Fuggertestamente des 16. Jahrhunderts.* Tübingen, 1960.

Simonsfeld, Henry. *Der Fondaco dei Tedeschi in Venedig und deutsch-venetianischen Handelsbeziehungen,* 2 vols. Stuttgart, 1887.

Soergel, Philip. *Wondrous in His Saints: Counter-Reformation Propaganda in Bavaria.* Berkeley, Calif., 1993.

Soly, Hugo. "The 'Betrayal' of the 16th-Century Bourgeoisie: A Myth?" *Acta historiae Neerlandicae* 8 (1979): 262–80.

Sommerlad, Bernhard. "Die Faktorei der Fugger in Leipzig." *Schriften des Vereins für die Geschichte Leipzigs* 28 (1938): 39–67.

Spranger, Carolin. *Der Metall- und Versorgungshandel der Fugger in Schwaz in Tirol 1560–1575 zwischen Krisen und Konflikten.* Augsburg, 2007.

———. "Der Metall- und Versorgungshandel der Fugger in Schwaz zwischen 1560 und 1580: Tiroler Landesherr, Montanverwaltung und Gewerken zwischen Krisen und Konflikten." In *Schwazer Silber—vergeudeter Reichtum? Verschwenderische Habsburger in Abhängigkeit vom oberdeutschen Kapital an der Zeitenwende vom Mittelalter zur Neuzeit,* ed. Wolfgang Ingenhaeff and Johann Bair, 181–98. Innsbruck, 2003.

Staudinger, Barbara. "Juden am Reichshofrat: Jüdische Rechtsstellung und Judenfeindschaft am Beispiel der österreichischen, böhmischen und mährischen Juden, 1559–1670." Ph.D. diss., University of Vienna, 2001.

Steinmeyer, Heinrich. *Die Entstehung und Entwicklung der Nördlinger Pfingstmesse im Spätmittelalter.* Nördlingen, 1960.

Steuer, Peter. *Die Außenverflechtung der Augsburger Oligarchie von 1500–1620: Studien zur sozialen Verflechtung der politischen Führungsschicht der Reichsstadt Augsburg.* Augsburg, 1988.

Stollberg-Rilinger, Barbara. "Gut vor Ehre oder Ehre vor Gut? Zur sozialen Distinktion zwischen Adels- und Kaufmannsstand in der Ständeliteratur der Frühen Neuzeit." In *Augsburger Handelshäuser im Wandel des historischen Urteils,* ed. Johannes Burkhardt, 31–45. Berlin, 1996.

Strieder, Jakob. *Aus Antwerpener Notariatsarchiven: Quellen zur deutschen Wirtschaftsgeschichte des 16. Jahrhunderts.* Stuttgart, 1930.

———. "Deutscher Metallwarenexport nach Westafrika im 16. Jahrhundert." In *Das Reiche Augsburg: Ausgewählte Aufsätze Jakob Strieders zur Augsburger und süddeutschen Wirtschaftsgeschichte des 15. und 16. Jahrhunderts,* ed. Heinz-Friedrich Deininger, 155–67. Munich, 1938.

———. "Ein Bericht des Fuggerschen Faktors Hans Dernschwam über den Siebenbürger Salzbergbau um 1528." *Ungarische Jahrbücher* 13 (1933): 262–90.

———. "Die Geschäfts- und Familienpolitik Jakob Fuggers des Reichen." In *Das Reiche Augsburg: Ausgewählte Aufsätze Jakob Strieders zur Augsburger und süddeutschen Wirtschaftsgeschichte des 15. und 16. Jahrhunderts,* ed. Heinz-Friedrich Deininger, 193–204. Munich, 1938.

———. *Die Inventur der Firma Fugger aus dem Jahre 1527.* Tübingen, 1905.

———. *Jakob Fugger der Reiche.* Leipzig, 1926. (English translation: *Jacob Fugger the Rich: Merchant and Banker of Augsburg, 1459–1525,* repr. ed. Washington, D.C., 2001 [1931].)

———. *Zur Genesis des modernen Kapitalismus: Forschungen zur Entstehung der großen bürgerlichen Kapitalvermögen am Ausgang des Mittelalters und zu Beginn der Neuzeit, zunächst in Augsburg,* 2d ed. Leipzig, 1935 (1904).

Stromer, Wolfgang von. *Die Gründung der Baumwollindustrie in Mitteleuropa: Wirtschaftspolitik im Spätmittelalter.* Stuttgart, 1978.

Tewes, Götz-Rüdiger. "Luthergegner der ersten Stunde: Motive und Verflechtungen." *Quellen und Forschungen aus italienischen Archiven und Bibliotheken* 75 (1995): 256–365.

Tietz-Strödel, Marion. *Die Fuggerei in Augsburg: Studien zur Entwicklung des sozialen Stiftungsbaus im 15. und 16. Jahrhundert.* Tübingen, 1982.

Tracy, James D. *Emperor Charles V, Impresario of War: Campaign Strategy, International Finance, and Domestic Politics.* Cambridge, 2002.

Trauchburg, Gabriele von. *Häuser und Gärten Augsburger Patrizier.* Berlin, 2001.

Trauchburg-Kuhnle, Gabriele von. "Auf den Spuren Augsburger Kaufleute in Flandern." In *Aus Schwaben und Altbayern: Festschrift für Pankraz Fried zum 60. Geburtstag,* ed. Peter Fassl et al., 261–71. Sigmaringen, 1991.

———. "Kooperation und Konkurrenz. Augsburger Kaufleute in Antwerpen." In *Augsburger Handelshäuser im Wandel des historischen Urteils,* ed. Johannes Burkhardt, 210–23. Berlin, 1996.

Unger, Eike Eberhard. *Die Fugger in Hall in Tirol.* Tübingen, 1967.

van der Wee, Hermann, and Jan Materné. "Antwerp as a World Market in the Sixteenth and Seventeenth Centuries." In *Antwerp: Story of a Metropolis (16th–17th centuries),* ed. Jan van der Stock, 19–32. Ghent, 1993.

Vlachović, Josef. "Die Kupfererzeugung und der Kupferhandel in der Slowakei vom Ende des 15. bis zur Mitte des 17. Jahrhunderts." In *Schwerpunkte der Kupferproduktion und des Kupferhandels in Europa, 1500–1650,* ed. Hermann Kellenbenz, 148–71. Cologne, 1977.

Völkel, Markus. "Der alte und der neue Adel: Johannes Engerds panegyrische Symbiose von Fugger und Montfort." In *Augsburger Handelshäuser im Wandel des historischen Urteils,* ed. Johannes Burkhardt, 107–17. Berlin, 1996.

Wallenta, Wolfgang. *Katholische Konfessionalisierung in Augsburg, 1548–1648.* Hamburg, 2003.

Warmbrunn, Paul. *Zwei Konfessionen in einer Stadt: Das Zusammenleben von Katholiken und Protestanten in den paritätischen Reichsstädten Augsburg, Biberach, Ravensburg und Dinkelsbühl von 1548–1648.* Wiesbaden, 1983.

Warnemünde, Christel. "Augsburger Handel in den letzten Jahrzehnten des 16. Jahrhunderts und dem beginnenden 17. Jahrhundert." Ph.D. diss., University of Freiburg, 1956.

Weber, Wolfgang E.J. "Das Vermächtnis des 'Wassermanns': Hans Jakob Fugger und die Münchener Hofbibliothek." In *Die Anfänge der Münchener Hofbibliothek unter Herzog Albrecht V.,* ed. Alois Schmid, 132–45. Munich, 2009.

Weitnauer, Alfred. *Venezianischer Handel der Fugger. Nach der Musterbuchhaltung des Matthäus Schwarz.* Munich, 1931.

Welt im Umbruch: Augsburg zwischen Renaissance und Barock, exhibition catalogue, 3 vols. Augsburg, 1980.

Westermann, Ekkehard. "The Brass-works of the Höchstetter at Pflach near Reutte in the Tirol, 1509–1529." In *Industry and Finance in Early Modern History: Essays Presented to George Hammersley to the Occasion of his 74th Birthday,* ed. Ian Blanchard et al., 161–86. Stuttgart, 1992.

———. "Gewichtsverhältnisse, Preise und Frachtkosten im Fuggerschen Kupfergeschäft zu Neusohl, Krakau, Breslau, Stettin, Stralsund und Danzig in der ersten Hälfte des 16. Jahrhunderts: Aus Vorarbeiten und -überlegungen zu einer möglichen Edition." In *"Vom rechten Maß der Dinge": Beiträge zur Wirtschafts- und Sozialgeschichte. Festschrift für Harald Witthöft zum 65. Geburtstag,* ed. Rainer S. Elkar et al., 166–81. St. Katharinen, 1996.

————, ed. *Die Listen der Brandsilberproduktion des Falkenstein bei Schwaz von 1470 bis 1623.* Vienna, 1988.

————. "Zur Silber- und Kupferproduktion Mitteleuropas vom 15. bis zum frühen 17. Jahrhundert: Über Bedeutung und Rangfolge der Reviere von Schwaz, Mansfeld und Neusohl." *Der Anschnitt* 38 (1986): 187–211.

Wölfle, Sylvia. *Die Kunstpatronage der Fugger, 1560–1618.* Augsburg, 2009.

Wüst, Wolfgang. "Das Bild der Fugger in der Reichsstadt Augsburg und in der Reiseliteratur." In *Augsburger Handelshäuser im Wandel des historischen Urteils,* ed. Johannes Burkhardt, 69–86. Berlin, 1996.

Wunder, Heide. *Er ist die Sonn', sie ist der Mond: Frauen in der frühen Neuzeit.* Munich, 1992. (English translation: *He Is the Sun, She Is the Moon: Women in Early Modern Germany.* Cambridge, Mass., 1998.)

Wurm, Johann Peter. *Johannes Eck und der oberdeutsche Zinsstreit, 1513–1515.* Münster, 1997.

Zorn, Wolfgang. *Augsburg: Geschichte einer europäischen Stadt,* 3d ed. Augsburg, 1994.

INDEX

Italicized page numbers refer to illustrations, and a "t" following a page number indicates a table.

Bruges, 25, 49

Brunswick, 135

Brussels, 54, 140, 145

Brüx (Most), 138

Bubenhofen, Hans Marx von, 74, 202

Bucer, Martin, 190

Budapest. *See* Ofen

Burgau, 36, 208–10

Burghausen, 215

Burgkmair, Hans (the Elder), 150, 155, 160–61

Burgos, 66, 77

Burgwalden (Swabia), 73, 202

Burkhardt, Johannes, 68, 90

Burkhart, Benedikt, 83

Burtenbach (Swabia), 11, 17

Bushart, Bruno, 154

Cajetan, Thomas de Vio, Cardinal, 181

Calatrava, 79

Cambrai, 50

Camerarius, Joachim (the Elder), 139

Canary Islands, 56

Capuchins, 193, 217

Carande, Ramón, 75, 95

Carinthia, 41, 85, 89, 122

cartels, 57, 89, 118. *See also* syndicates

Carvajal, Bernardino, 176

Castile, 75–77, 80

Catena, Vincenzo, 160

Catholicism, viii, 99–100, 116, 120, 133, 156, 168–69, 174–75, 185–87, 189–90, 192–97, 214, 217–19

Cavalli, Antonio (Anton vom Ross), 35

Centurione bank, 76

Charles the Bold, Duke (of Burgundy), 201

Charles V, Emperor, vii, 4, 54, 64–67, 75–77, 80, 82, 86, 90, 92, 95, 126, 128–29, 134, 140, 144, 151, 161, 164, 174, 177–78, 188–89, 191, 197, 222, 241n24

Charles VIII, King (of France), 37

Chile, 80

Chincha (Peru), 80

Christian II, King (of Denmark), 140

Christian III, King (of Denmark), 91, 143

chronicles, 1, 11, 14, 18, 21, 23, 67–68, 143, 172, 176–78, 182–83, 185, 194

Cieszyn. *See* Teschen (Cieszyn)

Civitavecchia, 47

Claes, Gerbrich, 142

Clemens VII, Pope, 49

clerics/clergy, 20, 29–30, 34, 46, 131, 173, 178–81, 184–87, 189, 195–97, 199, 213–19

Cochlaeus, Johannes, 166, 181

Colaus, Sidonia von, 215

Cologne, 15, 22, 106, 108, 111, 116–17, 131, 140, 182

common good, 6, 44, 66–67, 170, 176, 178, 181, 187, 222–23

Constance, 22, 48, 134, 180, 201, 216–19

Constantinople, 139, 166

copper, vii, 37–38, 41–42, 44, 47, 49–53, 56–57, 61, 63–65, 71–73, 80, 82–83, 85, 87–91, 96, 113–14, 122, 128, 140, 143, 151

Cordoba, 100

Cornelisz, Jakob, 142

corsairs, 54, 119

Cosimo I Medici, Grand Duke of Florence, 91

cotton, vii, 14, 20, 22, 24, 49, 51, 97, 212

Cranach, Lucas (the Elder), 160

credit, vii, 15–18, 22, 26, 35–38, 40, 42, 46, 59, 61, 73–77, 83–87, 90–92, 96–98, 102–4, 106, 109–12, 116, 120–24, 148, 180, 189, 208, 213, 215, 221–22

Cron, Ferdinand, 119

Cuspinianus, Johannes, 139

Custos, Dominicus, 172

Dachs, Johann, widow of, 12

Danzig. *See* Gdansk

Daucher, Adolf, 154

Daucher, Hans, 155

Dauser, Regina, 5

Denmark, 46, 90–91, 140, 143

Dernschwam, Hans, 70, 89, 133, 138–40, 142, 166

Dietrich, Wendel, 208

Dietrichstein, Adam von, 102, 110

Dillingen, 217

Dobrau, Jan von, 154

Fugger, Ulrich, I (1441–1510), 19–21, 26, 29–31, 33–35, 50, 58, 64, 128, 154, 166, 173, 176–77, 202

Fugger, Ulrich, II (1490–1525), 34, 67–68, 70, 160, 177

Fugger, Ulrich, III (1526–1584), 103, 166–69, 192, 204, 211

Fugger, Ursula, 165, 192, 202–3

Fugger, Viktor Augustus, 215

Fugger, Walburga, 21

Fugger ("von der Lilie"): genealogy, x–xi; tax payments of, 33t; map of territories of (Swabia, 1560 and 1618), 205

Fuggerau (Carinthia), 41–42, 88–89, 128

Furtenbach, Christoph, 107, 114, 121

Furtenbach, Paul, 121

Füssen, 40, 58

fustian, vii, 20, 22, 24–26, 28, 55, 80, 211–13, 223

Gabler, Stefan, 57

Gablingen (Swabia), 202, 206

Gabrieli, Giovanni, 165

Gama, Vasco da, 51

gardens, 53, 136, 149, 152, 156

Gasser, Achilles Pirmin, 167–68

Gassner, Lukas, 177

Gassner, Veronika, 177

Gassner family, 177, 202

Gastein (Salzburg), 37

Gdansk, 42, 44, 53, 88, 126, 140

Gefattermann, Elisabeth, 11–13; wealth of, 13t

Geffcken, Peter, 14, 30

Geizkofler, Katharina, 132

Geizkofler, Lukas, 133

Geizkofler, Zacharias, 117

Genoa, 25, 55, 76–77, 97, 100, 107, 114, 127, 134

Gentile bank, 76

Georgenthal (Thuringia), 41, 89

Georg of Saxony, Duke, 59, 65, 182

Gerhard, Hubert, 208

Gesner, Conrad, 167

Glasgow, 46

Glött (Swabia), 202–3, 206

Goa (India), 116

gold, 42, 55, 59, 79–80, 85, 89–90, 93, 97, 108, 134

goldsmiths, 13, 17–18

Goslar, 41, 63

Gossembrot, Georg, 38–39, 61

Gossembrot, Sigmund, 39

Gossembrot family, 38, 44, 52, 54, 56

Gossensass (Tyrol), 85, 112, 122

Gottenau (Swabia), 206

Graben (Swabia), 9, 12, 17, 26–27

Gran (Hungary), 46, 59

Grander, Georg, 40

Grander, Thoman, 14

Granvelle, Nicolas Perrenot de, 128, 189

Grasstein (South Tyrol), 85, 112

Gratt, Jacob, 84

Grau, Heinrich, 11

Graz, 216

Gregory XIII, Pope, 194

Gresham, Thomas, 91

Griesstetter, Melchior, 132, 146

Grimaldi, Giovanni Battista, 79

Grimaldi bank, 76, 79

Groebner, Valentin, 136

Grumbach, Wilhelm von, 145

Gryll, Lorenz, 167

Guadalcanal (Spain), 121

guaiacum wood, 82

guilds, 11, 14, 18–19, 22, 26–28, 56, 129–30, 134, 144, 173–75, 187, 190–91, 227n42

Gültlinger, Gumpold, 29

Günzburg, 24, 204

Günzer, Marx, 165

Gurk, 47

Gutenberg (Swabia), 132

Haberer, Stephanie, 5, 124

Habsburg dynasty, vii, 36, 45, 57–59, 64–65, 68, 71, 77, 82, 86, 88, 90–93, 96, 98, 107, 110, 114–15, 117, 138–39, 151, 164, 166, 191, 210, 212, 214, 216–17, 222

Hadrian VI, Pope, 49

Hagenauer, Friedrich, 138

Hainhofen (Swabia), 207

Hainhofer family, 98
Halberstadt, 48
Hall (Tyrol), 36, 38, 58, 71, 73, 84–86, 122, 129
Hamburg, 116, 119, 126, 131
Hämmerlin family, 25
Hanseatic League, 44
Hardt (Swabia), 206
Haro, Cristóbal de, 66
Harrach, Ursula von, 130, 215
Hase, Heinrich, 144
Hassler, Hans Leo, 165
Haug, Anton, 84, 132
Haug, David, 104
Haug, Gastel, 15–16
Haug-Langnauer-Linck company, 84, 92, 95, 98, 104, 112–13, 132, 134, 145
Haug-Neidhart company, 84–85
Heel, Carl, 165
Heidelberg, 103, 168
Heimertingen (Swabia), 206
Helfenbrunn (Bavaria), 215
Helffenstein, counts of, 204
Henry II, King (of France), 97
Henry VIII, King (of England), vii, 54, 64, 91
Herberstein, Bernhard von, 216
Herbrot, Jakob, 97, 187, 189, 191
Herbrot family, 174–75
Herrieden, 29–30
Herwart, Christoph, 66, 83–84, 95
Herwart, Georg, 187
Herwart, Hans Heinrich, 84, 96, 112
Herwart, Hans Paul, 84, 96, 104, 112, 152, 188
Herwart, Lukas, widow of, 33
Herwart family, 38, 40, 44, 52, 56, 96, 132, 173, 219
Hildebrandt, Reinhard, 4, 44, 88, 115–16, 119, 126, 129, 146
Hinderofen, Sigmund, 147
Hirblingen (Swabia), 206
Hirnheim, Hans Walter von, 203
Hirschvogel family, 52, 54, 61, 98
Höchstetter, Ambrosius (the Elder), 56–57, 62, 72–73, 95, 178, 202
Höchstetter, Ambrosius (the Younger), 73

Höchstetter, Georg, 56
Höchstetter, Hans, 56
Höchstetter, Joseph, 73
Höchstetter, Ulrich, 56
Höchstetter family, 52–54, 56–57, 67, 71–73, 83, 96, 98, 202
Hofmann, Wolfgang, 20
Hohenfreiberg (manor), 38
Hohenfurt, 85
Hohenkirchen (Thuringia), 41–42, 88–89, 126, 128
Hohenzollern, counts of, 204
Holbein, Hans (the Elder), 160–61
Holzapfel, Johann Jakob, 121, 147
Holzschuher, Gabriel, 119
Honold, Hans, 196
honor, viii, 6, 29, 104, 121, 123–24, 126, 133, 158, 169–72, 176, 178, 202, 208, 222–23
Hörl, Veit, 80
Hörmann, Christoph, 102, 104, 110, 132–33, 145
Hörmann, Georg, 83, 87, 100, 127, 131–32, 161, 222
Hörmann, Hans Georg, 132
Hörmann, Ludwig, 132
Hörnlin family, 28
horses, 58, 169
humanism, 99–100, 115, 131, 138–39, 142, 166–67, 169, 181–82, 185, 223
Hundt, Wiguleus, 191
Hungarian trade, 2, 34–35, 40–45, 53, 58–60, 63–64, 70–71, 87–90, 92, 94–95, 107, 125, 128–29, 138–39, 201, 222
Hungary, 7, 41, 46–47, 58–60, 63, 70, 82, 88, 98, 128, 138–39, 151, 197
Hünlein, Jakob, 126
Hurter, Christoph, 130
Hurter, Jobst, 109
Hutten, Ulrich von, 182, 223
Hyrus, Andreas, 146–48

Idria (Slovenia), 73, 79, 95
Ilsung, Anna, 216
Ilsung, Georg, 110
Ilsung, Sebastian, 180–81

Maximilian I, Emperor, vii, 3–4, 16, 28, 36–37, 40–42, 44, 50, 52–54, 56, 58, 61–62, 64, 66, 150, 177, 201, 222

Maximilian II, Emperor, 94, 102, 110, 215

Maximilian I of Bavaria, Duke, 215–17

Meckau, Kaspar von, 165

Meckau, Melchior von, 40, 60–62

Medici family, vii, 3, 46–47, 49, 173, 207

Megerler, Anna, 142

Meissen, 60

Meisterlin, Sigmund, 21, 23

Meitingen (Swabia), 206

Melanchthon, Philipp, 131

Memmingen, 22, 24, 38, 55, 97, 129–30, 203, 206

Mendel, Marquard, 25

Merano, 71

mercury, viii, 73, 79–80, 95–96, 108–10, 114, 120

Mering (Bavaria), 111, 206

Metzler, Hans, 20, 63, 126

Meuting, Bernhard, 96

Meuting, Hans (the Elder), 13, 25

Meuting, Hans (the Younger), 14

Meuting, Jörg, 128

Meuting, Konrad, 11, 20–21, 53, 128

Meuting, Lukas, 128

Meuting, Philipp, 96

Meuting, Ulrich, 13

Meuting family, 14, 25, 40, 53, 97, 128

Mexico, 108

Mickhausen (Swabia), 161, 184, 187, 202, 204, 206, 210–11

Middelburg, 131

Milan, 14–15, 20, 47, 55–56, 77, 97, 110, 119, 128, 134

military officers, 111–12, 123, 199, 213, 216–17

Miller, Thomas, 131

Mindelheim, 55, 206, 208

mining, viii, 18, 34–37, 41–45, 56, 60, 63, 65–66, 70, 73, 79, 82–90, 95–98, 103–4, 108–9, 112–14, 122–23, 129–31, 138–39, 144, 148, 161; map of major Fugger districts of (Alpine region), 40; map of major Fugger regions of (Silesia, Slovakia, and Transylvania), 43. See also copper; gold; lead; mercury; silver; tin

Moluccas, 65–66

Moncada, Hugo de, 87

monopolies, 66–67, 71, 73, 82, 118

Montafon, 117, 130

Montaigne, Michel de, 149

Monte, Philippe de, 164

Montfort, Barbara of, 153

Montfort, Haug of, 204

Montfort, Jakob of, 192

Montfort, Jörg of, 196

Montfort family, 206, 217

Moravia, 63

Moritz of Saxony, Elector, 144

Mörke, Olaf, 173–74

Mörsberg, Johann Jakob von, 204

Moschnitz (Moštenice), 42

Mühlberg on the Elbe, 188

Mülich, Christoph, 87

Mülich, Georg, 16

Mülich, Hektor, 21, 25

Mülich, Helena, 17, 28

Mülich family, 28, 40

Müller, Christoph, 15

Müller (Mylius), Georg, 195–96

Munich, 92, 97, 134, 152, 164–67, 169, 197, 214–16

Münster (Swabia), 211

Münster (Westphalia), 46

Münsterberg, Karl von, 59

Musculus, Wolfgang, 167

music, 116, 128, 143, 149–50, 164–65, 214

Nachtigall, Ottmar, 185

Nals (South Tyrol), 85, 112

Naogeorgius, Thomas, 167

Naples, 72–73, 82, 86–87, 110, 127–28, 132, 145

Neidhart, Sebastian, 84, 92, 96, 117

Netherlands, 15–16, 36, 53–54, 57, 66, 77, 79, 84, 91–94, 98, 102, 106, 109, 111, 118, 127, 130–31, 140, 142–43, 145–46, 157, 167, 169, 199, 212, 216

Neumarkt (Upper Palatinate), 165

Neusäß (Swabia), 207

Neusidler, Melchior, 150, 159, 164–65

Sacco di Roma, 71
Sailer, Hieronymus, 96, 188
Salamanca, Gabriel, 71
Salminger, Sigmund, 164
salt, 85, 90, 94, 139
Salzburg, 20, 37, 96, 216
Sambucus, Johannes, 139
Samland (East Prussia), 46
Santiago, Order of, 79, 130, 147
Santo Domingo, 80
Santori, Fazio, 59
Saragossa, 55
Saurzapf, Sebastian, 89
Savoy, 93, 216
Saxony, 56, 71, 89, 96, 182
Scalzi, Alessandro (named Padano), 152
Scandinavia, 46–47, 49, 140, 142–44
Scazuola, Julio Cesar, 147, 213
Schaffner, Martin, 160
Schattmannsdorf (Slovakia), 139
Schauer, Engelhard, 48
Schedel, Hartmann, 167
Schedel, Hermann, 167
Schedler, Hans, 131
Scheller, Benjamin, 5, 156–58
Schemel, Jeremias, 135
Scheppach (Swabia), 11
Schertlin of Burtenbach, Sebastian, 189
Schetz family, 76
Scheuermann, Ludwig, 148
Scheurl, Christoph, 16, 18, 181
Schick, Léon, 42
Schiersner, Dietmar, 209
Schilling, Johannes, 182
Schlackenwald (Bohemia), 129
Schleswig, 59
Schlipsheim (Swabia), 207
Schmalkaldic War. See War of the Schmalkaldic League
Schmid, Martin, 74
Schmiechen (Swabia), 201, 206
Schneeberg (Tyrol), 112
Schneeberger, Christoph, 119
Schöner, Johann, 168

Schönfeld (Bohemia), 129
Schrofenstein, Christoph von, 62
Schüren, Hans von, 52, 131
Schwab, Georg, 46
Schwab, Michael, 182
Schwarz, Kaspar, 134
Schwarz, Lukas, 134
Schwarz, Matthäus, 50, 58, 133–38, 137, 142, 164
Schwarz, Matthäus Ulrich, 134
Schwarz, Ulrich, 133–34
Schwarz, Veit Konrad, 134, 138
Schwarzenberg, Ottheinrich von, 196
Schwaz (Tyrol), 18, 35–36, 57, 65, 73, 83–86, 95, 100, 112–14, 122, 127, 131, 138, 148, 160–61, 189
Scrimger, Henricus, 168
Sebastian, King (of Portugal), 118
Seisenegger, Jakob, 163
Seitz, Simon, 51
Seitz family, 174
Seld, Georg Sigmund, 100, 191
Sender, Clemens, 67, 173, 176, 178, 182–84
Senftenau (manor), 127
Senj, 42
Senlis, 37
Serntein, Zyprian von, 61
Seville, 80, 82, 100, 109, 130, 212
Sforza, Bianca Maria, 37
Siedeler, Jörg, 194
Sieh-Burens, Katarina, 4, 173–74, 189, 191
Siena, 130
Sifanus, Laurentius, 100
Sigismund, Archduke (of Tyrol), 15, 26, 35–36, 38, 40, 60–61
Sigismund, Emperor, 22
Sigismund, King (of Poland), 88
Silesia, 24, 46–47, 55, 63, 88–90, 110
silk/silken cloth, 14, 20, 49, 55, 59, 96, 135
silver, vii, 15, 26, 35–38, 40–41, 47, 49–53, 61, 64–65, 71, 73, 79–80, 83–86, 93, 108–9, 113–14, 120–21, 128, 134, 145, 189; production at Falkenstein (1530–49), 84t
slaves/slave trade, 80, 82, 109, 239n36
Slovakia, 41, 50, 63, 70–71, 95, 127, 138–39